SCIENCE
In Your World

SENIOR AUTHORS

Dr. Jay K. Hackett
Dr. Richard H. Moyer

Macmillan/McGraw-Hill
School Publishing Com

ACKNOWLEDGMENTS

For permission to reprint copyrighted material, grateful acknowledgment is made to the following authors, publishers, and agents. All possible care has been taken to trace the ownership of every selection included and to make full acknowledgment of its use. If any errors have inadvertently occurred, they will be corrected in subsequent editions, provided notification is sent to the publisher.

Brandt & Brandt, Literary Agents, Inc.: "Benjamin Franklin" from *A Book of Americans* by Rosemary and Stephen Vincent Benet. Copyright 1933 by Rosemary and Stephen Vincent Benet, renewed © 1961 by Rosemary Carr Benet. Reprinted by permission of Brandt & Brandt, Literary Agents, Inc.

Harper & Row, Publishers, Inc.: Text from "The Question" from *Dogs & Dragons, Trees & Dreams* by Karla Kuskin. "The Question" originally appeared in *In the Middle of the Trees* by Karla Kuskin. Copyright © 1958 by Karla Kuskin.

Marian Reiner: From *Earth Songs* by Myra Cohn Livingston. Text copyright © 1986 by Myra Cohn Livingston. Published by Holiday House, New York. Reprinted with permission of Marian Reiner for the author.

William Morrow & Company, Inc.: "A Microscopic Topic" from *The New Kid on the Block* by Jack Prelutsky, copyright © 1984 by Jack Prelutsky by permission of Greenwillow Books (A Division of William Morrow & Co.).

CREDITS

Series Editor: Jane Parker
Design Coordinator: Kip Frankenberry
Series Production Editor: Helen Mischka
Level Editors: Shannon Moore, Carol MacPherson Bloom
Contributing Editors: Madelaine M. Meek, Joyce R. Rhymer, Jane Schott, Catherine P. Varca
Production Editor: Jillian C. Yerkey
Designer: Jeff Kobelt
Artist: Barton D. Hawkinberry
Photo Editor: Barbara Buchholz

Macmillan/McGraw-Hill School Division
866 Third Avenue
New York, New York 10022

Printed in the United States of America

ISBN 0-675-16230-0

9 8 7 6

SENIOR AUTHORS

Dr. Jay K. Hackett
University of Northern Colorado

Dr. Richard H. Moyer
University of Michigan-Dearborn

CONTRIBUTING AUTHORS

Stephen C. Blume
Elementary Science Curriculum Specialist
St. Tammany Public School System
Slidell, Louisiana

Ralph M. Feather, Jr.
Teacher of Geology, Astronomy, and Earth Science
Derry Area School District
Derry, Pennsylvania

Edward Paul Ortleb
Science Supervisor
St. Louis Board of Education
St. Louis, Missouri

Dr. Barbara Swanson Thomson
Associate Professor in Science Education
The Ohio State University
Columbus, Ohio

CONTRIBUTING WRITER

Ann H. Sankey
Science Specialist
Educational Service District 121
Seattle, Washington

READING CONSULTANT

Barbara S. Pettegrew, Ph.D.
Director of the Reading/Study Center
Assistant Professor of Education
Otterbein College, Westerville, Ohio

SAFETY CONSULTANT

Gary E. Downs, Ed.D.
Professor
Iowa State University
Ames, Iowa

GIFTED AND MAINSTREAMED CONSULTANTS

George Fichter
Educational Consultant
Programs for Gifted
Ohio Department of Education
Worthington, Ohio

Timothy E. Heron, Ph.D.
Professor
Department of Human Services, Education
The Ohio State University
Columbus, Ohio

CONTENT CONSULTANTS

Robert T. Brown, M.D.
Assoc. Prof. Clinical
Pediatrics Dir., Section for
Adolescent Health The Ohio State Univ.
Children's Hosp. Columbus, Ohio

Henry D. Drew, Ph.D.
Chemist, U.S. FDA
Div. of Drug Analysis
St. Louis, Missouri

Judith L. Doyle, Ph.D.
Physics Teacher
Newark High School
Newark, Ohio

Todd F. Holzman, M.D.
Child Psychiatrist
Harvard Com. Health Plan
Wellesley, Massachusetts

Knut J. Norstog, Ph.D.
Research Associate
Fairchild Tropical Garden
Miami, Florida

James B. Phipps, Ph.D.
Prof., Geol./Oceanography
Grays Harbor College
Aberdeen, Washington

R. Robert Robbins, Ph.D.
Assoc. Professor
Astronomy Department
University of Texas
Austin, Texas

Sidney E. White, Ph.D.
Professor
Dept. Geology/Mineralogy
The Ohio State Univ.
Columbus, Ohio

REVIEWERS: Teachers and Administrators

Annette Barzal, Walter Kidder Elementary School, Brunswick, OH; **Jack Finger,** Waukesha Public Schools, Waukesha, WI; **Rogerio Garcia,** Reynaldo Longoria Elementary, Brownsville, TX; **Shirley Gomez,** Luling Elementary School, Luling, LA; **Linda Harris,** Egly Elementary, Brownsville, TX; **Dr. Madelyn Jarvis,** West Carrollton School District, Dayton, OH; **Eddie Jordan,** Miami Edison Middle School, Miami, FL; **Shirley Larges,** Azalea Middle School, St. Petersburg, FL; **David Larwa,** Michigan Department of Education, Lansing, MI; **Janet McDonald,** Pine Middle School, Los Alamitos, CA; **Marsha McKinney,** Pope Elementary School, Arlington, TX; **Corinne Measelle,** Palm Beach County School Board, West Palm Beach, FL; **Sister Pauline Elizabeth Neelon,** St. Teresa Elementary School, Providence, RI; **Barbara Panzer,** P.S. 279, Brooklyn, NY; **Donald Paul,** Vineland Board of Education, Vineland, NJ; **Chris Rowan,** Palm Grove Elementary, Brownsville, TX; **Noe Sauceda,** Russell Elementary, Brownsville, TX; **Dr. Rosa White,** Cutler Ridge Elementary School, Miami, FL; **Jay Woodard,** Waukesha Public Schools, Waukesha, WI.

Table of Contents

Unit 1 — Physical Science 2

CHAPTER 1
Investigating Matter 4

Have You Ever...Wondered Why a Golf Ball Is Dimpled? 5

Lesson 1 Scientific Methods 6

You Can...Use Observations 7

Lesson 2 Measuring Matter 12

Activity: How Can You Compare Densities? 19

Lesson 3 Properties of Matter 20

Activity: How Can You Use Properties to Identify Materials?. . . . 26

Chapter Review. 27

CHAPTER 2
Matter and Its Changes. . . . 30

Have You Ever...Seen What Sugar Is Made Of? 31

Lesson 1 Elements and Atoms 32

You Can...Make an Electron Cloud Model 35

Lesson 2 Classifying Elements 36

I Want to Know About...Context Clues . . 41

Lesson 3 Compounds 42

Activity: How Is a Compound Formed? 47

Lesson 4 Mixtures 48

Activity: How Can You Separate and Compare Mixtures? 52

Chapter Review. 53

CHAPTER 3
Investigating Compounds . . 56
🔖 Have You Ever...Done an Acid Test? . . 57
Lesson 1 Classifying Compounds . . . 58
🔖 Activity: How Can You Prevent
Rust? 63
**Lesson 2 Acids, Bases, and
Salts** 64
🔖 You Can...Make an Indicator 66
🔖 Activity: How Can You Find Out if a
Solution Is an Acid or a Base? 69
I Want to Know About...Soil Scientists . . 70
Chapter Review 71

CHAPTER 4
Electricity 74
🔖 Have You Ever...Created Static
Electricity? 75
Lesson 1 Static Electricity 76
🔖 You Can...Do a Static Trick 77
Lesson 2 Current Electricity 80
🔖 Activity: How Are Circuits Different? . . . 85
Lesson 3 Electricity in Your Home . . 86
🔖 Activity: How Can You Make an
Electric Motor? 95
I Want to Know About...Pacemakers . . 96
Chapter Review 97

CHAPTER 5
Waves 100
🔖 Have You Ever...Cooked With a
Microwave Oven? 101
**Lesson 1 How Do Waves
Transfer Energy?** 102
🔖 Activity: What Are Some Properties
of Waves? 107
Lesson 2 Radio Waves 108
Lesson 3 Higher Frequency Waves . 112
🔖 You Can...Make a Color Wheel 114
Lesson 4 Lasers 116
🔖 Activity: How Much Does Light
Spread Out From Its Source? 118
Chapter Review 119

CHAPTER 6
Motion and Forces 122
🔖 Have You Ever...Compared Speed and
Distance? 123
Lesson 1 What Is Motion? 124
🔖 Activity: How Can You Find Your
Average Walking Speed? 129
Lesson 2 Forces in Your World . . . 130
**Lesson 3 Newton's Laws of
Motion** 138
🔖 You Can...Make a Come-Back Can . . 143
🔖 Activity: How Does Mass Affect
Acceleration? 145
I Want to Know About...Motion
Research 146
Chapter Review 147

CHAPTER 7
Work and Machines 150
🔖 Have You Ever...Made a Hovercraft? . . 151
Lesson 1 Working With Forces . . . 152
🔖 Activity: How Much Work Is Done
When an Object Is Lifted? 155
**Lesson 2 The Advantages of
Machines** 156
🔖 You Can...Use Marbles to Reduce
Friction 159
Lesson 3 Simple Machines 160
🔖 Activity: How Do Levers Change
Forces? 167
I Want to Know About...An Exercise
Expert 168
Chapter Review 169
Unit Review 172

Lesson 4 **People in Space** 220
Activity: How Will We Live in Space? . .227
I Want to Know About...Lightsailing
   in Space 228
Chapter Review. 229

CHAPTER 10
Soil and Land
Conservation 232
Have You Ever...Seen Soil Erode? . . .233
Lesson 1 **Soil: A Natural**
   Resource 234
Activity: How Do Roots Prevent Soil
   Erosion? 243
Lesson 2 **Conserving Forests**. . . .244
Lesson 3 **Disposing of Refuse** . . .248
You Can...Use It Again! 251
Activity: Which Items Are
   Biodegradable?. 253
I Want to Know About...Cause and
   Effect Relationships 254
Chapter Review. 255

CHAPTER 11
Water and Air
Conservation 258
Have You Ever...Wondered About Oil
   Spills? 259
Lesson 1 **Water Pollution**. 260
You Can...Observe the Effects of
   Pollution 262
Lesson 2 **Conserving Clean**
   Water 266
Activity: How Can Water Be Cleaned?. .273
Lesson 3 **Conserving Clean Air** . . .274
Activity: Where Can You Find Air
   Pollution? 281
I Want to Know About...A Biologist . .282
Chapter Review. 283
Unit Review 286

CHAPTER 8
Stars and Galaxies 176
Have You Ever...Studied the Colors of
   Stars? 177
Lesson 1 **The Vastness of**
   Space 178
Activity: How Can You Describe
   Your Location in Space?. 181
Lesson 2 **Stars**. 182
You Can...Compare the Sizes of the
   Stars 189
Lesson 3 **Galaxies** 190
Lesson 4 **Studying an Expanding**
   Universe. 194
Activity: How Do Galaxies Move in
   the Universe?. 198
Chapter Review. 199

CHAPTER 9
Exploring Space. 202
Have You Ever...Observed the Moon?. .203
Lesson 1 **Constellations** 204
You Can...Make Up a Constellation . .206
Lesson 2 **Telescopes**. 210
Lesson 3 **Satellites and Probes** . . .214
Activity: How Does Distance Affect
   Accuracy? 219

CHAPTER 12
Classifying Living Things . .290
🔖 Have You Ever...Classified Objects? . .291
Lesson 1 **Features of Life** 292
Lesson 2 **Grouping Organisms** 296
🔖 Activity: How Can You Use Cells
to Classify Organisms? 303
Lesson 3 **Scientific Naming**. 304
🔖 Activity: How Are Characteristics
Used in Classification? 311
Lesson 4 **Viruses** 312
🔖 You Can...Show How Viruses Are
Spread 314
Chapter Review. 317

CHAPTER 13
Simple Organisms 320
🔖 Have You Ever...Seen a Cell? 321
Lesson 1 **Monerans** 322
🔖 Activity: How Can the Growth of
Bacteria Be Controlled? 329
Lesson 2 **Protists** 330
Lesson 3 **Fungi** 334
🔖 You Can...Find the Fungus "Amongus" .335
🔖 Activity: What Are the Growth
Needs of Fungi? 337
I Want to Know About..."Flashlight"
Fish 338
Chapter Review. 339

CHAPTER 14
Growth and
Reproduction 342
🔖 Have You Ever...Examined an Egg?. . .343
Lesson 1 **Cells and Organisms** . . .344
🔖 You Can...Make a Cell Model 346
🔖 Activity: How Do Cells Divide? 351
Lesson 2 **Reproduction**. 352
🔖 You Can...Grow a New Plant 354
🔖 Activity: How Do Plants Reproduce
From One Parent?. 361
I Want to Know About...Summarizing
Paragraphs. 362
Chapter Review. 363

CHAPTER 15
Inheriting Traits 366
🔖 Have You Ever...Wondered About
Inherited Traits?. 367
Lesson 1 **Heredity** 368
🔖 You Can...Study Genetics With
Peanuts 374
🔖 Activity: How Common Are Dominant
and Recessive Traits? 377
Lesson 2 **Genetics in
Populations** 378
🔖 You Can...Show How Natural Selection
Occurs 383
🔖 Activity: What Are the Chances for
Tallness?. 385
Lesson 3 **Controlling Traits**. 386
I Want to Know About...A Geneticist. . .390
Chapter Review. 391
Unit Review 394

vii

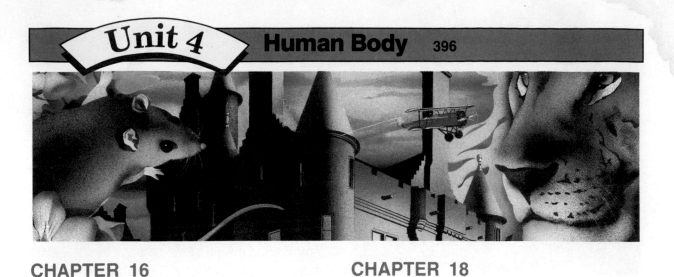

CHAPTER 16
Circulation and Respiration 398
- Have You Ever...Measured Your Breathing Rate?. 399
- Lesson 1 **Circulation** 400
- You Can...Check Your Pulse 403
- Activity: What Causes Blood to Circulate? 409
- Lesson 2 **Respiration**. 410
- Activity: What Do We Exhale? 420
- Chapter Review. 421

CHAPTER 17
Digestion and Excretion . . .424
- Have You Ever...Wondered About Digestion? 425
- Lesson 1 **Digestion** 426
- You Can...Change Starch to Sugar . . .427
- Activity: How Does Diffusion Take Place?. 435
- Lesson 2 **Excretion** 436
- Activity: How Do Kidneys Work? 443
- I Want to Know About...Kidney Transplants. 444
- Chapter Review. 445

CHAPTER 18
Caring for Your Body. 448
- Have You Ever...Wondered What Keeps Your Body in Balance? 449
- Lesson 1 **Healthful Eating** 450
- Lesson 2 **Exercise** 456
- Activity: What Happens When Muscles Are Overworked?. 461
- Lesson 3 **Prescription and Over-the-Counter Drugs** 462
- Activity: What Drugs Are Found in Over-the-Counter Medicines?. 465
- Lesson 4 **Effects of Drugs** 466
- You Can...Take a Caffeine Survey . . .469
- I Want to Know About...A Pharmacist . .476
- Chapter Review. 477
- Unit Review 480

Application Activities 482

Process Skill Models
Predicting 485
Interpreting Data 487
Defining Operationally 489
Controlling Variables 491
Hypothesizing 493
Experimenting 495

Problem Solving Activities
 The Sink/Float Dilemma 497
 Cat Burglar. 499

 The Great Egg Drop. 501
 To Take or Not to Take? 503
 Don't Refuse Refuse. 505
 Water Watch 507
 Living or Nonliving? 509
 Animal Scramble 511
 The Genie Game 513
 Digestive Detective 515

Glossary 517
Index 527
Photo Credits. 533

 denotes ACTIVITY. See page x for ACTIVITIES TABLE OF CONTENTS.

Activities

Have You Ever...

Wondered Why a Golf Ball Is Dimpled?. 5
Seen What Sugar Is Made Of ?. . . . 31
Done an Acid Test?. 57
Created Static Electricity? 75
Cooked With a Microwave Oven?. . .101
Compared Speed and Distance? 123
Made a Hovercraft? 151
Studied the Colors of Stars? 177
Observed the Moon? 203
Seen Soil Erode? 233
Wondered About Oil Spills? 259
Classified Objects? 291
Seen a Cell? 321
Examined an Egg? 343
Wondered About Inherited Traits?. 367
Measured Your Breathing Rate? . . .399
Wondered About Digestion? 425
Wondered What Keeps Your Body in Balance?. 449

You Can...

Use Observations 7
Make an Electron Cloud Model 35
Make an Indicator. 66
Do a Static Trick 77
Make a Color Wheel. 114
Make a Come-Back Can 143
Use Marbles to Reduce Friction. . .159
Compare the Sizes of the Stars. . .189
Make Up a Constellation 206
Use It Again! 251
Observe the Effects of Pollution. . .262
Show How Viruses Are Spread . . .314
Find the Fungus "Amongus" 335
Make a Cell Model 346
Grow a New Plant. 354
Study Genetics With Peanuts. . . .374
Show How Natural Selection Occurs. 383
Check Your Pulse. 403
Change Starch to Sugar 427
Take a Caffeine Survey 469

Activities

How Can You Compare Densities? . . 19
How Can You Use Properties to Identify Materials? 26
How Is a Compound Formed? 47
How Can You Separate and Compare Mixtures? 52
How Can You Prevent Rust?. 63
How Can You Find Out If a Solution Is an Acid or a Base? 69
How Are Circuits Different?. 85
How Can You Make an Electric Motor?. 95
What Are Some Properties of Waves? 107
How Much Does Light Spread Out From Its Source? . . .118

How Can You Find Your Average
Walking Speed? 129
How Does Mass Affect Acceleration? .145
How Much Work Is Done
When an Object Is Lifted? 155
How Do Levers Change Forces? . . .167
How Can You Describe Your
Location in Space? 181
How Do Galaxies Move in the
Universe? 198
How Does Distance Affect Accuracy? .219
How Will We Live in Space? 227
How Do Roots Prevent Soil
Erosion? 243
Which Items Are Biodegradable? . . .253
How Can Water Be Cleaned? 273
Where Can You Find Air Pollution? . .281

How Can You Use Cells to Classify
Organisms? 303
How Are Characteristics Used in
Classification? 311
How Can the Growth of Bacteria Be
Controlled? 329
What Are the Growth Needs of
Fungi? 337
How Do Cells Divide? 351
How Do Plants Reproduce From
One Parent? 361
How Common Are Dominant and
Recessive Traits? 377
What Are the Chances for Tallness? .385
What Causes Blood to Circulate? . . .409
What Do We Exhale? 420
How Does Diffusion Take Place? . . .435
How Do Kidneys Work? 443
What Happens When Muscles
Are Overworked? 461
What Drugs Are Found in
Over-the-Counter Medicines? 465

Process Skill Models

Predicting 485
Interpreting Data 487
Defining Operationally 489
Controlling Variables 491
Hypothesizing 493
Experimenting 495

Problem Solving Activities

The Sink/Float Dilemma 497
Cat Burglar 499
The Great Egg Drop 501
To Take or Not to Take? 503
Don't Refuse Refuse 505
Water Watch 507
Living or Nonliving? 509
Animal Scramble 511
The Genie Game 513
Digestive Detective 515

Science is ...

Understanding

"If it is exciting to probe the unknown and shed light on what was dark before, then more and more excitement surely lies ahead of us."

Isaac Asimov   American author and biochemist (1966)

What is electricity?
What causes cakes to rise?
Why are you able to see colors?
Science has some answers for you.

Science is ...

Discovering

Discovering

"I do not know what I may appear to the world; but to myself I seem to have been only like a boy playing on the seashore, and diverting myself in now and then finding a smoother pebble or a prettier shell than ordinary, whilst the great ocean of truth lay all undiscovered before me." Sir Isaac Newton English physicist (1642–1727)

Among other things, Sir Isaac Newton discovered the law of gravity, laws of motion, and that white light is composed of every color in the spectrum.

Discover science!

Science is...

Deciding

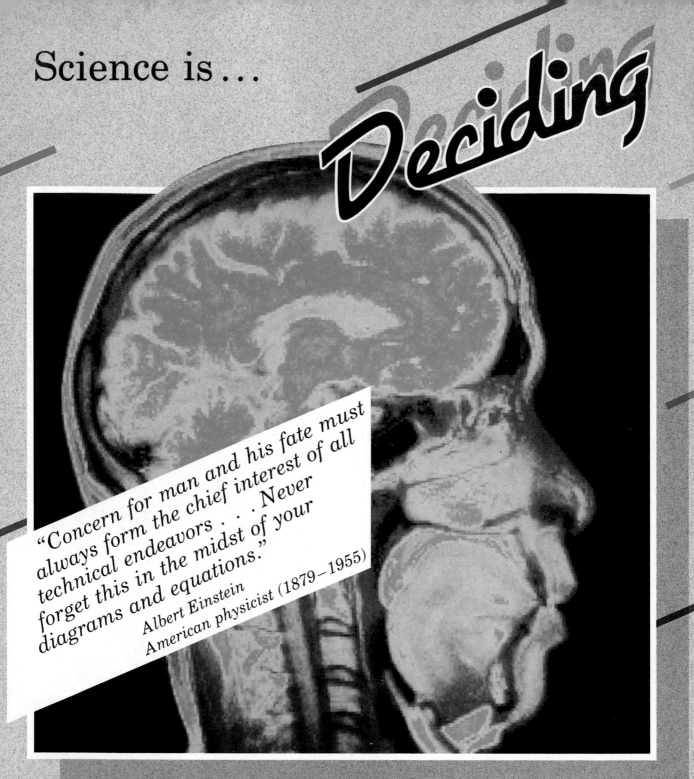

"Concern for man and his fate must always form the chief interest of all technical endeavors . . . Never forget this in the midst of your diagrams and equations."

Albert Einstein
American physicist (1879–1955)

Earth has limited amounts of water, air, and other resources. We must decide to use them wisely.
Science can help you decide.

Science is... *Applying*

"Genius is one percent inspiration and ninety-nine percent perspiration."
Thomas Alva Edison
American inventor (1847–1931)

Thomas Alva Edison was a genius
at making practical applications in science.
He invented many things that affect our
lives: the microphone, the record player, early
motion pictures, and the electric light bulb.
Have you used any of these things today?

Science is...

Predicting

Defining
Operationally

Interpreting Data

Controlling
Variables

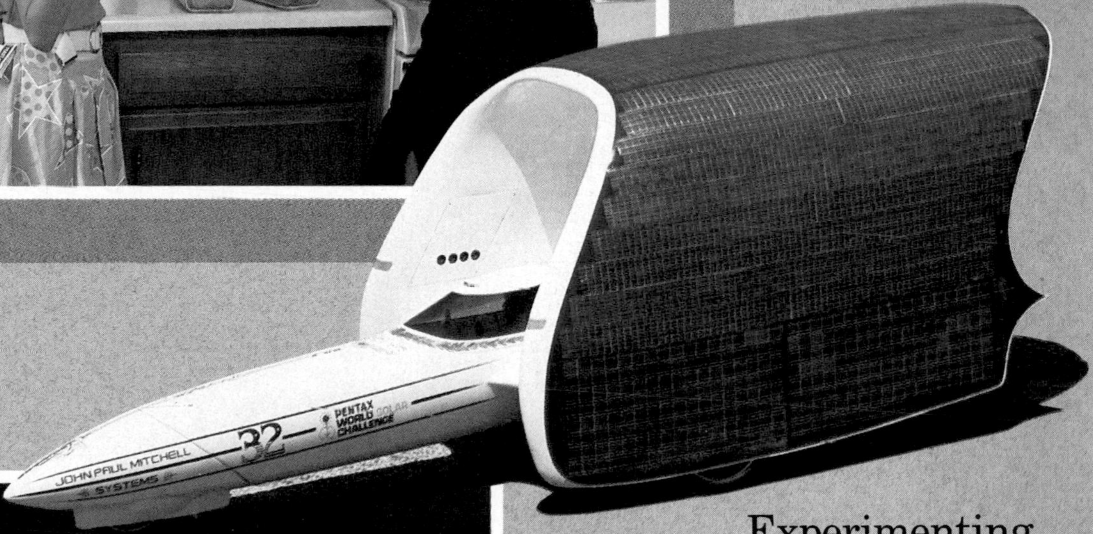

Experimenting

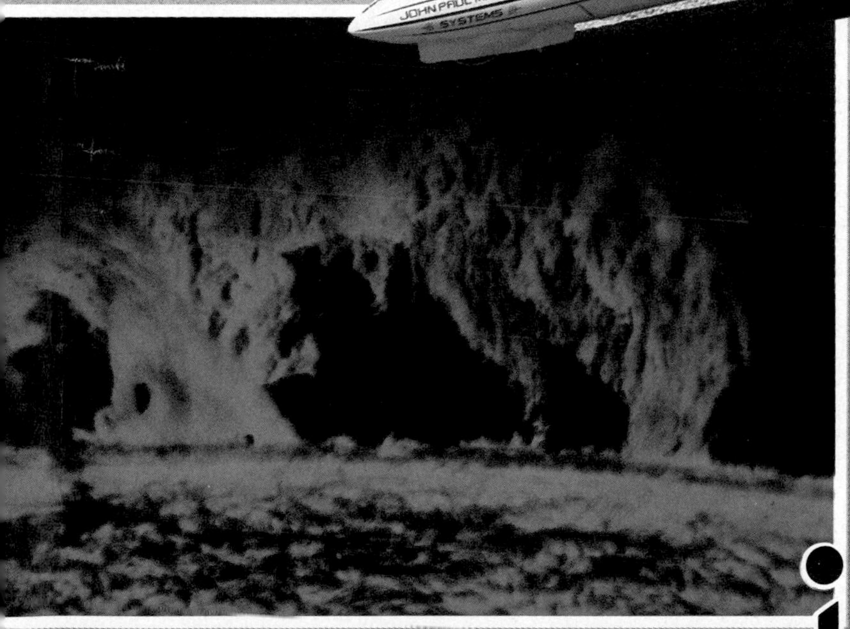

Hypothesizing

in your world...

Find out all about these process skills on pages 485-495 of this science book.

Physical Science

Ben Franklin made a pretty kite and flew it in the air
To call upon a thunderstorm that happened to be there,
—And all our humming dynamos and our electric light
Go back to what Ben Franklin found, the day he flew his kite.

from "Benjamin Franklin"
Rosemary and Stephen Vincent Benét

Investigating Matter

This young infant is not a trained scientist but, like all human beings, the infant is an observer. What does the infant see? The infant observes and gathers information about the world. That is the very nature of being human, our need to know. As an observer, this young child uses all five senses to understand the environment. Observations are our pathway to learning.

Have You Ever...

Wondered Why a Golf Ball Is Dimpled?

Look at a golf ball. Observe its size, shape, and design. Notice the rough-cut edges on the ball's surface. Imagine that two hundred years ago you had wanted to invent a golf ball that, once hit, would stay in the air for a long distance. Why would you have made it a dimpled ball?

Scientific Methods

LESSON 1 GOALS
You will learn
● that observations are made by using the five senses.
● that scientific methods are useful tools for solving problems.

Have you ever asked such questions as "Why is the sky blue?" and "What makes ice cold?" Most of us are curious about the world around us and why it's the way it is. You've probably explored the world outside your home to find answers to questions like "How do ants build colonies?" or "Why are some beaches cleaner than others?" If you have, then you are a scientist. You have something in common with other scientists like Thomas Edison. He had a natural curiosity about his world too.

Curiosity motivated Edison in his work. He noticed that people had to shout into telephone receivers to be heard at the other end of the line. He thought there had to be a way to fix this problem. After Edison observed how the telephone worked and studied what each part did, he was able to invent a part that allowed people to talk in a normal tone of voice.

Curiosity motivates us to learn about our world.

You Can...

Use Observations

Get an apple. Observe its properties and record your observations. Then put your apple in a pile with five other apples. Mix up the apples. Use your recorded observations to find your apple again. What senses did you use to make your observations?

Work with other students who have observed other apples. Trade observation sheets. Mix up all the apples in a pile. See if you can use another student's observations to find his or her apple. What type of observations were most useful?

Scientists—like you—want to gather information about the world and solve problems. Edison began by observing something that puzzled him. Observation is an important part of learning. Using your five senses helps you notice what's happening or changing in your environment. For example, you may look out the window to check on the weather before you get dressed for school. Based on what you observe, you choose an outfit that will make you comfortable.

Sometimes instruments are used to improve the observations we make using our senses. Because some objects are very small, very far away, or hidden from sight, they can't be observed easily. By using telescopes, for example, we can see distant planets and stars. A doctor uses a stethoscope to help listen to a patient's heartbeat. By using these and other instruments, we learn more exact information about our world.

Why must we sometimes use instruments to improve our senses?

The world you live in is an interesting place filled with different objects and events. Scientists observe, study, and explain these objects and events. They may observe how plants grow, study insects, or explain why there are earthquakes and volcanoes. To do these things, they use planned, orderly methods to organize their observations and findings.

When you have a question about the world around you, you may also have an orderly way of finding an answer. Let's take a look at one of the scientific methods you could use by seeing how another sixth grade student, Maria, used it to learn which brand of paper towels absorbs the most water.

First, Maria gathered samples of three different paper towel brands. By looking at and touching them, she picked one brand of towel she thought would absorb the most water. She predicted that the thickest towel would absorb the most water. Next, Maria placed each sample in water. She slowly counted to 15, squeezed the water into a measuring cup, and wrote down how much water each towel held. Her experiment showed that the thickest towel did absorb the most water.

Maria followed certain steps to find an answer to her question about paper towels. Scientists use

What information did Maria record?

Step 1
Problem

Step 2
Hypothesis

One scientific method includes five steps.

methods like Maria's to seek answers to even more puzzling questions. But because scientists work in many ways, there's not just one scientific method. Let's look at one method many scientists use.

Step 1. State the problem or ask a question. What question did Maria want to answer?

Step 2. Form a hypothesis. A **hypothesis** is a prediction of how something will work under certain conditions. It suggests a possible answer to a question.

Step 3. Plan and carry out an experiment to test your hypothesis. Because an **experiment** is done to solve a problem or answer a question, it's important to plan and do the experiment carefully.

Step 4. Record observations made during the experiment. As Maria did her experiment, she wrote down what she observed. Her recorded observations are called **data.** Data collected by one scientist can be studied and compared with data collected by other scientists.

Step 5. Write a conclusion. A **conclusion** is an answer to a problem or question. It's made by studying the data from the experiment. The conclusion may answer the question or solve the problem from step 1.   What was Maria's conclusion?

Step 3
Experiment

Step 4
Record data

Step 5
Conclusion

You may not always be sure of your conclusion. Sometimes the conclusion of an experiment shows that the hypothesis may not have been correct. In that case, steps 2 through 5 must be done again. A new hypothesis must be formed, and a new experiment must be done to test it.

Scientists sometimes repeat steps 2 through 5 many times in order to solve a problem. Often experiments raise more questions than they answer. Experiments must continue until a conclusion is reached that answers the question or questions. Maria reached a conclusion in her paper towel test. She could continue to ask more questions, such as "Which brand is strongest?" What other questions might she ask?

You may find yourself using the methods scientists use to answer questions about the world around you. For example, you may wonder why many of the houseplants in your home or school die or don't grow quickly. This may lead you to wonder what things affect plant growth. You could hypothesize that the amount of water plants get affects their growth. Then you could design and carry out experiments to test your hypothesis and come to some conclusions. The results would help you grow healthier plants.

Tyler's conclusion was based on his observation.

In the picture, Tyler has just said to Rosalind, "Oh, I see you own a dog." What did Tyler observe? Why does he think Rosalind owns a dog? Why could he be wrong? If Tyler had seen Rosalind at her house with a dog, he could have been more sure of forming a correct conclusion. It may be that she was buying food for a friend's dog. Tyler couldn't be sure, but he based his conclusion on the best information available. People must always be willing to change their conclusions as they learn new information.

Why do people change their conclusions?

Lesson Summary

- Observations are made using the five senses.
- One scientific method scientists use has five steps.

Lesson Review

1. List the steps in one scientific method.
2. Why is it sometimes useful to use instruments when making observations?
★3. Pretend that there are three ways for you to go home from school. Design an experiment to find out which way would be fastest.

Measuring Matter

LESSON 2 GOALS
You will learn
• that many properties of matter can be observed and measured.
• that weight is the measure of the force of gravity.
• that weight and mass are not the same.

You can describe matter because all matter has properties you can observe and compare. You use your senses to observe color, smell, taste, hardness, and texture. What properties of an ice cream cone can you sense? Some properties can be measured. Which properties of the cone could you measure? Often you will make measurements of matter when you do experiments. Keeping careful records of measurements is important because you use the data to form your conclusion.

Sense
Color
Taste
Odor
Texture

Measure
Volume
Mass
Density
Weight

Different size containers hold different volumes of matter.

Volume

Matter takes up space. Take a look at your desk. Your desk takes up space. How many desks do you think you could fit in your classroom? Next, pour some water into a glass. The water takes up space in the glass. Now, blow air into a balloon. The air takes up space and pushes on the sides of the balloon. The amount of space that matter occupies is called **volume** (VAHL yum). In Lesson 1, Maria used a measuring cup to find out how much water each paper towel held. Then she wrote down the volume of water she squeezed from each paper towel.

One unit you can use to measure volume is the cubic centimeter. For example, the volume of a rectangular object is found by multiplying the measure of its length, width, and height. Look at the cube on this page. The volume of the cube is

1 cm x 1 cm x 1 cm = 1 cubic centimeter.

Use a metric ruler to measure the length, width, and height of your science book. By multiplying these numbers, you will find the volume of your book. You will know how much space the matter of your science book takes up in your desk or on a shelf. If a math book in your desk is 25 cm long, 20 cm wide, and 2 cm high, what's its volume?

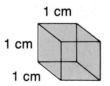

This cube is one cubic centimeter.

Two-liter bottles

Solids, liquids, and gases may be measured in cubic centimeter units. Liquids, however, usually are measured in units called liters (LEET urz). You're probably familiar with liters since soft drinks and other beverages come in two-liter bottles. One liter has the same volume as 1,000 cubic centimeters. This means that if you pour water into a container that has a volume of 1,000 cubic centimeters, you could pour the same amount of water into a one-liter container. The amount of space in both containers is the same.

The boys in the picture want to measure the volume of a cake pan. It is 30 cm long, 20 cm wide, and 5 cm deep. Remember, you find the volume by multiplying the length times the width times the depth. How many cubic centimeters of cake batter can it hold? How many liters is that?

SCIENCE AND . . .
Math

Arrange the following volumes of soft drink in order from the greatest to the least.
A. 1,162.04 cubic centimeters
B. 926.14 cubic centimeters
C. 1,126.4 cubic centimeters
D. 1 liter

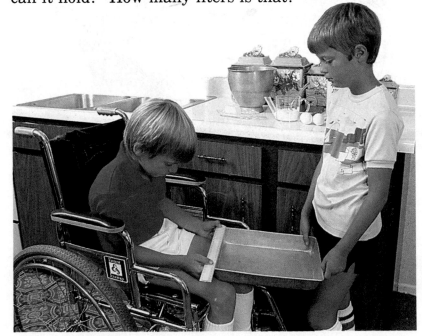

The boys can find the volume of the cake pan by measuring the length, width, and depth.

Mass

Another property of matter that can be measured is mass. **Mass** is the amount of matter that is in an object. All matter, including you, has mass. The amount of matter you have in your body is your mass. To measure mass, you may use a balance like the one in the photograph on this page. Mass is measured in units called grams. Two paper clips have a mass of about one gram. It would be inconvenient to use grams to measure the mass of many objects. For example, your body might have a mass of 36,000 grams. It would be simpler to say you have a mass of 36 kilograms. A kilogram is another unit used to measure mass. A kilogram is equal to 1,000 grams.

Pan balance

The pails hold the same volume.

Density

Suppose you have two pails that are exactly alike. They can hold the same volume of matter. One pail is full of rocks. The other pail is full of cotton balls. Which one would be easier to carry a long distance? Remember that the pails hold the same volume so the cotton balls take up the same amount of space as the rocks. But you know that the rocks would be harder for you to carry. Why? The volume of the pails is the same, but the pail filled with rocks has a much greater mass than the one filled with cotton balls. The density (DEN sut ee) of the rocks is greater than the density of the cotton balls.

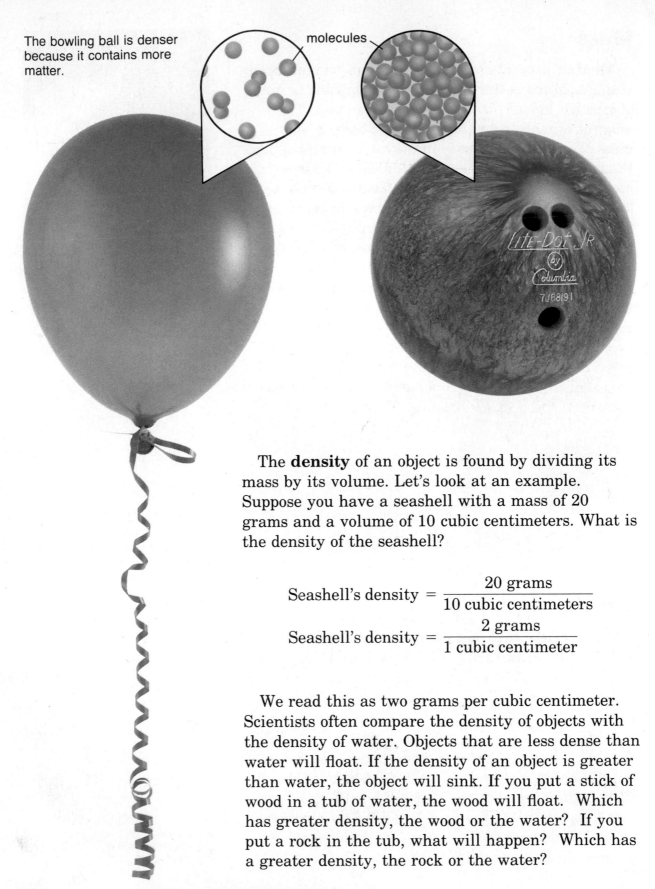

The bowling ball is denser because it contains more matter.

molecules

The **density** of an object is found by dividing its mass by its volume. Let's look at an example. Suppose you have a seashell with a mass of 20 grams and a volume of 10 cubic centimeters. What is the density of the seashell?

$$\text{Seashell's density} = \frac{20 \text{ grams}}{10 \text{ cubic centimeters}}$$

$$\text{Seashell's density} = \frac{2 \text{ grams}}{1 \text{ cubic centimeter}}$$

We read this as two grams per cubic centimeter. Scientists often compare the density of objects with the density of water. Objects that are less dense than water will float. If the density of an object is greater than water, the object will sink. If you put a stick of wood in a tub of water, the wood will float. Which has greater density, the wood or the water? If you put a rock in the tub, what will happen? Which has a greater density, the rock or the water?

Weight

Weight is not mass, and mass is not weight. Even though the two seem to be similar, they are in fact quite different.

If you held a large rock in one hand and a small pebble in the other hand, you would notice that the rock feels heavier than the pebble. That's because a rock is made up of more matter than a pebble. If a scientist measures the amount of matter in an object like a rock or pebble, he or she is measuring its mass not its weight. The number measurement would be in grams or kilograms.

The **weight** of the rock or pebble is the measure of Earth's gravitational pull on these objects. Your body's weight is the measure of Earth's gravitational pull on you. When you jump in the air, the force of gravity pulls you back to the ground. Weight is measured in a unit called a **newton**. Newtons can be measured using a spring scale. If you weigh a medium-sized apple, you will find that it weighs about one newton.

Define weight.

Spring scales are used to measure weight.

The force of gravity exists between all objects. The amount of pull between any two objects depends partly on the mass of each object. The greater the mass of the objects, the greater the force of gravity between them. The force of gravity between Earth and a large boulder is stronger than the force of gravity between Earth and a tiny pebble. So a boulder weighs more newtons than a pebble.

The force of gravity between objects becomes weaker as the objects move farther apart. The mass of an astronaut in space is the same as it is on Earth. However, the farther the astronaut moves away from Earth's gravitational pull, the less he or she weighs. Suppose you are an astronaut with a mass of 60 kilograms and a weight of about 600 newtons. If you travel into outer space, your mass will still be 60 kilograms. But your weight will be zero newtons.

Lesson Summary

- Volume, mass, and density are measurable properties of matter.
- The force of gravity acting between two objects can be measured. The unit used to record weight is the newton.
- Weight and mass are not the same. The location of objects does not affect their masses but does affect their weights.

Lesson Review

1. Name four properties of matter that can be measured.
2. A box of cereal measures 25 cm long, 20 cm wide, and 7 cm deep. What is its volume in cubic centimeters?
3. How many liters will take up the same space as 6,000 cubic centimeters?
4. Which is more dense, water or marbles? How do you know?
★5. How are mass and weight different?

How can you compare densities?

What you need

2 paper cups
popcorn (popped and unpopped)
water
small bowl
pan balance
pencil and paper

What to do

1. Fill one paper cup with unpopped corn. Fill the other cup with popped corn.
2. Place one cup on each pan of the balance. Record which cup has the greater mass.
3. Predict whether the popped or unpopped corn will float in water. Record your prediction.
4. Put some popped and unpopped corn into the bowl with water. Record your observations.

What did you learn?

1. How did the volume of the popped corn compare with the volume of the unpopped corn?
2. Which cup of corn has the greater mass?
3. Describe what you observed when both samples of corn were put in water.

Using what you learned

1. Does the popcorn become more or less dense after it is popped? How do you know?
2. What other foods change in density when they are cooked?
3. In supermarkets, why is popcorn usually sold unpopped rather than popped?

19

Properties of Matter

Think about the different kinds of things you see and use every day. All these objects are matter. The food you eat and the air you breathe are matter. You are also matter.

If you tried to list all the different kinds of matter you use or see in one day, the list would be very long. There are millions of different kinds of matter. Remember that matter is anything that has mass and takes up space. You may not be able to see some kinds of matter. Air can't be seen, but it is matter because it has mass and takes up space. Not everything you can see is matter. You can see light, but light isn't matter because it doesn't have mass or take up space.

We need to classify matter because there are so many different kinds. There are several ways scientists do this. One way to classify matter is by its state. Matter can be solid, liquid, or gaseous. Water is matter. It can exist as ice, liquid water, or water vapor. Another way to classify matter is by its composition.

The composition of something is what's in it. A baseball team is composed of nine players. A story is composed of words, and music is composed of notes.

All pure water has the same composition. It's made of hydrogen and oxygen. All pure water contains only these two kinds of matter. Water is a **substance** because it's matter that's always the same in composition. Table 1 shows some other substances.

You may think glass is a substance. Glass is matter, but it isn't a substance. The composition of glass is not always the same. Two pieces of glass may contain different kinds of matter or they may contain the same kinds of matter, but in different amounts.

Table 1	Substances and Their Uses
Substance	**Uses**
Aluminum	building material, aircraft and ships
Copper	electrical wire, plumbing
Gold	jewelry, coins, dentistry
Table Salt	flavoring food, making other chemicals
Baking Soda	cooking/baking, industry
Iodine	medicines, dyes
Propane	fuel

Chemical Properties

Objects are different because they are made of different substances. Substances have properties. Properties are characteristics such as color, hardness, and ability to combine with other substances. We use properties to tell one substance from another.

Some properties of substances are **chemical properties.** Chemical properties are observed when substances react with one another.

Oxygen in air reacts with the iron in some objects. When this happens the substance iron is changed into a new substance called rust. The ability to rust is a chemical property of iron. The ability to burn is a chemical property of substances such as wood and cotton. The burning of substances forms different kinds of matter such as ash, smoke, and gases.

Chemical Reactions

In a **chemical reaction,** two or more substances combine to form a new substance. For example, hydrogen and oxygen are both clear, colorless gases. A chemical reaction between hydrogen and oxygen forms water. The properties of water are very different from the properties of either hydrogen or oxygen.

Some chemical reactions cause a substance to be broken down into simpler substances. Water can be broken down into hydrogen and oxygen. Chemical reactions can build up or break down substances.

A chemical reaction occurs between silver nitrate and copper.

Silver nitrate reacts with sodium chloride and silver chloride is formed.

22

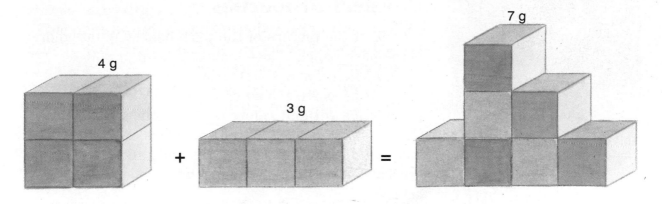

Matter can be rearranged but its total mass remains the same.

Have you ever used a camera with a flash bulb? If you have, you've caused a chemical reaction to occur. Now suppose that you measured the mass of your flash bulb before and after it flashed. If it had a mass of 20 grams before the flash, it would have a mass of 20 grams after it flashed. Though the substances have changed, there's the same total amount of substance you started with.

The **law of conservation of mass** states that mass is neither created nor destroyed in a chemical reaction. All the mass present in substances before a chemical reaction is present in the new substances after the chemical reaction. So when hydrogen and oxygen combine to form water, the mass of the water equals the mass of the hydrogen plus the mass of the oxygen. Conservation of mass applies to all chemical reactions.

Energy is involved in all chemical changes. Energy is either released or absorbed during a chemical reaction. The energy may be in the form of heat, light, or electricity. Burning is an example of a chemical reaction that releases energy. In what forms is energy released when a substance burns? A chemical reaction inside a flash bulb also releases energy. What kinds of energy are produced by this reaction?

Explain the law of conservation of mass.

This park bench has physical properties of color and hardness.

Physical Properties

Look at the picture of the park bench. What color is the park bench? Does it have a hard or soft surface? Its color and hardness are just two of its physical properties. You can observe **physical properties** without referring to another substance. Other examples of physical properties are volume, mass, and the boiling point of a substance. What are some other physical properties of the park bench?

Look at the pictures of water. Which picture shows water as a solid? As a liquid? Which picture shows where water as a gas is present? Notice that water can't be seen when it's a gas. When a substance changes state, its physical properties change. The state of a substance is another physical property.

Water exists in three states.

The boy has physically changed the wood.

In the picture, Jason has taken wood and created a model airplane. The size and shape of the wood has been changed, but the wood has not been changed into a new substance. It is still wood. The **physical change** in the wood's appearance hasn't changed its chemical composition. Physical change doesn't cause a new substance to be formed.

Lesson Summary

- A substance is composed of the same matter throughout.
- Chemical properties of substances depend on the behavior of those substances in a chemical reaction.
- Matter is neither created nor destroyed in a chemical reaction.
- Physical properties of substances can be observed without referring to another substance.

Lesson Review

1. Define substance. Give an example.
2. What is a chemical reaction?
★3. How are chemical and physical properties different?

Use Application Activity on pages 497, 498.

ACTIVITY

How can you use properties to identify materials?

What you need

baking soda
baking powder
cornstarch
materials A, B, C
vinegar
iodine solution
water

3 droppers
safety goggles
18 paper cups
pencil
3 spoons
aprons

What to do

1. Wear an apron and goggles.
2. Label three paper cups *baking soda*. Put a spoonful of baking soda into each cup.
3. Add one dropper of water to the first cup of baking soda. Record what you observe.
4. Add one dropper of iodine solution to the second cup. **CAUTION:** *Do not taste, touch, or spill the iodine solution.* Record what you observe.
5. Add one dropper of vinegar to the third cup. Record what you observe.
6. Repeat steps 2 through 5 using baking powder and cornstarch instead of baking soda.
7. Label three cups A, three cups B, and three cups C. Put samples of the three unknown materials in the cups.

   CAUTION: *NEVER taste an unknown material.*

8. Follow the same procedure you used in steps 3 through 5.
9. Compare your observations of the unknown materials with your observations of the known materials.

What did you learn?

1. What is each unknown material?
2. What properties of matter did you use to identify the unknown materials? Explain.
3. Why was it important to record your observations?

Using what you learned

1. How might scientists try to identify unknown materials in a laboratory?
2. What safety equipment must be used when identifying unknown materials?

Observations of Reactions			
Material	Liquid		
	water	iodine solution	vinegar
baking soda			
baking powder			
cornstarch			
A			
B			
C			

26

Summary

Lesson 1
- Observations are made using the five senses.
- One scientific method scientists use has five steps.

Lesson 2
- Volume, mass, and density are measurable properties of matter.
- The force of gravity acting between two objects can be measured. The unit used to record weight is the newton.
- Weight and mass are not the same. The location of objects does not affect their masses but does affect their weights.

Lesson 3
- A substance is composed of the same matter throughout.
- Chemical properties of substances depend on the behavior of those substances in a chemical reaction.
- The law of conservation of mass states that matter is neither created nor destroyed in a chemical reaction.
- Physical properties of substances can be observed.

Science Words

Fill in the blank with the correct word or words from the list.

hypothesis
experiment
data
conclusion
volume
mass
density
weight

newton
substance
chemical property
chemical reaction
law of conservation of mass
physical property
physical change

1. The amount of mass an object has for its volume is its ____.
2. ____ are recorded observations.
3. A(n) ____ is done to solve problems.
4. Matter that is the same throughout is a(n) ____.
5. Boiling point is a(n) ____.

6. When one substance changes into another, a(n) ____ takes place.

7. A change in the size, shape, or state of matter is a(n) ____.

8. A(n) ____ suggests a possible answer to a problem.

9. Ability to burn is a(n) ____.

10. Kilograms are used to measure ____.

Questions

Recalling Ideas

Correctly complete each of the following sentences.

1. Volume is measured in
   (a) grams.
   (b) density.
   (c) cubic newtons.
   (d) cubic centimeters.

2. Newtons are used to measure
   (a) mass.
   (b) density.
   (c) weight.
   (d) volume.

3. An example of a substance is
   (a) glass.
   (b) paper.
   (c) pure water.
   (d) salt water.

4. A chemical reaction is
   (a) evaporating.
   (b) rusting.
   (c) condensing.
   (d) boiling.

5. The attractive force between two objects is called
   (a) gravity.
   (b) mass.
   (c) density.
   (d) weight.

6. Burning is an example of
   (a) a physical change.
   (b) a chemical change.
   (c) a physical property.
   (d) a chemical property.

7. The basic unit of length is the
   (a) gram.
   (b) newton.
   (c) liter.
   (d) meter.

Examining Ideas

Determine whether each of the following statements is true or false. Rewrite the false statements to make them correct.

1. Physical properties depend on the way substances affect each other.

2. Air is matter because it has mass and takes up space.
3. Energy is involved in all chemical changes.
4. A new substance forms in a physical change.
5. Scientists use experimental data to form hypotheses.
6. Your mass would be the same on Earth and the moon.
7. A conclusion is an answer to an experimental question.
8. When water freezes, a physical change takes place.
9. Elements are substances.
10. Melting butter is a chemical change.

Understanding Ideas

Answer the following questions using complete sentences.
1. How do weight and mass differ?
2. Explain how observations are important in your everyday life.
3. What kind of property is the state of a substance?
4. How are chemical properties and physical properties different?
5. Why do astronauts weigh less two kilometers above Earth than on the surface of Earth?
6. What are the steps in one example of the scientific methods?
7. Which instruments aid you in seeing tiny organisms in a drop of pond water? craters on the moon? hearing your own heartbeat?

8. What is wrong with the statement, "Jose weighs 62 kilograms?"
9. What is the law of conservation of mass?

Thinking Critically

Think about what you have learned in this chapter. Answer the following questions using complete sentences.
1. Find the volume of water in a tank that is 50 cm high, 20 cm wide, and 50 cm long if the tank is full of water.
2. Your mother wants to find out which car wax gives the best shine. Help her use a scientific method to solve her problem.
3. What properties would you want in a material for baseball uniforms?
4. How would you use density to find whether the milk served in your cafeteria is skim, 2%, or whole?
5. Josh said, "Cork weighs less than iron. That's why cork floats in water and iron doesn't." Jan said, "I don't think that's exactly what you mean, Josh. It isn't the weight of the substances that is important . . ." Finish Jan's comment by explaining what she meant.
6. A window has light blue glass in it. Plants placed in this window either grow poorly or die. Suggest a hypothesis based on this observation.

CHAPTER 2

Matter and Its Changes

This bank, the Royal Bank of London in Toronto, Canada, has 70,000 grams of gold set in its glass windows. Gold is a scarce and beautiful element that naturally exists in Earth's crust. It is a difficult element to find because it usually occurs only as tiny grains or flakes inside rocks. Gold is almost indestructible. It doesn't tarnish like tin, or rust like iron. The gold in the bank's windows reflects the sun's rays in the summer and traps the sun's heat in winter. This temperature-control quality in gold helps maintain a constant temperature in the Royal Bank building.

Have You Ever...

Seen What Sugar Is Made Of?

Ask an adult to supervise you as you perform this activity. Put three tablespoons of sugar in a pie tin and place a jar upside down over the tin. As the sugar warms over low heat, notice the liquid that forms on the sides of the jar. What is that liquid? Remove the jar and continue to heat the sugar. Observe that the sugar has changed to a dark brown color. What remains in the tin?

Elements and Atoms

You've probably played with snap-together blocks similar to the ones pictured here. You may have built houses, airplanes, or spaceships with them. These blocks can be taken apart and rearranged into many shapes. As you know, all matter is composed of "building blocks." The building blocks of matter are tiny particles called **atoms.** Like snap-together blocks, a few atoms can be arranged in many combinations.

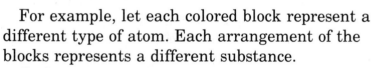

For example, let each colored block represent a different type of atom. Each arrangement of the blocks represents a different substance.

So far, scientists have found 109 kinds of atoms. They can combine to form an almost unlimited number of substances. But some substances are made of just one kind of atom. We call these substances **elements.** There is one element for each type of atom, 109 in all. We have found 90 elements that occur naturally in Earth's crust and atmosphere. Scientists have made 19 more in laboratories. One element you may know is iron. Iron is made of only iron atoms. What kind of atoms is the element sodium made of?

If we think about the blocks again, then we'd have to use only one type of block to represent an element. Say one blue block is a sodium atom. Then if we snapped together several blue blocks, we could represent the element sodium.

Atoms, like building blocks, can be arranged in many combinations.

Table 1 Common Natural Elements

Element	Symbol	State of Matter*	Some Properties and Uses	
Aluminum	Al	Solid	Lightweight metal	
Carbon	C	Solid	Found as coal, graphite, diamonds	
Chlorine	Cl	Gas	Greenish, poisonous gas	
Hydrogen	H	Gas	Lightest element, colorless, odorless gas	
Nitrogen	N	Gas	Colorless, odorless gas	
Oxygen	O	Gas	Colorless, odorless gas needed for life	

*at room temperature

Look at the table above. The first column shows you the names of some common natural elements. Which elements have you seen? Tell why you can't see some of them. We'll take a closer look at elements in the next lesson.

The Structure of Atoms

Look at the model of the helium atom on page 34. At the center you see the **nucleus.** The nucleus contains two kinds of particles called protons and neutrons. **Protons** have a positive electric charge. In the model they are shown with a plus (+) sign. **Neutrons** have no electric charge. They are shown with a zero (0). Protons and neutrons have almost identical masses. Together they make up most of the mass of an atom.

In the model you can see another type of particle. These are **electrons.** Electrons have negative electric charges. They are shown with a minus (−) sign.

Would You Believe?

If you could pack nuclei into a volume the size of a pea, they would weigh over 130,000,000 tons!

33

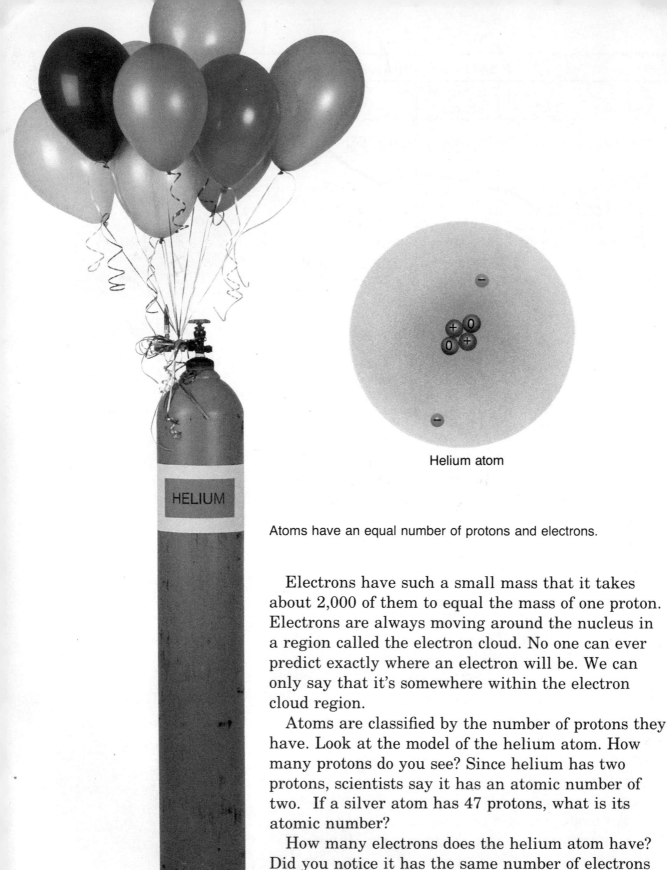

Helium atom

Atoms have an equal number of protons and electrons.

Electrons have such a small mass that it takes about 2,000 of them to equal the mass of one proton. Electrons are always moving around the nucleus in a region called the electron cloud. No one can ever predict exactly where an electron will be. We can only say that it's somewhere within the electron cloud region.

Atoms are classified by the number of protons they have. Look at the model of the helium atom. How many protons do you see? Since helium has two protons, scientists say it has an atomic number of two. If a silver atom has 47 protons, what is its atomic number?

How many electrons does the helium atom have? Did you notice it has the same number of electrons and protons? All atoms have equal numbers of

You Can...

ACTIVITY

Make an Electron Cloud Model

Put an X in the center of a sheet of paper. Use a hole punch to make ten paper dots. Hold the dots 30 cm above the paper. Drop them on the paper. Make a mark where each dot falls. Rotate the paper one-fourth turn, drop the ten dots again, and mark where they fall. Keep doing this until you have 100 marks on the paper. What do the X, the dots, and the paper represent? Where would protons be found?

electrons and protons. The positive charges of the protons cancel the negative charges of the electrons. Because of this, the helium atom itself has no electric charge.

Why don't atoms have an electric charge?

Lesson Summary

- All matter is composed of atoms.
- Different elements are composed of different atoms.
- Protons are particles with a positive charge. Neutrons are particles with no charge. Electrons are particles with a negative charge.

Lesson Review

1. What is an element?
2. Carbon has 12 protons. How many electrons does it have?
★3. If you could add extra neutrons to an atom, would the atom have a positive or negative electric charge? Explain.

35

Classifying Elements

LESSON 2 GOALS
You will learn
● how to use the periodic table.
● that elements can be grouped into chemical families.
● how elements can be classified.

Scientists classify elements into a table called the **periodic** (pihr ee AHD ihk) **table.** The periodic table is shown on pages 38 and 39.

As you look at the table, notice that the elements are arranged in order of their atomic numbers. At the upper left hand corner, you see hydrogen with the atomic number 1. Helium with the atomic number 2 is at the upper right hand corner. The second row begins with lithium which has the atomic number 3 and continues over to neon with the atomic number 10.

The periodic table also shows you a symbol for each element. The symbol is a short way to write the name of an element. The symbol for an element may be one, two, or three letters. When you look at carbon on the table, you see its symbol is C. The symbol for aluminum is Al. What is the symbol for neon? Did you notice that only the first letter is capitalized in symbols with more than one letter?

Some symbols come from the Latin names of the element. Find the symbol for iron. The Latin word for iron is *ferrum* so the symbol for iron is Fe. The Latin word for gold is *aurum.* What's the symbol for gold?

Naturally occurring elements are used to produce everyday products.

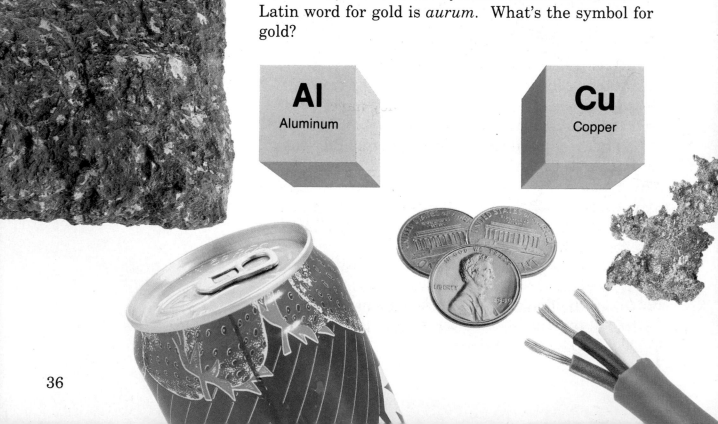

Al
Aluminum

Cu
Copper

Ne
Neon

   Besides being listed in order of their atomic numbers, the elements on the periodic table are grouped into columns. The element with the most mass in that column is found at the bottom. Likewise, the least massive element is on the top. Each of these columns makes up a **chemical family**. Elements in a chemical family have similar arrangements of electrons in their atoms. This gives them similar properties. For instance, look at the elements in the first column on the periodic table. All these elements are metals. They are different from many other metals because they have strong reactions with water. Lithium produces a flame when it contacts water. Sodium, potassium, and the other elements in this family have similar reactions with water. Why would it be useful for a scientist to know about this property of this particular family?

   Look for the family of elements in the eleventh column of the periodic table. These elements— copper, gold, and silver—are also metals. One of their properties is that they do not react to water. Why would a jeweler choose to make a ring from silver instead of sodium even though they're both shiny metals?

The Periodic Table

(Based on Carbon 12 = 12.0000)

Metals

Transition Elements

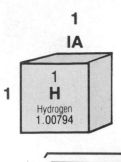

1 IA								
1 **H** Hydrogen 1.00794	**2** **IIA**							
3 **Li** Lithium 6.941	**4** **Be** Beryllium 9.01218	**3** **IIIB**	**4** **IVB**	**5** **VB**	**6** **VIB**	**7** **VIIB**	**8**	**9** **VIIIB**
11 **Na** Sodium 22.98977	**12** **Mg** Magnesium 24.305							
19 **K** Potassium 39.0983	**20** **Ca** Calcium 40.078	**21** **Sc** Scandium 44.95591	**22** **Ti** Titanium 47.88	**23** **V** Vanadium 50.9415	**24** **Cr** Chromium 51.9961	**25** **Mn** Manganese 54.9380	**26** **Fe** Iron 55.847*	**27** **Co** Cobalt 58.9332
37 **Rb** Rubidium 85.4678	**38** **Sr** Strontium 87.62	**39** **Y** Yttrium 88.9059	**40** **Zr** Zirconium 91.224	**41** **Nb** Niobium 92.9064	**42** **Mo** Molybdenum 95.94	**43** **Tc** Technetium 97.9072*	**44** **Ru** Ruthenium 101.07	**45** **Rh** Rhodium 102.9055
55 **Cs** Cesium 132.9054	**56** **Ba** Barium 137.33	**71** **Lu** Lutetium 174.967	**72** **Hf** Hafnium 178.49	**73** **Ta** Tantaium 180.9479	**74** **W** Tungsten 183.85	**75** **Re** Rhenium 186.207	**76** **Os** Osmium 190.2	**77** **Ir** Iridium 192.22
87 **Fr** Francium 223.0197*	**88** **Ra** Radium 226.0254	**103** **Lr** Lawrencium 260.1054*	**104** Unq Unnilquadium 261*	**105** Unp Unnilpentium 262*	**106** Unh Unnilhexium 263*	**107** Uns Unnilseptium 262*	**108** Uno Unniloctium 265*	**109** Une Unnilennium 266*

Lanthanide Series

57 **La** Lanthanum 138.9055	**58** **Ce** Cerium 140.12	**59** **Pr** Praseodymium 140.9077	**60** **Nd** Neodymium 144.24	**61** Pm Promethium 144.9128*	**62** **Sm** Samarium 150.36
89 **Ac** Actinium 227.0278*	**90** **Th** Thorium 232.0381	**91** **Pa** Protactinium 231.0359*	**92** **U** Uranium 238.0289	**93** Np Neptunium 237.0482	**94** Pu Plutonium 244.0642*

Actinide Series

38

Nonmetals

					18
					VIIIA
					2 **He** Helium 4.002602

13	14	15	16	17	
IIIA	**IVA**	**VA**	**VIA**	**VIIA**	
5 **B** Boron 10.811	6 **C** Carbon 12.011	7 **N** Nitrogen 14.0067	8 **O** Oxygen 15.9994	9 **F** Fluorine 18.998403	10 **Ne** Neon 20.179

10	11	12	13 **Al** Aluminum 26.98154	14 **Si** Silicon 28.0855	15 **P** Phosphorus 30.97376	16 **S** Sulfur 32.06	17 **Cl** Chlorine 35.453	18 **Ar** Argon 39.948
	IB	**IIB**						
28 **Ni** Nickel 58.69	29 **Cu** Copper 63.546	30 **Zn** Zinc 65.39	31 **Ga** Gallium 69.723	32 **Ge** Germanium 72.59	33 **As** Arsenic 74.9216	34 **Se** Selenium 78.96	35 **Br** Bromine 79.904	36 **Kr** Krypton 83.80
46 **Pd** Palladium 106.42	47 **Ag** Silver 107.8682	48 **Cd** Cadmium 112.41	49 **In** Indium 114.82	50 **Sn** Tin 118.710	51 **Sb** Antimony 121.75	52 **Te** Tellurium 127.60	53 **I** Iodine 126.9045	54 **Xe** Xenon 131.29
78 **Pt** Platinum 195.08	79 **Au** Gold 196.9665	80 **Hg** Mercury 200.59	81 **Tl** Thallium 204.383	82 **Pb** Lead 207.2	83 **Bi** Bismuth 208.9804	84 **Po** Polonium 208.9824*	85 **At** Astatine 209.98712*	86 **Rn** Radon 222.017*

63 **Eu** Europium 151.96	64 **Gd** Gadolinium 157.25	65 **Tb** Terbium 158.9254	66 **Dy** Dysprosium 162.50	67 **Ho** Holmium 164.9304	68 **Er** Erbium 167.26	69 **Tm** Thulium 168.9342	70 **Yb** Ytterbium 173.04
95 **Am** Americium 243.0614*	96 **Cm** Curium 247.0703*	97 **Bk** Berkelium 247.0703*	98 **Cf** Californium 251.0796*	99 **Es** Einsteinium 252.0828*	100 **Fm** Fermium 257.0951*	101 **Md** Mendelevium 258.986*	102 **No** Nobelium 259.1009*

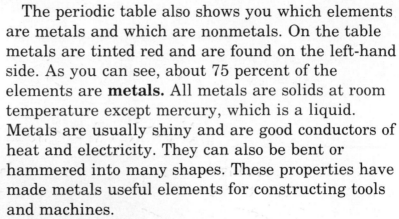

SCIENCE AND . . .
Math

In the following series of atomic numbers, what element would come next?

4, 8, 12, 16, . . .

A. Oxygen (O)
B. Magnesium (Mg)
C. Calcium (Ca)
D. Sulfur (S)

The periodic table also shows you which elements are metals and which are nonmetals. On the table metals are tinted red and are found on the left-hand side. As you can see, about 75 percent of the elements are **metals.** All metals are solids at room temperature except mercury, which is a liquid. Metals are usually shiny and are good conductors of heat and electricity. They can also be bent or hammered into many shapes. These properties have made metals useful elements for constructing tools and machines.

You can find the nonmetals, except for hydrogen, on the right-hand side of the periodic table. At room temperature, 10 nonmetals are solids, 11 are gases, and 1 is a liquid. **Nonmetals** are poor conductors of heat and electricity. The solids usually have dull surfaces and are too brittle to be hammered or bent.

Lesson Summary

- Elements are arranged in the periodic table according to their atomic structure.
- Elements within a chemical family have similar properties.
- Elements may be classified as metals or nonmetals.

Lesson Review

1. Look at the periodic table. Is helium a metal or a nonmetal?
2. What are the properties of most metals?
3. What are the five elements that have properties like calcium?
★4. What is the lightest element that has properties like those of iodine?

Gold can be reshaped for many uses.

40

I WANT TO KNOW ABOUT...

Context Clues

You can often guess the meaning of unfamiliar words by reading the sentence or paragraph they are used in. When you do this, you are using context clues. For example, read the following sentence to find the meaning of *periodic table.*

> Ellen looked at the **periodic table** to find the symbol and atomic number of silver.

From the sentence, you know that the periodic table is a table that gives you the symbol and atomic number of an element.

Read the following sentences and use the context clues to define the word in boldface type.

> **Atoms,** the tiny particles that make up matter, are composed of even smaller particles.

What part of the sentence helped you define the word *atoms?* In this case, the unfamiliar word is defined for you in the sentence.

> Iron, copper, and aluminum are all classified as **metals.**

How did you define *metals?* In what way did you need to apply your knowledge from previous experience to help you determine the meaning of *metals?*

When you come across unfamiliar words while reading, you can often find the meaning by using context clues in the sentence or paragraph in which the words are used. Sometimes the words are defined. Sometimes you must combine other clues with knowledge you already have.

Language Arts

LESSON 3 GOALS
You will learn
- what compounds are.
- that there are different kinds of compounds.
- how formulas show the elements in a compound.

Compounds

You have learned there are many known elements. Each is made of only one kind of atom. But there are many other substances on Earth that are not pure elements. You cannot find water on the periodic table. That's because water isn't made of only one kind of atom. Two kinds of atoms have combined chemically to form water. Water is a **compound.** Scientists have discovered about four million compounds formed from the 109 known elements.

Molecular Compounds

Let's take a look at how the compound water is formed. The diagram at the bottom of this page shows two hydrogen atoms and one oxygen atom combining to form a **molecule** (MAHL ih kyewl) of water. The atoms of hydrogen and oxygen combine in a chemical reaction because of the activity of their electrons. When the hydrogen and oxygen atoms join, they share electrons to form a molecule. We call water a molecular compound.

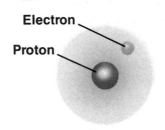

Electron

Proton

Hydrogen atom

+

Hydrogen atom

+

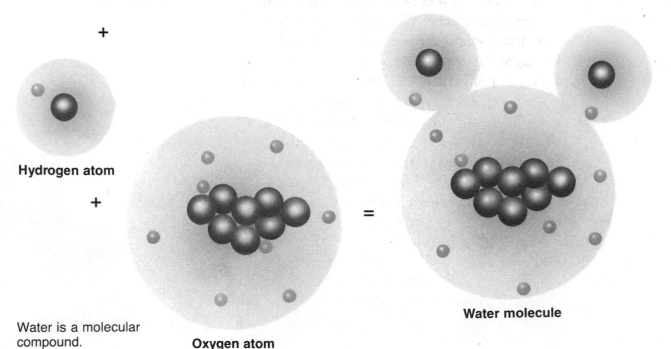

Water is a molecular compound.

Oxygen atom

=

Water molecule

Sugar granules still have properties of sugar.

The diagram on the previous page is a model of a water molecule. A molecule of water is extremely small. It takes trillions of them to form a single drop of water.

Another compound you're sure to know is table sugar. What are some of the properties of table sugar? Suppose you cut a cube of table sugar into smaller and smaller pieces. What do you think is the smallest amount a sugar cube could be divided into and still be sugar? A single grain of sugar? No, actually a sugar molecule is the smallest amount of sugar that still has all the properties of sugar.

If we break a sugar molecule apart into atoms, we would no longer have sugar. A sugar molecule is made up of hydrogen, oxygen, and carbon atoms. Hydrogen and oxygen are odorless, colorless gases. You may be familiar with carbon as charcoal or soot. When these three elements combine to form the compound sugar, they no longer have their individual properties. The new compound sugar has its own properties. You know it isn't an odorless, colorless gas like hydrogen and oxygen. And sugar is certainly different from charcoal or soot formed from carbon.

What elements are in sugar?

43

Model of table salt

Sodium Ion

Chloride Ion

Salt crystals

Ionic Compounds

How do atoms and ions differ?

Not all compounds are formed from molecules. Some compounds are formed when atoms lose or gain electrons instead of sharing them. Atoms that have gained or lost electrons are called **ions** (I ahnz). Remember that all atoms have an equal number of protons and electrons. Because of this, atoms have no electric charge. But when an atom gains an electron, it has more negative charges than positive ones, and the atom becomes an ion with a negative electric charge. If an atom loses an electron it has more positive charges, and the atom becomes an ion with a positive electric charge. Opposite charges attract, so negative ions attract positive ions. When this happens, **ionic compounds** form. Ionic compounds do not contain molecules.

The diagram on page 44 shows you the ionic compound sodium chloride, which we call table salt. Two kinds of atoms, sodium and chlorine, have become ions and joined to form sodium chloride. Chlorine is a poisonous green gas, and sodium is a shiny metal that bursts into flame in water. Yet table salt is nothing like either of these elements. So you can see that ionic compounds, like molecular compounds, don't have the same properties as the elements that form them.

Salt is formed from ions of sodium and chlorine.

Formulas

You have learned that a water molecule is formed from two hydrogen atoms and one oxygen atom. Scientists use hydrogen's symbol H and oxygen's symbol O to write the name for the compound water. These symbols written together as H_2O are the **formula** for water. The small number 2 after the H tells you there are two hydrogen atoms in water. The O has no number after it, which tells you there is only one atom of oxygen. It's not necessary to use a small number 1 in writing a formula.

Look at the photos below. Find the formula for hydrogen peroxide. Compare it to the formula for water. Here a different combination of hydrogen and oxygen atoms forms a different compound. This compound is used as a bleach and a disinfectant. How is the composition of hydrogen peroxide different from that of water? Perhaps you would like to make a diagram similar to the one on page 42 to show how a molecule of hydrogen peroxide is formed.

Common compounds and their formulas

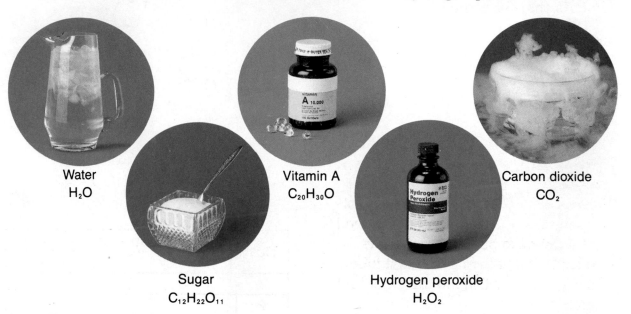

Water
H_2O

Sugar
$C_{12}H_{22}O_{11}$

Vitamin A
$C_{20}H_{30}O$

Hydrogen peroxide
H_2O_2

Carbon dioxide
CO_2

Lesson Summary

- A compound is formed when the atoms of different elements combine in a chemical reaction.
- In molecular compounds atoms share electrons. Ionic compounds contain ions formed when electrons are transferred from one atom to another.
- A formula shows the kind of atoms and number of atoms in a compound.

Lesson Review

1. What is an ion?
2. Vitamin C has the formula $C_6H_8O_6$. How many atoms of each of its elements does it have?
★3. How are elements different from compounds?

How is a compound formed?

What you need

steel wool
2 test tubes
beaker
water
masking tape
metric ruler
pencil and paper

What to do

1. Record the properties of the steel wool.
2. Place a small wet ball of steel wool in one test tube. Use the eraser end of a pencil to gently push the steel wool to the bottom of the test tube. Do not put anything in the other test tube.
3. Place both test tubes upside down in a beaker that's half full of water. Tape the test tubes so they will stand up in the beaker.
4. Measure the height of the water in each test tube. Make a data table like the one shown and record your measurements.
5. Observe the test tubes once a day for four more days. Measure the water levels in each test tube. Record your measurements and observations.

What did you learn?

1. Describe any changes you noticed in the steel wool.

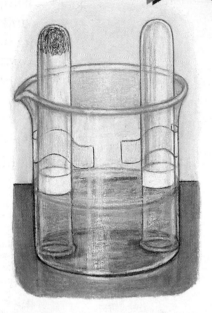

| Day | Height of water in test tubes | |
	Empty	Steel wool
1		
2		
3		
4		
5		

2. What compound was formed?
3. Explain any changes in the water levels in the test tubes.

Using what you learned

1. Where else does this compound form?
2. What combined to form the compound?
3. From where did the atoms of the compound come? How do you know?

Mixtures

LESSON 4 GOALS

You will learn
● how mixtures are formed.
● that there are different kinds of mixtures.
● several ways to separate mixtures.

Scott is helping his parents with lunch by making fruit salad. He mixes sliced apples, grapes, and oranges together to make the salad. Fruit salad is a combination of different substances, but it is not a compound. There's no chemical reaction taking place among the different pieces of fruit. Fruit salad is a mixture. A **mixture** is a combination of substances that forms without a chemical reaction.

Mixtures can be any combination of solid, liquid, and gaseous substances. Fruit punch is a mixture of liquids. The air you breathe is a mixture of gases. Soil is a mixture of solids. Ocean water is an example of solids and gases mixed with a liquid. A carbonated soft drink is an example of gas mixed with a liquid. The gas carbon dioxide is mixed with the liquid of a soft drink. The "fizz" you hear when you open a soft drink can is the carbon dioxide gas leaving the liquid.

Salads, concrete, and many rocks are mixtures.

48

Mixture of tea and sugar

Solution of tea and sugar

Saturated solution of tea and sugar

Solutions

A **solution** is a mixture in which a substance is spread evenly throughout another substance. A solution is exactly the same all the way through.

When you put a cube of sugar into a glass of tea, the cube sinks to the bottom of the glass and begins to dissolve. At this point the sugar and tea in the glass are a mixture but are not yet a solution. At first, the tea is sweeter at the bottom of the glass than at the top. When you stir the tea, what happens to the cube of sugar? The sugar breaks into smaller pieces and continues to dissolve. When the dissolved sugar is spread evenly throughout the tea, the entire mixture is a solution. All parts of the tea will taste equally sweet to you.

Some people put two cubes of sugar in their tea. Two cubes can easily dissolve in a glass of tea. However, you can't keep on dissolving sugar in the tea. After a few cubes, no more sugar will dissolve. We say the tea and sugar is a **saturated solution** when no more sugar will dissolve in it. But if you heat the tea, more sugar can be dissolved. Temperature is important in forming a saturated solution. More of a substance can usually be dissolved in a warmer liquid than in a cooler one.

When is a solution saturated?

Salad dressing is a suspension.

Suspensions

Why do you shake a bottle of salad dressing before you use it? The salad dressing is another kind of mixture called a suspension. In a **suspension** the substances that make it up are not dissolved. When you leave a suspension undisturbed, the materials in it separate. Look at the picture of the two bottles of salad dressing. What has happened in the second picture? The force of gravity causes the heavier materials to slowly settle out of the suspension.

Many medicines are also suspensions. Why do many medicine bottles include directions for shaking the medication before using it?

You may have seen dust particles in air form a suspension. When a ray of sunlight shines through a window, you can often see a cloud of dust particles. For a while dust will be suspended in the air, but eventually the force of gravity will cause it to settle onto the furniture and floor.

What type of mixture is dust and air?

Separating Mixtures

Substances in a mixture are not chemically combined. Each substance still has its own properties. The physical properties of substances can be used to separate mixtures. What properties could you use to separate a mixture of buttons?

50

You can separate some mixtures by using a filter. For example, a filter can be used to separate some solids mixed with liquids. The liquids pass through holes in the filter, while the solids are trapped. A strainer is a kind of filter. What have you seen filtered with a strainer?

Suppose you have a mixture of salt and sand and you want to separate them. How can you do this? Some mixtures of solids can be separated by dissolving one of the substances. First you can add water to the mixture. The salt will dissolve in the water but the sand will not. Then you can pour the mixture of sand, salt, and water through a filter. The sand will be trapped in the filter. The salt and water solution will go through the filter. Now you can separate the salt from the water by evaporation. Evaporating the water from the solution leaves only the salt.

An easy way to separate suspensions is to allow them to remain undisturbed. The force of gravity will cause the heavier materials to settle to the bottom of the suspension. Why do you think it's best to wait awhile after dusting the furniture before running the vacuum cleaner?

Some mixtures can be separated by filtering.

Lesson Summary

- Mixtures form without chemical reactions.
- Solutions and suspensions are types of mixtures.
- Mixtures may be separated by filtering, evaporation, or settling.

Lesson Review

1. What is a mixture?
2. How is a mixture different from a compound?
3. How could you use a filter to separate a mixture of raisins and flour?
★4. How is a solution different from a suspension?

How can you separate and compare mixtures?

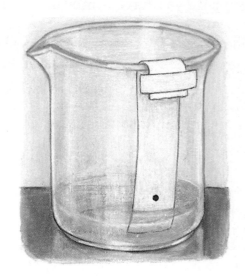

What you need

paper towel
metric ruler
scissors
black felt-tip pens
water
beaker
masking tape
pencil and paper

What to do

1. Cut a strip of paper towel about 4 cm wide and 15 cm long.
2. Make a large ink dot with a black felt-tip pen about 5 cm from the bottom of the strip.
3. Put water in the beaker. Make the water 3 cm deep.
4. Dip the bottom of the strip into the water, making sure the ink dot stays above the water. Bend the top of the strip over the edge of the beaker. Tape the top of the strip to the beaker.
5. Wait for the water to soak up to the top of the strip.
6. Observe the ink dot. Record your observations.
7. Repeat steps 1 through 6 using different pens. Record your observations.

What did you learn?

1. What color ink was in each pen you used?
2. What did you observe as the water moved up the paper strip?
3. What evidence do you have that the inks in the pens are mixtures? Explain your answer.

Using what you learned

1. Describe what might happen if you wrote a report in black ink and the paper got wet.
2. Suppose you stain your clothing. You try to clean the stain with water and a ring forms around the stained area. Explain why this might have happened.

CHAPTER REVIEW

2

Summary

Lesson 1
- All matter is composed of atoms.
- Different elements are composed of different atoms.
- Protons are particles with a positive charge. Neutrons are particles with no charge. Electrons are particles with a negative charge.

Lesson 2
- Elements are arranged in the periodic table according to their atomic structure.
- Elements within a chemical family have similar properties.
- Elements may be classified as metals or nonmetals.

Lesson 3
- A compound is formed when the atoms of different elements combine in a chemical reaction.
- In molecular compounds atoms share electrons. Ionic compounds contain ions formed when electrons are transferred from one atom to another.
- A formula shows the kinds of atoms and number of atoms in a compound.

Lesson 4
- Mixtures form without chemical reactions.
- Solutions and suspensions are types of mixtures.
- Mixtures can be separated by filtering, evaporation, or settling.

Science Words

Fill in the blank with the correct word or words from the list.

atoms	molecule	electrons	saturated
elements	ion	periodic table	solution
nucleus	formula	compound	suspension
protons	mixture	chemical family	nonmetals
neutrons	solution	metals	ionic compounds

1. Particles in the nucleus with no electrical charge are ____.

2. Elements are classified in the ____.

3. The negative particles outside the nucleus of an atom are ____.
4. In a(n) ____ , heavier materials may settle to the bottom.
5. Atoms of different elements react to form a(n) ____.
6. Charged particles with the same mass as the neutron are ____.
7. An atom that has lost or gained an electron is called a(n) ____.
8. When two or more atoms share electrons, they form a(n) ____.
9. Symbols of the elements in a compound make a(n) ____.
10. A(n) ____ has the same composition throughout.

Questions

Recalling Ideas
Correctly complete each of the following sentences.

1. All atoms of an element have the same number of
   (a) protons.
   (b) neutrons and protons.
   (c) neutrons.
   (d) neutrons and electrons.

2. An example of an element and its symbol is
   (a) I-iron.   (c) Hg-mercury.
   (b) H-helium.   (d) Ne-nitrogen.

3. The particles of atoms that have a negative charge are
   (a) electrons.   (c) neutrons.
   (b) protons.   (d) nuclei.

4. Compounds are made of at least two
   (a) mixtures.   (c) suspensions.
   (b) ions.   (d) elements.

5. The formula of a compound with one sodium atom, one oxygen atom, and one hydrogen atom is
   (a) SH_2O.   (c) SOH.
   (b) NaOH.   (d) HO_2Na.

6. Elements that are usually shiny and good conductors of heat and electricity are known as
   (a) gases.   (c) solids.
   (b) metals.   (d) nonmetals.

7. A copper atom that has lost two electrons is
   (a) a molecule. (c) an alloy.
   (b) a compound. (d) an ion.

8. Electrons are shared in
   (a) an element. (c) a molecule.
   (b) an ion.   (d) an ionic compound.

9. A solution in which no more substance can be dissolved is
   (a) saturated.   (c) ionic.
   (b) filtered.   (d) separated.

10. An example of a compound is
    (a) Co.   (c) NO.
    (b) N.   (d) Fe.

Examining Ideas
Determine whether each of the following statements is true or false. Rewrite the false statements to make them correct.

1. Atoms combine physically to form compounds.

2. Elements are made of atoms.
3. Atoms that share electrons with other atoms form ionic compounds.
4. If an atom loses an electron, it becomes a molecule.
5. Symbols put together in a certain way to show the elements in a compound make a formula.
6. The nucleus of an atom contains protons and electrons.
7. A solution is a mixture in which a substance is spread evenly throughout another substance.
8. Salt can be separated from a salt water solution by settling.
9. A mixture is a combination of substances that forms during a chemical reaction.
10. More sugar can be dissolved in cold water than in hot water.

Understanding Ideas

Answer the following questions using complete sentences.

1. How are all atoms alike?
2. Contrast and compare elements and compounds.
3. An atom of platinum, Pt, has 78 protons. How many electrons does it contain?

Thinking Critically

Think about what you have learned in this chapter. Answer the following questions using complete sentences.

1. How are the elements in a chemical family different?
2. What are some elements that have properties similar to helium. Explain how you know.
3. Tell how to separate
   (a) sand-water.
   (b) oil-vinegar.
   (c) salt-water.
   (d) sand-salt
   (e) pennies-nickels.

CHAPTER 3

Investigating Compounds

Water covers over two-thirds of Earth's surface. In fact, of all nine planets in our galaxy, Earth has the most water. All living things on Earth require the compound water to survive. Though we have found water on other planets, only on Earth does it exist as a liquid, gas (vapor), and solid (ice).

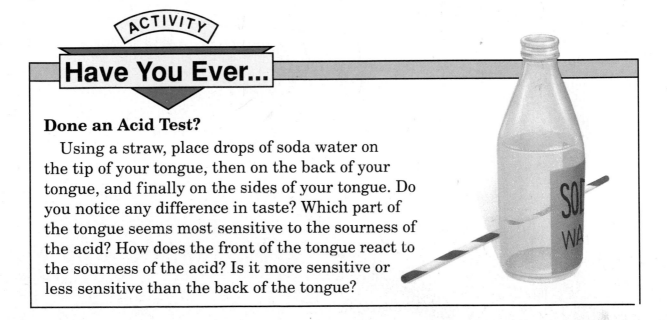

ACTIVITY

Have You Ever...

Done an Acid Test?

Using a straw, place drops of soda water on the tip of your tongue, then on the back of your tongue, and finally on the sides of your tongue. Do you notice any difference in taste? Which part of the tongue seems most sensitive to the sourness of the acid? How does the front of the tongue react to the sourness of the acid? Is it more sensitive or less sensitive than the back of the tongue?

LESSON 1 GOALS
You will learn
● that compounds can be classified.
● what organic compounds are.
● how inorganic and organic compounds differ.

Classifying Compounds

On the way home from school one day, Jake stopped at the grocery store. His mother had given him a list of ten items she needed. The grocery store was very large, and Jake was worried he might not be able to find everything his mother wanted. As he pushed his cart up and down the aisles, he noticed that each aisle had a sign listing the items that could be found there. The grocery items were grouped to help make shopping easier.

Classifying items can be helpful.

milk   bread
hamburger   tomatoes
foil   yogurt
lettuce   oranges
potatoes   butter

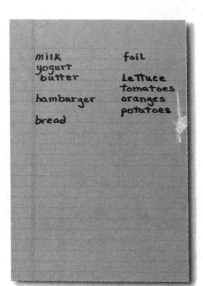

milk   foil
yogurt
butter   lettuce
            tomatoes
hamburger   oranges
            potatoes
bread

Jake studied his list. If he grouped the items by similarities, he could finish shopping quicker. Milk, he knew, could be found in the dairy case. He knew that the butter and yogurt he needed were also found there because they have properties similar to milk. To help Jake, what similar properties would you use to group, or classify, the rest of the items on his list?

Just as Jake organized his list to make it useful, scientists classify matter so they can study it.

58

As you have learned, there are millions of compounds on Earth. Even though all these compounds are formed by chemical reactions, no two compounds are the same. Each compound has a set of properties that scientists use to classify it. One way to classify a compound is by its composition. You can tell the composition of a compound by looking at its formula. The formula for table sugar is $C_{12}H_{22}O_{11}$. What three elements make up table sugar?

Organic Compounds

Sugar and many other compounds that contain carbon are called **organic compounds**. In organic compounds, carbon is combined with other elements. These other elements are usually hydrogen and oxygen, and may include nitrogen, phosphorus, or sulfur.

At one time scientists thought organic compounds could be found only in organisms or in matter that was once alive. But about 150 years ago, scientists discovered they could make organic compounds in laboratories. Since then several million organic compounds have been made in laboratories. Many compounds you use every day are organic compounds. Look at the pictures on this page. All these items contain organic compounds.

What elements are usually found in organic compounds?

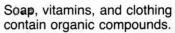

Soap, vitamins, and clothing contain organic compounds.

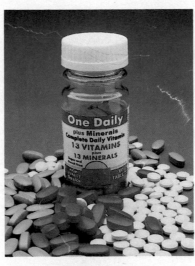

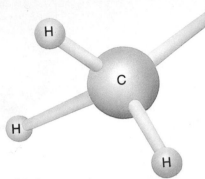

Methane molecule

An organic compound that contains only carbon and hydrogen is called a **hydrocarbon**. We often use hydrocarbons for fuels. Methane is a common hydrocarbon found in marshes. When organisms in a marsh die and decay, methane is produced.

Methane mixed with other gases makes up natural gas. You may use natural gas as a fuel for heating and cooking in your home.

Petroleum is another example of a mixture of hydrocarbons. The gasoline used in your family's car and in the bus you ride to school is made from petroleum. Many of the medicines, cosmetics, paints, plastics, and clothes you use are also made from petroleum.

Petroleum for gasoline, cosmetics, and plastics is produced at oil refineries.

Inorganic Compounds

Some compounds that contain carbon aren't classified as organic compounds. For example, carbon dioxide (CO_2) is made of carbon and oxygen. Yet it's not classified as an organic compound. Compounds that are not classified as organic compounds are called **inorganic compounds**. An inorganic compound may be made of any elements and can be classified as an oxide, acid, base, or salt. In the next lesson you will learn about acids, bases, and salts. Now let's investigate oxides.

C   + O_2 = CO_2

Carbon dioxide is an inorganic compound.

Oxides

An **oxide** (AHK side) is formed when oxygen combines with another element. When oxygen, for example, combines with aluminum, aluminum oxide is formed. This oxide forms a protective coating on aluminum. Oxygen can also combine with silicon to form silicon dioxide. Perhaps you have built a castle out of silicon dioxide at a beach. What is another name for silicon dioxide?

Most elements can combine with oxygen to form oxides. What is the composition of each oxide listed in Table 1 on page 62? Where can you find these oxides?

This sculpture is made of silicon dioxide.

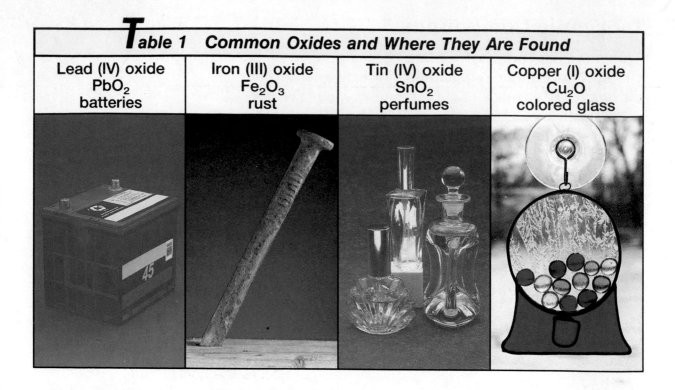

Table 1 Common Oxides and Where They Are Found			
Lead (IV) oxide PbO_2 batteries	Iron (III) oxide Fe_2O_3 rust	Tin (IV) oxide SnO_2 perfumes	Copper (I) oxide Cu_2O colored glass

Some oxides can be harmful. Oxides of nitrogen are produced when some fuels are burned. Two common ones are nitrogen oxide and nitrogen dioxide. They are produced in high temperature engines. They can kill plants and may be harmful to animals, including humans. High amounts of nitrogen oxides in the air can lead to lung diseases.

Lesson Summary

- Scientists classify compounds by their physical and chemical properties and by their composition.
- Organic compounds contain carbon.
- Most inorganic compounds do not contain carbon.

Lesson Review

1. What do scientists need to know about a compound in order to classify it?
2. How are some organic compounds helpful to you?
★3. Why are there so many more compounds than there are elements?

How can you prevent rust?

What you need

iron nails
galvanized nails
2 or more large corks
shallow pan
water
2 small jars
paint and brushes
motor oil
petroleum jelly
other materials as needed
clay

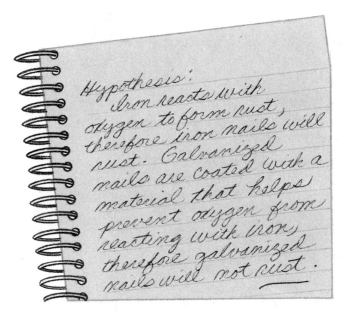

Hypothesis:
Iron reacts with oxygen to form rust, therefore iron nails will rust. Galvanized nails are coated with a material that helps prevent oxygen from reacting with iron, therefore galvanized nails will not rust.

What to do

1. Read the hypothesis that a student made.
2. To test the student's hypothesis, insert each kind of nail into a different cork.

3. Secure the corks in a pan of water with clay. Invert a jar over each cork and nail as shown in the picture.
4. Observe the nails each day for 5 days. Record your observations.
5. Make a hypothesis about how you might prevent nails from rusting.
6. Test your hypothesis.

What did you learn?

1. Does your data support the student's hypothesis? Explain.
2. What did you do to prevent the nails from rusting? Did it work?

Using what you learned

1. Change your hypothesis into a conclusion based on your data.
2. If you were building a house, what kind of nails would you use to attach shingles to the roof? What are some other things you would want to consider besides whether the nails rust?

Acids, Bases, and Salts

How would you describe the taste of a lemon? What about a grapefruit? Most likely, you'd say they taste sour. Many foods contain acids that give them a sour taste. If you've ever eaten too many green apples, you know they make your stomach hurt. There's more acid in the green apples than your stomach can handle at one time. Taking an antacid tablet or drinking milk of magnesia helps your stomach. These medicines are classified as bases. Bases react with acids and produce salt and water. As a result, your stomach contains less acid and you begin to feel better.

You're probably familiar with many common acids, bases, and salts. Let's take a closer look at these types of compounds.

Acids

Acids are substances that form hydrogen ions as they dissolve in water. Because of these ions, all acids have similar properties. Acids cause some foods to taste sour. Vinegar, for example, tastes sour because of the organic acid compound. Yet carbonated soft drinks, which contain carbonic acid, taste sweet. This is because sugar and other sweeteners are added to them.

Acids

Bases

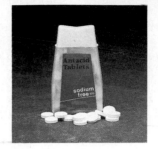

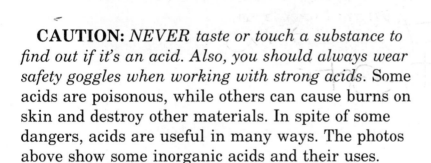

CAUTION: *NEVER taste or touch a substance to find out if it's an acid. Also, you should always wear safety goggles when working with strong acids.* Some acids are poisonous, while others can cause burns on skin and destroy other materials. In spite of some dangers, acids are useful in many ways. The photos above show some inorganic acids and their uses.

Bases

Some inorganic compounds are classified as bases. A **base** is a substance that dissolves in water to form hydroxide ions. A hydroxide ion is a unit of hydrogen and oxygen. As the photos show, some inorganic bases are used to make soaps, detergents, and other household cleansers. You could use one of these cleansers to clean a greasy frying pan because bases break up fats and oils. Bases taste bitter and feel slippery. Like acids, bases can be very dangerous and especially harmful if they are splashed into your eyes. **CAUTION:** *NEVER taste or touch a substance to find out if it's a base. You should always wear safety goggles when working with strong bases.*

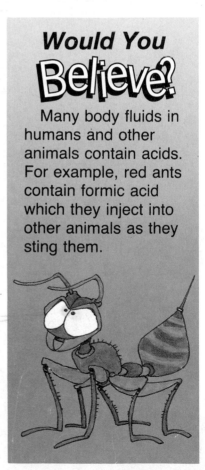

Would You *Believe?*

Many body fluids in humans and other animals contain acids. For example, red ants contain formic acid which they inject into other animals as they sting them.

You Can...

Make an Indicator

Get an adult to help you with this activity. Do not do it without an adult's help! Put some shredded red cabbage in a pan of hot water. Stir until the water is bright red. Strain the mixture and collect the liquid in a jar or cup. Mix 5 drops of the liquid with a little vinegar and 5 drops with a little window cleaner. What color indicates acids? bases? Test liquids, such as tea, shampoo, fruit juices, and so on. Which are acids? Which are bases?

Acid and Base Indicators

How do scientists identify acids and bases?

Scientists never taste or touch a substance to find out if it's an acid or a base. Instead, they use an indicator as a safe way to find out if a substance is an acid or a base. An **indicator** (IHN duh kayt ur) is a compound that changes color when added to acids and bases. Litmus is an indicator made from lichen plants. People use paper coated with litmus to find out if substances are acids or bases. Litmus paper can be red or blue. Blue litmus paper turns red when dipped in an acid. Red litmus paper turns blue when dipped in a base.

Litmus paper is used to indicate acids and bases.

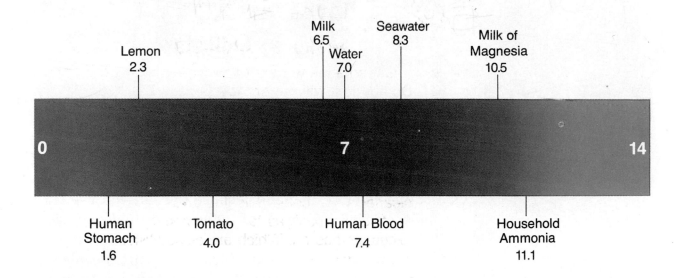

A scale called the **pH scale** can be used to indicate the strength of acids and bases. The pH scale ranges between 0 and 14. A pH between 0 and 7 indicates an acid. A pH between 7 and 14 indicates a base. A substance that is neither an acid nor a base has a pH of 7. Such a substance is **neutral.** Pure water has a pH of 7, therefore, water is a neutral substance.

Salts

An acid and a base can be combined in a chemical reaction. The chemical changes that occur produce water and a **salt**. The water and salt have properties different from those of the acid and base from which they were formed. As you know, water is neutral and the salt produced may also be neutral.

There are many kinds of salts. Most salts are composed of a metal and a nonmetal and can be made by combining a certain acid and base.

SCIENCE AND . . .
Reading

If household ammonia has a pH of 11.1, it is classified as a(n) ____
A. oxide.
B. acid.
C. base.
D. salt.

At dinner, do you ever say "Please pass the salt"? Do you know you could say instead, "Please pass the sodium chloride"? That's because the salt you use to flavor your food is made of sodium and chloride ions. The element sodium, however, keeps water in the body, and that can be harmful to the heart. People have to watch the amount of sodium they use to help keep their hearts healthy. Many people use a salt substitute instead. One such substitute is potassium chloride. Potassium chloride is also a salt, but potassium doesn't cause your body to hold water as sodium does.

There are other salts that can be found in your home. On icy days, you may use calcium chloride on your front steps or sidewalk to melt the snow and ice. This salt lowers the freezing point of water, and the ice and snow soon turn to liquid water.

What's another name for table salt?

Lesson Summary

- Acids, bases, and salts are three kinds of compounds.
- Indicators are compounds that change color to indicate whether a solution is acidic or basic.

Lesson Review

1. How are inorganic compounds often classified?
2. What are some properties of acids? of bases?
★3. Combining NaOH, a base, and HCl, an acid, produces the salt NACl and what other substance?

How can you find out if a solution is an acid or a base?

What you need

5 small jars
5 labels
safety goggles
vinegar
lemon juice
liquid detergent
baking soda
   solution
distilled water
5 strips red litmus
   paper
5 strips blue litmus
   paper
pencil and paper

What to do

1. Put on your safety goggles and copy the data table below.
2. Label the jars 1–5.
3. Fill each jar one-fourth full of the following liquids:
   Jar 1: vinegar
   Jar 2: lemon juice
   Jar 3: detergent
   Jar 4: baking soda solution
   Jar 5: distilled water
4. Dip one end of a strip of red litmus paper into the liquid in jar 1. Record your observations.
5. Dip one end of a strip of blue litmus paper into the liquid in jar 1. Record your observations.
6. Using new strips of red and blue litmus paper for each test, repeat steps 4 and 5 with each liquid.

What did you learn?

1. Blue litmus paper turns red in acids. Which liquids are acids?
2. Red litmus paper turns blue in bases. Which liquids are bases?
3. Which liquids are neutral (neither acids nor bases)?

Using what you learned

1. How can you use litmus paper to find out if a substance is an acid?
2. Predict 2 liquids used in this experiment that may be combined to form a neutral solution. Combine these liquids. Use litmus paper to test your prediction.

Jar Number	Contents	Litmus Paper	
		Red	Blue
1	vinegar		
2	lemon juice		
3	detergent		
4	baking soda solution		
5	distilled water		

I WANT TO KNOW ABOUT...

Soil Scientists

Every morning Donald R. Ballinger laces his sturdy hiking boots and packs an assortment of bottles and small tools into his knapsack. His daily work assignments take him to many of the farms and fields in the county. Don is a soil scientist.

One of the chemical properties of soil that Don studies is soil pH. To determine the pH of a soil sample, Don uses an indicator solution. He places a few drops of the solution in a jar containing a small amount of soil. If the soil is acidic, the colorless indicator solution will turn dark green. If the soil is basic, the solution will turn bright red.

Don then takes another small soil sample and compares its natural color to color charts designed to determine the exact soil pH.

It's important to know the pH of soil. Farmers need to know what types of plants will grow best on their land. For example, tomatoes and asparagus require slightly acidic soil with a pH between 5.5 and 7.0. Certain types of wheat, on the other hand, require slightly basic soil with a pH between 7.5 and 8.0. Soil scientists, like Don, help farmers choose which crops to grow.

Summary

Lesson 1
- Scientists classify compounds by their physical and chemical properties and by their composition.
- Organic compounds contain carbon.
- Most inorganic compounds do not contain carbon.

Lesson 2
- Acids, bases, and salts are three kinds of compounds.
- Indicators are compounds that change color to indicate whether a solution is acidic or basic.

Science Words

Fill in the blank with the correct word or words from the list.

organic compound   base
hydrocarbon   indicator
inorganic compound   pH scale
oxide   neutral
acid   salt

1. A compound containing carbon is called a(n) ____.
2. A compound containing only hydrogen and carbon is known as a(n) ____.
3. A compound containing oxygen and one other element is a(n) ____.
4. A substance that produces hydrogen ions when dissolved in water is a(n) ____.
5. A substance that produces hydroxide ions when dissolved in water is a(n) ____.
6. A compound that changes color when added to acids or bases is a(n) ____.
7. A range of numbers to measure the strength of an acid or base is the ____.
8. A compound that is neither an acid nor a base is ____.
9. A compound that does not contain carbon is classified as a(n) ____.

Questions

Recalling Ideas

Correctly complete each of the following sentences.

1. A substance with a pH of 7 is
   (a) neutral.
   (b) an acid.
   (c) a base.
   (d) saturated.
2. Litmus turns red in
   (a) a salt.
   (b) a base.
   (c) an acid.
   (d) an element.
3. Sand is an example of
   (a) an oxide.
   (b) an acid.
   (c) a base.
   (d) a salt.
4. All of the following are hydrocarbons EXCEPT
   (a) CH_3COOH.
   (b) CH_3CH_3.
   (c) C_8H_{18}.
   (d) CH_4.
5. Two compounds that are formed when an acid reacts with a base are
   (a) water and an oxide.
   (b) water and a salt.
   (c) a salt and an oxide.
   (d) organic and inorganic.
6. The pH of a strong base would be closest to
   (a) 14.
   (b) 9.
   (c) 7.
   (d) 3.
7. The reaction of an acid with a base is a(n)
   (a) chemical change.
   (b) physical change.
   (c) organic reaction.
   (d) negative reaction.

Examining Ideas

Determine whether each of the following statements is true or false.

Rewrite the false statements to make them correct.

1. A chemical compound may be classified by its physical and chemical properties.
2. Most organic compounds do not contain carbon.
3. Salts are made by combining water and acids.
4. A pH value of 4 indicates that a solution is neutral.
5. Blue litmus paper turns red when dipped into acid.
6. Bases taste sour and feel slippery.
7. A hydrocarbon is a compound of carbon and water.
8. Scientists may use indicators to find out if a solution is an acid or a base.
9. Petroleum is a compound containing different hydrocarbons.
10. No inorganic compounds contain carbon.

Understanding Ideas

Answer the following questions using complete sentences.

1. How is the composition of every oxide alike?
2. How are the properties of acids and bases different?
3. Which of the following household items contain acids? Which contain bases?
   (a) orange juice

(b) ammonia

(c) tomato sauce

(d) tea

(e) soap

4. Which of the following are NOT organic compounds?
   (a) alcohol (C_2H_6O)
   (b) water (H_2O)
   (c) antifreeze ($C_2H_6O_2$)
   (d) table sugar ($C_{12}H_{22}O_{11}$)
   (e) zinc oxide (ZnO)
   (f) methane (CH_4)
   (g) octane (C_8H_{18})

5. Why does litmus paper not change color in distilled water?

6. What are two ways organic compounds are made?

Thinking Critically

Think about what you have learned in this chapter. Answer the following questions using complete sentences.

1. How are all compounds alike?

2. Why do scientists classify compounds? How do they classify them?

3. Baking soda (sodium bicarbonate) is often sprinkled on spilled acid. Give a possible explanation.

4. Name and write the formula for the salt that forms when hydrochloric acid (HCl) reacts with potassium hydroxide (KOH). What other compound forms? Write its formula.

5. When science fiction writers discuss life on different planets, they often identify Earth as having a carbon-based life form. Explain what they mean.

CHAPTER

4

Electricity

The average hurricane is over 400 kilometers in diameter. But a hurricane begins as a small tropical storm. The rain and wind build in size and intensity. A hurricane's energy is about equal to the amount of electricity used in one day in the United States. And one bolt of lightning from that storm can provide enough electricity for 200,000 homes for one day.

ACTIVITY

Have You Ever...

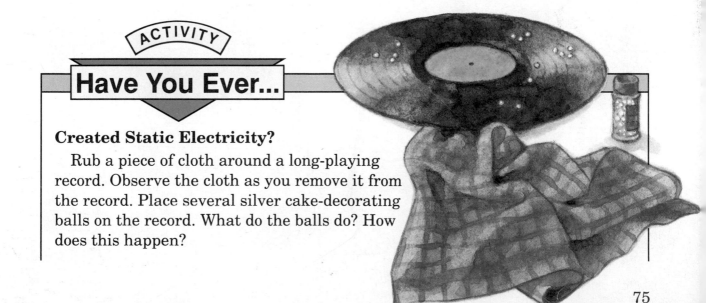

Created Static Electricity?

Rub a piece of cloth around a long-playing record. Observe the cloth as you remove it from the record. Place several silver cake-decorating balls on the record. What do the balls do? How does this happen?

Static Electricity

LESSON 1 GOALS
You will learn
● how static electricity occurs.
● the effects of like and unlike electric charges.
● what a static electric discharge is.

Have you ever unloaded the clothes dryer and found your socks sticking to your sweater? When you pulled them apart, did you hear a crackling noise and see the fibers in the fabrics standing up as though pulled by a magnet? What you experienced is static electricity. Let's find out what causes it.

While the dryer is operating, the clothes are tumbling around and rubbing against each other. The constant rubbing causes electrons to move from one piece of clothing to another. <u>Th</u>e extra electrons that some pieces of clothing gain cause them to have a negative charge. The clothes that have lost electrons are left with a positive charge. You have learned that opposite electric charges attract. This causes some of the clothes to cling together.

Positive or negative electric charges on objects are called static electric charges. **Static electricity** is electric charge built up in one place. So the charges you experienced on the clothes are static electric charges.

You Can...

Do a Static Trick

Get a clear plastic cup, a nickel, a plastic comb, and a narrow strip of paper about 1 cm long. Fold the paper in half. Place a nickel on end on a table. Balance the paper on the nickel. Place the plastic cup over the setup, as shown. Challenge friends to move the paper off the nickel without touching or blowing on the cup or banging the table. *(If you run a comb through your hair and place the comb near the cup, the paper will lift off the nickel and move toward the cup.)*

Sometimes objects have the same static charge. In that case they repel or push away from one another. You may have noticed this while combing your hair. What happens is that your hair loses electrons to the comb, causing your hair to have more protons than electrons. In other words, your hair gains a positive charge. For this reason, the hairs repel each other, making your hair stick up. Strands of your hair may also move toward the comb. What is the charge on the comb?

What happens when objects have the same static charge?

Each hair repels another.

In the first picture on this page, two balloons hang side by side. Neither one has an electric charge. If you rub a balloon with a piece of wool, electrons are rubbed off the wool onto the balloon. This gives the balloon a negative charge. The balloons in the second picture have both been given a negative charge. What happens to them when they are brought near one another?

Perhaps you have felt an effect of static electricity when you touched a metal doorknob after walking across a carpet. You may have felt a shock. If the room was dark, you may even have seen a spark. The shock was caused by electrons moving from your hand to the doorknob. These electrons came from atoms in the carpet. They were picked up by your body as you walked across the rug.

What is a static discharge?

When a static electric charge moves from one place to another, we say there is a static discharge. Remember that only electrons move. Protons don't move. You may actually hear static discharges when you pull apart clothes you take from the dryer.

Sometimes you may see a static discharge in the sky. Charges may jump from one cloud to another cloud. They may also move from clouds to the ground. What do we call a static discharge from a cloud?

Static electricity has many uses. For example, dust and smoke particles often have an electric charge. Static electricity is used in special filters to remove these charged particles from the air.

Lesson Summary

- Static electricity is the buildup of charge in one place.
- Like charges repel and unlike charges attract one another.
- The movement of static electricity from one place to another is static discharge.

Lesson Review

1. What happens when objects lose electrons? gain electrons?
2. What happens when two objects with negative charges are placed beside each other?
★3. Explain the difference between static electricity and static discharge.

LESSON 2 GOALS
You will learn
● what current electricity is and how it flows.
● how a conductor differs from an insulator.
● how electricity flows through series and parallel circuits.

What is current electricity?

Current Electricity

What do turning on a lamp, pushing a button to raise a garage door, heating your dinner in an electric oven, or listening to a transistor radio have in common? You're right! Electricity makes all these activities possible. Until now we have talked about static electricity—electric charge that stays in one place. The type of electricity used to operate appliances is called **current electricity.** In current electricity, electric charges move through a material in a continuous flow. Currents of electrons flow through some materials much like currents of water flow in a river.

Only certain materials, called **conductors,** allow electrons to flow through them easily. Look at the picture of the inside of an electric cord. You can see the copper wires that provide a pathway for the electric currents. Most metals are good conductors.

Some materials, called **insulators**, are poor conductors of electricity. Electrons don't flow easily through insulators. Wood and plastic are good insulators. So are rubber and glass. Why do you think copper wires are covered with plastic?

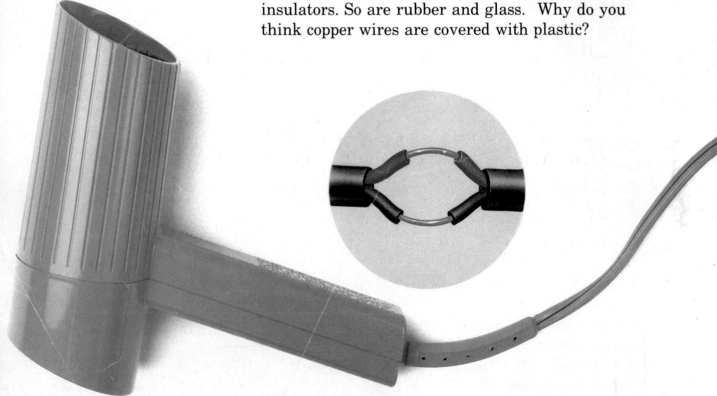

Where do the electrons come from that are needed to produce electric currents? A **battery** is one source of electrons. A chemical reaction inside the battery produces the electrons. But certainly not all the electricity in your home comes from batteries! Electric currents for your home are most likely produced at an electric power plant. The source of electrons at these plants is a generator. **Generators** cause electrons to flow by rotating coils of wire through a magnetic field. Generators at power plants can produce much more electric current than batteries can. But can you think of an advantage a battery might have over a generator as a source of electric current?

What are two sources of electrons for electric currents?

Electric circuit

Circuits

Imagine you are playing baseball. The pitcher throws the ball, and you hear that wonderful solid sound as your bat sends the ball flying hard and fast. It looks like a home run! You take off racing around the bases. When you get back to home base, you have returned to where you started. You have made a home run, and you have completed a circuit.

Electric currents, like a baseball player rounding the bases, follow circuits. There must be a continuous path called an **electric circuit** for electrons to travel. Conductors, such as the copper wire inside an electric cord, form circuits for current electricity. Look at the picture of an electric circuit. Remember that a battery supplies electrons. Electrons move from a place where there are more negative charges—the negative terminal—to a place with more positive charges—the positive terminal. The wires provide a path as the electrons flow from one terminal of the battery to the other.

Describe a complete circuit.

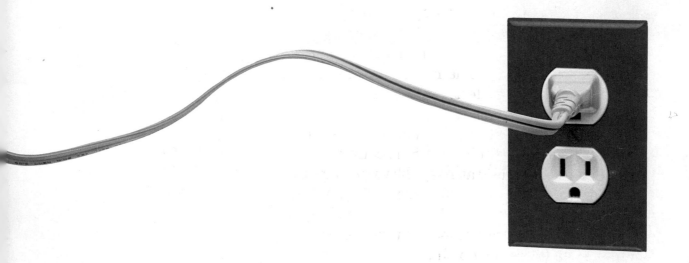

Electric current can flow along the wires and through the light bulb only if there is a complete circuit. If you disconnect the wire from one of the terminals, the circuit is broken, and the current will stop flowing.

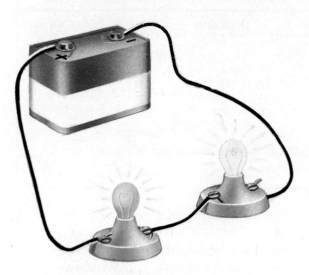

Series circuit

Parallel circuit

Electricity can flow through two different types of circuits—series and parallel. Study the picture of a **series circuit**—the one with the yellow and green bulbs. Electric current must flow first through the yellow bulb in order to flow through the green bulb. A series circuit has only one path for current. To understand a series circuit, think about runners running around a track. The runners all run in the same direction, just as electrons travel in the same direction in a series circuit.

Now look at the **parallel circuit** with the red and blue bulbs. Here the electric current can flow through more than one pathway. Electric current does not have to flow through the blue bulb in order to flow through the red one. Think about riding your bike to a friend's house. Suppose there are two paths, one easier to ride on than the other. If the easy path is clogged with other bicycle riders, you might choose the more difficult path that has less traffic. Both paths in a parallel circuit will have electrons traveling on them—with more electrons traveling on the easier path. Unlike a series circuit, a parallel circuit can have a burned-out bulb and other bulbs in the circuit will still operate.

What are two types of electric circuits?

Why do you think a burned-out bulb on a parallel circuit does not break the circuit?

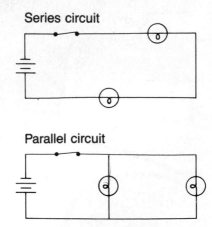

Series circuit

Parallel circuit

$\boldsymbol{T}$*able 1* *Symbols for Electric Currents*		
Item	**Purpose**	**Symbol**
Wire	Conducts electric current	
Battery	Stores and supplies electricity	
Light bulb	Provides electric light	
Switch	Completes or breaks a circuit	

How do electricians use electrical symbols?

Have you ever seen a blueprint of a house? The architect uses symbols to represent the windows, doorways, closets, stairs, plumbing, and other parts of the house. Electricians also use diagrams to make their jobs easier. The symbols they use help them illustrate how they designed a circuit. Drawing these symbols is easy to learn. Some common symbols used in diagrams of circuits are shown in Table 1. The diagrams on this page show you one way a series circuit and a parallel circuit would be drawn.

Lesson Summary

- Current electricity is the flow of charged particles through a conductor.
- Conductors are materials through which electrons flow easily, while electrons don't flow easily through insulators.
- A series circuit provides one pathway for electric current. A parallel circuit provides more than one.

Lesson Review

1. Explain the difference between current and static electricity.
2. Name two materials that are good conductors of electricity. Name two that are insulators.
★3. If one bulb burns out in a parallel circuit, will the other bulb remain burning? Explain your answer.

Use Application Activity on pages 499, 500.

How are circuits different?

What you need

2 flashlight batteries (size D)
2 light bulbs in sockets
masking tape
insulated electric wire
switch
pencil and paper

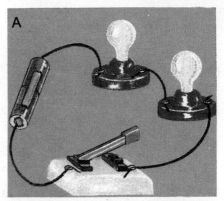

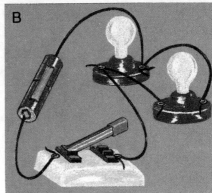

What to do

Part A

1. Tape two flashlight batteries together with the positive end of one touching the negative end of the other, as shown. Tape wires to the ends of this "battery pack."
2. Connect the batteries, the sockets, and the switch to make the circuit shown in drawing A.
3. Turn the switch on and off. Observe.
4. Loosen one of the bulbs. Turn the switch on and off again. Observe.

Part B

1. Make the circuit shown in drawing B.
2. Turn the switch on and off. Observe.
3. Loosen one of the bulbs.
4. Turn the switch on and off again. Observe.

What did you learn?

1. What happened when you loosened one bulb in Circuit A?

2. What happened when you loosened one bulb in Circuit B?
3. Draw each circuit using the symbols in Table 1.

Using what you learned

1. Explain what you observed when you loosened the bulbs.
2. Circuit A is a series circuit. Circuit B is a parallel circuit. Are the lights in your home part of a series circuit or a parallel circuit? How do you know?

LESSON 3 GOALS
You will learn
- how circuits are protected.
- how a simple electric motor operates.
- how electricity use is measured.

Electricity in Your Home

Just how busy is your house in the early morning during the school year? Is your father making a pot of coffee, while your mother is making toast for breakfast? Are you styling your hair with a hair dryer, while your sister is ironing a blouse? Most of the time-saving appliances that busy families rely upon today use electric current.

Electric current enters your home through wires. The wires are connected to either a service panel or a fuse box. The panel or box provides a place to connect the many different circuits inside your home to the outside wires. Each circuit provides electric current to a different area of your home. Any electric appliance or device you are using is part of a circuit. Some devices, such as electric clocks, are constantly part of a circuit. Other devices, such as an electric fan, are part of a circuit only when you switch them on. What are some other electric devices you use at home? Which of these devices have switches?

86

Utility worker repairs damaged power lines.

A simple switch makes it easy for you to complete or to break an electric circuit. A switch is like a drawbridge. Suppose there is a drawbridge between your home and your school. In the morning the drawbridge is down. You can cross the drawbridge and go to school. But on your way home after school, you discover the drawbridge is up. This means you can't get home until the drawbridge is lowered. As long as the drawbridge is down, your circuit to and from school is complete. When the drawbridge is up, your circuit to and from school is broken.

When you turn a switch on, the electric circuit is complete. Current then flows through the circuit. When you turn a switch off, the electric circuit is broken, and current doesn't flow.

A circuit may be broken in ways other than by using a switch. During storms a circuit between your home and the electric power plant may break when power lines are knocked down by wind or struck by lightning. Electricity can't flow into your home until workers have repaired the circuit.

What does a "broken circuit" mean?

Sometimes a circuit is broken inside your home. You may blow a fuse. A **fuse** is a safety device that is installed in an electrical panel box as part of a circuit. Heat is produced when electric current flows through the wires of a circuit. When too much electric current flows through a circuit, the wires get very hot and can cause a fire. Before the wires get too hot, the metal strip in a fuse melts and breaks the circuit. In this way fuses help to prevent fires. After a circuit is broken and the fuse has blown, you must replace the fuse with a new one. Look at the picture of a fuse. Find the metal strip in it.

Your home may have circuit breakers instead of fuses. A **circuit breaker** is an automatic switch in an electrical panel box. The switch automatically breaks a circuit when electric wires carry too much current. A piece of metal holds the switch in the *on* position. If the circuit carries too much current, the metal becomes hot. As it gets hot, it expands and releases the switch. After a circuit has been broken, you simply flip the circuit breaker back on.

A fuse

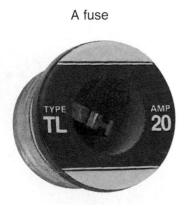

But, when a fuse or circuit breaker breaks a circuit in your home, you know there is a problem with that circuit. Perhaps you have several appliances connected in that circuit, and you overloaded the circuit by using too many of them at the same time. This causes the circuit to be broken. You must correct the problem by turning off some of the appliances before you flip the circuit breaker on again or replace the fuse. Why do you think fuses and circuit breakers are called safety devices?

Because you use electricity in many ways each day, you sometimes forget that it can be dangerous. In your home, check electric cords for broken insulation. Never overload a circuit by using extension cords and extra plugs. Never handle appliances when you have wet hands.

When playing outside, stay off electric poles. Fly kites far away from power lines. If you see fallen electric wires, don't touch them. Call the power company immediately. Warn others to stay clear of the danger.

Remember to always think of safety first!

SCIENCE AND . . .
Reading
What should be done FIRST when a fuse or a circuit breaker breaks an electric circuit in your home?
A. Replace it with one of equal size.
B. Switch it back on.
C. Shut off appliances that may be overloading the circuit.
D. Nothing.

What others rules of safety about electricity can you add?

Don't overload circuits.

Electric Motors

Quite by accident nearly 200 years ago, a physics teacher made an important discovery. Hans Christian Oersted was setting up an experiment for his college students. He planned to show them the effects of electric currents flowing through wires. He laid a wire carrying an electric current down on top of a small compass and noticed that the compass needle moved. Oersted thought his eyes had played a trick on him! He repeated his actions again and again. Each time the wire came near the compass, the needle moved. After many more experiments, Oersted concluded that any wire carrying an electric current has a magnetic field around it. This was the first time anyone realized that electricity and magnetism are related.

The pictures on this page will help you understand what Oersted's discovery says about electricity and magnetism. In the picture on the left, you see a coil of wire wrapped around an iron nail, a good conductor. The ends of the wire are connected to a battery, a source of electric current. Together the coil, nail, and battery make a simple **electromagnet**. The electric current flowing through the coil produces a magnetic field that will pick up paper clips. Why is the electromagnet no longer operating in the second picture?

Electromagnet

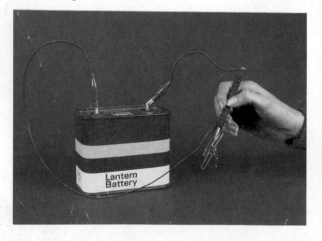

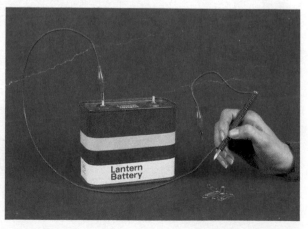

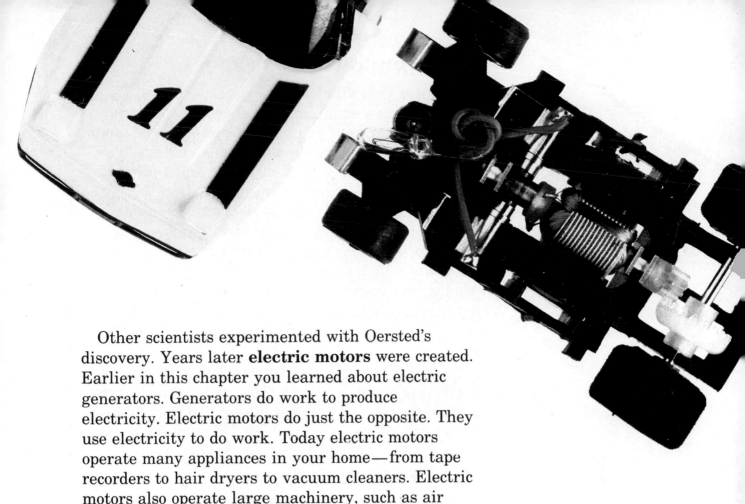

Other scientists experimented with Oersted's discovery. Years later **electric motors** were created. Earlier in this chapter you learned about electric generators. Generators do work to produce electricity. Electric motors do just the opposite. They use electricity to do work. Today electric motors operate many appliances in your home—from tape recorders to hair dryers to vacuum cleaners. Electric motors also operate large machinery, such as air conditioning systems and subway trains. Let's look more closely at how a simple electric motor works.

Study the electric motor in the car and the drawing below it. First, find the two opposite magnetic poles that are fixed in place. A magnetic field exists between these two poles. A coil of wire with an iron rod through its center has been mounted in the magnetic field in such a way that the coil is free to turn. Current flowing through the wire produces a magnetic field around the coil. The two magnetic fields interact to create a force that causes the coil to turn. As the coil turns, the interaction of the fields keeps changing, and the coil continues to spin. The shaft of the motor, which is attached to the turning coil, moves the car's wheels. Electric motors also move the hands of a clock or operate a drill. Where in your home are electric motors used? How is the motor's spinning motion used in these devices?

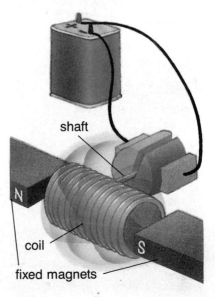

Simple electric motor

shaft

coil

fixed magnets

N

S

Measuring Electric Usage

What is power?

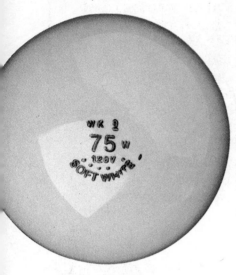

You know that all electric devices use energy. A light bulb uses a small amount of energy compared to an electric oven. If you had the oven and the lamp on all day, the oven would use far more energy. The rate at which a device uses energy is called **power**. The **watt** is the unit used to measure power.

Most electric devices are labeled with the number of watts they use. Devices labeled with a low number of watts use electricity at a slower rate than those with a high wattage. Household light bulbs usually have power ratings of 25 to 100 watts. Small night-lights are usually four or seven watts. An electric toaster may use energy at the rate of 1,000 watts.

The electric energy used in your home is measured in kilowatt-hours. A kilowatt is equal to 1,000 watts. A **kilowatt-hour** is the energy required to produce 1,000 watts of power in one hour. How many hours would a 100-watt light bulb have to burn to use one kilowatt-hour of electric energy?

Would You Believe?

A pear-shaped light bulb will burn out after about 1,000 hours of use.

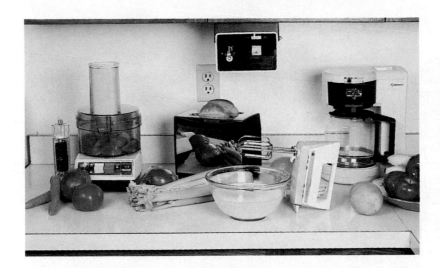

SCIENCE AND . . .
Math

Calvin wants to find what it costs to watch TV. He knows his TV uses 460 watts and that electricity costs 8 cents per kilowatt-hour. What else does he need to know?
A. number of hours
B. size of the fuse
C. cost of the TV
D. size of the screen

*T*able 2   **Cost of Electricity in Household Appliances**

appliance	wattage	hours used monthly	kilowatt-hours used monthly	rate	monthly cost
Hair dryer	600	8	4.8	12¢	58¢
Stereo	110	90	9.9	12¢	$1.19
Color TV	200	100	20	12¢	$2.40
Microwave oven	1450	12	17.4	12¢	$2.09
Clock	2	720	1.44	12¢	17¢

Your electric company charges you for the number of kilowatt-hours you use. Suppose the cost of electricity is 12 cents for each kilowatt-hour. How much would it cost you to use a 2,000-watt heater for four hours? To calculate this cost you must use two formulas that look like this:

watts × hours = watt-hours or kilowatt-hours
2,000 watts × 4 hours =
8,000 watt-hours, or
8 kilowatt-hours

kilowatt-hours × rate = cost
8 kilowatt-hours × $0.12 = $0.96.

It would cost 96 cents to use the heater four hours.

You are charged for the electricity you use.

Your home has a kilowatt-hour meter that measures the amount of electricity in your home. The meter is read regularly, and the cost of electricity you used in the past month is calculated. How can you find out how many kilowatt-hours of electricity were used in your home last month?

Lesson Summary

- Fuses and circuit breakers protect circuits by breaking them when there is too much electric current.
- An electric motor is made up of an iron core wrapped with a coil of wire turning between opposite poles of a fixed magnet.
- Electricity use is measured in kilowatt-hours.

Lesson Review

1. A hair dryer is plugged in, but its switch is off. Is it part of a complete circuit? Explain.
2. What is the difference between a circuit breaker and a fuse? How are they alike?
3. List the basic parts of a simple electric motor.
★4. What is meant by the wattage of an appliance?

How can you make an electric motor?

What you need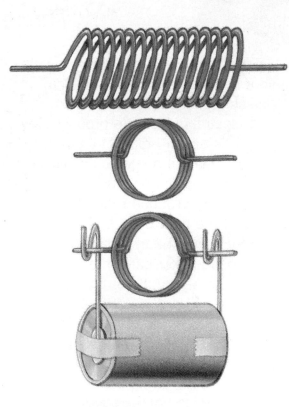

1 enameled wire
1 flashlight battery (size D)
sandpaper
2 jumbo paper clips
masking tape
bar magnet

What to do

1. Wrap the enameled wire around a flashlight battery 15 times to make a coil.
2. Remove the coil from the battery. Loop each free end twice around the center of each side of the coil, as shown. Leave the ends sticking out. Remove the insulation by sanding the enamel off the ends.
3. Straighten the big bend of each jumbo paper clip. See the diagram. Tape the paper clips to the ends of the battery. Wrap tape tightly around the battery to hold the paper clips firmly in place.
4. Place the coil in the paper clips, as shown.
5. Hold one end of the bar magnet near the coil. Use your finger to spin the coil gently to start the motor. Move the magnet around until you find the position where the coil spins the fastest.

What did you learn?

1. Why did you need to remove the enamel from the ends of the wire?
2. How did you make a complete circuit?

Using what you learned

1. Why should you remove the coil from the clips when you are not using your motor?
2. Design and carry out an experiment that would change the speed of the spinning coil. Record your procedure and results.

I WANT TO KNOW ABOUT...

Pacemakers

Sixty to eighty times every minute your heart produces tiny electric pulses that cause your heart to beat. The electric pulses are produced by cells in a small region of the heart. These cells are sometimes called pacemaker cells, because the electric pulses they produce regulate the pace of the heartbeat.

People with heart disease may have pacemaker cells that fail to function properly. If the pacemaker cells do not send out the electric pulses properly, the heart will have an irregular beat or may stop beating. To correct this problem, medical scientists have invented a device to do the job of the pacemaker cells.

The electronic pacemaker produces regular pulses of electricity that start and control the rate of the heartbeat. Some electronic pacemakers produce pulses all the time. Other pacemakers operate only when the natural pacemaker cells don't work properly.

An electronic pacemaker has small wires that are implanted in or near the heart. The pacemaker itself is quite small (2 cm x 2 cm x 1 cm) and can be inserted just below the skin. Most pacemakers are battery powered.

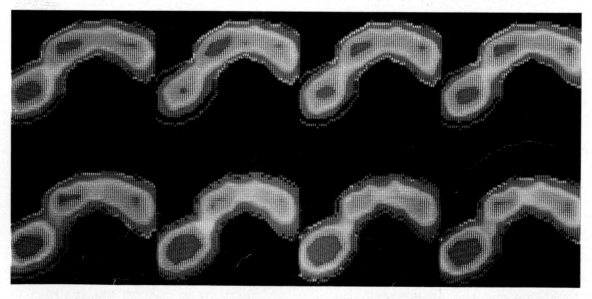

Science and Technology

Summary

Lesson 1
- Static electricity is the buildup of charge in one place.
- Like charges repel and unlike charges attract one another.
- The movement of static electricity from one place to another is a static discharge.

Lesson 2
- Current electricity is the flow of charged particles through a conductor.
- Conductors are materials through which electrons flow easily, while electrons don't flow easily through insulators.

- A series circuit provides one pathway for electric current. A parallel circuit provides more than one.

Lesson 3
- Fuses and circuit breakers protect circuits by breaking them when there is too much electric current.
- An electric motor is made up of an iron core wrapped with a coil of wire turning between opposite poles of a fixed magnet.
- Electricity is measured in the energy unit kilowatt-hours.

Science Words

Fill in the blank with the correct word or words from the list.

static electricity	fuse
current electricity	circuit breaker
conductor	power
insulator	watt
electric circuit	kilowatt-hour
series circuit	battery
parallel circuit	generators
electric motors	electromagnet

1. One thousand watts of electricity used for sixty minutes is called a(n) ____.
2. How fast a device uses energy is called ____.
3. An automatic switch that stops the flow of electricity when a circuit is carrying too much current is a(n) ____.

4. A continuous conducting path is a(n) ____.
5. Electric charge built up in one place is ____.
6. A material, such as glass, through which electricity does not flow easily is called a(n) ____.

7. Electricity flows through only one path in a(n) ____.
8. The flow of electrons through a conductor is called ____.
9. Electric current can flow through two or more paths in a(n) ____.

Questions

Recalling Ideas
Correctly complete each of the following sentences.

1. An atom that has taken on an electric charge is called
   (a) a proton.   (c) neutral.
   (b) an ion.   (d) a molecule.
2. A material through which electrons flow easily is
   (a) a fuse.   (c) a conductor.
   (b) a switch.   (d) an insulator.
3. To produce an electric current, you need a continuous source of
   (a) electrons.   (c) watts.
   (b) protons.   (d) neutrons.

4. An electric circuit with more than one path is
   (a) in series.   (c) in parallel.
   (b) balanced.   (d) positive.
5. The buildup of charge in one place is called
   (a) static discharge.
   (b) static electricity.
   (c) electromagnetism.
   (d) a kilowatt.
6. Meters measure home electricity use in units of
   (a) kilograms.   (c) watts.
   (b) kilowatt-hours. (d) liters.

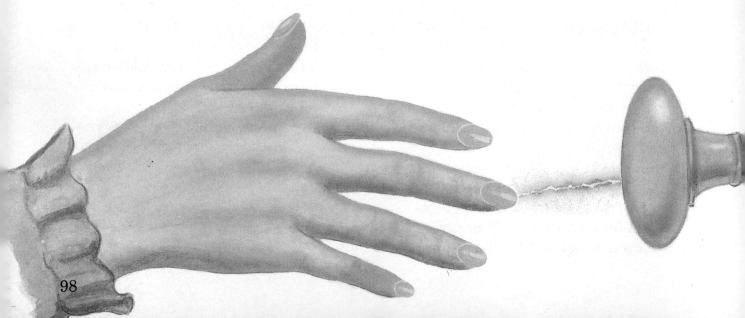

7. A kilowatt-hour is a unit to measure
   (a) force.
   (c) power.
   (b) strength.
   (d) energy.
8. Static electricity is responsible for all of the following EXCEPT
   (a) a lighted lamp.
   (b) lightning.
   (c) dried clothes stuck together.
   (d) hair crackling when combed.

Examining Ideas
Determine whether each of the following statements is true or false. Rewrite the false statements to make them correct.
1. A lightning flash is an example of a static charge.
2. Ions with the same electric charge attract each other.
3. A continuous source of electrons is needed to produce an electric current.
4. Circuit breakers act as safety devices in electric circuits.
5. A circuit breaker has a metal strip that can melt to break a circuit.
6. Electric devices labeled with a low number of watts use electricity at a faster rate than those with a higher wattage.
7. Most metals are good conductors of electricity.
8. In a parallel circuit, when one bulb goes out, so will all others.
9. Current flowing through a wire wrapped around an iron nail produces an electromagnet.

Understanding Ideas
Answer the following questions using complete sentences.
1. How does a conductor differ from an insulator? Give examples.
2. What are the advantages of a circuit breaker over a fuse?
3. Explain the difference between current electricity and static electricity.
4. Explain how switches control electricity.
5. Tell how the structure of the atom relates to static electricity.

Thinking Critically
Think about what you have learned in this chapter. Answer the following questions using complete sentences.
1. Why are the circuits in your home parallel? Are there any series circuits?
2. Suppose the price of electricity is nine cents per kilowatt-hour. How much would it cost to operate
   (a) a 100,000-watt stove for 1 hour?
   (b) a 60-watt bulb for 8 hours?
3. A family's electric bill for one month is $60.50. Suppose one kilowatt-hour of electricity costs 10 cents. How many kilowatt-hours of electricity did the family use that month?
4. You learned that generators and motors do opposite jobs. Suggest changes to the motor on page 91 that would make it a generator.

CHAPTER 5

Waves

These magnificent streams of color are the Northern Lights. A solar flare sends a stream of charged particles called the solar wind to Earth. These particles enter the atmosphere over the north or south magnetic poles. There, they collide with particles in the upper atmosphere, creating great shimmering sheets of light. These lights in the Northern Hemisphere are called Aurora Borealis, or Northern Lights. In the Southern Hemisphere, the lights are called Aurora Australis, or Southern Lights.

ACTIVITY

Have You Ever...

Cooked With a Microwave Oven?

Put an uncooked potato in a microwave oven for seven minutes. Remove the potato. Measure the internal temperature in the center of the potato. What do you think the temperature will be if you wait two minutes and then take another reading? Test your prediction by checking the temperature agtain after two minutes. Did the temperature increase, decrease, or remain the same?

How Do Waves Transfer Energy?

LESSON 1 GOALS
You will learn
● how mechanical and electromagnetic waves are different.
● the characteristics common to waves.

Have you ever thrown a rock into a pond or puddle of water? What happened when the rock hit the water? Did you know when you threw the rock that you were using and transferring energy? You were the source of energy that caused the rock to move. When that rock hit, part of its energy was transferred to the water. How can you be sure? The water rippled with waves.

There are two types of waves—mechanical and electromagnetic. Both types transfer energy. With a **mechanical wave,** energy is transferred as the wave travels through matter. The water wave created by the rock is an example of a mechanical wave. When the wave traveled through the water, the water moved up and down as the wave passed. The water, however, was not carried along with the wave because the wave transfers only energy and not matter.

Waves transfer energy.

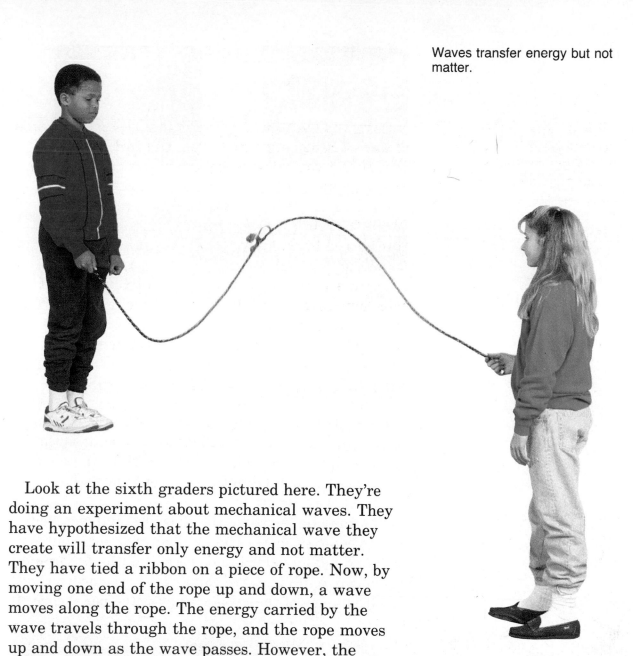

Waves transfer energy but not matter.

Look at the sixth graders pictured here. They're doing an experiment about mechanical waves. They have hypothesized that the mechanical wave they create will transfer only energy and not matter. They have tied a ribbon on a piece of rope. Now, by moving one end of the rope up and down, a wave moves along the rope. The energy carried by the wave travels through the rope, and the rope moves up and down as the wave passes. However, the ribbon stays tied in the same place and does not move from left to right with the wave. If the wave transferred matter as well as energy, the ribbon would move from one end of the rope to the other. From their experiment, the students conclude that matter is not transferred along the wave.

The second type of waves is **electromagnetic waves**. These waves don't have to travel through matter. They can transfer energy through empty space. The energy we receive from the sun is transferred through space by electromagnetic waves.

Which type of wave can travel through empty space?

103

The electromagnetic spectrum.

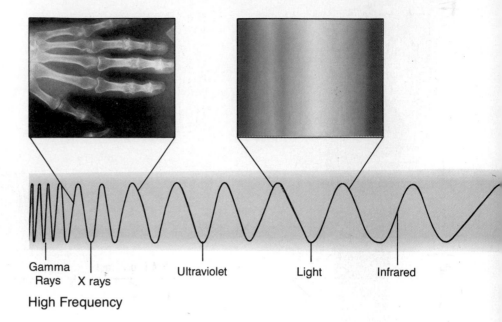

Gamma Rays   X rays   Ultraviolet   Light   Infrared

High Frequency

Wave Properties

Look at the drawing of a wave. The highest point of the wave is its **crest** and its lowest point is the **trough**. The distance from one trough to the next trough is the **wavelength.** Different waves have different wavelengths.

You may have visited the seashore and watched waves come to shore. The number of waves you watched pass a point in one second is the **frequency** of the wave. If one wave comes to shore each second, the frequency of the waves is one wave per second. If

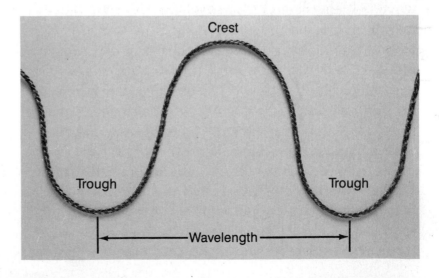

Crest

Trough   Trough

←————Wavelength————→

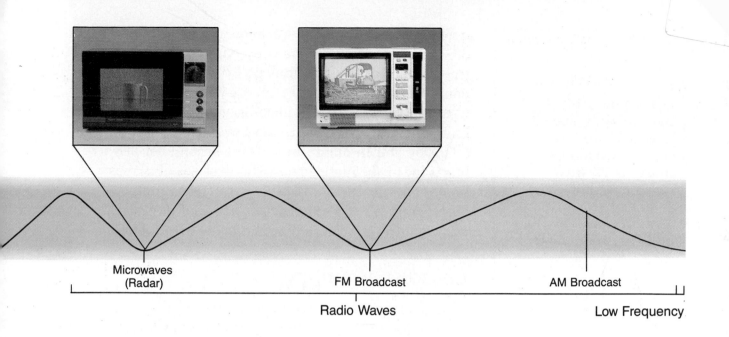

Microwaves
(Radar)

FM Broadcast

AM Broadcast

Radio Waves

Low Frequency

two waves come to shore each second, then the frequency is two waves per second. What would the frequency be if three waves came to shore each second?

Electromagnetic Waves

Electromagnetic waves have a wide range of wavelengths, frequencies, and levels of energy. But the speed at which these waves travel through space is the same. Electromagnetic waves all travel at the speed of light. The chart shows the **electromagnetic spectrum,** an arrangement of electromagnetic waves according to their wavelengths. Most of the waves of the electromagnetic spectrum are invisible. Our eyes can detect only those waves in the portion of the spectrum labeled light. Each color of the spectrum has a distinct wavelength all its own. You see a particular color because a wave of a particular wavelength reaches your eye. Notice that waves with the highest frequencies have the shortest wavelengths and the waves with the lowest frequencies have the longest wavelengths. Let's see why this is true.

✓At what speed do electromagnetic waves travel?

105

Suppose you have a way of watching electromagnetic waves as they pass by. If you count the number of troughs that go by in one minute, you'll know the frequency of the wave. Now suppose a second set of waves is passing you. These waves have a longer wavelength, so fewer troughs are going by you in one minute. This second set of waves has a lower frequency than the first set of waves. Look again at the chart of the electromagnetic spectrum. What kind of wave has the longest wavelength and, therefore, the lowest frequency?

Lesson Summary

- Mechanical waves transfer energy as they travel through matter, while electromagnetic waves transfer energy without matter.
- Electromagnetic waves have various wavelengths and frequencies and transfer different amounts of energy.

Lesson Review

1. How is wavelength related to frequency?
★2. Sound waves are mechanical waves. If you and a friend were on the moon's surface, would you be able to hear your friend calling to you without using a transmitter? Why or why not?

What are some properties of waves?

What you need

spring toy
meter stick
safety goggles
pencil and paper

What to do

1. Have a partner hold one end of the spring toy. Take hold of the other end and stretch the spring to a length of three meters along a smooth floor.
2. Give one quick side-to-side motion to your end of the spring. Observe the spring.
3. Make a steady side-to-side motion so that one wave is formed with the entire spring.
4. Now make the spring move twice as fast. Observe the wavelength.
5. Repeat, trying to move the spring twice as fast as in step 4. Note the wavelength.

What did you learn?

1. What happened in step 2 when the wave reached your partner?
2. How did the length of the wave in step 4 compare with the length of the wave in step 3?
3. How did the length of the wave in step 5 compare with the length of the wave in step 4?

Using what you learned

1. What evidence do you have that waves transmit energy?
2. If the frequency of a wave increases, what happens to its wavelength?
3. Based on what you observed, how does a wave behave when it reaches a barrier?

Radio Waves

LESSON 2 GOALS
You will learn
- the characteristics of radio waves.
- some uses of radio waves.

Did you know you are surrounded by electromagnetic waves? Well, you are. These waves make it possible for you to see. They keep you warm and even cook your food. Electromagnetic waves are also used to transmit information. When you turn on a radio or TV, you can detect some of these waves. Let's see how this happens.

When you tune your radio to a certain station to listen to your favorite music, you're really using your radio to detect radio waves. **Radio waves** have the longest wavelengths in the electromagnetic spectrum. They can have wavelengths as long as 10,000 kilometers or as short as one millimeter. Because you can't hear radio waves, you must use your radio to detect them.

Radio waves from many stations reach your radio's antenna at the same time. The various stations in your area broadcast at different frequencies. You must tune your dial so you can choose the frequency of the station you wish to listen to. Back at that

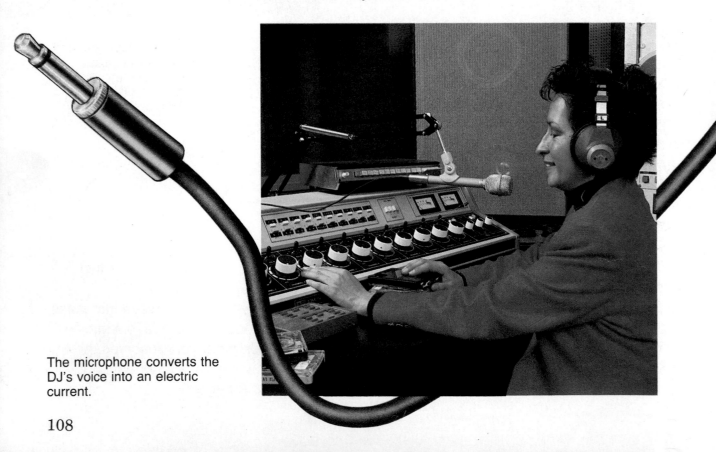

The microphone converts the DJ's voice into an electric current.

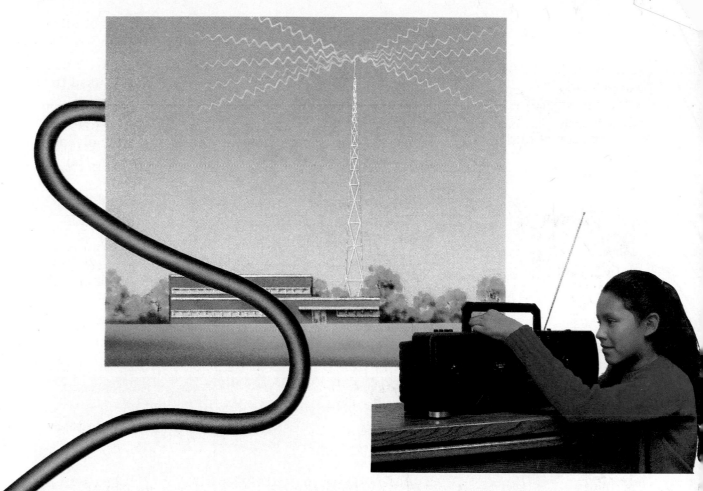

station, the disk jockey's voice creates vibrations in a microphone. The microphone changes these vibrations into electric currents that are then used to produce radio waves. The station's transmitter broadcasts the radio waves through the atmosphere. These waves pass through the walls of your home and reach the antenna in your radio. There, the radio waves from the station are changed back into electric currents. Speakers change the electric currents into sound vibrations so you can hear the disk jockey's voice.

Radio waves are also used to broadcast television programs. These waves carry both audio and video information. Inside your TV, circuits separate the two types of information. Speakers change the audio information into sounds. A picture tube changes the video information into patterns of light that appear as a picture on your screen.

An electric current is converted into radio waves at the transmitter. Your radio changes the waves back into an electric current and then into sound.

What type of wave is used to broadcast TV programs?

109

Microwaves have the highest frequencies of all radio waves. Microwaves pass easily through fog, smoke, and rain, so they are well-suited for communication. That's why microwaves are used to transmit telephone calls. You're probably familiar with microwave ovens. In these ovens, microwaves transfer their energy to food, causing some molecules in the food to move more rapidly. As a result, the food becomes warmer.

The word radar is made from the letters of the phrase "*ra*dio *d*etection *a*nd *r*anging." **Radar** is a device that uses radio waves to locate objects by working like an echo. Radio waves are sent out from a transmitter and travel through the atmosphere of space until they meet an object. Upon meeting the object, the waves bounce off it and are received by an antenna when they return.

How do microwaves heat food?

Satellites receive and transmit microwaves.

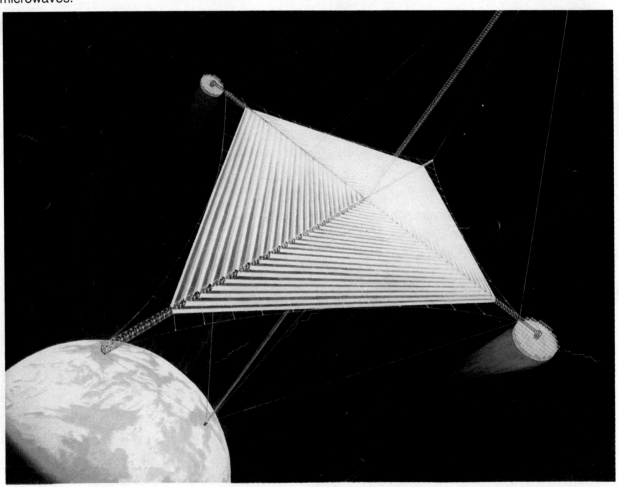

Radar is used to track airplanes.

Flight controllers use radar to track airplanes. Radio waves are sent out from a transmitter. When they strike an airplane, they are bounced back to the observation tower. The airplanes appear as bright spots on a radar screen. By tracking the air traffic in an area, flight controllers prevent planes from colliding while in the air.

Meteorologists use radar to help predict the weather. Radar can detect raindrops as far away as 400 kilometers. Strong radar echoes may mean a violent thunderstorm. Knowing this early enough allows meteorologists to send out storm warnings.

Lesson Summary

- Radio waves have the longest wavelengths in the electromagnetic spectrum.
- Uses of radio waves include transmitting information, cooking food in microwave ovens, and tracking airplanes and severe weather.

Lesson Review

1. How does radar work?
2. Why are microwaves used in communication?
★3. Waves with short wavelengths have more energy and pass through more matter than waves with long wavelengths. Would you expect an AM or FM radio broadcast to sound better on rainy days?

Higher Frequency Waves

Recall that the electromagnetic spectrum is an arrangement of electromagnetic waves according to their wavelengths. Radio waves have long wavelengths and low frequencies. In this lesson you will be introduced to waves with higher frequencies. These higher frequency waves have shorter wavelengths and more energy than radio waves.

Infrared Waves

An **infrared wave** is an electromagnetic wave with a wavelength slightly shorter than those of microwaves. When an object absorbs infrared waves, it becomes warmer. That's why restaurants use infrared lamps to keep cooked food warm.

All materials give off some infrared waves. Have you ever wondered how mosquitoes find you? The antennas of mosquitoes can detect the infrared waves from your body. Cameras sensitive to infrared waves are used to detect places where heat leaks from buildings. Adding insulation in these places helps conserve energy. Cameras can also be used to detect tumors because they are often warmer than the tissue around them.

Infrared waves show heat loss from buildings and brain damage from a stroke.

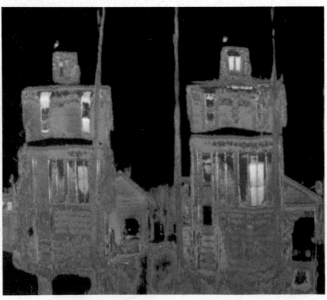

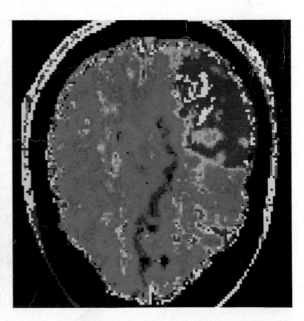

A prism separates white light.

Light

The part of the electromagnetic spectrum that human eyes can see is called **light.** It's a small part of the whole spectrum. Red, along with orange, yellow, green, blue, indigo, and violet make up white light. White light is a mixture of all colors. Each color has a different wavelength. Red light has the longest wavelength, while violet light has the shortest. You can use a prism to separate white light into its colors. A **prism** causes light to bend. Light with shorter wavelengths is bent more than light of long wavelengths. Therefore, violet with the shortest wavelength bends more than red with the longest wavelength. The colors separate as they pass through a prism. Rainbows are produced in a similar way. Sunlight shines on drops of water in the atmosphere. When the white light of the sun hits the water droplets, the droplets act like tiny prisms and separate the white light into its many colors.

113

You Can...

Make a Color Wheel

Get a small round piece of white cardboard. Divide it into 9 pie sections. Color the cardboard as shown. Glue a new unsharpened pencil to the back of the cardboard. Spin the color wheel in bright light. What colors do you see?

Ultraviolet Waves

Name the benefits and dangers of ultraviolet waves.

Ultraviolet waves have wavelengths just shorter than the wavelengths of light. Ultraviolet waves are present in sunlight but cannot be seen by people. Ultraviolet waves help your body produce vitamin D, which is important in forming teeth and bones. Vitamin D is also needed to keep your skin healthy. However, ultraviolet waves can also be harmful to your skin. They cause your skin to darken or burn, and with too much unprotected exposure you could develop skin cancer. Earth's atmosphere blocks much of the ultraviolet light coming from the sun. But pollution in the atmosphere may be destroying the part of our atmosphere that protects us. This is why it's important to use sunblock ointment when you're outside for a long time.

Ultraviolet waves are useful in hospitals because they kill germs and bacteria on hospital equipment. Some hairstylists use ultraviolet waves to kill bacteria on the combs and scissors they use for their customers.

X rays and Gamma Rays

Another type of electromagnetic wave, **X rays**, has a large amount of energy and a wavelength just shorter than an ultraviolet wave. This electromagnetic wave can penetrate many materials such as the soft tissues of your body. You've probably seen X-ray machines used in your doctor's or dentist's office to "see" inside your body.

Because X rays have so much energy, they are harmful to living tissue and should be used carefully. Technicians who take X-ray pictures are careful not to expose themselves to X rays while they work. If you've ever had your teeth x-rayed, the dentist probably covered your body with a lead apron. This apron protects the part of the body that it covers. Why do you suppose an apron made of lead is used? X rays can't pass through lead, so they're stopped before they can get to your body.

Gamma rays have the shortest wavelengths in the electromagnetic spectrum, so they have very high energy. Gamma rays can damage or destroy body cells. But there is an advantage to this property of gamma rays. Doctors use them to kill cancer cells.

Would You Believe?

X rays are used to reveal a painting on a canvas covered over by another painting.

Lesson Summary

- Infrared waves, light, ultraviolet waves, X rays, and gamma rays all have higher frequencies than do radio waves.
- Higher frequency waves have a variety of uses including communication, sterilization, and treatment of tumors and cancer.

Lesson Review

1. How does a prism cause white light to separate into its colors?
2. What are the uses and dangers of ultraviolet waves?
★3. How is light different from all other electromagnetic waves?

Lasers

LESSON 4 GOALS
You will learn
● the differences between laser light and light.
● the uses of lasers.

When you turn on a lamp, the light travels out in all directions. A **laser**, however, is a device that produces a very strong light beam. This light has one wavelength that travels in only one direction. So instead of spreading out, as the light from an ordinary light bulb does, the laser light moves straight ahead for a longer distance. These properties make lasers useful tools. For example, scientists have bounced laser beams off mirrors placed on the moon to measure the distance between the moon and Earth.

Laser light is also used in communications. Some of the newest telephone cables are made of very small glass fibers. Messages are sent through these fibers as laser beams.

Lasers have other important uses. Because a laser beam can be so sharply focused, it is used to perform delicate surgery, such as repairing parts of the eye. In such cases, laser beams are used in place of

Optical fibers

Lasers are used to read
product codes.

surgical knives. Doctors also use laser beams to
destroy some kinds of tumors. The intensity and
high energy of the beams kill the cells of tumors.

You will also find supermarket checkouts using
lasers to identify each item purchased. The product
code is sent to a computer where the price for each
item has already been stored. The price is then
automatically sent back to the cash register. This
process produces a record of the total number of
items sold so managers can use this record to reorder
items as needed.

What medical tool do lasers
sometimes replace?

Lesson Summary

- A laser beam is made up of only one wavelength
  of light, while white light is a mixture of many
  wavelengths.
- Laser light has a variety of uses including
  communication, "reading" codes, and medical
  applications.

Lesson Review

1. What properties of laser light make it useful as a
   medical tool?
★2. Why will you never see a laser beam that is
   white?

How much does light spread out from its source?

What you need

masking tape
flashlight
meter stick
pencil and paper

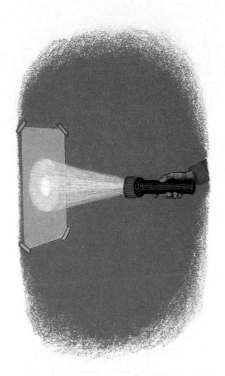

What to do

1. Mark an X in the center of a sheet of paper. Tape the paper on the wall. Darken the room.
2. Hold the flashlight 1 cm from the X on the wall. Have your partner mark the diameter of the circle of light on the wall.
3. Measure and record this distance in a table like the one shown.
4. Repeat steps 2 and 3, placing the flashlight at 2, 4, 8, 16, and 32 cm from the wall. Keep the center of the flashlight beam on the X.
5. Make a line graph of your results. Across the bottom of the graph put the distance of the flashlight from the wall. Along the side of the graph put the light circle diameter.

Distance from wall (cm)	1	2	4	8	16	32
Diameter of light circle (cm)						

What did you learn?

1. What happened to the circle of light as you moved the flashlight farther from the wall?
2. What happened to the brightness of the circle of light as you moved the flashlight farther from the wall?

Using what you learned

1. What is the relationship between the flashlight distance and the diameter of the light circle? Explain.
2. Why is it easier to read when a lamp is beside you than when the lamp is across the room?

Summary

Lesson 1
- Mechanical waves transfer energy as they travel through matter, while electromagnetic waves transfer energy without matter.
- All waves have wavelength and frequency, and carry different amounts of energy.

Lesson 2
- Radio waves have the longest wavelengths in the electromagnetic spectrum.
- Uses of radio waves include transmitting information over radios, TVs, and telephone lines; cooking food in microwave ovens; and tracking airplanes and severe weather with radar.

Lesson 3
- Infrared waves, light, ultraviolet waves, X rays, and gamma rays all have higher frequencies than do radio waves.
- Higher frequency waves have a variety of uses including communication, sterilization, and treatment of tumors and cancer.

Lesson 4
- A laser beam is made up of only one wavelength of light, while white light is a mixture of many wavelengths.
- Laser light has a variety of uses including communication, "reading" codes, and medical applications.

Science Words

Fill in the blank with the correct word or words from the list.

mechanical wave	radar	crest
electromagnetic wave	infrared waves	prism
wavelength	light	
electromagnetic spectrum	ultraviolet waves	
radio waves	X rays	
microwaves	gamma rays	
trough	laser	
	frequency	

1. A wave that must travel through matter in order to transfer its energy is a(n) ____.
2. A pattern of electromagnetic waves according to their wavelengths is called the ____.
3. Light of only one wavelength that travels in one direction is produced by a(n) ____.

4. ____ are used to cook food.
5. The electromagnetic waves we can see are called ____.
6. Long exposure to ____ can cause skin cancer.
7. The distance from one wave crest to the next is a(n) ____.

8. A device that uses radio waves to locate objects is ____.
9. Electromagnetic waves that produce warmth are ____.
10. Electromagnetic waves that have wavelengths just longer than those of gamma rays are ____.

Questions

Recalling Ideas
Correctly complete each of the following sentences.
1. Lasers are used for all of the following EXCEPT
   (a) measurement. (c) ovens.
   (b) cutting.   (d) surgery.
2. All of the following are used in communication EXCEPT
   (a) radar.   (c) microwaves.
   (b) lasers.   (d) gamma rays.
3. Waves produced by heat lamps are
   (a) X rays.   (c) mechanical.
   (b) infrared. (d) microwaves.
4. Waves that can transfer energy through empty space are
   (a) mechanical.   (c) electromagnetic.
   (b) sound.   (d) both a and c.
5. Waves that can be used to examine internal body parts are
   (a) microwaves. (c) X rays.
   (b) radio.   (d) visible.
6. White light is made up of
   (a) red and blue waves.
   (b) red and ultraviolet.
   (c) orange, yellow, and green.
   (d) all colors.

Examining Ideas
Determine whether each of the following statements is true or false. Rewrite the false statements to make them correct.
1. Waves with the longest wavelengths have the highest frequencies.
2. Gamma rays and radio waves travel through space at the same speed.
3. In order to transfer energy, waves must travel through matter.
4. Waves transfer matter and energy.
5. A prism can be used to separate infrared into colors.
6. Microwaves are a type of radio waves.
7. X rays are shorter than light waves, which are shorter than ultraviolet waves.
8. Humans can see ultraviolet waves.
9. The intensity and high energy of laser beams kill the cells of tumors.

Understanding Ideas

Answer the following questions using complete sentences.

1. Explain how mechanical waves and electromagnetic waves are different.
2. Make a chart listing the waves of the electromagnetic spectrum from shortest to longest wavelength and give two uses for each type.
3. How do microwaves cook food?
4. The unit used to measure wave frequency is the hertz (Hz). One hertz equals one complete wave (1 cycle) passing a given point per second. What do you mean when you say that a certain sound has a frequency of 440 Hz?

radiation, the larger the detector must be. For this reason, would you expect the eyes of small insects to be sensitive to infrared or ultraviolet waves?

4. Sound is a type of mechanical wave that may travel at about 344 meters per second. You can discover how far away a thunderstorm is by measuring the interval between the time you see the lightning and the time you hear the thunder. Suppose you find that the thunder arrives 3 seconds after the lightning that caused it. Use the formula

$$distance = speed \times time$$

to find how far away the storm is.

Thinking Critically

Think about what you have learned in this chapter. Answer the following questions using complete sentences.

1. Explain why gamma rays damage living tissue more than light.
2. A science fiction movie shows a rocket ship exploding in outer space with a loud boom. Explain why this is incorrect.
3. In general, the longer the wavelength of electromagnetic

CHAPTER 6

Motion and Forces

How can this baseball player move the bat in order to make contact with a fast-moving ball? The player's bat moves from its stationary position near the player's ear to the waist in seconds. Why is the speed of the bat so important? First of all, the faster the bat is moving, the more energy it will have to hit the ball. Using a heavy bat won't necessarily affect the amount of force that hits the ball. In fact, a heavy bat might slow down the swing.

Have You Ever...

Compared Speed and Distance?

Using tape, mark off two 15-meter-long paths side-by-side down a hall. Divide each path into meter-long segments. Now, stand at the beginning of the first path, and have your partner stand at the beginning of the second path. Have someone clap five times at a slow and steady rate. At each clap, you move one meter, and your partner moves three meters. How is the pattern of movement different between you and your partner? Compare your movements to movements of cars on a highway.

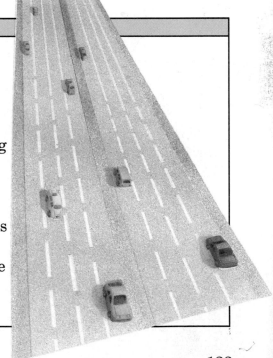

LESSON 1 GOALS
You will learn
● that motion is the changing of position.
● that speed is a measure of how far an object moves in a given time.
● how speed and velocity differ.

What Is Motion?

Two sixth-graders find themselves in similar predicaments! Janna goes to a large department store to buy a baseball mitt for her younger brother's birthday. She can't seem to find the sporting goods department. Pedro is spending the day at the county fair. He has finished looking at the horses in the animal barns and wants to get to the double Ferris wheel on the midway. These students need information. They need to find out how to get to where they want to go.

When you want to know where something is, what you really want to know is its position (puh ZIHSH un). **Position** is the place or location where something is. Suppose you are going to describe to new students in your class where the lunchroom is. What would you need to say so they could find it? How would your directions be different if you were standing by the office instead of your classroom as you talked to the students?

Pedro needs to know his starting position.

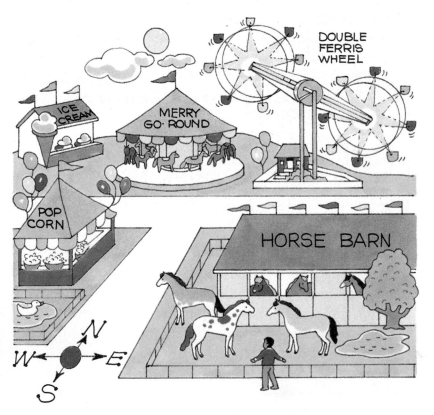

ICE CREAM

MERRY GO ROUND

DOUBLE FERRIS WHEEL

POP CORN

HORSE BARN

Cyclists in motion

How you describe the position of an object depends on where you are. Pedro wants to go to the double Ferris wheel. Look at the picture of the fairgrounds on page 124. What is the position of the Ferris wheel in relation to the horse barns? Yes, the horse barns are directly south of the Ferris wheel. Since Pedro's position is on the south side of the horse barns, what directions would you give Pedro to get to the ride?

Look at the picture of the cyclists. When the cyclists change their positions, they are in motion. **Motion** is simply the changing of position. The cyclists are constantly in motion as they change position during the race.

The motion of the ball looks different to people depending on their position.

How do you calculate average speed?

When you describe motion, part of your description depends on your position. Look at the picture of a ball game. When the batter hits the ball from her position, she sees the ball moving away from her bat. The player in the field sees the motion of the ball from a different position. She sees the ball moving toward her glove. How do the people watching the game see the motion of the ball?

You spend much of your time in motion—changing position. Sometimes you move fast, sometimes slowly. When you walk to school, you walk slowly to talk with friends. But then you suddenly remember something you need to do before class, so you walk more quickly the rest of the way. You've increased your speed. You don't usually travel at the same speed all the time. However, you do have a certain average speed. To find your **average speed,** you divide the distance you moved by the time it took you to move that distance.

average speed = total distance ÷ total time

Suppose you travel two hours in the car to reach a friend's home 150 kilometers away. What's the car's average speed?

Her speed is how far she moves in a given time.

So far we've talked about the speed of motion. Sometimes it may be necessary to describe the direction of motion as well. For example, suppose you want your friend Lauren to meet you after school. If you tell her that you'll be riding your bike from your house at an average speed of 16 kilometers per hour, how will she know where to find you? She won't, because you didn't give her enough information. Not only do you need to give the speed at which you'll be riding, but you also need to tell Lauren in which direction you'll be traveling. You need to give her your velocity. **Velocity** describes both your speed and direction. If you had said "I'll be riding north at 16 kilometers per hour," Lauren would more likely know where to look for you.

Each girl's velocity depends on the direction she travels.

After you and Lauren meet and talk, suppose you both decide to head home. You return home by riding south at 16 kilometers per hour, and Lauren rides east at 16 kilometers per hour. You and she have the same average speed but not the same velocity. For two bikes to have the same velocity, they must be traveling at the same speed and in the same direction.

Lesson Summary

- Motion is the changing of position.
- Average speed is a measure of how far an object moves divided by the time it takes to move the distance.
- Velocity is the speed and direction of a moving object.

Lesson Review

1. What is position? motion?
2. What is the difference between speed and velocity?
★3. If you rode your bicycle for three hours and went 48 kilometers, what would your average riding speed be?

How can you find your average walking speed?

What you need

watch or clock
meter stick
masking tape
large area for walking
pencil and paper

What to do

1. Use the meter stick to measure a distance of 10 meters on the floor. Mark the distance with masking tape.
2. Have a person walk the 10-meter distance 5 times. Time how long the person takes to walk this distance. Record the time in a table like the one shown.
3. Time yourself and several other people walking the same distance. Record the times for each person.
4. Divide the total distance by each person's total time to find the average walking speed for each person.

Name	Time to walk 50 meters	Average Speed

What did you learn?

1. What is your average walking speed?
2. How is your average walking speed different from the average walking speeds of your friends?

Using what you learned

1. What is the average walking speed for your class?
2. At your average walking speed, how far could you walk in 20 seconds? 60 seconds?
3. How could you find your average running speed?

Forces in Your World

Forces are at work when you push the buttons on a telephone, your dog pulls at the rubber toy in your hand, or the wind pushes your kite into the sky. Forces are a very important part of your world.

You use forces and forces act on you when you work and play. If there weren't any forces, you couldn't play ball or ride a bicycle. You couldn't talk on the telephone with a friend or play video games. There wouldn't be any electric lights to use for reading at night. You couldn't pour a glass of milk for a bedtime snack. Without forces your world would be very different.

Forces are all around you. Sometimes forces act together, and sometimes they act against each other. Some forces hold objects together, and others keep objects apart. Forces are needed to start, stop, or change any motion. Force is the push or pull one body exerts on another. Gravity is one of these forces.

Force is the push or pull one body exerts on another.

130

Force of Gravity

Remember that the **force of gravity** is the pulling force of every object on every other object. You can't see the force of gravity, but you can see what it does. You know that no matter how high you throw a ball into the air, it will always fall to the ground. The force of gravity between Earth and the ball slows the upward motion of the ball, until the ball changes direction and falls to the ground. The force of gravity affects all objects.

What is the force of gravity?

Gravity is a force.

Magnetic and Electric Forces

You have learned that the area around a magnet is called a magnetic field. Magnetic fields can exert a force that attracts or repels some objects. You can't see a magnetic field, but you can see what it does. What happens if you place iron filings near a magnet? The magnetic field exerts a force on the filings. Each filing turns in the direction of the field. The pattern the filings make creates a picture of the magnetic field.

Magnetic field

Another force you have studied is **electric force.** An object with an electric charge creates an electric force field around itself. This electric field exerts a force that attracts or repels the fields of other charged objects. It is electric force that holds atoms and molecules together.

People have learned to make use of magnetic and electric forces. Electric lights, TVs, and telephones use magnetic and electric forces. Name other ways we use these two forces.

Friction

Imagine you are riding a bicycle down a straight, flat road. You pedal as hard as you can. Then you stop pedaling and start coasting. You keep coasting until your bicycle finally wobbles to a stop. Why couldn't you just keep on coasting? Your coasting bicycle was stopped by **friction**, a force that slows down and stops moving objects. Friction occurs when two objects move across each other.

These tires increase friction.

These tires reduce friction.

Suppose you could roll a bowling ball down an endless bowling lane. It would move easily down the long, smooth surface. What would happen if you tried to roll a bowling ball down a lane covered with carpet? You can see that different surfaces result in different amounts of friction. But no matter what the surface, the ball eventually would stop rolling because of friction. The ball would also be slowed by friction with the air it moved through. Where did the friction occur that caused the bicycle to stop?

Friction can be useful. You experience the force of friction every day just in walking around. Friction between your shoes and the floor allows you to start moving and stop moving. Have you ever tried to walk on ice? You probably found that you had trouble because your shoes kept slipping. Because ice is so smooth, there was very little friction to hold your shoes in place. If there wasn't any friction, you wouldn't be able to stand at all. Think of some different surfaces you walk on. Which ones create the most friction with your feet? the least?

How is friction useful?

133

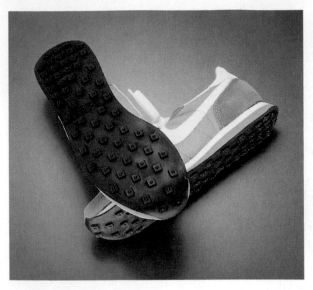

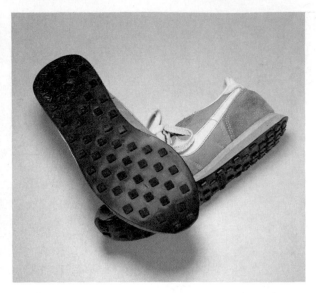

Friction often wears down surfaces.

Oil reduces friction between moving parts.

Have you ever found a round, smooth rock? As rocks tumble about in the current of a stream or the waves of an ocean, they are often worn smooth by the friction of water and other rocks. Sometimes friction causes problems. Moving parts of machinery sometimes need to be replaced because friction wears them away. They are often coated with oil, because two surfaces covered with oil have less friction. Look at the bottoms of your shoes. If you have worn them for awhile, how has friction changed them? Can you think of some other objects that become worn because of the effects of friction?

Forces and Pressure

Gently press the eraser end of your pencil against the palm of your hand. Now, using the same amount of force, press the pointed end against your palm. Do you feel a difference? The pencil point is much smaller than the eraser. When you applied the same force to a smaller area, you increased the pressure on the palm of your hand. **Pressure** is a measure of the amount of force applied to a given area. If you stand with both feet on the floor, the weight of your body applies pressure to the area of the floor covered by both feet. If you stand on one foot, the force on the entire floor is the same, but the pressure on that area of the floor under your foot doubles. Your weight does not change, but the area on which your weight rests is only half the size it was when you were standing on both feet. What happens to the force on the floor if you lie down? What happens to the pressure?

What is pressure?

The student applies the same amount of force in the standing and sitting positions, but more pressure in the standing position.

Solids, liquids, and gases all apply pressure. If you dive into a swimming pool, you can feel the pressure of the water on your body. The air around you is always applying pressure to your body. You don't notice it, because you're used to it. The air pressure on the inside of tires provides enough force to support the weight of a car or truck. Have you ever used a can of spray paint? The gas pressure inside the spray can is greater than the air pressure outside the can. When you press down on the nozzle, liquid inside the can is pushed out. In what other ways have you seen gas pressure used?

Air exerts pressure.

136

It's amazing to realize how many forces surround us every day. For example, while you're listening to your newest cassette tape on your headset, electric force helps play your favorite song. And your report card may even be posted on the refrigerator with a magnet. How many other ways do you see forces at work around you?

Lesson Summary

- Some forces in the world include the force of gravity, magnetic forces, electric forces, and the force of friction.
- Friction occurs when two objects move across each other. It is a force that slows down and stops moving objects.
- Pressure is a measure of the amount of force applied to a given area by solids, liquids, or gases.

Lesson Review

1. Name three forces in the world.
2. What force causes some objects to wear smooth?
3. Does pressure increase or decrease when you reduce the area to which a force is applied?
★4. Explain how friction helps you walk around.

Water exerts pressure on the scuba diver.

Newton's Laws of Motion

LESSON 3 GOALS
You will learn
● about three laws of motion.
● when motion occurs.
● that acceleration is any change in an object's speed or direction.

Your homeroom has been challenged to a tug-of-war contest by Mr. Sakawa's homeroom across the hall. Your class's plan is to make up a team with the strongest students. In a tug-of-war one team pulls on one end of a rope, and another team pulls on the other end of the same rope, each trying to avoid moving across a line drawn between them. The rope won't move as long as your class's team pulls with the same strength or amount of force as Mr. Sakawa's team. Neither team will win if the forces on each side are balanced. Balanced means the two teams' forces are equal in size, and they are pulling in opposite directions. What will happen if your class's team is stronger? The rope will start to move in your direction, because your class's force on the rope is greater than the force of Mr. Sakawa's team. The forces acting on the rope are then unbalanced, and the stronger team—yours—becomes the winner! Without an unbalanced force acting on an object, there is never any change in its motion.

What causes an object to move?

SCIENCE AND . . .
Math

Carrie, Sheelah, and Tom are in a tug-of-war. How much force do they need to balance their opponents' forces of 125, 165, and 148 newtons?
A. 146 newtons
B. 438 newtons
C. 328 newtons
D. 142 newtons

Young Isaac Newton with some of his inventions

Would You Believe?

Newton did not tell anyone or write anything about his discoveries for 20 years, when his astronomer-friend Edmund Halley found out.

Questions about what caused things to move in different ways filled the thoughts of a young man from England many years ago—a boy who liked to daydream. Rather than help his mother with the farm chores, Isaac sat under a tree in the countryside and read books. The books gave him many ideas to think about, raising questions about the world around him. Isaac also loved to invent machines—from clocks to windmills. When he grew up, Isaac Newton spent the rest of his life studying science and mathematics. During the 1600s he made many important discoveries about position, motion, and forces. Today Newton's laws of motion are important in any scientific study about motion. Let's take a look at these laws and see how they affect our work and play every day.

During what time period did Newton make his discoveries?

An orbiting spacecraft maintains the same speed because there's no friction from air molecules to slow it down.

What does the first law of motion say about objects at rest?

First Law of Motion

Look at the books and papers lying around your classroom. They will continue to lie there unless a force—a student or an air current, for example—moves them. The **first law of motion** that Newton described states that objects at rest stay at rest. The law also states that objects moving in a straight line will stay in motion in a straight line and at the same speed unless acted on by an unbalanced force. Suppose you are riding in the car with your father and an animal runs out in front of the car. To avoid hitting the animal, your father quickly steps on the brake pedal. The force of the brakes will stop the car, but without a seat belt your body will continue to move forward until you hit the dashboard. These two ideas in Newton's first law say that objects tend to keep doing what they are already doing unless some kind of unbalanced force makes them change.

Second Law of Motion

If you are riding your bicycle and are stopped for a red light, you accelerate when you start pedaling again. You move forward, and your speed increases. **Acceleration** (ihk sel uh RAY shun) is any change in the speed or direction of an object. If you turn onto a side street, you are also accelerating even though you may not change speed, because you are changing direction. It takes an unbalanced force to change either direction or speed of motion.

Suppose you are pulling a wagon. It is easier to accelerate an empty wagon than to accelerate a wagon full of bricks. A wagon filled with bricks has more mass than an empty wagon. More force is needed to accelerate more massive objects. Suppose a friend comes to help you push the wagon. If you both move in the same direction, the wagon accelerates more rapidly than if you pull alone. Newton's **second law of motion** states that an object's acceleration depends on the size and direction of the forces acting on it and on the mass of the object.

What does the second law of motion say about an object's acceleration?

The car is accelerating around the curve.

Third Law of Motion

What is the third law of motion?

Jessica was roller skating one day. She stopped when she came to a brick wall. Jessica faced the wall and pushed on it with her hands. She rolled backward on her skates away from the wall. Newton's **third law of motion** describes what happened to Jessica. It states that for every force there is an equal and opposite reaction force. These pairs of forces are often called **action-reaction forces**. Jessica pushed on the wall with her hands. She exerted a force on the wall, while at the same time the wall exerted in the opposite direction an equal amount of force on Jessica. The wall pushed back on Jessica when she pushed on it. Because Jessica was on roller skates, the wall's push on Jessica was enough to overcome the force of friction, and Jessica rolled backward.

Remember action and reaction forces always work in pairs. There will always be two objects involved. The reaction force could just as easily be called the action force because the forces happen at the same instant in time. Jessica pushed on the wall, and the wall pushed back on Jessica. Or you could say the wall pushed on Jessica, and Jessica pushed back on the wall.

Jessica and the wall push on each other.

You Can...

Make a Come-Back Can

Get a coffee can (453 or 906 gram size) with a plastic lid. Have an adult help you put two holes in the bottom of the can and in the plastic lid. Cut a long, thick rubber band. Thread it through the holes and through 5 large heavy washers on the inside of the can. (See the picture.) Tie the rubber band back together as shown in the picture. Now roll the can on the floor away from you. Watch what happens. Why does it come back?

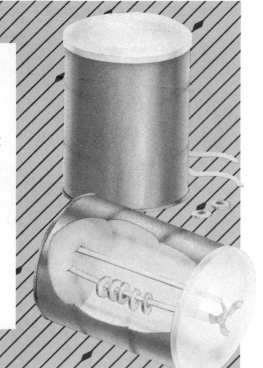

Here's another example of Newton's third law of motion. Look at the picture. At the moment the dog jumps from the boat to the dock, the boat moves backward in the water. The dog exerts a force on the boat, and the boat pushes back on the dog with an equal amount of force. Is the dog the action force or the reaction force? Remember you can say the dog pushes on the boat or the boat pushes on the dog.

Newton's laws help us design more efficient cars.

Why does Newton receive credit for the three laws of motion?

Many scientists believe that Newton's description of what happens to objects in motion was one of the greatest scientific achievements in history. Newton wasn't the first to discover each of these laws, but he was the first to write down the laws and show proof. His work still helps scientific study today with research on rockets, automobiles, and sports.

Lesson Summary

- Newton's three laws describe the properties of objects at rest and in motion.
- Objects in motion continue in motion in a straight line unless acted on by an unbalanced force.
- An object's acceleration depends on its mass and the force acting on it.

Lesson Review

1. What were the three important laws Isaac Newton formed that scientists still use today?
2. What is needed to start, stop, or change the direction of objects?
3. What is acceleration?
★4. Make up your own example of the third law of motion.

How does mass affect acceleration?

What you need

string
paper clip
Puller Pal or spring scale
3 chalkboard erasers
pencil and paper

What to do

1. Using the Puller Pal, slowly pull 3 erasers across a table as shown.
2. Record the amount of force needed to accelerate the 3 erasers by placing a mark on the Puller Pal.
3. Remove 1 of the erasers. Pull the remaining 2 erasers across the table, using the same amount of force you used in step 1.
4. Repeat step 3 again using only 1 eraser. Try to use the same amount of force.

What did you learn?

1. What happened to the acceleration as you used fewer erasers?
2. What was being decreased as you used fewer erasers?
3. How does mass affect acceleration?

Using what you learned

1. Why are bicycle racers concerned about the materials used to make their bikes?
2. Why do some very long freight trains have more than one engine?
3. Why do race cars have more powerful engines than family cars?

I WANT TO KNOW ABOUT...

Motion Research

For many years motion research relied on film. A person or object was filmed in motion to find out the most efficient way to do a task. Scientists would then view the film—frame by frame—and measure changes in position. Scientists now have new techniques to make motion analysis less time-consuming.

One new technique uses a video camera to record motion. A video processor determines the outlines of moving objects, which are stored in a computer. The computer charts the paths of the objects. This method has been used by a shoe manufacturer to analyze foot motion so the company can make better shoes for sports activities.

Another motion analysis technique uses electronic devices attached to a moving object. These devices flash on and off when the object moves, and the motion is recorded by a special camera. The information goes into a computer that analyzes the positions of the flashes and the motion of the object. This technique has been used to study various movements—from a dancing ballerina to a person throwing a javelin, as in the photograph below.

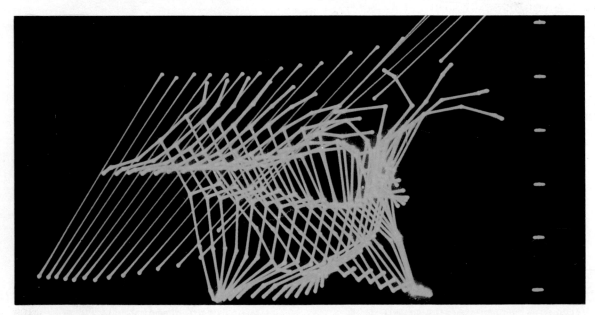

Science and Technology

Summary

Lesson 1
- Motion is the changing of position.
- Average speed is a measure of how far an object moves divided by the time it takes to move the distance.
- Velocity is the speed and direction of a moving object.

Lesson 2
- Some forces in the world include the force of gravity, magnetic forces, electric forces, and force of friction.
- Friction occurs when two objects move across each other. It is a force that slows down and stops moving objects.
- Pressure is a measure of the amount of force applied to a given area by solids, liquids, or gases.

Lesson 3
- Newton's three laws describe the properties of objects at rest and in motion.
- Objects in motion continue in motion in a straight line unless acted on by an unbalanced force.
- An object's acceleration depends on its mass and the force acting on it.

Science Words

Fill in the blank with the correct word or words from the list.

average speed	velocity	action-reaction	second law of motion
forces	friction	forces	third law of motion
position	electric force	pressure	force of gravity
motion	acceleration	first law of motion	

1. The ____ states that for every force there is always an equal but opposite force.
2. The measure of the amount of force applied to a certain area is ____.
3. ____ is the distance moved by an object in a certain direction in a given time.
4. The ____ states that acceleration depends on an object's mass and the unbalanced force acting on it.
5. The ____ states that it takes an unbalanced force to change an object's motion.
6. ____ is the changing of position.
7. An object's location is its ____.
8. A force that slows down objects moving across each other is ____.

Questions

Recalling Ideas

Correctly complete each of the following sentences.

1. Changes in motion occur only when forces acting on an object are
   (a) equal.　　(c) unchanged.
   (b) balanced.　(d) unbalanced.

2. A runner runs a 100-meter race in 20 seconds. The average speed of the runner is ____.
   (a) 2,000 meters/second.
   (b) 5 meters/second.
   (c) 80 meters/second.
   (d) 50 meters/second.

3. The rate at which the motion of an object changes is called
   (a) speed.　　(c) acceleration.
   (b) gravity.　(d) friction.

4. Friction can be reduced by
   (a) applying more pressure.
   (b) making surfaces rougher.
   (c) using lubricants.
   (d) adding mass.

5. If you tell a friend that your house is two doors north of the corner of Broad St. and High St. and on the east side of the street, you are describing a(n)
   (a) area.　　(c) action.
   (b) motion.　(d) position.

6. A car is driven around a circular track at 90 kilometers per hour. All of the following are changing EXCEPT
   (a) speed.　　(c) acceleration.
   (b) velocity.　(d) distance.

7. Suppose your science book is lying flat on your desk. If you stand it on end, you increase the ____ on the desk.
   (a) weight　　(c) pressure
   (b) force　　(d) gravity

8. The change in an object's position is
   (a) velocity.　　(c) speed.
   (b) acceleration.　(d) motion.

Examining Ideas

Determine whether each of the following statements is true or false. Rewrite the false statements to make them correct.

1. Velocity measures only how fast you are moving.
2. Any object with a force acting on it will accelerate.
3. The action force and reaction force act on the same object.
4. Friction slows down motion.
5. When you ride your bike around a curve, your velocity will not change.
6. The action force is always produced before the reaction force.
7. Modern scientists no longer use Newton's three laws of motion.
8. Pressure can be measured in newtons per square centimeter.

Understanding Ideas

Answer the following questions using complete sentences.

1. List some everyday forces and tell how they are useful.
2. Explain and give examples of Newton's three laws of motion.

3. You push on a box with a force of 10 newtons. A friend pushes on the box in the opposite direction with a force of 20 newtons.
   (a) Are these two forces an action-reaction pair of forces? Explain.
   (b) Will these two forces cause the box to accelerate? Why?
4. What happens to a moving object if it is acted on by several forces that balance each other?
5. Give three examples of when friction is necessary and three examples of when friction is a problem.

Thinking Critically

Think about what you have learned in this chapter. Answer the following questions using complete sentences.

1. To make a squirt gun shoot farther, how should you change the size of the opening? Explain.
2. Sometimes Newton's first law is incorrectly stated as, "An object will continue in motion unless it is acted on by a force." Explain what is wrong with this statement.
3. Why might a car slide off an icy road when the car goes around a curve?
4. A gymnast lands on a trampoline and bounces upward. Identify the
   (a) action-reaction force pair.
   (b) unbalanced force.

Work and Machines

There is an old saying that you can't get something for nothing. A weight lifter is able to lift a heavy object. Might a machine make lifting easier? Suppose a pulley were attached to the weight. Would lifting the weight be easier? A pulley might make it easier, but it may take longer. Each pull only moves the bar a short distance. Both ways equal the same result because the distance the weight moves is the same. Which way would you prefer?

ACTIVITY

Have You Ever...

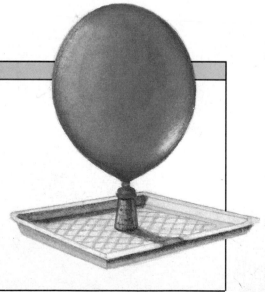

Made a Hovercraft?

Poke a hole in the middle of a plastic foam tray. Poke a similar hole through the middle of a cork. Line up the holes. Glue the wide end of the cork to the tray, making sure there are no air gaps. Attach a blown-up balloon over the cork. Place the craft on the floor and give it a gentle push. What happens? How does the craft move?

LESSON 1 GOALS
You will learn
- that work is done when a force is used to move an object through a distance.
- that work equals force used times the distance the object moves.
- how work is measured.

Working With Forces

One day Drew and Keisha were walking out of school when Keisha suddenly stopped.

"Drew, will you hold my books for me?" she asked. "I have to run back into school. I forgot my hat."

Drew didn't want to wait, but Keisha said, "I'll pay you for the work you do."

"OK," he said, taking Keisha's books.

Drew stood outside school, holding Keisha's books for about five minutes. Then Keisha returned.

"Thanks, Drew," she said.

"You can pay me now," he answered.

"But Drew," Keisha said. "I don't *have* to pay you. You didn't do any work."

Is Keisha right? Didn't Drew do work when he held her books? It really depends on how you define work. To a scientist **work** is using a force to move an object through a distance. Every time you ride a bicycle, move a saw through wood to cut it, or open a door, you are using a force to move something. In each case you are doing work. If work is using a force to move an object through a distance, do you think Drew did any work? No, he didn't. He may have used a force to hold the books, but he didn't move them anyplace.

You do work when you move a saw.

Pushing the sled is work!

When you lift an object, you are doing work. Work is one way of transferring energy from one object to another. When you lift a box or push a box across the floor, the work you do is transferring your energy to the box.

You can measure the amount of work you do, if you know the amount of force and the distance that the force moved an object. To measure work, multiply the force (in newtons) times the distance (in meters). The answer will be expressed in newton-meters, or the metric unit for work—**joule** (JEWL). The formula looks like this:

What is the formula for measuring work?

$$\text{work} = \text{force} \times \text{distance object moved}$$

The girl in the picture is climbing a rope in gym class. She is doing work because she must use a force to pull herself up the rope. How much force is she using? If the girl weighs 300 newtons, she must apply a force of 300 newtons in order to pull herself up the rope. How much work will she do if she pulls herself up a three-meter rope? You can use the formula below to find the answer.

$$\text{work} = \text{force} \times \text{distance object moved}$$
$$\text{work} = 300 \text{ newtons} \times 3 \text{ meters}$$
$$\text{work} = 900 \text{ newton-meters or } 900 \text{ joules}$$

The girl has done 900 joules of work to pull herself up the rope.

153

Suppose Keisha uses three newtons of force to push a box across the floor a distance of two meters. Suppose Drew uses three newtons of force to lift the box on a table that is one meter from the floor. Who has done more work?

Lesson Summary

- Work results when a force moves an object through a distance.
- The amount of work done is equal to the amount of force used times the distance an object is moved.
- Work is measured in newton-meters or joules.

Lesson Review

1. When is work done?
2. In what metric unit is work measured?
★3. A woman is lifting boxes. Each box requires a force of 120 newtons to move. She lifts 15 boxes from the ground onto the back of a truck that is 1 meter off the ground. How much work does the woman do in lifting 1 box? 15 boxes?

How much work is done when an object is lifted?

What you need

meter stick   string
small objects   pencil and paper
spring scale

What to do

1. Attach an object to the spring scale. You may need to tie some objects with string.
2. Slowly lift the object at a steady rate. Record how much force you used to move the object.
3. Ask a classmate to measure the distance you moved the object. Record the distance in meters.
4. Find out how much work you did by using the formula—work = force × distance object moved. Record your answer.
5. Repeat steps 2 through 5 with other objects.

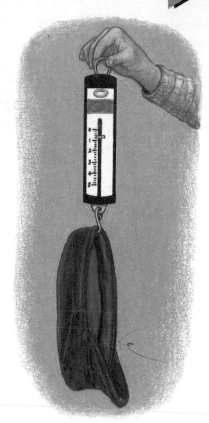

Work Measurement Table			
Object	Force (N)	Distance (m)	Work (J)

What did you learn?

1. Why did you record the distance in meters?
2. Which object required the most force?
3. How did you find which object required the most work?

Using what you learned

1. What are you measuring when you weigh an object with a newton spring scale?
2. How much more work is done by lifting an object two meters instead of one meter?

LESSON 2 GOALS
You will learn
- how machines can change the direction or amount of force needed to do work.
- how machines help you in doing work.
- that the amount of work put out by a machine is never more than the work put into it.

The Advantages of Machines

Keisha's sister works in a large warehouse. When she first began her job, she lifted boxes by hand. She quickly discovered that boxes were heavy and hard to lift. Luckily, she now uses a machine. The machine Keisha's sister uses makes her job seem easier and go faster.

Machines are devices that can make a job seem easier to do. That does not mean, however, that less work is done. Many people use machines every day to do work because machines can increase or decrease a force. They can also change the direction of a force. What machines have you used to do work today?

Mechanical Advantage

To get work out of any machine, work must first be put into it. For many machines, a person is the source of this needed work. A person must exert a force on a machine. The amount that a machine increases a force is called the **mechanical** (mih KAN ih kul) **advantage** of the machine. Different machines increase forces by different amounts. This means they have different mechanical advantages.

Machines make work seem easier.

This machine increases the force put into it.

You find the mechanical advantage for each machine by dividing the force exerted by the machine by the force you used on the machine. The formula looks like this:

How can you find a machine's mechanical advantage?

$$\text{mechanical advantage} = \frac{\text{force exerted by machine}}{\text{force used}}$$

Suppose Drew's father is driving him to school and the car's front tire goes flat. His father uses a jack to lift the front of the car near the flat tire so it can be changed. Suppose the tire supports 4,000 newtons of the car's weight. His father uses a force of only 40 newtons on the jack. You can use the formula below to find the mechanical advantage of the jack.

$$\text{mechanical advantage} = \frac{\text{force exerted by machine}}{\text{force used}}$$

$$\text{mechanical advantage} = \frac{4,000 \text{ newtons (to lift car)}}{40 \text{ newtons (applied to jack)}}$$

$$\text{mechanical advantage} = 100$$

This means the force Drew's father used was increased 100 times by using a jack.

Machine Efficiency

When Drew's father used a machine to help him lift the car, he still had to do work. He had to put work into the machine before it would do work for him. The **efficiency** (ih FIHSH un see) of a machine is a measure of the work put into it compared with the work it does. The amount of work Drew's father puts into his machine is more than the amount of work done by the machine. Some of the work he puts in is used to overcome friction between parts of the machine. Because of friction the amount of work done by any machine is never more than the amount of work put into the machine.

A machine can do more work if there is less friction. The more efficient a machine is, the closer the amount of work done by the machine comes to the amount of work put into the machine. For this reason it makes sense to try to reduce a machine's friction. Oil is often used to lubricate parts that move against each other. Another way to reduce friction between surfaces is by using small, smooth spheres called ball bearings. Since there is less contact between a bearing and a surface, there is less friction. Ball bearings are used to reduce friction in skate wheels, for example, and between machine parts.

You Can...

Use Marbles to Reduce Friction

Get two large cans and some marbles. Turn one can upside down. Place the second can right-side-up on top of the first can. Put the marbles between the bottoms of the cans. How do the surfaces move across each other when the top can is rotated? What would happen if you tried to rotate the top can without the marbles in between?

Increasing a machine's efficiency is very important. Reducing friction protects machine parts from wear and makes them last longer. In addition, an efficient machine requires less fuel to operate.

Why does reducing friction help conserve fuel?

Lesson Summary

- Machines can change the direction or the amount of force needed to do work.
- The mechanical advantage of a machine equals the force exerted by the machine divided by the force used.
- Machine efficiency is a measure of the work put into a machine compared with the work the machine does.

Lesson Review

1. How are forces changed by machines?
2. A girl weighing 300 newtons lifts her teacher on a seesaw. The teacher weighs 600 newtons. What is the mechanical advantage of the seesaw?
★3. Explain why increasing a machine's efficiency is very important.

LESSON 3 GOALS
You will learn
● about six types of
simple machines.
● that most machines are
made of two or more
simple machines.

Simple Machines

If your teacher asked you to list some machines, you might say lawn mower, tractor, or blender. The machines you first think of may seem very complicated, but they are all combinations of a few simple machines. A simple machine is made of only one part. You could have listed any of six types of simple machines—a lever, inclined plane, screw, wedge, wheel and axle, or pulley. The knife you use to cut bread is a simple machine called a wedge. A bottle opener is a simple machine called a lever. Let's find out how simple machines help make a job easier.

Machines are used to perform work. You know now that work is done when something is moved by a force through a distance. A lever is a very useful simple machine because it can be used to move objects. A lever may change the direction of a force or the amount of force used.

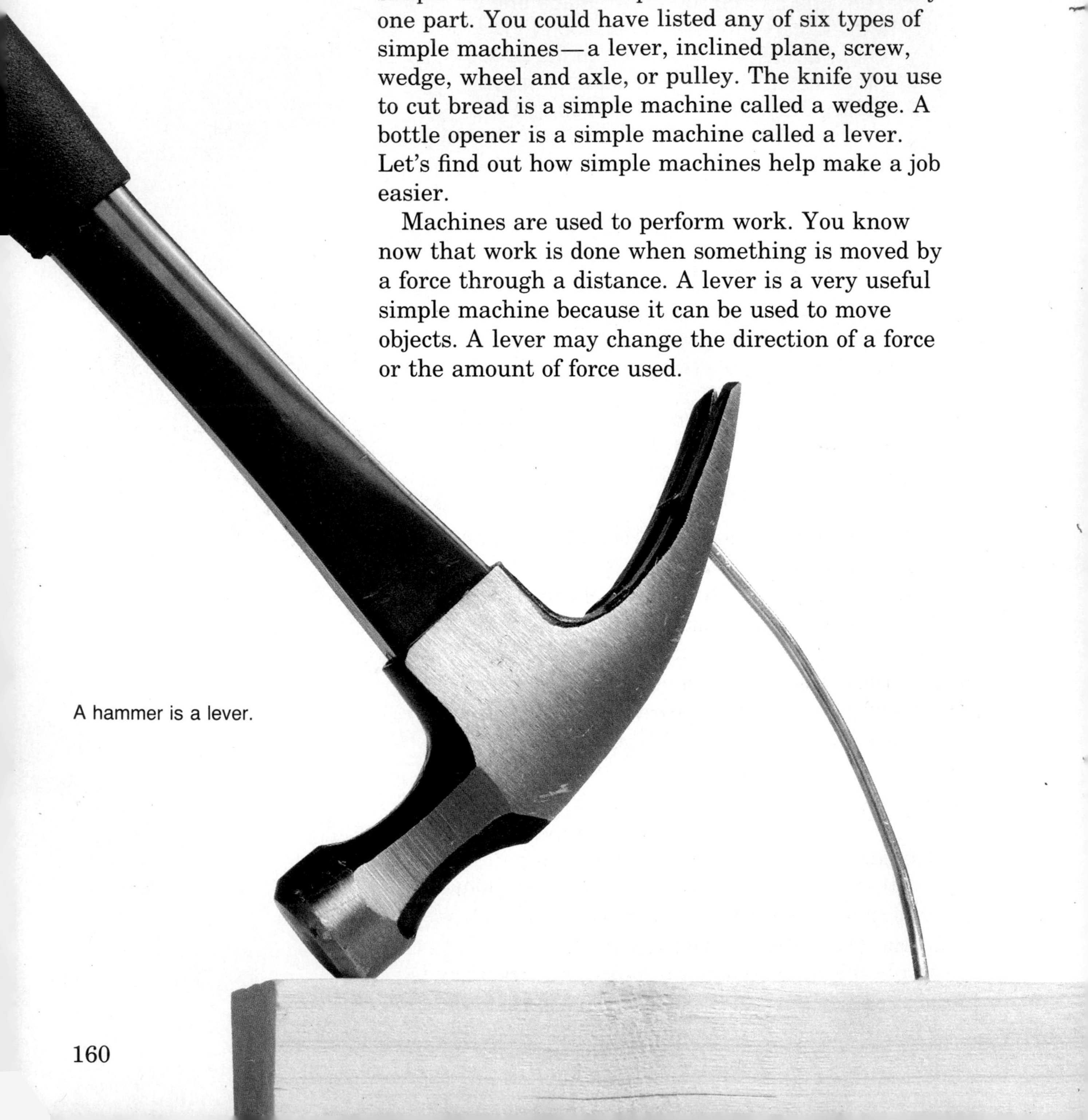

A hammer is a lever.

160

A **lever** is a bar that turns around a fixed point. The fixed point is called a **fulcrum**. Suppose Carol and Hung in the picture want to put the next large stone on top of the wall they are building, but the stone is too heavy for them to lift. Since they know about simple machines, they make a lever by using a board and a log. The board acts as the lever, and the log is the fulcrum. When they apply a force to the other end of the lever, the board will turn on the log and lift the stone off the ground. The end of the lever to which they apply force is called the effort arm. The force they apply to the machine is called the **effort force**. The end of the lever where the stone rests is called the **resistance** (rih ZIHS tuns) **arm**. The stone's weight exerts a **resistance force**. Since Carol and Hung need to increase the force they can exert, they've put the log fulcrum closer to the resistance force than to their effort force. As they apply an effort force by pushing down on their end of the lever, the stone on the other end is lifted to the top of the wall.

How do effort force and resistance force differ?

Look at the picture of the nutcracker. This is a lever with the fulcrum at the end rather than in the middle. When you crack the nut, your effort force is at the end opposite the fulcrum. The nut's resistance force occurs in the middle. As you apply force to the handle, the lever intensifies the force, and the nut is cracked.

The boy raking the leaves is also using a lever—the rake. His upper hand acts as the fulcrum, while his lower hand applies the effort force. Each time he pushes against the rake, he applies effort force. Where do you think the resistance force occurs? Why does the lever intensify the force he exerts with his lower hand?

Levers can be found in the most surprising places. You probably never thought of your arm as a lever. Yet it is. Watch tennis players during a match. A player's arm acts as a lever during the serve. The shoulders are the fulcrum, the upper arms provide the effort force, and when the ball hits the racket, resistance occurs. Can you think of any other levers?

The rake is a lever.

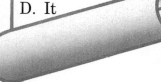

SCIENCE AND . . .
Writing
Choose the word that belongs in the space.
The movers used a great deal of force to push our refrigerator up the ramp. ____ did a lot of work and were tired.
A. I
B. They
C. She
D. It

A second simple machine that is found almost everywhere is an inclined plane. An **inclined plane** is a slanted surface used to help raise or lower objects. It makes work seem easier because it reduces the amount of force required.

A ramp is a good example of an inclined plane. You use less force to push a cart up a ramp than you would use to lift the cart the same vertical distance. In fact, whether you lift a box straight up to a shelf or slide it up a ramp, you do the same amount of work on the box. However, when you use a ramp, you exert a smaller force but over a longer distance. It is good to know that you can put a heavy box on a shelf more easily by using a ramp than by lifting it. There are many examples of inclined planes, such as freeway and wheelchair ramps. What inclined planes do you see on the way to school?

Two more examples of simple machines related to inclined planes are the screw and the wedge. A **screw** is an inclined plane wrapped in a spiral around a cylinder. You may have used a screw to hold pieces of wood or metal together. Because it is useful for pushing two objects together or moving materials, it is also used in some types of car jacks and for well-drilling and oil-drilling equipment. For underground drilling, screws remove long columns of dirt from the ground.

What is an inclined plane?

A **wedge** is made of one or two inclined planes. A wedge, in the form of the head of an axe, splits firewood. One of the world's oldest machines—over 5,000 years old—is a farmer's wooden plow, which is a wedge. Knife blades and scissors blades are also wedges. Would you consider a doorstop a wedge?

Both the screwdriver and doorknob are wheels and axles.

A fifth simple machine is a wheel and axle. Bicycles, pencil sharpeners, doorknobs, some can openers, and fishing reels all contain wheels and axles. A **wheel and axle** is made up of a large wheel—the wheel—attached to a wheel with a smaller diameter—the axle. The wheel and axle are attached so they can turn together. Often, for example in the doorknob, the axle is not a wheel but a cylinder or shaft that is inside the mechanism. Remember how Carol and Hung used a lever to lift a stone that required more force than they could exert? A wheel and axle intensifies force in the same way. A small force is applied to turn the wheel a longer distance so the axle will apply a greater force over a short distance. How is the screwdriver a wheel and axle?

Look closely at the pedals of a bicycle. Consider your feet as they go around on the pedals as the large wheel. The axle is the small gear wheel that is attached to the chain. Your feet and the axle rotate at the same speed. However, your feet move a long distance applying a moderate force, while the axle moves a shorter distance applying a greater force to the rear wheel.

The sixth simple machine is a **pulley**. Like other simple machines, pulleys can change the direction or amount of a force. The pulley on a flagpole doesn't change the amount of force but does change the direction. When you pull down on one side of the rope, the flag attached to the other side goes up. By combining pulleys, the amount of force needed can also be changed. Pulleys are often used for lifting heavy objects. An elevator is a motorized lifting machine made of pulleys.

For what kind of work are pulleys often used?

A pulley is a simple machine.

165

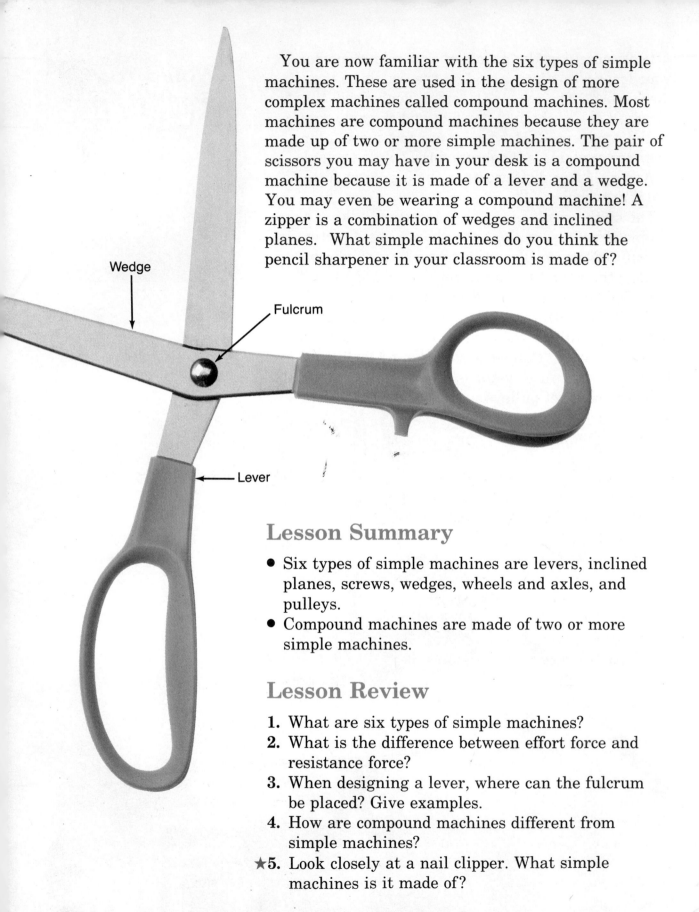

Wedge

Fulcrum

Lever

You are now familiar with the six types of simple machines. These are used in the design of more complex machines called compound machines. Most machines are compound machines because they are made up of two or more simple machines. The pair of scissors you may have in your desk is a compound machine because it is made of a lever and a wedge. You may even be wearing a compound machine! A zipper is a combination of wedges and inclined planes. What simple machines do you think the pencil sharpener in your classroom is made of?

Lesson Summary

- Six types of simple machines are levers, inclined planes, screws, wedges, wheels and axles, and pulleys.
- Compound machines are made of two or more simple machines.

Lesson Review

1. What are six types of simple machines?
2. What is the difference between effort force and resistance force?
3. When designing a lever, where can the fulcrum be placed? Give examples.
4. How are compound machines different from simple machines?
★5. Look closely at a nail clipper. What simple machines is it made of?

How do levers change forces?

What you need

meter stick
2 chairs
metric ruler
string
2 large paper clips
4 large washers
pencil and paper

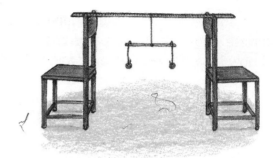

What to do

1. Set up the ruler balance as shown. Hang a large paper clip on each end of the ruler.
2. Place one washer on each paper clip. Move the paper clips so that the ruler is balanced. Read and record how far each paper clip is from the string.
3. Add a second washer to one paper clip. Leave only one washer on the other clip. Move the paper clips so the ruler is balanced. Read and record the distances from the string to each paper clip.
4. Repeat step 3 using three washers on one paper clip and one washer on the other paper clip.

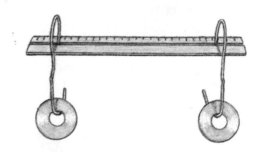

What did you learn?

1. How did the distances from the string to the paper clips change with two washers?
2. What are the forces on the lever?

Using what you learned

1. If one washer is placed 10 centimeters from the fulcrum, where will the other washer have to be placed to balance it?
2. If one washer is placed 15 centimeters from the fulcrum, where will you have to place three washers to balance it?
3. How is this balance like a seesaw? Explain how a child can balance an adult on a seesaw.

167

I WANT TO KNOW ABOUT...

An Exercise Expert

Lee Jones is a salesperson for an exercise equipment company. He has to know how the equipment works and how it uses motion and force. He also has to know how it will affect the muscles of the body. Lee tells his customers how the machines work and the best ways to use them.

Lee explains that some machines are endurance builders and some are strength builders. The endurance-building machines Lee sells are rowers and bicycles. The strength-builders include free weight, cable-and-pulley, and isokinetic (i soh kuh NET ihk) machines. Part of Lee's job is to explain their differences.

Some of the strength-building weight machines are set at a certain load, such as 15 kilograms. You have to lift 15 kilograms to complete the movement. But with an isokinetic machine, your effort determines the machine's resistance. If you exert enough force to lift 10 kilograms, the machine provides 10 kilograms of resistance. The machine will adjust to resist any amount of force. No matter how hard you push or pull, the machine provides an equal resistance. Your stronger muscles pull harder, and the machine offers greater resistance. It offers less resistance to weaker muscles.

Career

Summary

Lesson 1
- Work results when a force moves an object through a distance.
- The amount of work done is equal to the amount of force used times the distance an object is moved.
- Work is measured in newton-meters or joules.

Lesson 2
- Machines can change the direction or the amount of force needed to do work.
- The mechanical advantage of a machine equals the force exerted by the machine divided by the force used.
- Machine efficiency is a measure of the work put into a machine compared with the work the machine does.

Lesson 3
- Six types of simple machines are levers, inclined planes, screws, wedges, wheels and axles, and pulleys.
- Compound machines are made of two or more simple machines.

Science Words

Fill in the blank with the correct word or words from the list.

work   lever   fulcrum   screw
joule   resistance arm effort force   wheel and axle
mechanical wedge   resistance force pulley
  advantage efficiency   inclined plane

1. A measure of the amount a machine can increase a force is the ____.
2. Work is measured in a unit called the ____.
3. The force that is applied to a lever is called the ____.
4. A force causes an object to move through a distance. This is called ____.
5. A measurement of the amount of work put into a machine compared to the amount of work done by the machine is the machine's ____.
6. The point around which a lever rotates is called the ____.

Questions

Recalling Ideas
Correctly complete each of the following sentences.

1. An example of a simple machine is a
   (a) bicycle.
   (b) motor.
   (c) wheel and axle.
   (d) sewing machine.
2. The resistance force divided by the effort force is called
   (a) mechanical advantage.
   (b) power.
   (c) efficiency.
   (d) work.
3. A force of 10 newtons is applied to a machine. The machine exerts a force of 20 newtons. The mechanical advantage of the machine is
   (a) 1/2.   (c) 10.
   (b) 2.   (d) 20.
4. A building maintenance person uses 50 newtons of force to move a desk 2 meters. The amount of work done on the desk is
   (a) 25 joules.   (c) 52 joules.
   (b) 50 joules.   (d) 100 joules.
5. A nutcracker is an example of a
   (a) screw.   (c) lever.
   (b) pulley.   (d) wedge.
6. Every lever has a
   (a) wheel and an axle.
   (b) resistance arm and fulcrum.
   (c) wedge and screw.
   (d) fulcrum and plane.
7. In a very efficient machine, the amount of work produced by the machine compared to the work put into the machine is
   (a) high.   (c) constant.
   (b) zero.   (d) low.

Examining Ideas
Determine whether each of the following statements is true or false. Rewrite the false statements to make them correct.

1. A compound machine is made of more than one simple machine.
2. The mechanical advantage of a simple machine is always greater than one.
3. Decreasing friction decreases efficiency.
4. Work is a way of transferring energy by motion.
5. Work is measured in watts.
6. A screw is a lever wrapped around a cylinder.
7. If there were no friction, the work produced by a machine could be greater than the work put into a machine.
8. A crowbar is a form of screw.

Understanding Ideas
Answer the following questions using complete sentences.

1. It takes less force to push a box up a ramp into the back of a pickup truck than it does to lift it straight up. However, it takes more work. Explain why this is true.

170

2. A pulley changes the direction of a force applied to it, but it doesn't increase the force. What is the mechanical advantage of the pulley?
3. Explain how a lever can make a job easier and still put out no more work than was put into it.
4. Describe the wheel and axle and give an everyday example of it.
5. A machine in which the efficiency is 100% is called an ideal machine.
   (a) Why is this type of machine considered an ideal machine?
   (b) Tell which of the six simple machines you think probably comes closest to being an ideal machine and explain why.

Thinking Critically

Think about what you have learned in this chapter. Answer the following questions using complete sentences.

1. A 20-newton box must be moved 2 meters. However, you find you need to exert 22 newtons of force to move it that distance. How large is the force of friction?
2. Explain this statement: "Work is energy transferred as a result of motion."
3. Name the simple machines in each of the following tools.
   (a) shovel   (c) fishing reel
   (b) axe   (d) screwdriver
4. Power is the rate at which work is done. It is measured in joules per unit of time; for example, joules per second. Suppose you have two motors operating to lift 500-newton boxes to a loading dock 1.5 meters above the ground. The first motor lifts one box every 2 seconds; the second motor takes 4 seconds to lift each box.
   (a) Which motor does the most work?
   (b) Which motor produces the most power?
   Explain your answers.

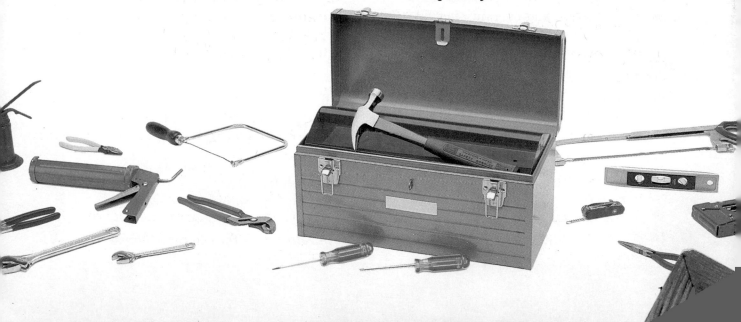

Checking for Understanding

Write a short answer for each question or statement.

1. How are all atoms alike?
2. Distinguish among volume, density, mass, and weight and give a unit for each.
3. How are elements classified in the periodic table?
4. Name the kind of change that occurs in each of the following (a) wood burning, (b) paper tearing, (c) ice melting, (d) glass breaking.
5. Distinguish among elements, compounds, and mixtures.
6. List the characteristics of acids and of bases.
7. Explain how ions are formed.
8. State the law of conservation of mass and explain what it means.
9. What is a static charge?
10. What is the difference between static and current electricity?
11. What is power? What is a unit used to measure power?
12. How are mechanical and electromagnetic waves alike? How are they different?
13. List three types of electromagnetic waves and one practical use for each.
14. What is a laser, and how are laser beams used?
15. Explain how velocity and speed are different.
16. What causes the motion of objects to change?
17. What is work?
18. Indicate which one of the following statements is true and explain why.
    (a) Simple machines require less work to do a job.
    (b) Simple machines make a job easier to do.

Recalling Activities

Write a short paragraph for each question or statement.

1. How can you compare densities?
2. How can you use properties to identify materials?
3. How is a compound formed?
4. How can you separate and compare mixtures?
5. How can you prevent rust?
6. How can you find out which liquids are acids?
7. How are circuits different?
8. How can you make an electric motor?
9. What are some properties of waves?
10. How much does light spread out from its source?
11. How can you find your average walking speed?
12. How does mass affect acceleration?
13. How much work is done when an object is lifted?
14. How do levers change forces?

Project Ideas

1. Design each of these words in a way that shows what each word means: force, motion, evaporate, solid, liquid, gas.
2. Find out how magnets are used in electric motors. Take apart a small motor and identify the parts.
3. Build a circuit to control one light with two three-way switches. Obtain or make two three-way switches. Use a flashlight bulb, dry cells, and wire to make a circuit in which the bulb may be turned on by either switch.

Books to Read

Fireworks! Pyrotechnics on Display by Norman D. Anderson and Walter R. Brown, Dodd., Mead & Co.: New York, 1983.

This is an explosively entertaining book!

Gobs of Goo by Vicki Cobb, Lippincott Junior Books: New York, 1983.

Try some "gooey" experiments and learn about chemical reactions.

Electricity by Alan Cooper, Silver Burdett: Morristown, NJ, 1983.

Explore the world of electricity.

Super Motion by Philip Watson, Lothrop, Lee, and Shepard: New York, 1983.

Do interesting motion activities.

Earth Science

"Little O, small earth, spinning in space,
face covered with dizzy clouds, facing,
chasing sunlight through the Milky Way,
say your secrets, small earth, little O,
know where you lead, I follow. I go.

Patched together
With land and sea.
I am earth,
Great earth.
Come with me!

from *Earth Songs*
Myra Cohn Livingston

Stars and Galaxies

The Earth's sun, a shining globe of hot gas, is average in size when compared to other stars in our galaxy. Yet if the sun were hollow, well over a million Earths could fit inside it. The sun is not only the center of our planetary system, it is also vitally important in sustaining life here on Earth. This star, a great ball of intense heat, is the nearest star to Earth. But in fact, had Earth been a little closer to the sun, our surface temperature might have been too hot to support life.

ACTIVITY

Have You Ever...

Studied the Colors of Stars?

Go outside on a clear night with binoculars. Study the stars in the sky. Focus on one bright star. Study that star for a few moments. Now move across the sky and focus on another bright star. Study that star for a moment. Does it shine a particular color? Go back to the first star. Does it shine a particular color? What do you think creates the color in stars?

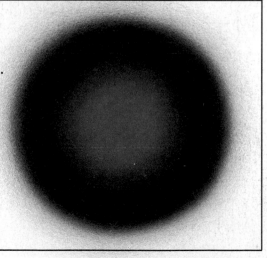

The Vastness of Space

LESSON 1 GOALS
You will learn
● that space is all the area beyond Earth's atmosphere.
● that the universe is composed of space, matter, and energy.
● why light-years are used to measure distance in space.

Have you ever stood outside at night studying the stars twinkling against the black sky? Perhaps you wondered how far away the stars were and if a spaceship could ever reach one of them. The starlight that you saw had traveled hundreds or thousands of years through space before reaching Earth. Space is so large it's hard to imagine. It is all the area beyond Earth's atmosphere. Even with the most powerful telescope, you see only a tiny part of space.

Long ago, early people observed and studied the night sky. Some wrote records of their observations of the stars and planets. These people were some of the earliest **astronomers.** Today's astronomers still use these records to help them understand the universe and how it's constantly changing.

Astronomers study space.

The **universe** that astronomers study is space and all the matter and energy in space. Our sun, surrounded by Earth and the other planets, is part of the Milky Way Galaxy. A galaxy is a large group of stars and gas. There are so many stars in the Milky Way that scientists have not yet counted them all. The Milky Way is just one of a huge unknown number of galaxies scattered throughout the universe. These individual galaxies are separated by great distances and empty space. It's impossible to imagine the vastness of space. The Milky Way Galaxy is just a tiny speck in the universe, and Earth is an even tinier speck in the Milky Way. Distances in space are unlike any we experience on Earth.

Just for fun, imagine a road that goes from your house to the sun. One morning, you get in your car and start on a journey to the sun. The speed limit for cars on many highways is 88 kilometers per hour. If you could drive at 88 kilometers per hour, 24 hours per day, it would take almost 200 years to get to the sun! The sun is the closest star; imagine how long it would take to get to another star in the Milky Way.

In which galaxy is our solar system located?

Distances in space are so huge we don't measure them in kilometers. Instead, astronomers use light-years to measure most distances in space. A **light-year** is equal to 9.5 trillion kilometers, the distance light travels in one year. In one second, light travels 300,000 kilometers. Compare the speed of light to the 88 kilometers per hour your car travels. Traveling at the speed of light, it would take your car about eight minutes to reach the sun.

The star closest to Earth, other than the sun, is Proxima Centauri (PRAWK sih muh ● sen TAWR ee). The distance to Proxima Centauri is over four light-years. It takes light from Proxima Centauri over four years to reach Earth. What were you doing four years ago when the light left Proxima Centauri that we can see today? Other stars are hundreds of light-years from Earth. Many are millions of light-years away. Imagine seeing starlight that left a star hundreds or even thousands of years before you were born! You do just that every time you look at the stars.

What is a light-year?

Lesson Summary

- Space is all the area beyond Earth's atmosphere.
- Space, matter, and energy make up the universe.
- Light-years are used to measure distances in space.

Lesson Review

1. Why do we use light-years rather than kilometers to measure distance in space?
2. What is the universe?
★3. Why is it so hard for people to imagine the size of the universe?

How can you describe your location in space?

What you need

globe or world map
pencil and paper

What to do

1. Write your name and school address by listing the following information in order:
   a. name
   b. desk position
   c. room number
   d. school name
   e. school address
   f. city
   g. county
   h. state or province
   i. nation
   j. continent
   k. hemisphere
   l. longitude and latitude
   m. planet
   n. solar system
   o. galaxy
   p. galaxy cluster
2. Compare your address in space to the addresses of other students in your class and school.

What did you learn?

1. How did you find the information for each part of your address?

2. How is your address different from the addresses of other students in your class and school?

Using what you learned

1. How might you address a letter to a friend living on the moon?
2. Design a universal zip code for your address. Be sure to include a designation that will locate the sun in our galaxy and the position of our planet around the sun.

181

Stars

LESSON 2 GOALS
You will learn
● that stars are different sizes, colors, and temperatures.
● that energy is released in stars by fusion.
● that stars go through a series of stages.

As you walk on a sandy beach, the tiny grains of sand slide between your bare toes. They seem to be all the same size and color. But if you sit down and examine the sand grains closely, you will discover they are not alike at all. Some are larger than others. Colors may be white, tan, or gray. Some may even have a pink, green, or blue tinge.

Like grains of sand, the stars probably appear alike to you when you stand outside your door and look at them in the night sky. If you could view the stars away from the brightness of city lights, you would probably be able to see a slight variation in color. The color of a star depends on its surface temperature. A very hot star gives off blue light. A much cooler star, like Betelgeuse (BEET ul joos) or Antares (an TER eez), gives off red light.

From the star color and temperature chart, you can see that the surface temperature of our sun is about 6,000 degrees Celsius.

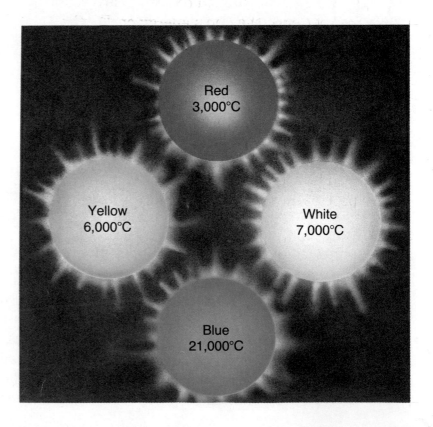

Red
3,000°C

Yellow
6,000°C

White
7,000°C

Blue
21,000°C

Star colors depend partially on their temperature.

Stars like our sun are mostly made of hydrogen and helium gases. Hydrogen gas is changed to helium gas inside stars during the fusion process. In fusion, the nuclei of two hydrogen atoms are combined to form the nucleus of a helium atom. Fusion produces huge amounts of energy. The energy production causes stars to get hot and glow as energy is released into space. What are some ways we experience the sun's energy on Earth?

The Life Cycle of Stars

When you go to the grocery store, you see people of many different ages. You might see a mother pushing a baby in a cart. Older children may be choosing their favorite cereals. Perhaps a teenager has stopped at the magazine counter. Possibly some elderly people are shopping for the freshest vegetables. How can you tell what stage of life these different people are in? Do height, weight, and general appearance give you some clues?

Stars also go through a series of stages. Astronomers have observed that, like people, younger stars have features different from older stars. Let's find out about the life cycle of a star.

Astronomers have seen large clouds of hydrogen gas and dust in space. These clouds are called **nebulas.** Stars like our sun may begin as nebulas.

Define nebula.

183

Our sun is about half way through its fuel supply.

Stage 1. The force of gravity causes the gas and dust in a nebula to come closer and closer together. When this happens, the gases become very hot. A core is formed as the very hot gases become densely packed.

Stage 2. When the densely packed gases reach a certain temperature, fusion begins. Hydrogen nuclei fuse into helium nuclei. Huge amounts of energy are produced when this fusion occurs. Young stars have lots of hydrogen in the core. In older stars, most of the hydrogen has been changed into helium. Our sun is a middle-aged star. It's about halfway through its fuel supply of hydrogen.

Stage 3. After a star uses its fuel supply, the outer layer of gases begins to expand, and the star grows very large. This outer layer cools and glows red as the star grows larger. That's why we call these very large red stars **red giants**. Red giants are hundreds of times larger than our sun.

Stage 4. As the hydrogen and helium of the red giant are used up, the force of gravity causes it to shrink. This shrinking causes the star to become hotter. When the red giant has shrunk to about the size of Earth, it has become hot enough to glow white. Astronomers call these very old stars **white dwarfs**.

Stage 5. Eventually a white dwarf loses all its energy and can no longer give off heat or light. It may take billions of years for the star to cool to the small, dense, **black dwarf** stage. This last stage is the final one in the life cycle of stars similar to our sun.

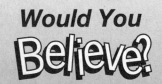

Would You Believe?

The iron in your blood and the calcium in your bones were formed in the interior of a star, billions of years ago.

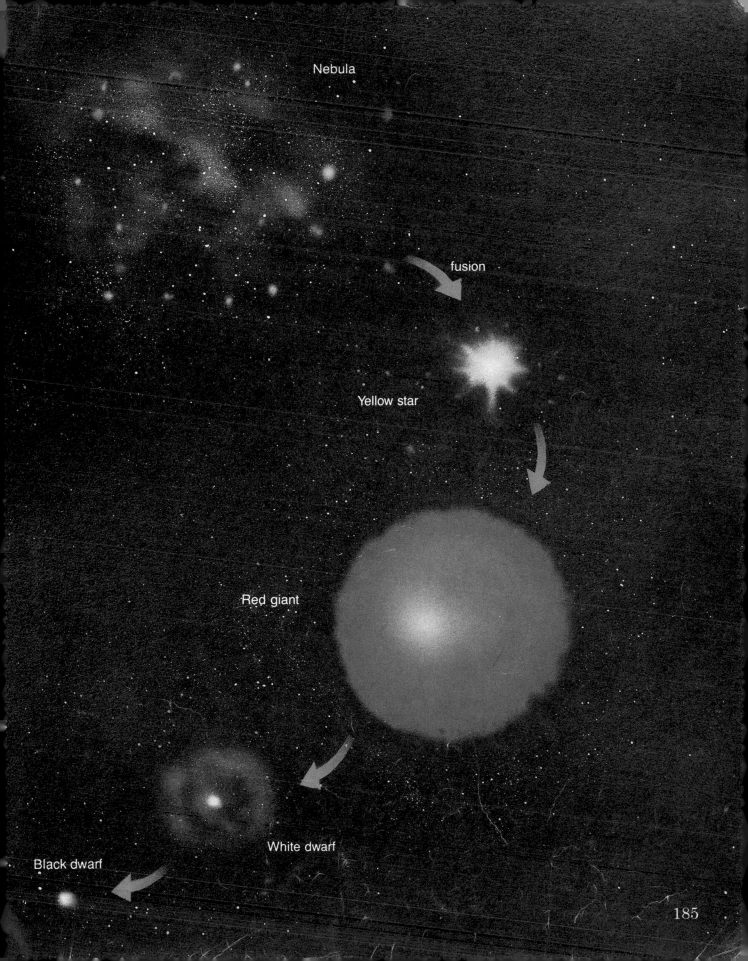

Nebula

fusion

Yellow star

Red giant

White dwarf

Black dwarf

Other Kinds of Stars

On the night of February 23, 1987, a telescope operator at an observatory in the Andes mountains of Chile was scanning a galaxy known as the Cloud of Magellan. He noticed a bright light and realized it was an exploding star, or a **supernova.** No supernova had been sighted since 1604, a time before the invention of the telescope. Word of the supernova was soon circling the globe, and telescopes were swiveling to get a view of this wondrous astronomical event.

The most spectacular supernova ever recorded occurred in 1054. The exploding star was so bright it could even be seen during the day. A nebula formed where that supernova occurred. It's called the Crab Nebula because some people thought it looked like a crab. The gas and dust left over from this supernova may someday be used in the formation of a new star.

The supernova observed in 1987

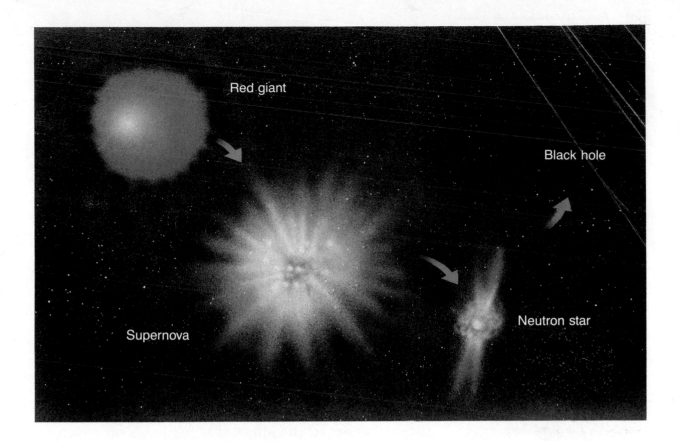

Red giant

Black hole

Supernova

Neutron star

Supernovas occur in only the most massive red giants. When the fuel of these stars runs out, the inner layers collapse rapidly. The collapse ends in a violent explosion. Astronomers have hypothesized about the events occurring after a supernova. Atomic particles left over from the explosion join to form neutrons. These neutrons then pull together and a **neutron star** is formed. The force of gravity is so strong in a neutron star that its matter is forced into a very small space. A neutron star is about 20 kilometers in diameter.

Astronomers have found that sometimes neutron stars spin and give off radio waves. A spinning neutron star is called a **pulsar**. The radio waves from a pulsar form a pattern, or pulse, blinking on and off many times a second. The pattern is used by astronomers to find out how fast the pulsar is spinning. One pulsar rotating about 30 times per second has been observed in the Crab Nebula.

Would You Believe?

One teaspoon of a neutron star has the same mass as a mountain.

187

A model of a black hole and its effect on a nearby star

Perhaps you've heard of black holes in space. But what are they and how do they form? Suppose a red giant that's very large and massive explodes in a supernova. As you know, the particles left over from the explosion will begin to clump together as gravity pulls them. With so many particles, the gravitational pull will be very strong. As the particles pull closer and closer together, the star keeps getting smaller and smaller. Eventually the gravity becomes so strong that nothing can stop the collapse of the particles. The star is crushed to a single point! This object is known as a **black hole**. The gravity surrounding a black hole is so strong that even light can't escape it. Any light coming within about ten kilometers of a black hole will fall into it. In other words, if you tried to shine a light on a black hole, you still wouldn't be able to see it because the light would disappear into the hole. Scientists can't observe black holes because they don't emit any light or energy. But they think they've observed the effect of black holes on nearby stars.

You Can...

Compare the Sizes of the Stars

Compare the diameters of the sun and a white dwarf. Find a place where you can make a chalk mark on pavement outside. Tie a piece of chalk to the end of a string 87 cm long. Have someone hold the end of the string to a point on the pavement. Pull the string tight and use the chalk to draw a circle on the pavement. Put a raisin in the center. What represents the sun? What represents a white dwarf? Our sun is over 100 times larger than a white dwarf.

Lesson Summary

- Stars vary in size, temperature, and color.
- Energy is released from stars through fusion.
- There are five stages in the life cycle of most stars. Some large red giants go to a supernova stage and may eventually become neutron stars or black holes.

Lesson Review

1. What color light is given off by the hottest star? The coolest?
2. What element is hydrogen changed into during fusion within a star?
3. What stage of a star's life cycle is the sun in?
4. Our sun is estimated to be 5 billion years old. About how old will it be when it eventually dies?
★5. Why can't astronomers use large telescopes to see black holes?

Galaxies

LESSON 3 GOALS
You will learn
● that galaxies can be classified based on their shapes.
● that the Milky Way Galaxy is classified as a spiral galaxy.
● that the Milky Way Galaxy belongs to a group of galaxies called the Local Group.

Ancient people looked at the night sky and saw what looked like a milky white path. What they were seeing was the huge galaxy of stars to which our sun belongs. We call it the **Milky Way Galaxy.** A **galaxy** is a large group of stars, gas, and dust containing billions of stars. The Milky Way Galaxy is made up of between 100 and 200 billion stars. Most of the stars you see in the sky are part of the Milky Way. On a clear night, our galaxy appears as a bright band stretching across the sky.

No one knows how many galaxies there are in the universe. Astronomers have identified about one billion. Each one differs in size and shape. Galaxies have been classified by their shapes. They may be elliptical, irregular, or spiral.

Elliptical galaxy

190

Some galaxies appear to have an oval shape. Astronomers call these elliptical galaxies. Through a telescope, you would be able to see many individual stars around the edges of an elliptical galaxy.

An irregular galaxy doesn't have any certain shape or form. You wouldn't be able to identify any pattern in the arrangement of the stars. Each irregular galaxy has a different shape.

A spiral galaxy has the flat shape of a disk. It has arms spiraling, or curving, out from its center. Our galaxy is believed to be a spiral galaxy. At its center the Milky Way is about 10,000 light-years thick. Its diameter is about 100,000 light-years. Our sun is located in a spiral arm of the Milky Way, about 30,000 light-years from the center. How long would it take light from a star on one side of the Milky Way to reach a star on the other side?

How is the Milky Way Galaxy classified?

Irregular galaxy

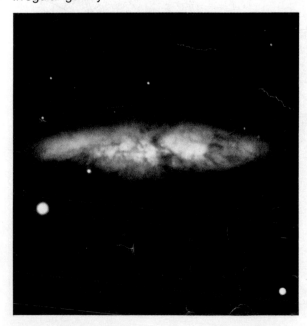

Spiral galaxy

191

If you could look at a map of the universe, you would notice that many galaxies seem to be in groups or clusters. The Milky Way is part of a cluster called the **Local Group.** Astronomers know of 28 galaxy members in the Local Group. The distance between two galaxies in the same cluster is small compared to the distance between two galaxies that aren't in the same cluster.

To help you imagine galaxy clusters, you might think of them as towns or cities. A galaxy cluster would be like a number of towns or cities located close together on a map. Farther away might be another group of towns representing another galaxy cluster. The universe is made up of these galaxy clusters and the space around them.

Diagram of the Milky Way Galaxy.

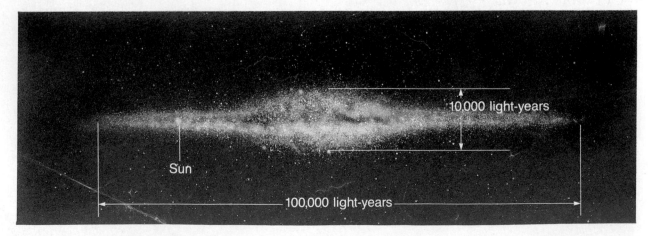

10,000 light-years

Sun

100,000 light-years

Andromeda is the nearest galaxy in the Local Group. Andromeda is often called our twin galaxy because it's a spiral galaxy of about the same size and shape as the Milky Way. Andromeda is about 2,250,000 light-years from our galaxy. On a very clear, dark night, away from city lights, you can see Andromeda without a telescope. It looks almost like a star, appearing as a fuzzy patch of light. The light that you see left Andromeda 2,250,000 years ago!

What galaxy is nearest to ours?

Lesson Summary

- Galaxies are large groups of stars, gas, and dust.
- Our solar system belongs to the Milky Way Galaxy, which is a spiral galaxy.
- The Milky Way Galaxy belongs to a galaxy cluster called the Local Group.

Lesson Review

1. How are different types of galaxies classified?
2. Describe the size and shape of the Milky Way.
★3. Explain how it's possible that some of the stars we observe today may have actually died millions of years ago.

Studying an Expanding Universe

LESSON 4 GOALS
You will learn
● that star spectra can be used to study the motions of stars and galaxies.
● one theory astronomers use to explain how the universe began.

Sometimes after a rain shower, a rainbow shimmers briefly in the sky. The white light from the sun has been separated into a spectrum by drops of water in the atmosphere. You can also see a spectrum of sunlight by using a prism. Where else have you seen the sun's spectrum?

Astronomers have found a way to look at a spectrum of starlight. First they attach a tool that works like a prism to their telescopes. The tool splits light from a star into a spectrum. The spectrum looks like a rainbow with dark lines in certain places. The dark lines are caused by elements such as hydrogen or helium that may be present in the star. Since the lines form a particular pattern for each element, we use them to tell us which elements are present in a star.

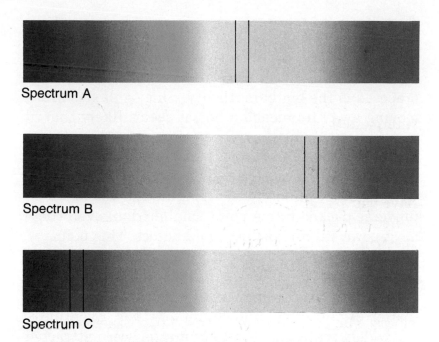

Spectrum A

Spectrum B

Spectrum C

Look closely at Spectrum A. It's an example of a standard spectrum produced in a lab. The dark lines indicate the presence of sodium. Now look at Spectrum B. Here you see an example of a spectrum of a star containing sodium that's moving away from us. The dark lines are in a different place on the spectrum than they were on the lab spectrum. They are closer to the red end of the spectrum. Astronomers have observed that this "red shift" of dark lines shows that a star is moving away from Earth. The faster it is moving away, the greater the red shift of dark lines. Spectrum C is an example of a spectrum of a star containing sodium that's moving toward us. Notice that the black lines have shifted toward the blue end of the spectrum. This is called a "blue shift."

Astronomers also look at the spectra of distant galaxies. A mixture of light from the billions of stars in the galaxy is split into a spectrum. Every one they have studied shows a red shift of dark lines. This red shift in all the galaxy spectra supports the idea that galaxies are moving away from each other. Does this mean the universe is expanding? Astronomers believe it is.

Why do we think the universe is expanding?

195

Origin of the Universe

For centuries people have wondered how the universe began. One answer that scientists have proposed is the big bang theory. Since galaxies are moving away from each other, it seems likely that at one time they must have been closer together. The **big bang theory** explains that about 20 billion years ago all the matter and energy that now exist were together at one place. Imagine the whole universe packed into a point smaller than even the most powerful microscope could detect! This point began to expand, pushing the matter and energy outward in all directions. At first this rapidly expanding matter was incredibly hot. Later the matter began to cool and clump together. Eventually the widely scattered clumps of matter were attracted to each other, forming huge clouds. Within these clouds, stars formed as matter continued to pull together into smaller, denser clumps. As time went on, galaxies came into existence as billions of stars formed within each cloud. Between the galaxies was empty space. The big bang theory is supported by the fact that star spectra indicate that the galaxies are still moving apart. Some astronomers believe that the universe will continue to expand forever.

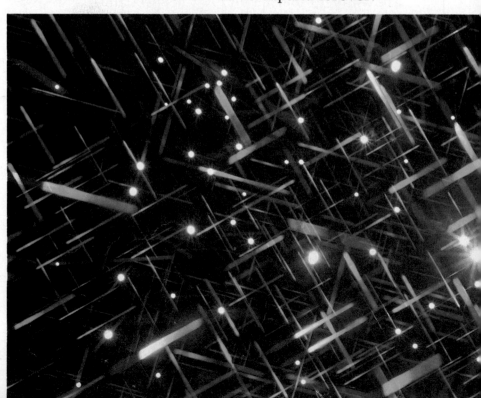

Will the universe expand forever and its stars eventually die, or will it end in a "big crunch" and then expand again?

Other astronomers believe that the outward movement of galaxies has slowed during the last several billion years. They believe that the universe may eventually stop expanding. If this happens, gravity will begin pulling everything back together. If everything comes back to one point, another big bang could occur. The universe could expand and shrink over and over again. This idea is called the **pulsating theory.**

Lesson Summary

- Star spectra can be used to determine if stars are moving toward or away from Earth.
- The big bang theory is one explanation of the way the universe may have begun.

Lesson Review

1. How can astronomers tell if a star is moving away from us?
2. Why do astronomers believe the universe is expanding?
3. What is the big bang theory?
★4. If the pulsating theory were true, how many times could the universe expand and shrink?

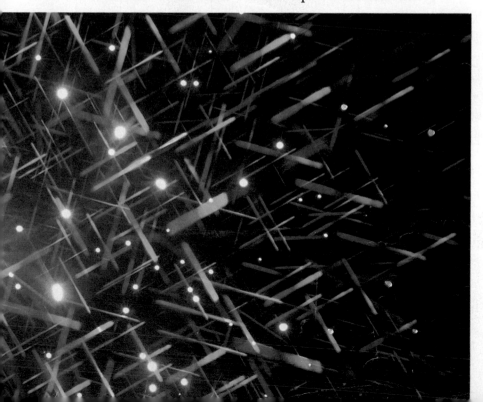

How do galaxies move in the universe?

What you need

round balloon
clothespin
felt-tip marker
metric ruler
string
pencil and paper

What to do

1. Copy the table to record your data.
2. Inflate a balloon to a small shape. Fold the neck and clip it shut with a clothespin so air doesn't escape.
3. Draw six dots, evenly spaced on the balloon. Label the dots A through F.
4. Use the string and ruler to measure the distance in millimeters from dot A to each of the other dots. Record the distances in your table.
5. Remove the clothespin from the balloon neck. Inflate the balloon to a medium size. Clip the neck shut. Repeat step 4.
6. Remove the clothespin. Inflate the balloon to a larger size. Clip the neck shut. Repeat step 4.

Model of the Universe Data			
Distance (in mm)	Size of balloon		
	small	medium	large
A to B			
A to C			
A to D			
A to E			
A to F			

What did you learn?

1. What happens to the distance between the dots as the balloon expands?
2. Which distances changed the most? the least?

Using what you learned

1. Let dot A be the Milky Way and the other dots be other galaxies. How would you describe the motion of the galaxies?
2. How is your balloon model like the universe?

Summary

Lesson 1
- Space is all the area beyond Earth's atmosphere.
- Space, matter, and energy make up the universe.
- Light-years are used to measure distances in space.

Lesson 2
- Stars vary in size, temperature, and color.
- Energy is released from stars through fusion.
- There are five stages in the life cycle of most stars.

Lesson 3
- Galaxies are large groups of stars, gas, and dust.
- Our solar system belongs to the Milky Way Galaxy, which is a spiral galaxy.
- The Milky Way belongs to a galaxy cluster called the Local Group.

Lesson 4
- Star spectra can be used to determine if stars are moving toward or away from Earth.
- The big bang theory is one explanation of the way the universe may have begun.

Science Words

Fill in the blank with the correct word or words from the list.

astronomers	**supernova**	**Milky Way Galaxy**	**pulsating theory**
universe	**red giants**	**galaxy**	**white dwarfs**
light-year	**neutron star**	**Local Group**	**pulsar**
nebulas	**black hole**	**big bang theory**	**black dwarf**

1. Space and everything in it is called the ____.
2. One scientific model that states all matter in the universe was together in one place about 20 billion years ago and then exploded is the ____.

3. A very large exploding star is called a(n) ____.
4. A large group of stars, gas, and dust is a(n) ____.
5. The cluster of galaxies to which the Milky Way Galaxy belongs is called the ____.

6. Scientists that study stars, planets, and other objects in space are ____.
7. A theory that states that the universe will expand and shrink over and over is the ____.
8. The length measurement that is equal to the distance that light travels through space in one year is a(n) ____.
9. Large clouds of gas and dust in space are ____.

Questions

Recalling Ideas
Correctly complete each of the following sentences.

1. Stars are thought to form from
   (a) empty space.   (c) white dwarfs.
   (b) nebulas.   (d) black holes.
2. Astronomers think that our sun is
   (a) very old.   (c) very young.
   (b) middle-aged.   (d) almost dead.
3. Young stars are mostly
   (a) hydrogen.   (c) carbon.
   (b) helium.   (d) oxygen.
4. Distances in space are usually measured in
   (a) meters.   (c) newton-hours.
   (b) kilometers.   (d) light-years.
5. Compared to our sun, the surface temperature of a red star is
   (a) hotter.   (c) brighter.
   (b) cooler.   (d) the same.
6. Galaxies with an oval shape are classified as
   (a) irregular.   (c) circular.
   (b) elliptical.   (d) spiral.
7. When the nucleus of one atom is joined with the nucleus of a different atom, the process is called
   (a) fission.   (c) gravitation.
   (b) fusion.   (d) formation.
8. Our sun will probably end its life as a
   (a) white dwarf.   (c) pulsar.
   (b) black dwarf.   (d) neutron star.

9. The life cycle of a very massive star may end with a
(a) white dwarf. (c) black hole.
(b) black dwarf. (d) nebula.

Examining Ideas
Determine whether each of the following statements is true or false. Rewrite the false statements to make them correct.

1. As a red giant shrinks, it becomes cooler.
2. The core of a star forms when hydrogen atoms begin to fuse into helium atoms.
3. The color of a star depends on its size.
4. A black hole is a star with a strong gravity field from which light cannot escape.
5. According to the big bang theory, the universe is contracting.
6. Space is larger than our solar system.
7. It would be possible to visit Proxima Centauri in a modern spacecraft in your lifetime.
8. A star's composition can be determined by its spectrum.
9. A pulsar is a neutron star that rotates and gives off radio waves.
10. The last stage in the life cycle of most stars is a black hole.
11. The Local Group is a cluster of stars to which our sun belongs.
12. A blue shift in a star's spectrum indicates that the star is moving toward the sun.

Understanding Ideas
Answer the following questions using complete sentences.

1. Why is it so hard to imagine the size of the universe?
2. How do astronomers tell younger stars from older ones?
3. Where in its life cycle is our sun?
4. What can scientists learn from studying the spectrum of a star?
5. How is a pulsar different from other neutron stars?
6. What do the spectra of all distant galaxies have in common? What does this tell us?
7. How do dwarf stars compare in size and density to our sun?
8. Tell how galaxies are classified. Give the classification of the Milky Way Galaxy and describe it.

Thinking Critically
Think about what you have learned in this chapter. Answer the following questions using complete sentences.

1. What kind of evidence would indicate the universe was contracting?
2. Why is the big bang idea considered to be a theory instead of a law?
3. Explain the statement, "When you look at a star, you look back in time."
4. What is a black hole? Why do you think these structures are called black holes?

CHAPTER
9

Exploring Space

Hans Lippershey, who made eyeglasses in seventeenth-century Holland, built one of the first telescopes in 1608. The story is told that one day Hans's son was playing with two of his father's lenses. When the young child held one lens near his eye and the other lens at arms distance away, he was surprised to see how much larger and closer a weather vane on the roof of a house down the street seemed. The father, very pleased with his child's discovery, mounted the two lenses on a piece of board and made the first refracting telescope.

ACTIVITY

Have You Ever...

Observed the Moon?

The moon is bigger than it looks. If set on Earth's surface, it would stretch from the Great Lakes to the Pacific Ocean! Observe the moon every night for four weeks. Use binoculars if they are available. Sketch the shape of the moon and date each sketch. Look at your drawings. What changes do you see in the apparent shape of the moon? Why does the moon appear to change?

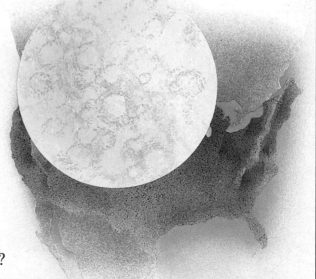

Constellations

LESSON 1 GOALS
You will learn
● that constellations are star patterns that aid in mapping the sky.
● that some constellations come and go with the seasons of the year.

If you look out your window tonight, you may see stars or maybe just a cloudy night sky. On a clear night, you may see between 1000 and 3000 stars. And there are far more stars that can be seen by using a telescope. In fact, there may be more stars in the universe than there are grains of sand in the world.

When you gaze at the night sky, notice that the stars are scattered all over the sky. As you continue to observe them, you may begin to organize the stars into groups or patterns. A group of stars in a recognized pattern or arrangement is called a **constellation.**

Constellations have been studied for centuries. To find their way around the night sky, the people of long ago gave names to the star patterns. These names came from objects, animals, or famous people who were important to them. The early Greeks named the constellation pictured here after Queen Cassiopeia (kas ee uh PEE uh) because it looked like a queen sitting on her throne.

Early people discovered that constellations could be found in the same place in the sky at a certain time of the year. Because of this, constellations were

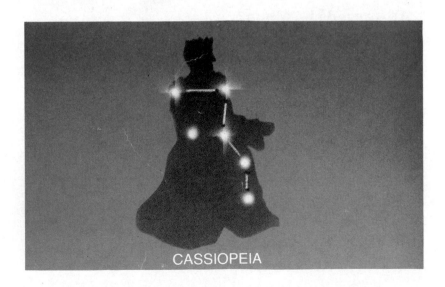

CASSIOPEIA

used to map the sky. It would be very difficult to find a particular star or other object in the sky without a way to organize the thousands of stars you can see. For example, suppose you wish to find the North Star. How could you find it among all the stars in the sky? The North Star can be located by first locating the constellation called the Big Dipper.

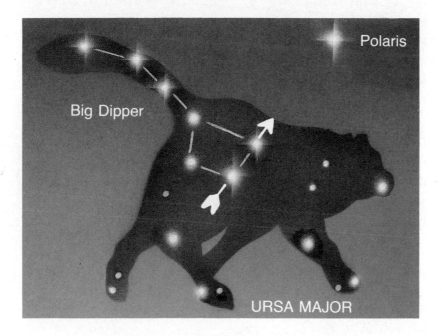

As you can see in the picture, the Big Dipper is part of a larger constellation called Ursa Major, or the Great Bear. Notice that the Big Dipper is formed by seven stars. Four stars make the bowl, and three stars form its handle. The two bright stars on the end of the bowl are called the pointers. They point to the North Star, which is located almost directly above the North Pole and about 50 light-years from Earth. **Polaris** (puh LER us) is another name for the North Star. Lost travelers locate Polaris because it shows them which way is north. By knowing this, travelers are then able to find their way. There is no star directly above the South Pole. People in the southern hemisphere use a constellation, the Southern Cross, to find their way.

How far away is Polaris?

Some constellations are seasonal; they are visible for only part of the year. Constellations above Earth's poles are visible all year, though they do appear to change their positions. You can do an experiment to observe this for yourself. Pick a night when you can see a constellation. Then, once a week at the same time for the next month stand in the same place and locate your constellation. You will notice that it appears to change its location in the sky. This happens because of Earth's rotation and revolution.

Imagine you are sitting on a merry-go-round and facing out looking at a park bench. As the merry-go-round begins to rotate, you can see the bench for only a short period of time. It appears to move away from you. Has the bench really moved? No, but the merry-go-round has. The bench's apparent movement is similar to what happened in your experiment with the constellation. Although the stars appeared to have moved, they didn't.

Which constellations are visible year-round?

ACTIVITY You Can...

Make Up a Constellation

Get 10 gummed stars and a black sheet of paper. Hold the stars above the paper. Drop the stars and stick them on the paper wherever they fall. Use your imagination to "see" the outline of a familiar object, animal, or person in the stars. Draw lines with white chalk to connect them in a way that represents what you imagined. Give your constellation to some friends and see if they can guess what it represents. Does it look like any of the Greek constellations?

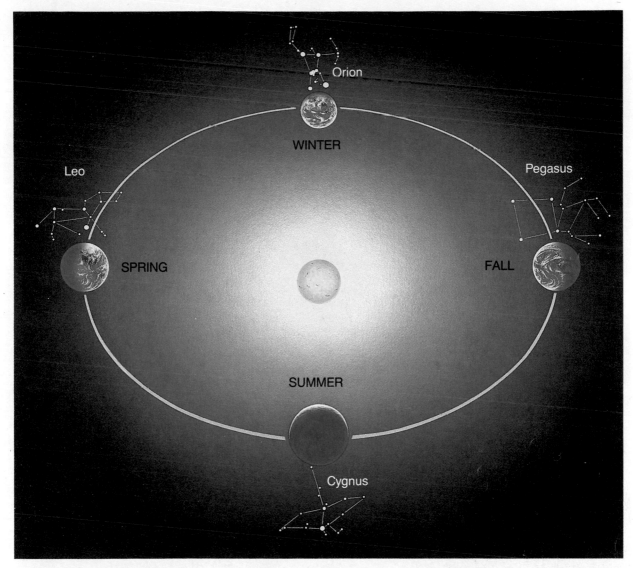

As Earth revolves around the sun, different constellations become visible.

If you think of Earth as a giant merry-go-round, its rotation causes the apparent movement of stars. So as Earth rotates on an imaginary axis, the sun and other stars appear to move.

While Earth rotates on its imaginary axis, it also revolves around the sun. It's because of Earth's revolution around the sun that some constellations are visible for only certain times of the year. People of long ago studied the appearance and apparent movement of the constellations and used this to mark the seasons of the year. They would plant their crops and hold festivals and other events based on the appearance and movement of the stars.

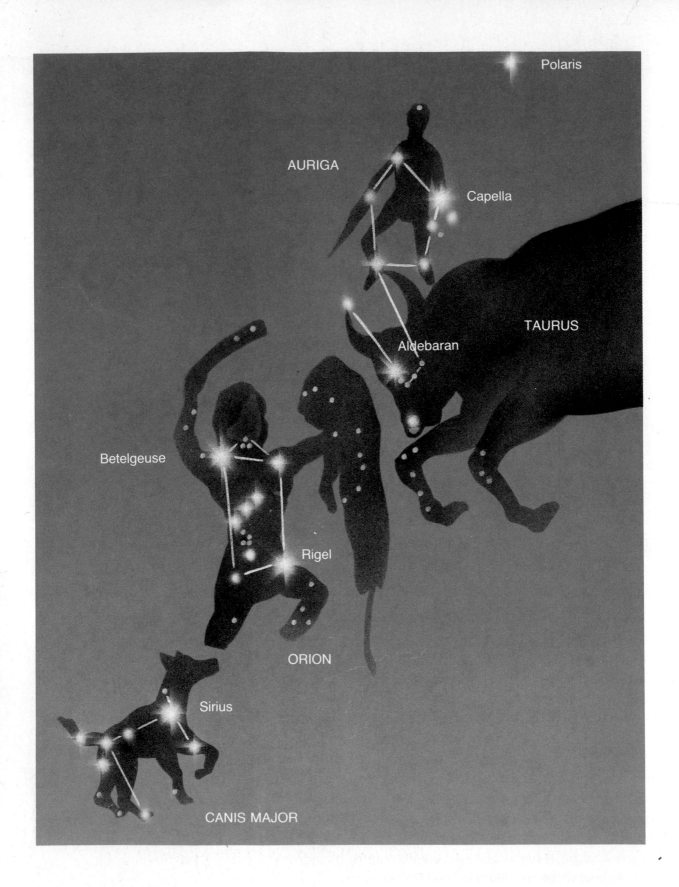

Polaris

AURIGA

Capella

TAURUS

Aldebaran

Betelgeuse

Rigel

ORION

Sirius

CANIS MAJOR

In the star pattern pictured on the preceding page, the early Greeks saw a mighty hunter, and they named it after the mythical hunter Orion. They'd know winter had arrived when this large constellation with its two brightest stars—red supergiant, Betelgeuse, and a blue-white star, Rigel (RI jul)—appeared in the sky. Can you find these two stars? Betelgeuse is located at Orion's right shoulder; Rigel is located near the hunter's left knee. Three other bright stars seem to form Orion's belt.

What type of star is Betelgeuse?

Orion has a dog to help him in the hunt. His faithful dog, Canis Major, is near Orion's right heel. Sirius (SIHR ee us), or the Dog Star, is in Canis Major. It's the brightest star in the winter sky.

When the early Greeks studied the constellation west of Orion, they saw a V-shape similar to the horns of a bull. They called the constellation Taurus and gave Orion a bull to hunt in the winter sky.

Lesson Summary

- Constellations are star groups with a recognized pattern that aid in mapping the night sky.
- Stars appear to move across the sky because of Earth's rotation and appear in different seasons because of Earth's revolution.

Lesson Review

1. In what ways did ancient people depend on the stars?
2. Why do constellations appear to move?
★3. Suppose you are standing at the North Pole. How far are you from Polaris?

Telescopes

LESSON 2 GOALS
You will learn
● that telescopes aid in the observation of space objects.
● that Earth's atmosphere makes it difficult to view space objects.
● the difference between optical and radio telescopes.

From early times, people have wondered about the stars, the planets, and the moon. The more they observed the night sky, the more questions they had. People of long ago could only observe the stars with their eyes. They had no tools like binoculars or telescopes.

However, today's astronomers have telescopes to help them observe space objects. These modern telescopes are the results of people like Galileo Galilei, who lived in Italy almost 400 years ago. With Galileo's early telescope, he was able to see objects in space, like the moons around the planet Jupiter, that no one had ever seen before. His telescope was an **optical telescope** because it had glass lenses to collect and focus light. Do you own a pair of binoculars? If you look through them, you are really looking through a small optical telescope.

The Hale telescope

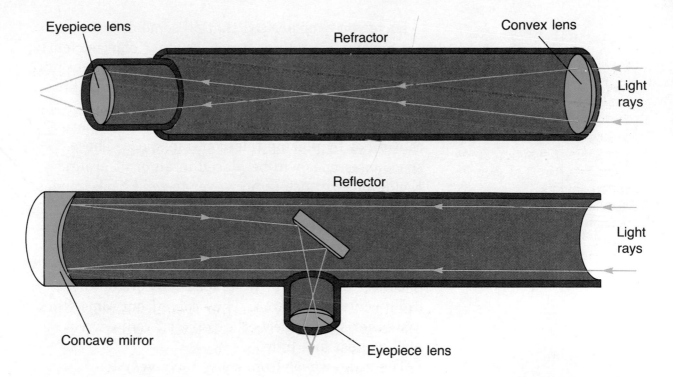

Eyepiece lens

Refractor

Convex lens

Light rays

Reflector

Light rays

Concave mirror

Eyepiece lens

Refracting telescopes use lenses and reflecting telescopes use mirrors to magnify objects.

Since the human eye is too small to collect much light, and the lens of the eye can't magnify what is seen, people need telescopes to help them observe space objects. Telescopes aid us because they magnify objects by using lenses and mirrors that gather the light from dim objects.

Today's optical telescopes are much better than the one used by Galileo. They are built in different sizes so they can be used by people at home or by astronomers for research. Research telescopes are so large that they are mounted in buildings called observatories.

Some of these large telescopes are not made to be looked through with the human eye. Instead, the telescope transmits an image to a camera, television, or computer. Astronomers can then see the object that the telescope is focused on. The Hale Telescope shown on page 210 is mounted at the Mount Palomar Observatory in California. It has a mirror 508 centimeters across and is an example of a telescope that uses computers, cameras, and televisions to aid astronomers.

What advantage do orbiting telescopes provide?

Have you ever noticed that on some days you can see far-away buildings, trees, or other objects clearly, but on other days these objects appear hazy and hard to see? This is a result of small particles of pollution, dust, and water in the Earth's atmosphere.

Astronomers plan to avoid Earth's atmosphere altogether by placing telescopes in space. These space telescopes will be placed in an orbit around Earth and will use radio waves to send back images. From space these telescopes will help us observe stars too faint to be seen from Earth's surface.

Scientists also use another type of telescope to study space. A **radio telescope** is an antenna used to collect radio waves from space. Where do these radio waves come from? They come from some stars and other space objects that give off radio waves as well as heat and light.

The radio waves from space have very long wavelengths, so radio telescopes must be quite large to collect the waves. The largest radio telescope in the world is in Puerto Rico. It is 305 meters in diameter, about the length of three football fields! Like other radio telescopes, its large, metal, dish-shaped antenna collects the waves. The radio waves are then put through a computer. The computer changes the signals into a picture or other useful form. It was by using a radio telescope that scientists found pulsars.

Radio telescope in Puerto Rico

The Very Large Array

The dishes of some radio telescopes can be turned to collect radio waves coming from any direction. The Very Large Array in New Mexico has 27 dishes that can be moved to collect radio waves from different areas of space.

Do you think Galileo would be surprised by the changes made in telescopes of today compared to his optical telescope?

Lesson Summary

- Optical telescopes have lenses or mirrors to collect and focus light.
- The atmosphere scatters light from space objects and causes very dim objects not to be visible.
- A radio telescope is an antenna used to collect radio waves from space.

Lesson Review

1. What did Galileo observe through his telescope?
2. How do telescopes aid the human eye?
★3. What are the differences between an optical telescope and a radio telescope?

Satellites and Probes

LESSON 3 GOALS
You will learn
● the difference between a natural and an artificial satellite.
● how artificial satellites orbiting Earth aid people.
● the uses of a space probe.

Can you define the term satellite? Did you know the moon is a satellite? A **satellite** can be defined as any object that moves in an orbit around another object.

Besides natural satellites like the moon, there are also objects placed in Earth's orbit by people. These are called **artificial satellites**.

The first artificial satellite launched into orbit around Earth was *Sputnik I.* The Soviet Union launched this artificial satellite in October 1957. The United States followed with its own space satellite, *Explorer I,* in January 1958.

Once a satellite enters space, it tends to travel in a straight line at a certain speed. However, the force of Earth's gravity causes the satellite to fall toward Earth. The result of these two actions is that the satellite travels in a curved orbit around Earth. *Sputnik I*, for example, circled Earth about once every 95 minutes at a speed of 29,000 kilometers per hour.

If a satellite slows down, the force of gravity causes it to fall back to Earth, which is what happened when *Sputnik I* fell to Earth on January 4, 1958, three months after its launch.

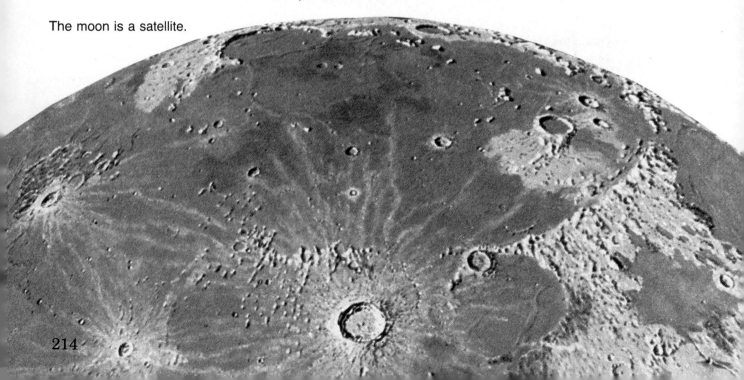

The moon is a satellite.

214

Photos made of Landsat images

Since the 1950s, scientists have launched many artificial satellites to aid them in their space research, as well as in other areas of interest. Some satellites are used to receive and relay messages, such as telephone calls and television programs, between the United States and other countries.

You may see pictures from weather satellites in newspapers or on television each day. Weather satellites provide these pictures of clouds and Earth's surface. The pictures then provide data about temperature, humidity, and the speed and direction of winds. Scientists use this information to understand and forecast weather on Earth.

Landsat satellites are used for studying Earth's surface. *Landsat 5* is orbiting Earth at an altitude of 710 kilometers. It sends radio signals back to computers on Earth. The computers change the signals into pictures. Many facts can be learned from these *Landsat* pictures. For example, the types of crops in an area can be surveyed. Crops that are diseased or affected by insects can be identified. How would this information be helpful to a farmer? *Landsat* pictures are also used to estimate the amount of water that will run off when winter snows melt. Why do you think this is important to know?

How do space probes differ from satellites?

Not all spacecraft become Earth satellites. A **space probe** is a spacecraft sent beyond Earth to gather data about space objects. The United States launched spacecraft *Viking 1* and *Viking 2*, which landed on Mars in 1976. These space probes tested Martian air and soil. Data about the composition and temperature were sent back to Earth.

Voyager 1 and *Voyager 2* have been very important space probes. Both probes were launched in 1977 and have since traveled farther than any human-made space object. Their flights through the solar system took them past Jupiter in 1978 and Saturn in 1980 and 1981. The probes sent back data to computers that produced spectacular pictures. Scientists learned much about the composition of the rings around Jupiter and Saturn. Some of the pictures showed volcanoes erupting on one of Jupiter's moons. These were the first volcanic eruptions seen anywhere except on Earth.

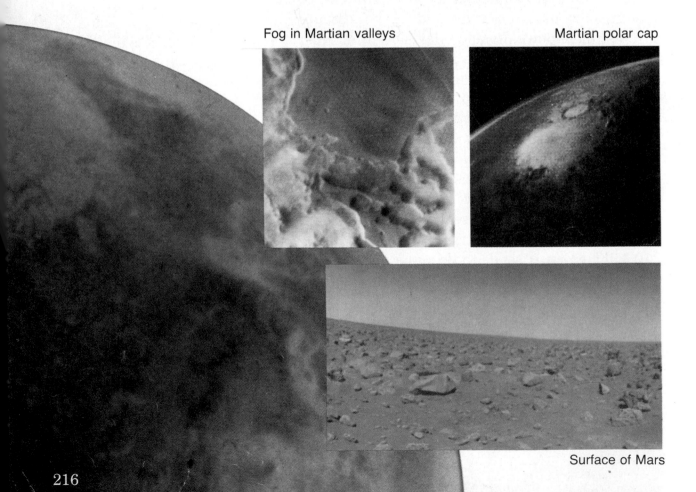

Fog in Martian valleys

Martian polar cap

Surface of Mars

Jupiter and one of its moons, Io

In August 1989, after 12 years in space, the space probe *Voyager 2* reached Neptune and transmitted data about the planet. Scientists discovered that Neptune has active storms and constantly changing clouds and winds that may reach 1000 kilometers per hour. They also discovered four new moons. And Triton, one of Neptune's moons, is the coldest known object in the solar system. Scientists think that Triton has ice volcanoes that spew liquid nitrogen.

Voyager 1

217

In the next century, you will see scientists gather greater information about space through the use of space probes. Both *Voyagers* will be sending signals back to Earth from beyond the solar system for at least 25 more years. By then the *Magellan* mission to Venus should be completed, and NASA's *Galileo* spacecraft will send a probe on a parachute ride into Jupiter's clouds. Do you think these space probes will answer all our questions about space? Or do you think each new discovery will bring with it more questions?

Galileo mission

Lesson Summary

- The moon is a natural satellite of Earth.
- Artificial satellites orbit Earth and aid people in many ways.
- Space probes have been used to study most of the other planets.

Lesson Review

1. What was the first artificial satellite?
2. Why are *Voyager 1* and *Voyager 2* classified as space probes rather than satellites?
★3. Humans have never sent a satellite or probe to the planet Pluto. Yet there is a satellite orbiting Pluto. Explain how this can be.

How does distance affect accuracy?

What you need

wastebasket   masking tape
small rubber ball   pencil and paper
meter stick

What to do

1. Mark a tape line on the floor. Place the wastebasket 1 m from the line. Stand at the line.
2. Toss the ball underhanded into the wastebasket 10 times. Record how many times the ball landed in the wastebasket.
3. Predict how many times you can toss the ball into the wastebasket at 2 m. Move the wastebasket to 2 m from the line. Repeat step 2. Do it again for 4 m and 6 m.
4. Predict how many times you can toss the ball into the wastebasket at 37 m. Move the wastebasket to 37 m from the line. Repeat step 2.
5. Make a bar graph showing how many times the ball landed in the wastebasket from each distance.

What did you learn?

1. How close were your predictions to the actual number of times you tossed the ball into the wastebasket at each distance?
2. At which distance was the wastebasket easiest to hit?

Using what you learned

1. Why is the target harder to hit as the distance increases?
2. If the target were moving, would your ability to hit it change? How?
3. The apparent size of the wastebasket at 37 m is about the same as the apparent size of the moon from Earth. What problems do scientists have when they try to land a spacecraft on the moon?

219

People in Space

LESSON 4 GOALS
You will learn
• that exploring space requires a lot of preparation.
• about plans to build a new space station.
• about products developed from knowledge gained from the space program.

An exciting chapter of space exploration began in 1961. In that year Yuri Gagarin from the Soviet Union became the first person to ride into space. Gagarin's trip in April 1961 lasted one hour and 48 minutes. He circled Earth at a speed of more than 27,000 kilometers per hour. Later that year Alan Shepard became the first American in space. Unlike Gagarin, Alan Shepard didn't orbit Earth. His ride into space and back lasted only 15 minutes.

In early 1962 John Glenn became the first United States astronaut to orbit Earth. Glenn's flight was followed by a series of more complex missions in space. The early missions were called Mercury and Gemini. The next series of missions, Project Apollo, landed people on the moon.

Apollo rocket and capsule

The Apollo program resulted in people landing on the moon.

On July 20, 1969, astronauts Neil Armstrong and Edwin Aldrin, Jr., landed on the moon's surface, while their fellow astronaut, Michael Collins, orbited above them. Armstrong became the first person to walk on the moon. Between 1969 and 1972, six lunar landings were completed. During the landings astronauts did experiments and gathered rock and soil samples that they brought back to Earth. From these missions, we have been able to learn a great deal about the solar system.

Exploring space requires preparation. On Earth people have air to breathe, food to eat, and water to drink. The environment in space is very different from that on Earth. It doesn't provide the air, food, or water that people need. So an earthlike environment must be made in a spacecraft so astronauts can live in space.

Astronauts simulate weightlessness by working underwater.

Astronauts have a problem called weightlessness when their spacecraft is in orbit. **Weightlessness** is a condition of objects that are falling freely. For example, if you jump on a trampoline, your body is falling freely while it is going both up and down. You are weightless because you do not feel the pull of gravity. Astronauts are constantly free-falling when they are in orbit. Long periods of weightlessness can cause people's muscles to become weak, and their bones can become soft from loss of minerals. To prevent this from happening, astronauts must exercise in space, eat a proper diet, and get the necessary amounts of sleep.

Before they travel in space, astronauts go through a training program. To prepare for weightlessness, they work underwater because weightlessness can be imitated by working underwater. Other conditions of space travel can also be imitated so astronauts learn what it's like to work in space. Each step of a space mission is rehearsed over and over again. By doing this, astronauts are prepared for the mission and can react calmly and correctly in a crisis.

Living in Space

A **space station** is a spacecraft used for living and working in space. A space station called *Skylab* was launched in 1973. It orbited Earth until 1979, when most of it burned up in the atmosphere as it fell back to Earth. *Skylab* had a telescope that was used to observe the sun and other stars. Views of objects in space were very good from *Skylab*. Why do you think the views were better from *Skylab* than from Earth?

One of the most useful spacecraft is a space shuttle. A **space shuttle** is a system composed of a giant fuel tank, two large rockets, and an orbiter. The orbiter is a reusable spacecraft with its own rockets. The orbiter can also glide and land like an airplane when in Earth's atmosphere. After two large rockets launch the orbiter into space, they separate and drop into the ocean. These rockets can be recovered and used in future launches.

The stages of a space shuttle mission include: liftoff (a), separation of rocket boosters (b), separation of fuel tank (c), completion of daily activities while orbiting Earth (d), and landing (e).

About nine minutes after launch, the fuel tank also separates from the orbiter. Unlike the rockets, the fuel tank burns up as it falls through Earth's atmosphere. After the rockets and fuel tank fall off, the orbiter goes into orbit, completes its mission, and returns to Earth.

Space shuttle orbiters can be launched into space and returned to Earth many times. They can carry satellites, space laboratories, and supplies. While in space, space shuttle crews record much data during the experiments they conduct. These data are returned to the scientists on Earth to aid in their space research.

The United States has plans to build a large space station called *Freedom*. This space station will be in orbit, and people and equipment will be brought to it by a space shuttle. Scientists will conduct experiments that can't be done on Earth. One type of experiment involves preparing medicines because these medicines must be prepared in a weightless environment. The space station will also serve as a base to launch and repair other satellites.

How will *Space Station Freedom* be useful?

Model of proposed *Space Station Freedom*

Computer chips and printed circuit boards are a result of space technology.

Space Technology and You

Scientists have learned a lot as a result of building spacecraft and sending people into space. What scientists have learned has changed life on Earth.

Many products you use daily were developed with space technology. You may have used a small portable radio or tape player. You may have a digital watch with an alarm. These are all products of space technology. One of the first uses of space technology was in building tiny electronic circuits that made the microcomputer and hand-held calculator possible. All types of spacecraft use electronic equipment. For this equipment to be lifted into space, it must be small. So electronic circuits, whose parts are so small they can be seen only with a microscope, were developed for spacecraft.

Use Application Activity on pages 501, 502.

SCIENCE AND . . .
Reading

You can tell that the author of this lesson—

A. is opposed to space technology.
B. is in favor of space technology.
C. has traveled in space.

Space technology has also been useful in developing devices that aid health and handicapped people. Heart pacemakers are used to keep a person's heart beating with a steady rhythm. Pacemakers were the result of space technology and have saved many lives. Another device that helps the handicapped converts ink to a vibrating form. This allows a person who is blind to read any printed material because the person can feel the vibrating letters to determine what they are. Another device that aids people who are blind is one that scans paper money and "announces" what the amount is. Switches also have been developed that can be worked by eye movements. These switches allow a person who's paralyzed to control objects such as a television, a light, or a book page turner.

Space technology has produced many new products. Freeze-dried foods and vacuum-sealed foods prepared for use in space have led to packaged foods that don't need to be refrigerated. Better batteries, paints, and plastics have been made. Solar cells, smoke detectors, and metal alloys have also been developed with space technology.

Lesson Summary

- An earthlike environment must be made in a spacecraft so astronauts can survive in space.
- *Space Station Freedom* will be the next U.S. space station.
- Technology from the space program has produced many products that improve our lives.

Lesson Review

1. What is an earthlike environment? How is it important in space travel?
2. What was *Skylab?*
★3. The space program developed solar cells—devices that convert light from the sun into electricity. Why would this technology be useful for space stations and other spacecrafts?

Use Application Activity on pages 503, 504.

How will we live in space?

What you need

reference materials
cardboard
white glue
scissors
pencil and paper
other materials as needed

What to do

1. Read in books and magazines about space stations.
2. Make a list of things that people who live in a space station would need, such as places to sleep, prepare and eat food, exercise, experiment, and control the space station.
3. Design a space station that will provide for the needs you have identified. Draw it on paper. Be sure to indicate where incoming space shuttles will dock so people and supplies can be transported.
4. Gather materials you need and build a model of your space station.
5. Give a presentation to your class describing your space station.

What did you learn?

1. How does your space station provide for the needs of the people who live in it?
2. What type of structure seems the best for a space station? Explain.

Using what you learned

1. How will living in space be different from living on Earth?
2. What materials used by people on Earth might be useful in a space station?
3. Why do you think building a space station might be important?

I WANT TO KNOW ABOUT...

Lightsailing in Space

In the 1950s, the dream of space travel became a reality when the first satellite orbited Earth. Since then, scientists have constantly studied ways to improve space travel.

The vehicle for propelling things into space has been the rocket. Large amounts of fuel are needed to accelerate ships, and once in space, ships are often drained of fuel and can only coast. A way is needed to enable vehicles to travel in space without bringing large quantities of fuel from Earth.

One promising method for travel resembles the type used by early explorers like Columbus and Magellan. Scientists would like to hoist sails to power space vehicles. But instead of using wind, spaceships would use light energy.

The pressure of the sun's energy would exert force against a "lightsail." The force of sunlight is weak, but the quantity of sunlight would make up for its weakness. A lightsail could accelerate a vehicle steadily, causing it to continually gain speed. Rockets, on the other hand, must coast after using up their fuel. Lightsails could reduce the time needed to travel to other planets.

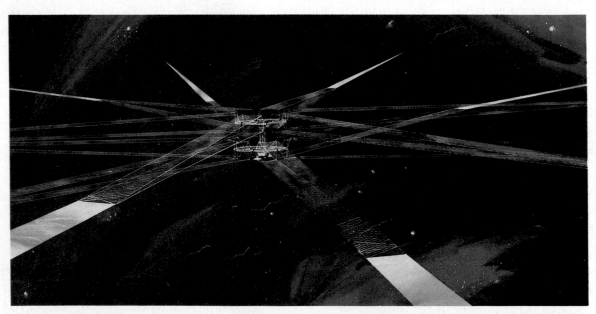

Science and Technology

Summary

Lesson 1
- Constellations are star groups with a recognized pattern that aid in mapping the night sky.
- Stars appear to move across the sky because of Earth's rotation and appear in different seasons because of Earth's revolution.

Lesson 2
- Optical telescopes have lenses or mirrors to collect and focus light.
- The atmosphere scatters light from space objects and causes very dim objects not to be visible.

Lesson 3
- The moon is a natural satellite of Earth.
- Artificial satellites orbit Earth and aid people in many ways.
- Space probes have been used to study most of the other planets.

Lesson 4
- An earthlike environment must be made in a spacecraft so astronauts can survive in space.
- *Space Station Freedom* will be the next U.S. space station.
- Technology from the space program has produced many products that improve our lives.

Science Words

Fill in the blank with the correct word or words from the list.

constellation
optical telescope
radio telescope
satellite
Polaris

space probe
weightlessness
space station
space shuttle
artificial satellites

1. A star group with a definite pattern or arrangement is a(n) _____.

2. A spacecraft sent into orbit to gather information about other planets is called a(n) _____.

3. Radio waves from space are collected by a(n) _____.

4. An orbiting base for people working in space is a(n) _____.

5. Objects that are falling freely in space are said to be in a condition of ____.

6. A(n) ____ is a device with lenses or mirrors used by astronomers to collect light.

7. The spacecraft that can be launched like a rocket and land back on Earth like an airplane is the ____.

8. An object orbiting around another object is a(n) ____.

Questions

Recalling Ideas
Correctly complete each of the following sentences.

1. Galileo was able to see new objects in space by using
   (a) a radio telescope.
   (b) an optical telescope.
   (c) a satellite.
   (d) binoculars.

2. Stars appear to move because
   (a) of Earth's rotation.
   (b) of Earth's revolution.
   (c) constellations actually move.
   (d) both a and b

3. A star that always appears in about the same spot in the sky is
   (a) Rigel.   (c) Orion.
   (b) the sun.   (d) Polaris.

4. A famous large winter constellation is
   (a) Orion.   (c) Leo.
   (b) Scorpio.   (d) Cassiopeia.

5. A familiar constellation visible all year is
   (a) Orion.   (c) Andromeda.
   (b) Ursa Major.   (d) Betelgeuse.

6. Pictures of Jupiter, Saturn, and Uranus were sent to Earth by
   (a) *Voyager 2.*   (c) *Mariner.*
   (b) *Viking.*   (d) *Landsat.*

7. America's first orbiting space station was called
   (a) *Landsat.*   (c) *Freedom.*
   (b) the orbiter.   (d) *Skylab.*

8. Astronauts can suffer from weak muscles and bones because of
   (a) their diet in space.
   (b) the difficult launch.
   (c) weightlessness.
   (d) high temperatures.

9. All of these are products of space technology EXCEPT
   (a) lightweight insulation.
   (b) electronic circuits.
   (c) heart pacemakers.
   (d) aluminum.

10. Facts about Earth's surface are learned from a satellite called
    (a) *Voyager 1.*   (c) *Landsat.*
    (b) *Viking 2.*   (d) *Echo 1.*

Examining Ideas
Determine whether each of the following statements is true or false. Rewrite the false statements to make them correct.

1. One advantage of a space shuttle is that the orbiter and rockets can be launched, return to Earth, and be reused.

2. Optical telescopes gather radio waves.

3. Polaris is located in the Big Dipper.

4. Betelgeuse is the brightest star in the winter sky.

5. *Sputnik I* was the first American artificial satellite.

6. Long periods of weightlessness don't cause any health problems.

7. Mars has been explored by *Viking 1* and *Viking 2*.

8. A space station is a spacecraft sent beyond Earth's orbit to gather data about space objects.

9. Radio waves from space can be collected and focused in the dishes of radio telescopes.

10. Astronauts and many other people benefit from space technology.

11. *Landsat* satellites show fractures where earthquakes may occur.

Understanding Ideas

Answer the following questions using complete sentences.

1. How do satellites stay in orbit?
2. List special preparations astronauts make for space.

3. In what ways is the space shuttle different from other spacecraft?

4. What is the advantage of putting a telescope in space?

5. Which Earth motion causes some constellations to appear in certain seasons?

6. How did people long ago use constellations?

7. Native Americans called Polaris "the star that doesn't move." Why?

Thinking Critically

Think about what you have learned in this chapter. Answer the following questions using complete sentences.

1. How could you find south on a clear night?
2. Why are weather satellites important to people?
3. How has space technology aided in improving the lives of people?

CHAPTER
10

Soil and Land Conservation

In a football game, the ball carrier looks for an opening in the line in order to score a touchdown. In a similar way, running rainwater seeks pathways on sloped ground, taking rich topsoil with it. This causes soil erosion. Did you know that rain falling on one acre of barren, sloping land can wash away about 60 truckloads of soil in one year?

Have You Ever...

Seen Soil Erode?

To observe how soil can erode, partially fill two cake pans with soil. Use a stick to make small, shallow trenches going across one pan. In the other, make trenches going down the pan. Hold each pan at an angle and slowly pour water in the top end of each pan. Which pan had more soil wash to the bottom?

233

Soil: A Natural Resource

LESSON 1 GOALS
You will learn
● why soil is an important natural resource.
● that a soil profile describes soil layers.
● about methods of soil management and conservation.

At 6:30 A.M. David's alarm clock buzzes. Yawning and stretching, he tumbles from bed and opens the window to see what the weather is like. The icy air filling his lungs tells him he'd better wear his wool socks and shirt to school. Dressing quickly, he runs downstairs for his coat and then out to the sidewalk for the morning newspaper. As he returns to the warm house, he smells the toast his mother is making in the kitchen. As David gets ready for school, he doesn't give much thought to the shirt and socks he's wearing, the newspaper he retrieved, or the bread that he's eating. But as David will learn in school today, a lot of energy and natural resources went into making the products he's using.

A **natural resource** is a material from Earth's atmosphere or crust that is useful to people. Trees, air, petroleum, and water are natural resources. One of our most important natural resources is **soil**. Let's see how soil was important to David this morning. Soil was used to grow the grain that was made into flour to bake the bread for his toast. Soil was used to grow food for the sheep that produced the wool in his shirt and socks. And the trees that were used to make the pages of his newspaper grew in soil.

When you were younger, you probably played with soil. Perhaps you examined the little bits and pieces of materials you found in it. There are many kinds of soil, over 15,000 types just in the United States. But all soils are made of two basic ingredients— weathered rocks and organic matter. As rocks are weathered, they are broken into small pieces. The weathered rocks in soil may be as large as pebbles or smaller than grains of sand. The organic matter is partly decayed plant and animal matter such as pieces of leaves, bark, bones, feathers, or insect bodies. About half the volume of soil is made up of weathered rocks and organic matter. The other half is open spaces filled with air or water.

Soil needs to be a mixture of both weathered rocks and organic matter for most plants to grow. Many soils that produce healthy plants are alive with all sorts of underground dwellers. With a small shovel you could easily find ants, millipedes, earthworms, and grub worms in a garden. You might see an occasional mole or chipmunk as it quickly escapes to its underground burrow. With a hand lens, or microscope, you could observe fungi and bacteria. All these organisms are constantly mixing and loosening the soil. This helps water and air get into the soil. Plants use this water and air as they grow. Plants also break up soil as they push their roots into cracks in rocks, wedging the rocks apart and breaking them into ever smaller pieces. Soil is constantly changing.

What are the two main components of soil?

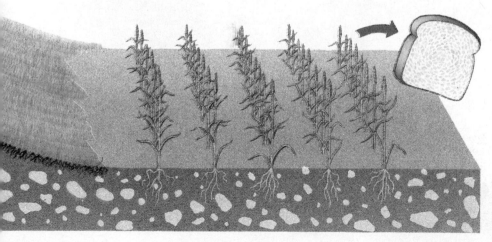

We depend on soil for many everyday products.

Soil Profile

If you dig a hole anywhere in the world, you will eventually hit solid rock. Soil is only a thin layer over this rock. It forms very slowly. In some places it takes about 300 years for a layer one centimeter thick to form.

If you could see a slice of soil, it would look something like this picture. Notice the colored layers in this soil profile. Remember there are over 15,000 types of soil, so no two profiles are exactly alike. The depth and color of the layers vary from place to place. Some soils have more weathered rock; some have more organic materials.

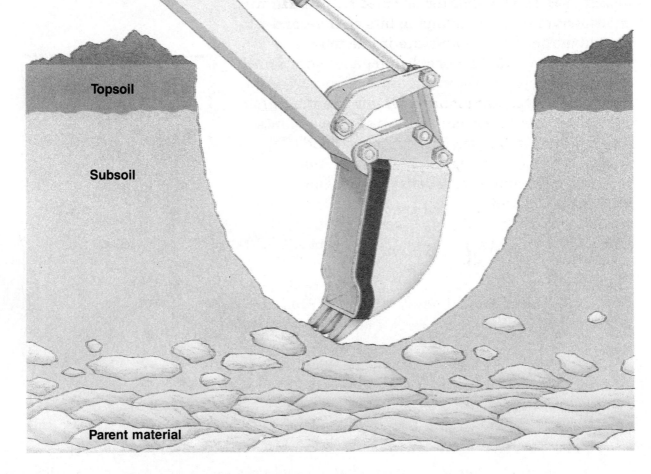

Topsoil

Subsoil

Parent material

Garden soils are a good mixture of minerals and organic matter.

The top layer in the soil profile is **topsoil**. In some soil profiles it is thicker than in others. Most of the organic matter in a soil profile is found in the topsoil. This organic matter is called humus. **Humus** is formed from all the decaying bits of plant and animal matter that accumulate in the topsoil. Humus works like a sponge, helping to hold water in the soil where plant roots can use it. And humus is rich in minerals that plants need. For plants, topsoil is the most necessary part of the soil profile.

Below the topsoil you can find the **subsoil**. This layer is thicker than topsoil and usually contains clay. If you've rubbed clay between your fingers, you know it feels smooth. That's because the clay particles are very small. In the subsoil the clay particles pack tightly together, and it's difficult for plant roots to penetrate the clay. Usually only roots of large plants such as trees grow down into the subsoil. Water carries minerals into the subsoil, but you would find very little humus there.

Now look at the bottom layer of the soil profile. Here are large rocks. These rocks are called the **parent material** because it's from them that the soil above is partly formed. Over time, the big rocks can be broken into gravel, sand, and clay that become part of the subsoil.

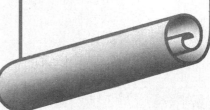

SCIENCE AND . . .

Math

While digging you stop to measure the thickness of the topsoil and subsoil. The topsoil is 15.1 cm, and the subsoil is 22.9 cm. What is the total thickness?
A. 3.8 mm
B. 38 mm
C. 380 mm
D. 3800 mm

Conserving Soil

When the pilgrims came to America in 1620, they may have brought some money with them, but they soon discovered that the soil in America was worth far more than any silver or gold. There was no food for sale, but they could grow crops in the soil of their new land.

Topsoil is one of our country's most valuable resources. As you've discovered, there's only a thin layer of it covering Earth's rocky crust. In many places topsoil is being used up more quickly than it can be replaced naturally.

The worst enemy of topsoil is **erosion**. In the photo you can see how topsoil has been carried away by water. In other places soil is eroded by wind, ice, or gravity. Much of it then ends up in the bottom of a lake or ocean. All of us depend on soil for the products we use each day and for the food we eat. It's important that we prevent it from ending up in lake and ocean basins. As you can imagine, this is especially important to farmers. Let's take a look at the methods they use to prevent erosion and manage the soil.

What happens to much of the topsoil?

Running water carries away topsoil.

Clover

Many farmers plant cover crops after the autumn harvest. A **cover crop** is a fast-growing plant with many shallow roots. The roots help hold the soil in place during the winter rains and snows. The stems and leaves slow the water running over the surface, preventing it from carrying away topsoil. Alfalfa and clover are two plants used as cover crops. These crops also add nutrients to the soil. The farmer's main crop of corn, wheat, or soybeans will need these nutrients the following spring.

During the main growing season, farmers sometimes use strip cropping. In **strip cropping** several rows of cover crops are planted between rows of a main crop. The cover crop holds water in the soil, which helps the main crop grow better. The next year the locations of cover crops and main crops are switched. This enables the cover crop to replace nutrients used by the main crop the previous year.

What is the purpose of strip cropping?

Farmers with hilly land have difficult erosion problems to solve. If they plant crops in rows up and down a hillside, rain washes the topsoil from the top of the hill down the rows to the bottom. By combining strip cropping with contour planting, farmers can keep much of the topsoil in place. In **contour planting** the crops are planted in rows that follow the shape, or contour, of the land. When rain falls it's caught in the rows and held where the plants can use it.

Have you ever seen a row of trees planted along the edge of a field? Trees are sometimes planted in this way to help reduce erosion by wind. A **shelter belt** is a row of trees or shrubs planted to prevent the wind from blowing soil away. In winter shelter belts also prevent snow from blowing off a field. On warm days when the snow melts, the water seeps into the soil and adds moisture.

Contour planting

Shelter belt

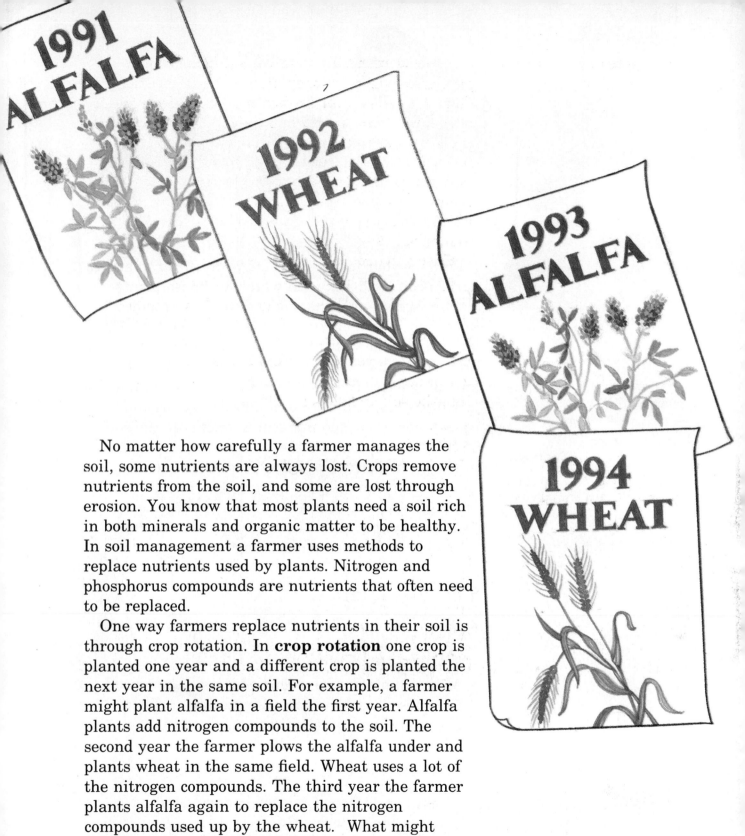

No matter how carefully a farmer manages the soil, some nutrients are always lost. Crops remove nutrients from the soil, and some are lost through erosion. You know that most plants need a soil rich in both minerals and organic matter to be healthy. In soil management a farmer uses methods to replace nutrients used by plants. Nitrogen and phosphorus compounds are nutrients that often need to be replaced.

One way farmers replace nutrients in their soil is through crop rotation. In **crop rotation** one crop is planted one year and a different crop is planted the next year in the same soil. For example, a farmer might plant alfalfa in a field the first year. Alfalfa plants add nitrogen compounds to the soil. The second year the farmer plows the alfalfa under and plants wheat in the same field. Wheat uses a lot of the nitrogen compounds. The third year the farmer plants alfalfa again to replace the nitrogen compounds used up by the wheat. What might happen if a farmer planted wheat several years in a row? In many areas poor soil management has led to abandoned farms and ruined soil.

These fertilizer spikes are often used around trees and shrubs.

Perhaps your family has bought fertilizer to add to garden soil or to mix with water for house plants. **Fertilizers** are materials added to soil to replace nutrients. They help increase healthy plant growth by adding minerals and humus. Some fertilizers contain organic matter such as dead plants and animal wastes. They add humus to the soil. Other fertilizers are a mixture of minerals and organic compounds. They add mineral nutrients to the soil. The fertilizers rich in mineral nutrients are often available in convenient bags. A label on the bag gives the amount of each mineral contained in the fertilizer. By careful use of soil management, farmers can reduce erosion and replace nutrients needed to produce abundant crops.

Lesson Summary

- Soil is an important natural resource because it's used to provide food, materials for clothes, and other items.
- Most soil profiles have three layers—the topsoil, the subsoil, and the parent material.
- Good farming practices improve and conserve soil.

Lesson Review

1. What percentage of soil is air and water?
2. How is humus formed?
★3. What types of soil management would you recommend for a farmer with hilly land? Explain your answer.

How do roots prevent soil erosion?

What you need

2 large shallow pans   books
sprinkling can   water
piece of sod   scissors
soil   pencil and paper

What to do

1. Cut off the blades of grass from the piece of sod so only the roots remain. Place the piece of sod in one end of a pan.
2. In the second pan, pack enough loose soil so it's about the size and height of the soil in the piece of sod.
3. Tilt each pan by resting each on 3 books.
4. Use the sprinkling can to water the contents of the pans. Use the same amount of water for each pan. Pour the water slowly.
5. Observe the runoff materials in each pan. Record your observations.

What did you learn?

1. How were the piece of clipped sod and pan of loose soil different? Why did you need to cut off the blades of grass?
2. Which pan contained the least amount of runoff materials? Why?
3. What did you find in the runoff from each pan?

Using what you learned

1. What do the roots of trees and forest plants do for the soil?
2. In addition to soil erosion, what other problems are caused by completely clearing a forest area?
3. Why is reforestation important?

Conserving Forests

LESSON 2 GOALS
You will learn
• why reforestation is important.
• about methods and goals of forest management.
• about national forests and wildlife reserves.

Perhaps you live where there are many trees, or maybe there are only a few. Imagine what our world would be like if there were no trees. It would seem an empty place. And just as importantly, we would be missing one of our most valuable natural resources. Because, just as we depend on soil, we also depend on trees for our everyday lives. Your notebook paper is made from trees, and the oxygen in the air that you breathe is made by trees. Though animals don't make paper from trees, they do build their homes in them, rest in their shade, and breathe the oxygen they produce.

There's no doubt that trees are important to us, but how can we be sure we'll always have them? Let's look at some of the problems and solutions to managing our forests.

The forest in the photo has had all its trees removed by **clear cutting.** When an area is clear cut, all the trees are cut down. In this area, erosion has washed away soil because plants and root systems were destroyed. The wildlife has died or left the area. And when new trees begin to grow, insects and diseases easily damage them. Clear cutting is used less often today, and when it is, the areas are often replanted with trees that grow well in the open.

Clear cut forest

244

The replanting of new trees on land where trees have been removed or destroyed is called reforestation. Some trees grow more quickly than others, but all take many years to produce usable timber. Forests must be used wisely if we want to continue to use them as a source of natural resources. As trees are taken from forests, they must be replaced.

Selective cutting leaves small, young trees to grow.

Ways of Managing Forests

Good forest management provides a continuous supply of trees and prevents damage to the forest and land. One such method is selective cutting. **Selective cutting** is a method of removing mature trees from a forest. Only the older trees are cut and hauled away to the lumber mills. The remaining young trees will grow larger in the spaces left by this thinning. With selective cutting, reforestation occurs naturally from the seeds that fall from the remaining mature trees.

245

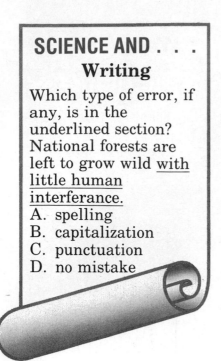

SCIENCE AND . . .
Writing

Which type of error, if any, is in the underlined section? National forests are left to grow wild <u>with little human interferance.</u>
A. spelling
B. capitalization
C. punctuation
D. no mistake

Name several reasons for establishing national forests.

Forest fires, of course, are something we all need to help prevent. But sometimes forest rangers use fire to improve and protect forests. **Controlled burning** can control certain insects and diseases. It is also used to clear the forest floor of dry materials that can spread wildfires. Such uncontrolled wildfires destroy large areas of land.

Controlled burning also causes plants to grow that otherwise wouldn't. As you know, pine cones hold the seeds of pine trees. But some types of cones open only if they become extremely hot. Fires are necessary to open these cones and release the seeds that they contain.

National Forests

Another way to conserve forests is through a system of national forests and wildlife reserves. The United States Forest Service was started in 1905 and now manages 155 national forests in the United States and Puerto Rico. Some areas in the forests and wildlife reserves are left to grow wild with little human interference. These areas provide protected homes for wildlife, including some endangered species. Other areas are used for timber, but the Forest Service makes sure new trees are planted.

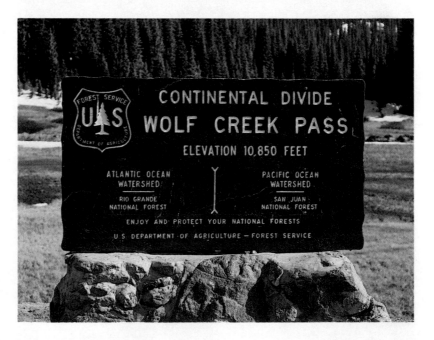

Recreation in the national parks

The Forest Service runs the national forest system in a way that best serves all people. Perhaps you've visited a national forest to go camping, hiking, or mountain biking. Every year many vacationers enjoy outdoor recreation in the national forests. But at the same time, the timber, water, and wildlife are conserved and protected.

Lesson Summary

- Reforestation is the planting of new trees where old trees have been removed.
- Clear cutting, selective cutting, and controlled burning are methods of forest management.
- National forests and reserves are created to aid in forest, plant, and animal conservation.

Lesson Review

1. Why is reforestation needed?
2. Name two ways of removing trees from forests.
★3. Tell why it would be better for a lumber company to use selective cutting rather than clear cutting when removing timber.

Disposing of Refuse

LESSON 3 GOALS
You will learn
• some methods of disposing of refuse.
• the value of biodegradable materials.
• why recycling is becoming necessary.

If you put a bag of trash out at the curb, where does it go when the truck comes and takes it away? Perhaps you haven't really thought about what happens to trash, garbage, and other waste. All this waste material is called refuse, and every person in the United States is throwing away 1.5 kilograms of it every day. Getting rid of refuse is a big problem.

Sanitary Landfills

Today large amounts of land are being used for disposal of refuse. These areas are called landfills. For many years refuse was just dumped in open mounds. Such dumps polluted the air and water. And not only were they ugly, but they wasted acres of land.

Many communities now operate sanitary landfills. In a **sanitary landfill,** the refuse is covered with layers of soil. First, a machine is used to dig a large trench. Trucks then dump the refuse into the trench. At the end of the day, the trench is covered with soil. The soil keeps insects and animals from getting into the refuse. It also keeps it from blowing away. Every day another trench is dug and filled. In time some of the refuse decomposes and becomes part of the soil. If a landfill is well cared for, the land can later be put to another use. The flat surface can be planted with grass and trees to create recreational

Our refuse includes items that are recyclable, biodegradable, nonbiodegradable, and hazardous.

Final soil cover (0.6 m)

Daily soil cover (15 cm)

Compacted solid waste

Original ground

areas where people can enjoy nature as well as picnicking and sports. It may be that your local soccer field or baseball diamond is built on the site of an old sanitary landfill.

Types of Waste

When landfills are not properly managed, rain seeps through the refuse, picking up harmful chemicals. These chemicals are then carried into the groundwater, polluting the water supply. This problem is made even more serious by hazardous waste. **Hazardous waste** can't be placed in ordinary landfills because it should never be allowed to enter the environment. These poisonous and radioactive materials must be sealed in containers and put in underground chambers.

No matter what kind of container is used to seal up hazardous waste, the container will eventually break or rust apart. Once this happens its poisonous or radioactive contents will be free to enter the environment. One possible way to prevent the waste from spreading is to put the sealed containers in abandoned salt mines. Scientists hope the salt will act as a wall between the leaking hazardous waste and our water supplies.

Why must most hazardous waste be buried?

249

Some nonhazardous refuse is broken down by organisms in soil and returned to the environment. This type of refuse is **biodegradable waste.** Many paper and wood products are biodegradable. Some detergents, soaps, and industrial cleaning materials are also biodegradable. Many products that were once made of plastics that couldn't be broken down by organisms are now made of biodegradable materials. For example, some garbage bags and disposable diapers are now biodegradable.

Power From Trash

Another way some communities dispose of refuse is by burning. Refuse that will burn must first be separated from refuse that won't burn. Then, inside a trash-burning plant, refuse is mixed with another fuel such as coal. As the refuse and fuel burn, energy is produced that is used to provide electricity. These **trash-burning power plants** are very expensive to build, however. Problems also occur when explosive materials are accidentally mixed in with the burnable refuse. The explosions that occur have injured workers and temporarily closed the power plants for repairs.

Trash burning power plant

ACTIVITY

You Can...

Use It Again!

Find out what materials are accepted at the recycling center in your community. Then set up a system for separating wastes at home for recycling. For example, you could get some boxes and label them Aluminum Cans, Glass Bottles, Newspaper, Recyclable Plastic, and so on. Then tell the others in your family that when they throw away a recyclable item, such as an aluminum can, they should put it in the correct box. When the boxes are full, take them to the recycling center.

Recycling

You have probably seen refuse tossed out along highways or dumped in other improper places. Not only is refuse ugly to look at, but it is polluting our environment. But how can we reduce the amount of refuse and litter we produce?

A lot of things you put in the trash each day could be used again. Reusing items or resources is called **recycling**. Perhaps you already recycle aluminum cans or paper by taking them to collection centers. Some states have passed laws that require most beverage containers to be recycled. When you buy a beverage, you pay a small deposit. When you return the empty can or bottle to be recycled, your money is returned. Bottles are cleaned and reused, while cans are melted and made into new containers. Recycling

How have some states encouraged recycling?

Compost

helps reduce the amount of refuse going to landfills. It also reduces litter. Since people receive money for their garbage, they're less likely to just throw it out along roadways. You can help reduce refuse by using recyclable packaging. If a store offers a choice of nonrecyclable plastic bags or recyclable paper bags, which might you choose? Can you think of some other ways you can help reduce the amount of refuse going to landfills?

A large share of refuse going to landfills is yard waste. Each week people fill trash bags with grass clippings. In the autumn you may rake and bag leaves for trash pickup. There is an alternative to this, however. The grass clippings and leaves, along with food wastes, can be recycled and used to make compost.

Compost is a mixture of decaying vegetable matter. Compost is a good organic fertilizer that adds humus to the soil. Some people have compost piles in their yard. After the grass clippings and leaves have decomposed, they are added to gardens. Some cities collect yard waste and make compost that they sell to gardeners and farmers.

Lesson Summary

- Refuse can be disposed of in landfills or by burning it in power plants.
- Biodegradable materials return resources to the environment when they are broken down by organisms in the soil.
- Recycling of materials decreases the amount of refuse.

Lesson Review

1. What is refuse?
2. How is a sanitary landfill different from an open dump?
★3. Explain how recycling helps conserve Earth's natural resources.

Use Application Activity on pages 505, 506.

Which items are biodegradable?

What you need

rubber gloves
safety goggles
refuse: aluminum can,
  glass jar, plastic bag,
  paper napkin, orange
  peel, milk carton,
  ink pen, foam cup
4 stakes
string
meter stick
shovel
pencil and paper

What to do

1. Wear rubber gloves and goggles when you handle the refuse or dig.
2. Use stakes and string to mark off a one square meter area in the schoolyard. Remove the soil to a depth of 30 cm in the area.
3. Place the refuse in the bottom of the pit you have made. Separate the items so they don't touch.
4. Make a top-view map of the pit. Mark the location of each item.
5. Carefully replace the soil in the pit. Do not disturb the refuse as you cover it with soil. Wait 30 days.
6. Carefully reopen the pit. Observe. Write a description of each item.
7. Remove the items and dispose of them in a refuse container. Try to make the area look better than it did before you dug the pit.

What did you learn?

1. What changes occurred in the pit?
2. Were these results what you expected? Explain.

Using what you learned

1. Suppose you put all the items back in the pit and closed it. What would you expect to observe if you reopened it after 30 more days?
2. What items could you use in place of the nonbiodegradable items?
3. What happens to refuse that is disposed of in a sanitary landfill?

253

I WANT TO KNOW ABOUT...

Cause and Effect Relationships

The relationship between an event and why it occurred is known as *cause and effect.* What happened is the *effect.* Why it happened is the *cause.* Scientists and others needing to solve problems often seek to learn why an event occurs.

Read the following paragraph and decide what are the causes and what are the effects.

A few years ago, this area was a forest. Builders came in to build houses. They built streets with bulldozers. They cut down trees to make space for houses. With the trees gone, the soil began to lose moisture and dry out. Small plants began to die because there was little moisture. The plants also had little food, because there were no leaves to enrich the soil. The sun further dried out the ground. Then a windstorm blew much of the topsoil away. The ground was dug up for house foundations, and more soil blew away each day. Rains washed even more soil away. When I moved into my new house, the soil in the yard was clay. I wanted a beautiful green lawn, so I sowed grass seed. I've lived here three months and planted grass seed several more times. No grass will grow.

1. What first caused the ground to lose moisture?
2. What two events caused small plants to die?
3. What events caused the loss of topsoil?
4. What effect did the loss of topsoil have on the remaining soil?
5. What effect did the loss of topsoil have on the grass seed?

Language Arts

Summary

Lesson 1
- Soil is an important natural resource because it's used to provide food, materials for clothes, and other items.
- Most soil profiles have three layers—the topsoil, the subsoil, and the parent material.
- Good farming practices improve and conserve soil.

Lesson 2
- Reforestation is the planting of new trees where old trees have been removed.

- Clear cutting, selective cutting, and controlled burning are methods of forest management.
- National forests and reserves are created to aid in forest, plant, and animal conservation.

Lesson 3
- Refuse can be disposed of in landfills or by burning it in power plants.
- Biodegradable materials return resources to the environment when they are broken down by organisms in the soil.
- Recycling of materials decreases the amount of refuse.

Science Words

Fill in the blank with the correct word or words from the list.

natural resource	fertilizers	selective cutting	erosion
cover crop	clear cutting	controlled burning	recycling
strip cropping	humus	sanitary landfill	compost
contour planting	soil	hazardous waste	trash-burning power
shelter belt	topsoil	biodegradable waste	plants
crop rotation	subsoil	parent material	

1. ____ are added to soil to replace nutrients.
2. When fire is used to clear away unwanted parts of a forest, it is called ____.
3. Refuse is dumped and covered with layers of soil at a(n) ____.
4. Refuse that can be broken down by organisms into harmless compounds is called ____.

5. Refuse that is poisonous or radioactive is ____.

6. The planting of different crops year after year in the same soil is called ____.

7. The planting of a cover crop between rows of a main crop is called ____.

8. A row of trees or shrubs planted to prevent wind erosion is a ____.

9. A mixture of decaying organic matter such as food wastes, leaves, and grass clippings is ____.

10. A fast-growing plant with many shallow roots that is planted to prevent erosion is called a(n) ____.

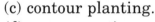

Questions

Recalling Ideas

Correctly complete each of the following sentences.

1. All of the following are methods of managing the soil EXCEPT
   (a) irrigation.
   (b) contour planting.
   (c) strip cropping.
   (d) erosion.

2. A soil mixture of decayed organisms is
   (a) inorganic.
   (b) a soil profile.
   (c) humus.
   (d) subsoil.

3. A shelter belt is used to prevent erosion of soil by
   (a) gravity.   (c) water.
   (b) wind.   (d) ice.

4. The soil layer that contains the most humus is the
   (a) topsoil.
   (b) subsoil.
   (c) rock layer.
   (d) parent material.

5. The planting of crops in rows that follow the shape of the land is
   (a) strip cropping.
   (b) crop rotation.
   (c) contour planting.
   (d) cover cropping.

6. The layer of soil that is most important to crops is
   (a) parent material.
   (b) the rock layer.
   (c) the subsoil.
   (d) the topsoil.
7. Fertilizers may add all of the following to the soil EXCEPT
   (a) minerals.   (c) humus.
   (b) water.   (d) nutrients.
8. All of the following are ways of managing and conserving forests EXCEPT
   (a) controlled burning.
   (b) selective cutting.
   (c) clear cutting.
   (d) reforestation.

Examining Ideas
Determine whether each of the following statements is true or false. Rewrite the false statements to make them correct.

1. Subsoil is the bottom layer of a soil profile.
2. If hazardous wastes are not disposed of properly, they can pollute groundwater.
3. Strip cropping is the planting of one crop one year and a different crop the next year in the same soil.
4. Erosion is the removal of soil by wind, water, ice, or gravity.
5. Forest fires have no benefit for the forest.
6. Biodegradable products can be put into a compost pile, and later the decayed material can be used for fertilizer.
7. The two basic ingredients of soil are weathered rock and inorganic material.
8. National forests are a method of forest conservation.
9. Humus is important in soil because it lets plant roots get air.
10. The profiles of most soil samples are alike.

Understanding Ideas
Answer the following questions using complete sentences.

1. How is soil affected by the organisms that live in it?
2. Describe the layers in a soil profile.
3. What happens at a sanitary landfill?
4. List six methods of soil conservation.
5. What is the purpose of national forest systems and wildlife reserves?

Thinking Critically
Think about what you have learned in this chapter. Answer the following questions using complete sentences.

1. Name some products you use daily that are related to soil.
2. How can you conserve soil around your home?
3. What are some possible solutions to the problem of too much refuse?
4. Explain the statement: "Eventually all waste is recycled."

SCIENCE
In Your World

CHAPTER 11

Water and Air Conservation

Water becomes so scarce in certain areas and at certain times of the year that people are told when they can water their yards or wash their cars. Only fountains or water displays that recycle the same water may be used.

All of Earth's water eventually ends up in the ocean, flowing out from rivers or from melting polar snow or ice. Unfortunately these water supplies are often contaminated by such things as fertilizers, pesticides, or oil spills.

Have You Ever...

Wondered About Oil Spills?

To understand how oil disperses in water, add two or three drops of oil to water in a glass jar. What happens to the oil? Add a few drops of detergent, put on the lid, and shake hard. Can you still see the oil? Why would it be difficult to clean up an oil spill in an ocean?

Water Pollution

LESSON 1 GOALS
You will learn
- about the two main sources of drinking water.
- how water becomes polluted.
- about the dangers of water pollution.

How much water do you think you and your family use every day? How much water do you use by taking baths or showers; washing cars, clothes, and dishes; drinking water; and watering plants and lawns? Could it be 50 liters a day? 100 liters a day? Actually, each American family uses an average of 260 to 560 liters of water daily. Every time you turn on the faucet you use one of Earth's most important resources—water.

Water is needed by all living things. You couldn't survive without a supply of clean water. You turn on the faucet, and out comes clean water, right? But it's not that simple. Because people carelessly use and pollute water faster than it can be cleaned or replenished by nature, clean water is becoming a prized natural resource.

Water covers more than 71 percent of Earth's surface. It can be found in Earth's oceans, lakes, streams, other bodies of water, ice, atmosphere, and ground. Earth's water is used over and over again. Today's clean water is tomorrow's wastewater. And the wastewater you produce today is tomorrow's clean water.

2% Ice caps

1% Streams, lakes, groundwater, and water vapor

97% Ocean water

Nearly all of the water on Earth's surface is ocean water.

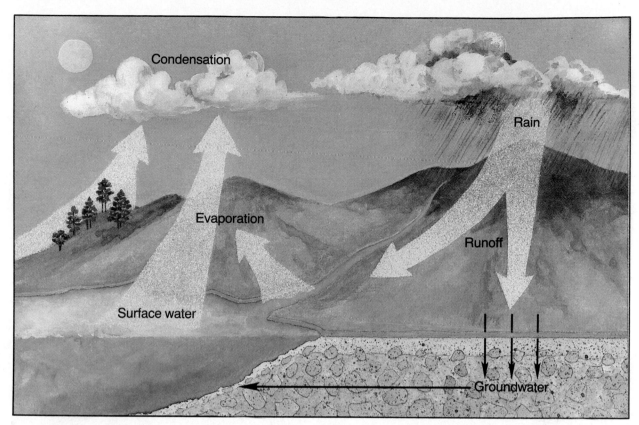

Condensation

Rain

Evaporation

Runoff

Surface water

Groundwater

The water on Earth continually moves from one place to another within the water cycle.

You may remember studying about the water cycle. Water travels through a cycle in which it continually changes form—from a liquid to solid ice to water vapor. The sun begins the cycle when it evaporates water from oceans, lakes, and streams, making it water vapor. Water vapor is also produced from plants and animals. This water vapor then rises into the air, where it cools and condenses into liquid droplets, forming rain or snow. When rain or snow falls, water returns to the ground, where it may flow back to oceans, lakes, or streams. The water cycle continues. During any part of this cycle, water may become polluted. Polluted water is water that has impurities.

Over half the people in the United States get their drinking water from underground wells. This underground water supply is called **groundwater.** Most of the rest comes from surface water sources such as rivers and lakes. How do these sources of drinking water become polluted?

Where do people get drinking water?

If wastes are not stored properly they may seep into groundwater.

Groundwater becomes polluted in several ways. Chemicals from dumps and landfills seep into the ground and pollute groundwater. Industrial wastes also pollute groundwater. You may have read about industrial chemical waste containers buried years ago. Some are now leaking into the ground, contaminating local water supplies.

Besides this chemical seepage, the cleaning agents and other chemicals an industry uses to produce its product may cause water pollution. The water used to wash away excess chemicals is often dumped into nearby rivers, lakes, or oceans.

Some industries use water to cool machines that get very hot. The cool water becomes hot as it absorbs the heat from the machines. This hot water is then dumped into nearby rivers or lakes. This causes the temperature in parts of these rivers or

ACTIVITY

You Can...

Observe the Effects of Pollution

Plant four radish seeds in each of three different pots of soil. Water each pot daily until you observe seedlings. Then, instead of using water, use vinegar to "water" the second pot. Use salt solution to "water" the third pot. (To make the salt solution, mix a large spoonful of salt in a half-liter of water.) Continue using plain water for the first pot. "Water" the plants every other day for two weeks. What happens to the plants? Why? Where might you find plants in nature that are affected by similar conditions? Use the results of your experiment to explain how "acid rain" might affect wild plants.

Wastes pollute surface water.

lakes to rise, killing organisms and increasing the evaporation rate of the water. Scientists call this dumping of hot water **thermal pollution.** It's a type of pollution that reduces the amount of oxygen dissolved in water. Living things then die from lack of oxygen. Dissolved oxygen helps decompose organic wastes in water, so wastes break down very slowly when there's a lack of oxygen. As a result, scientists warn that thermally polluted water will stay polluted for a long time.

What is thermal pollution?

Another type of water pollution is sewage. The liquid and solid wastes carried in your city or town sewers and drains are **sewage**. Much of this sewage is made up of human wastes as well as food particles and cooking wastes that go down the drain of your kitchen sink. You will learn later in this chapter about how sewage is treated before it's returned to the environment.

Thermal pollution threatens living things.

Agricultural wastes enter water supplies and endanger life.

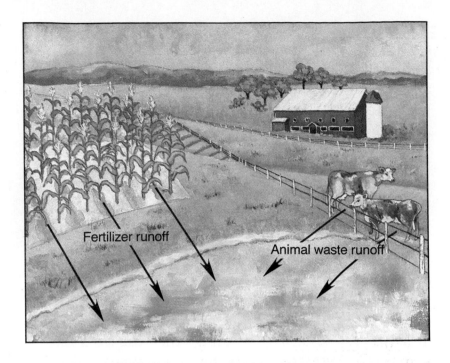

Fertilizer runoff

Animal waste runoff

Besides industrial chemical wastes and sewage, animal wastes also pollute water. Animal wastes from barns and pens sometimes seep into rivers and lakes, causing disease and decreasing the amount of oxygen in the water.

How do pesticides get into rivers and lakes?

Have you ever seen your parents use a spray to kill ants or other insects that entered your house? Farmers use such **pesticides** to kill insects and other organisms that harm crops. And many use **herbicides** to kill weeds. These pesticides and herbicides can pollute if they dissolve in water that runs off farmlands into rivers and lakes.

Pesticides may pollute water in nearby rivers and lakes.

264

The price of water pollution is high. Industrial wastes may poison living things that use or live in the water. Thermal pollution causes some to die from lack of oxygen. Since human wastes contain bacteria, disease can develop if sewage is not treated properly. It is clear that water pollution threatens life on Earth.

In what ways is water pollution costly?

Lesson Summary

- Water is a natural resource needed for life. Drinking water comes from groundwater or surface water sources.
- Pollution occurs when impurities enter water. Waste heat and chemicals from industry, agriculture, and sewage are common sources of water pollution.
- Water pollution may kill living things that use or live in the water and may spread disease among living things.

Lesson Review

1. From what two natural sources does most drinking water come?
2. List four sources of groundwater pollution.
3. What are some dangers of water pollution?
★4. List several ways water pollution could be reduced in your home and community.

Conserving Clean Water

LESSON 2 GOALS
You will learn
- how water is treated.
- how sewage is treated.
- how to conserve water.

Have you ever visited a local reservoir? You saw a large artificial or natural lake. You may even have gone swimming or boating there. Often the future drinking water supplies for a community are collected and stored in a **reservoir.** Since most water must be treated before it can be used, treatment may begin there.

When water is stored in a reservoir, some materials in the water settle to the bottom. The water on the top then flows through a filter. The filter keeps out twigs, fish, and other large objects as the water is pumped through a nearby water-treatment plant.

Water-treatment plants often add chemicals to water before it's pumped to your house. These chemicals kill bacteria and remove color and small particles. **Chlorine**, which kills bacteria, is usually one of the chemicals added. The water is filtered again, and more chlorine is added. The treated water is then pumped to the community through pipes.

What chemical is most often used in water treatment?

Reservoirs often store future drinking water supplies.

Today people are using more natural ways to clean water.

Some cities also add **fluorine** to water supplies. They do this because dental research says fluorine helps keep teeth healthy. Six states require fluoridation in cities with a population of more than 20,000 people. However, there are many other people who refuse fluoridation in their cities or states because they disagree that fluorine is really needed. Does your community add fluorine to your drinking water? Do you know what compounds your local water-treatment plant adds to your water?

Some water-treatment plants, like the one pictured here, are using new experimental techniques to provide clean water to the public. This treatment plant uses living plants called water hyacinths to produce more than 75,000 liters of clean water from wastewater each day.

Every time you wash your face, brush your teeth, flush the toilet, or empty the rest of your glass of milk in the kitchen sink, you make sewage. In many cities sewage is first cleaned in a sewage-treatment plant before it's returned to the environment. Let's look more closely at how this is done.

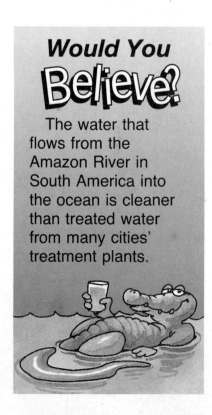

Would You Believe?

The water that flows from the Amazon River in South America into the ocean is cleaner than treated water from many cities' treatment plants.

267

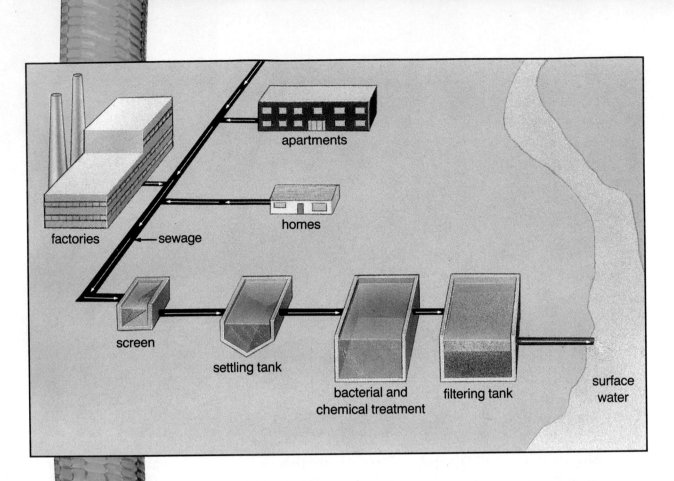

factories

sewage

apartments

homes

screen

settling tank

bacterial and
chemical treatment

filtering tank

surface
water

In sewage-treatment plants, sewage is first screened to remove large objects. It's then pumped to large tanks or ponds where solid pieces settle to the bottom. Then the liquid sewage is pumped to tanks. Here, helpful bacteria are added that feed on sewage, thus removing some of the pollution. At a later stage, chlorine and other chemicals are added to kill bacteria and to break down other polluting materials. The sewage water then runs through layers of sand and gravel, which filter out most remaining impurities. The treated sewage water is finally released to nearby lakes or streams. This water becomes part of the water cycle again.

If sewage is treated properly, wastewater can be cleaned and returned to the environment with very little pollution. But in some areas, wastewater and untreated sewage are dumped directly into streams and lakes. This kills living things in the water and pollutes the freshwater supply needed by people and other animals.

Water Conservation

Do you ever find yourself spending more time in the shower than necessary—singing or daydreaming? How about running the water while you're brushing your teeth? Sometimes you forget that water is a limited resource. Knowing that Earth's surface is more than two-thirds water, you might think that water is plentiful enough that you needn't worry about wasting some of it. But only one percent of Earth's water is usable for drinking. Nearly all the rest is ocean salt water. While you can fish or swim in ocean water, you can't drink it. The limited sources for clean drinking water must be used wisely or they will run out. When we carefully plan their use, we are conserving these resources.

How much of Earth's water can be used for drinking?

People often waste water without thinking about it.

269

Preventing water pollution is an important part of water conservation. A United States law called the **Clean Water Act** fights pollution. It has helped clean up some lakes and rivers in this country. It helps prevent thermal pollution. For example, industries are encouraged to cool water in cooling towers or ponds before they dump it into lakes or streams. Instead of dumping it, industries in some places are using their hot wastewater to heat buildings.

To combat agricultural wastes, some farmers are practicing organic farming. Only natural fertilizers, such as farm animal wastes, are being used on these farms. Instead of pesticides, farmers may use **biocontrols,** or living things that feed on other living things. Ladybugs are biocontrols that eat such crop-destroying insects as aphids.

Cooling towers

Organic farming

SCIENCE AND . . .
Writing

You have just learned that pesticides from local farms are running off into a lake. Write a speech to present to the local farm community. Describe how pesticide run-off is polluting the lake. Explain how biocontrols can be used instead.

270

In the Southwest water is limited.

When people try to make dry land green, water supplies diminish.

As more and more people continue to move into previously unpopulated areas, the demand for water continues to rise. Conserving water is necessary because this increased demand can diminish water supplies. This is already happening in such areas of the southwestern United States as Arizona and New Mexico. Water in these desert areas is a scarce resource, and has to be carefully used by residents. People moving into these areas can't expect to have as much water available for recreational activities as they may have once had in areas where water was more plentiful. Can you think of some of these activities?

Even cities where water shortages were never a problem have to be concerned with water conservation. Research studies have shown that some cities have water systems that waste drinking water because of leaks in old underground pipes.

Conserving water is the responsibility of all persons on Earth. If this responsibility is ignored, we may find ourselves repeating the words of an ancient mariner in an old English poem, "Water, water, everywhere. Nor any drop to drink."

It's everyone's responsibility to conserve water.

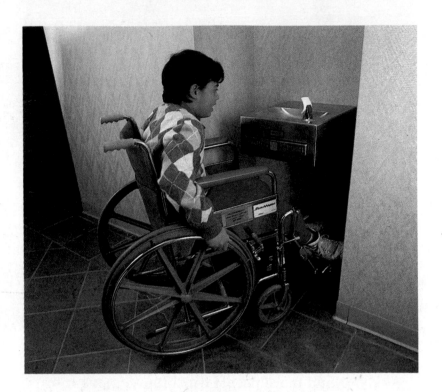

Lesson Summary

- Water is treated to make it safe to drink.
- Sewage is treated before it's returned to the environment.
- Water conservation must be practiced to avoid water shortages in the future.

Lesson Review

1. How is water treated to make it fit for drinking?
2. What harm may untreated sewage cause?
3. Why is it necessary to conserve water?
4. In what ways are industry and agriculture helping prevent water pollution?
★5. Explain what this saying means: "Today's wastewater is tomorrow's clean water."

Use Application Activity on pages 507, 508.

How can water be cleaned?

What you need

crushed charcoal
sand
soil
crushed gravel
3 jars
3 plastic foam cups with 5 holes poked
in bottoms
metric ruler
measuring cup
spoon
liter of water

What to do

1. Place crushed charcoal in a plastic foam cup to a depth of 5 cm. Put 5 cm of sand in another cup. Put 5 cm of crushed gravel in a third cup.
2. Set the cups in the jars so the bottoms of the cups are not touching the bottoms of the jars.
3. Mix one large spoonful of soil in 1 liter of water.
4. Pour the same amount of dirty water into each cup.
5. Observe what happens to the water. Record your observations.

What did you learn?

1. What happened to the dirty water when you poured it into the cups?
2. Which filter cleaned the water best? Why do you think so?
3. Why was it important to use the same amount of dirty water each time?

Using what you learned

1. What could you do differently to get the water cleaner?
2. How is water filtered for use on a large scale?
3. Why might a device for filtering water be used in your home?

Conserving Clean Air

LESSON 3 GOALS
You will learn
● how air becomes polluted.
● about effects of air pollution.
● how to conserve clean air.

Lee Wong and Frances, members of Mrs. Putnam's sixth-grade class, are sitting in the cafeteria discussing their project for science class. It's going to be about air pollution, and they plan to use information they learned from Mr. Cord. He was from the Environmental Protection Agency (EPA) and had just visited their class to talk on air pollution. Let's listen to what Lee Wong and Frances are saying about their project.

"I couldn't believe it when Mr. Cord listed all the ways air can be polluted. I didn't know there were so many," Lee Wong said. "Did you?"

"I knew that smoke from the factories around here and car exhausts caused pollution. But I didn't think about cigarette smoke or other kinds of indoor pollution. Mr. Cord said one of the EPA's studies said the air inside homes is often more polluted and dangerous than outdoor air on a smoggy day. He gave us lots of examples of indoor pollutants—fumes from aerosol spray cans, gas stoves, furnaces, and cleaning products. I was really interested in the natural ways air is polluted. I think we should list them in our project. My notes say seed particles, pollen, forest fires, and volcanoes are natural sources of air pollution.

Particulates from factory smoke pollute the air.

"I agree. But we definitely should put down some of the ways that *people* pollute the air. What did Mr. Cord say about that farmer and his cattle?"

"He said that a factory polluted the air with particulates. Scientists found out the cattle on a nearby farm became sick and died. They died from grazing in a pasture where the grass was coated with these particulates."

"But what exactly are particulates? I think we should give examples of them," Lee Wong said.

"Well," Frances answered, "have you ever seen smoke pouring out of a factory's smokestack? That smoke is made up of small particles of solid matter."

"And those particles are called **particulates,**" finished Lee Wong. "Mr. Cord also said that there are harmful gases like sulfur and nitrogen oxides in the smoke from factories and coal-burning power plants. Scientists think these gases combine with water in the atmosphere."

"That's how **acid rain** forms," concluded Frances. "Mr. Cord said that when the gases combine with water it forms acid. The acid then falls as rain or snow. Acid rain and acid snow poison any body of water they fall into. They also make soils have a lower pH."

What are particulates?

275

Chemicals in automobile exhaust fumes harm the air we breathe.

Some large cities alert their citizens when air pollution levels are seriously high.

"And many plants can't grow in acid soils," finished Lee Wong. She added, "I remember reading that some ponds have become so polluted by acid rain that some of the organisms that once lived in them can no longer survive."

"Right. I think we should also include examples of motor-vehicle pollution in our report."

"Good idea," Lee Wong said. "My notes say that city streets and highways are overcrowded with automobiles and trucks. Their exhausts have harmful hydrocarbons, lead, nitrogen oxides, and carbon monoxide. These chemicals are very harmful to the air we breathe."

"I remember hearing Mr. Cord say that in some parts of the southwestern United States the air pollution has become so great the fruit trees are producing only half as much fruit as they once did."

"I also heard him say that the air pollution from large cities has been rising into the mountains, producing acid rain and killing millions of pine trees. And sometimes it's so bad that these cities have air quality alerts. These alerts tell people with allergies or breathing problems to stay indoors until the air becomes safer to breathe."

Mr. Cord also told the class that scientists have noticed a warming of Earth's surface in recent years. To explain this, he drew a diagram on the chalkboard much like the one below. The sun's rays pass through the atmosphere and reach Earth's surface. There, surface features such as plants, soil, water, buildings, blacktop, and concrete absorb the rays. As they absorb the sun's energy, the surface features warm up and give off heat as infrared waves. Infrared waves have longer wavelengths and less energy than the light that came through the atmosphere from the sun. The carbon dioxide and other gases in the atmosphere absorb the infrared waves, and they send some of this energy back to Earth's surface. This process is often compared to what happens inside a greenhouse, even though it is somewhat different. That's why the warming of the atmosphere is often called the **greenhouse effect**.

Earth's atmosphere warms the inside of a greenhouse.

Mr. Cord pointed out that carbon dioxide is added to the atmosphere by burning coal, oil, and natural gas, and motor-vehicle exhausts. If Earth continues to warm, world temperatures could rise enough to melt parts of the polar ice caps. This would cause oceans to rise and shoreline areas to flood.

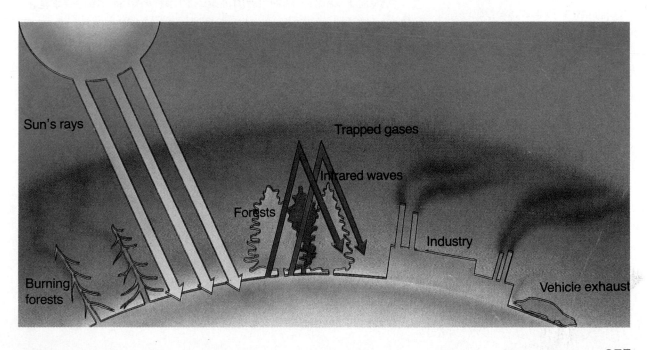

Mr. Cord emphasized to Mrs. Putnam's students that air pollution is not only harmful but costly. "Besides making people with respiratory illnesses like asthma and bronchitis even sicker, it damages crops, harms livestock, and causes concrete, steel, and nylon to wear out faster. These materials are used to build bridges, buildings, and homes. When polluted air damages them, repairing them is costly."

Frances remembered something Mr. Cord had said, and repeated it, "We can often choose food and water that aren't polluted by being careful of what we eat and drink. But we can't choose the air we breathe. When air is polluted we all breathe polluted air."

"Yes, I remember that too. That gives me an idea. Besides telling the causes of air pollution and its dangers to our environment, we should also include the things we can do to help clean the air."

"Okay, what do you think we should say? How can we help? We don't own a factory or a car."

"True, but our parents own cars. Maybe we could get them to car pool so there would be one less car on the road," Frances said.

"I like that. What else can we do?"

"We can probably do more things to help with indoor pollution," said Frances. "We can help people we know who smoke to stop smoking. We can choose not to sit in smoking areas of restaurants and public buildings. And buying pump sprays instead of aerosol cans will help some. Let's call Mr. Cord and see what else he suggests."

Air Conservation

"Although we may not be able to end all air pollution, we can control it," Mr. Cord said on the telephone to Frances. "Laws have been passed to combat air pollution. The federal government sets limits on air pollutants from car exhausts. Particulates are cleaned from engine exhausts before the exhaust is released into the air. We also see more unleaded fuels used. To reduce the amounts of particulates, some states forbid the open burning of trash within city limits."

Mr. Cord went on to say that another way industries prevent particulates and smokestack gases from polluting air is by using scrubbers. A **scrubber** is a device that fits in a smokestack or chimney. It uses water to remove particulates and some polluting gases. Some of the materials removed by a scrubber can actually be used to make other products.

When Lee Wong and Frances told Mr. Cord about their car pooling idea, he thought it was great. He also suggested they walk or ride a bicycle whenever possible. He told them that he rode a bike to work, and his office building had shower facilities he used before starting his work day.

Car pooling and riding bicycles help conserve clean air.

Because trees take in carbon dioxide and absorb particulates, planting trees helps lessen air pollution.

Lee Wong and Frances's science project was a success. At the end of their oral report, they said that clean air is important because we can't live healthful lives without it. Because of this, they asked their classmates to think of other ways to reduce air pollution. Can you think of any?

Lesson Summary

Cigarette smoke, smoke from industries, and motor-vehicle exhaust are some common sources of air pollution.

Air pollution is not only harmful but costly.

Lesson Review

1. What are some sources of air pollution?
2. How is air pollution harmful to humans? to the environment?
3. If you lived in a large city, what would an "air quality alert" mean?
★4. What ways can you help lessen air pollution in your community?

Where can you find air pollution?

What you need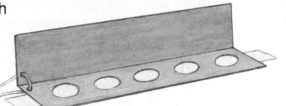

2 strips of thin   nickel
  cardboard   transparent tape
scissors   hand lens
hole punch
string
pencil
paper

What to do

1. Punch a hole in one end of each strip of cardboard.
2. Put a piece of string through the hole in each strip. Tie the string to make a loop for hanging it.
3. Fold each strip in half lengthwise. Trace five nickel-sized circles in a row on one half of each strip. Then cut out the circles.
4. Put tape on the outside of each strip so that the sticky side shows through the holes. Then fold the strip in half to cover the holes. Seal it with tape.
5. Find a different place to hang each strip. Choose one place that is inside and one that is outside.
6. Label each strip with the location. Open the strip so the sticky part of the tape is exposed. Then hang it.
7. Collect the strips the next day. As you collect each strip, fold it again and seal it with tape.
8. Use a hand lens. Observe the tape. Record your observations.

What did you learn?

1. What did you observe on the tape?
2. What caused it?

Using what you learned

1. What would you expect to detect on a windy day?
2. What types of air pollution might not be detected with your strips?

281

I WANT TO KNOW ABOUT...

A Biologist

Far from the busy city, biologist James Kabotie often paddles his canoe across a serene wilderness lake in the taiga. The taiga is a large biome south of the tundra. Jim has studied the ecology of the taiga for 20 years. In that time, he has observed alarming changes in the freshwater and conifer forest ecosystems. Many trees have died, and the lakes have produced fewer and fewer fish. Common loons and other fish-eating birds have become rarer as their food supplies dwindled.

After years of intense investigation, Jim learned that the pH of the lakes was very acidic. The source of the problem was acid rain. Acid rain forms when nitrogen oxides and sulfur dioxide are released into the atmosphere. A major source of nitrogen oxides is the exhaust from automobiles. Sulfur dioxide is produced from coal- or oil-burning power plants.

Taiga lakes can't neutralize acid rain. But lime can. Lime reacts with acid and lessens its effect. The lime is sprayed on frozen lakes so it can neutralize the acid in the snow and ice before they melt in the spring.

Career

Summary

Lesson 1
- Water is a natural resource needed for life. Drinking water comes from groundwater or surface water sources.
- Pollution occurs when impurities enter water. Waste heat and chemicals from industry, agriculture, and sewage are common sources of water pollution.
- Water pollution may kill organisms that use or live in the water and may spread disease among humans.

Lesson 2
- Water is treated to make it safe to drink.

- Sewage is treated before it's returned to the environment.
- Water conservation must be practiced to avoid water shortages in the future.

Lesson 3
- Cigarette smoke, smoke from industries, and motor-vehicle exhaust are some common sources of air pollution.
- Air pollution is not only harmful but costly.

Science Words

Fill in the blank with the correct word or words from the list.

thermal pollution	pesticides
Clean Water Act	herbicides
acid rain	reservoir
greenhouse effect	sewage
biocontrols	chlorine
particulates	fluorine
scrubbers	groundwater

1. ____ occurs when industries raise the temperature of bodies of water by dumping hot water into them.

2. Chemicals that farmers use to destroy organisms that may harm crops are ____.

3. Another method of controlling crop-destroying organisms, less damaging to the environment, is to use other organisms called ____ to destroy the pests.

4. To reduce air pollution, industries can install ____ in their smokestacks to wash out particulates and some polluting gases.

5. A(n) ____ is a natural or human-made lake used to store water.

6. Chemicals used to kill weeds are called ____.

7. Small particles found in smoke are ____.

Questions

Recalling Ideas

Correctly complete each of the following sentences.

1. All of the following are water pollutants EXCEPT
   (a) sewage.　　(c) reservoirs.
   (b) chemicals.　(d) heat.

2. The fraction of all the water on Earth that can be used as drinking water is
   (a) 1 percent.　　(c) 20 percent.
   (b) 10 percent.　(d) 50 percent.

3. Organisms that are used in place of chemical pesticides to prevent other organisms from harming crops are
   (a) particulates.　(c) herbicides.
   (b) fertilizers.　　(d) biocontrols.

4. A chemical added to water in a water treatment plant to kill bacteria is
   (a) sulfur.　　(c) fluorine.
   (b) chlorine.　(d) nitrogen.

5. Of the following air pollutants, one that is a cause of acid rain is
   (a) lead.　　　　(c) hydrocarbons.
   (b) particulates.　(d) sulfur oxide.

6. Of the following pollutants, the one that does NOT come from a natural source is
   (a) pollen.
   (b) seed particles.
   (c) nitrogen oxides.
   (d) dust.
7. A way to purify water without adding chemicals is to use
   (a) bacteria.
   (b) chlorine and settling.
   (c) water hyacinths.
   (d) both a and c.

Examining Ideas
Determine whether each of the following statements is true or false. Rewrite the false statements to make them correct.

1. Chlorine is added to water in water treatment plants to remove color from the water.
2. There are no natural sources of air pollution.
3. Seventy-one percent of Earth's water is usable as drinking water.
4. Some farmers use biocontrols.
5. Thermal pollution reduces the amount of oxygen that is dissolved in water.
6. Organic farming is a method that uses no pesticides and no human-made fertilizers.
7. Motor vehicles are only a minor source of air pollution.
8. In most large cities in the United States, water comes into homes directly from wells or reservoirs.

9. Placing scrubbers in industrial smokestacks would end acid rain.
10. Indoor air is free from pollutants.

Understanding Ideas
Answer the following questions using complete sentences.

1. List the two main sources of drinking water and tell how each becomes polluted.
2. Explain how thermal pollution affects water organisms.
3. How can pollution of water by sewage be controlled?
4. List several sources of air pollution.
5. Describe the causes and effects of acid rain.

Thinking Critically
Think about what you have learned in this chapter. Answer the following questions using complete sentences.

1. How can organic farming reduce water pollution?
2. Tell what might be done about each of these instances of pollution.
   (a) a power plant dumping hot water into a river
   (b) air pollution caused by heavy traffic near a school
3. Make a list of the ways that you use water in one day. Then suggest several ways that you might conserve water.
4. Discuss how the rapidly increasing human population is affecting the supply of clean air and water.

Checking for Understanding

Write a short answer for each question or statement.

1. Compare the sizes of the sun, red giants, white dwarfs, and neutron stars.
2. How does the surface temperature of a red star compare with the temperature of a blue star?
3. What is the Local Group?
4. What causes the apparent change in location of stars?
5. What are the stages in the life cycle of most stars?
6. What evidence leads to the idea of an expanding universe?
7. Why must astronauts exercise in space?
8. How has space technology been useful to people other than astronauts?
9. Compare the big bang theory with the pulsating theory.
10. List and describe three methods of conserving forests.
11. What is a light-year?
12. Why are space probes such as *Voyager* and *Viking* important?
13. Describe three different types of galaxies.
14. List the ways that topsoil can be eroded.
15. What is refuse?
16. Why are some wastes considered hazardous?
17. What is a biodegradable material?
18. Describe the layers in a soil profile.
19. List and describe five methods of soil conservation.
20. What is pollution, and what causes air and water pollution?
21. What are biocontrols and how are they better than pesticides?
22. Name two indoor air pollutants and suggest ways in which they could be controlled.
23. What are five important benefits of forests?
24. What is the purpose of an optical telescope?
25. Why can astronomers not see black holes?
26. What is Polaris and why is it important to people in the northern hemisphere?

Recalling Activities

Write a short paragraph for each question or statement.

1. How can you describe your location in space?
2. How do galaxies move in the universe?
3. How does distance affect accuracy?
4. How will we live in space?
5. How do roots prevent soil erosion?
6. Which items are biodegradable?
7. How can water be cleaned?
8. Where can you find air pollution?

Project Ideas

1. Consider everything that is required for an astronaut to exist in space. Design a spacesuit that would allow an astronaut to function freely on the moon. Draw a picture of your suit.

2. Some items normally referred to as "wastes" and "pollution" are really valuable resources. They are thrown away because there has been a lack of planning for their use. Choose three "wastes" or "pollutants" and research how these could be used, or how they could be prevented from becoming refuse.

Books to Read

The Macmillan Book of Astronomy by Roy A. Gallant, Macmillan Publishing Co.: New York, 1986.

More With Less: The Future World of Buckminister Fuller by Nathan Asseng, Lerner Publication Co.: Minneapolis, 1986.

To Space and Back by Sally Ride, with Susan Okie, Lothrop, Lee & Shepard Books: New York, 1986.

Waste by Christina G. Miller and Louise A. Berry, Franklin Watts, Inc.: Danbury, CT, 1986.

SCIENCE FAIR ➡

Life Science

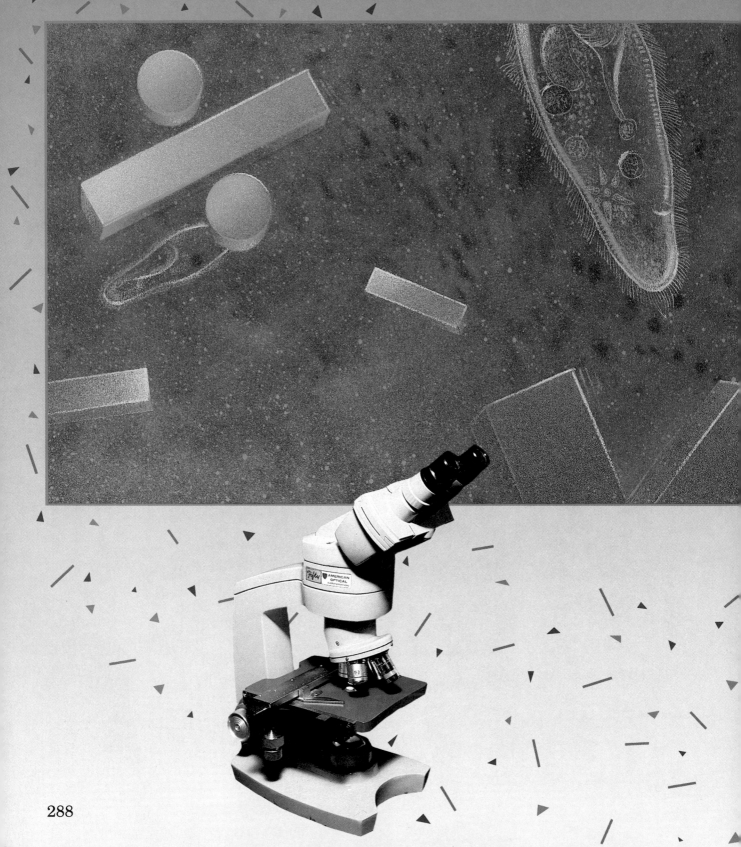

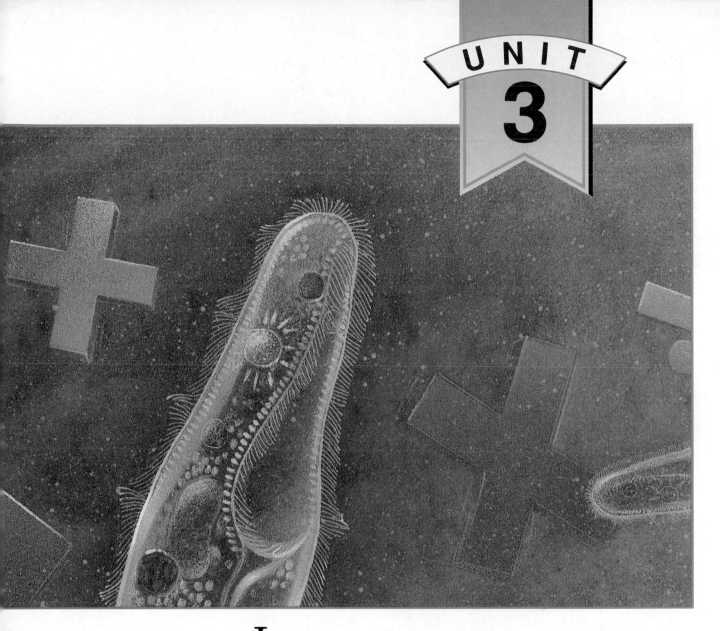

I am a paramecium
that cannot do a simple sum,
and it's a rather well-known fact
I'm quite unable to subtract.

If I'd an eye, I'd surely cry
about the way I multiply,
for though I've often tried and tried,
I do it backward . . . and divide.

"A Microscopic Topic"
Jack Prelutsky

Classifying Living Things

A school orchestra is divided into sections according to the similarity of the instruments' sounds. The unique sound of each instrument is produced by its structural materials and design. A saxophone and bassoon don't look the same, but they belong to the same section because their sound is made by a reed.

Living things can also be grouped by certain common characteristics that they share. How are such groupings, or classifications, helpful?

Have You Ever...

Classified Objects?

Collect ten items from the classroom. Divide a piece of paper into three columns. In the first column, write the name of each object. In the second column, tell how each item is used. In the third column, jot down any specific characteristic of the item, such as its color or size. Then see how many ways you can group the items.

How many ways were you able to group the items?

Features of Life

LESSON 1 GOALS
You will learn
● about six features all organisms have in common.
● about the parts of a cell and their functions.

Imagine you are sitting in the grass on a warm summer day. Your dog lies lazily beside you. The air is filled with the buzzing sound of grasshoppers as a light breeze rustles the leaves of the tree above your head. As you glance up, you notice a robin returning to a nest. Three baby robins stretch their necks to grasp the earthworm the adult robin has brought.

It's certainly interesting to observe the living things on Earth. You, your dog, the grasshoppers, the tree, and the robins are all called **organisms** because they are living things. You can separate organisms from nonliving things, such as rocks and water, by looking at their features. Let's use the robin as an example as we look at the features of living things.

Feature 1. *Organisms reproduce.* A female robin builds a round nest of grass. She shapes it into a bowl, then lines it with more dry grass. In the nest she lays three to six blue eggs. When the young

One of the features of life is that organisms need food.

birds hatch, they have speckled breasts. But they will grow up, and their features will become like those of adult robins—including dark gray backs and rusty-red breasts.

Feature 2. *Organisms grow.* Young robins are very small when they hatch. With the help of constant feeding by their parents, young robins grow to full size in several months.

Feature 3. *Organisms develop.* When robins first hatch, they are blind and helpless. As they develop, they're able to hold their heads up and open their mouths for food. Soon their eyes open, and they're able to move about the nest. Later they develop feathers and eventually learn to fly.

Feature 4. *Organisms use energy.* All birds use a tremendous amount of energy because they are almost constantly moving. The robin uses energy to fly, find food, sing, and even sleep.

Feature 5. *Organisms need food.* When the baby robins are still in the nest, the mother bird feeds them. Later they learn to find fruit, earthworms, and insects for themselves. Food gives the robins energy.

Feature 6. *Organisms are made of cells.* Robins, like all other organisms, are made of cells. Let's take a closer look at cells because **cells** are the basic units of life.

What are all organisms made of?

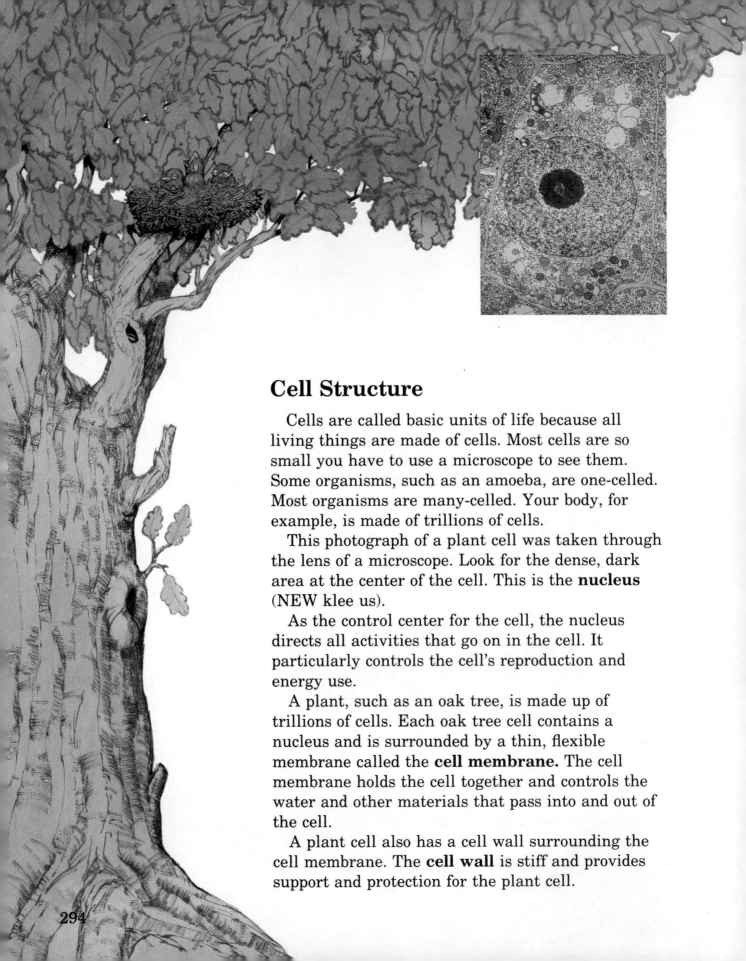

Cell Structure

Cells are called basic units of life because all living things are made of cells. Most cells are so small you have to use a microscope to see them. Some organisms, such as an amoeba, are one-celled. Most organisms are many-celled. Your body, for example, is made of trillions of cells.

This photograph of a plant cell was taken through the lens of a microscope. Look for the dense, dark area at the center of the cell. This is the **nucleus** (NEW klee us).

As the control center for the cell, the nucleus directs all activities that go on in the cell. It particularly controls the cell's reproduction and energy use.

A plant, such as an oak tree, is made up of trillions of cells. Each oak tree cell contains a nucleus and is surrounded by a thin, flexible membrane called the **cell membrane.** The cell membrane holds the cell together and controls the water and other materials that pass into and out of the cell.

A plant cell also has a cell wall surrounding the cell membrane. The **cell wall** is stiff and provides support and protection for the plant cell.

Plant cells like those that Robert Hooke observed

Robert Hooke was the first person to observe plant cells. When he saw the cells, he thought they looked like the little rooms in which monks live. For this reason, he called the tiny units cells. All basic units of life, both plant life and animal life, are now called cells.

Lesson Summary

- All organisms reproduce, grow, develop, use energy, need food, and are made of cells.
- The nucleus of a cell controls cell activities. A cell membrane holds the cell together and controls what passes into and out of it. A cell wall provides support for a plant cell.

Lesson Review

1. Name six features of life.
2. What is the function of a nucleus?
3. What is the function of a cell membrane?
4. Robert Hooke first saw plant cells in the 1600s. Why do you think no one had seen them before that?
★5. Choose an organism and explain how it has each of the features of living things.

Use Application Activity on pages 509, 510.

Grouping Organisms

LESSON 2 GOALS
You will learn
• that organisms can be grouped according to their likenesses.
• how all organisms are grouped into five kingdoms.

Do you have fun collecting baseball cards? Gathering cards of all the players you admire, trading with your friends, and seeing how quickly you can get a complete set of your favorite team makes this quite an enjoyable way to spend your free time.

If you do collect baseball cards, you know how important it is to sort the cards into groups. It can be very frustrating if your friend Emilio wants to trade one of his cards for one of your cards and you have to rustle through a large shoe box of loose, unsorted cards. You know you have the player, but it takes too long to find the card. It would be much faster to find it if the cards were sorted into categories.

Scientists would experience the same kind of frustration if someone asked them questions about an organism and they had to look for information in a gigantic trunk labeled *Organisms*. Without any way to sort Earth's 1.5 million known organisms into smaller groups, scientists could not easily study them.

Scientists have developed a way to sort organisms into groups according to how they are similar. This sorting system is called classification.

Slime mold

Bacteria

Your sorting system for grouping baseball cards is also classification. The first step in your sorting system is to break down all the cards of players into the largest groups they belong to. In this case, sorting players into the National League and the American League would be your first step.

What would be the first step in classifying organisms? Take a look at the pictures shown on this page. Does each have features of living things? If so, then you can say that each is an organism. Yet all of these living things are very different. If you were to group them according to other similar characteristics, which organisms would you group together? You would probably put the dog and elephant together because you know they are animals. The rose and tree belong together because you know they are plants. But what would you do with the bacteria, slime mold, and mushrooms? Are they plants, animals or something else? Let's find out how scientists group them.

The first step in classifying organisms is to group them according to the largest groups they belong to. Many years ago organisms were grouped into only two large groups—plants and animals. But after tools such as microscopes were invented, scientists discovered new organisms that did not have the same characteristics as plants or animals. Today most scientists group organisms into five large groups called kingdoms.

Even though simple and complex organisms both eat, complex organisms have many more steps in their digestion process.

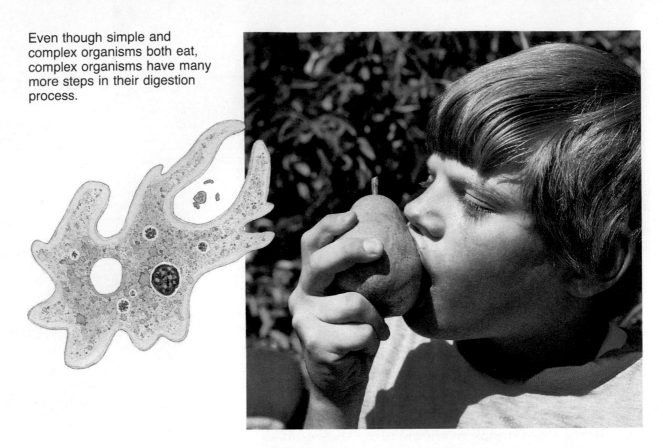

How many cells do simple organisms have?

The kingdoms are the largest groups organisms belong to. They are the moneran kingdom, the protist kingdom, the fungus kingdom, the plant kingdom, and the animal kingdom. The bacteria in the photograph belong to the moneran kingdom, the slime mold is a member of the protist kingdom, and the mushrooms are in the fungus kingdom.

Organisms are placed into the kingdom with which they share the most characteristics. You would look at a player's characteristics—such as what team he plays for—in classifying the player into one of the two baseball leagues. Likewise, scientists look at three general characteristics to see which kingdom an organism belongs to. One of the three characteristics is whether the organism is one-celled or many-celled. Because one-celled organisms carry out their life processes in an uncomplicated way, they are called simple organisms. Many-celled organisms are called complex organisms because their cells are organized in much more involved ways.

298

The second characteristic scientists look at is whether or not a cell of an organism has a nucleus. The third characteristic is how an organism gets food. An organism that makes its own food, such as the apple tree, is called a **producer.** It contains chlorophyll and can capture the sun's energy. Can you name the other producers pictured on page 297? A **consumer,** such as the dog, eats other organisms. Consumers don't contain chlorophyll. Can you name the other consumers pictured on page 297? Let's take a closer look at each of the five kingdoms.

Moneran Kingdom. A moneran (muh NIHR un) is the smallest living thing. It's a one-celled organism that has no nucleus. There is material in a moneran that controls the cell's activities, but it is not contained in a central part as in other cells. Monerans are the simplest organisms. They may be producers or consumers. Moneran cells are often found in groups or long chains. Bacteria are monerans. Some kinds of bacteria take in their food from outside their cells. They are consumers. Other bacteria have chlorophyll and are producers. Another name for producer bacteria is **cyanobacteria.** You may have seen groups of cyanobacteria in a pond or lake.

In what kingdom are bacteria placed?

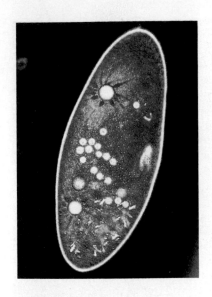

Protozoan

Protist Kingdom. A **protist** (PROHT ust), like the moneran, is a one-celled simple organism, but a protist has a nucleus. Protists may be producers or consumers. The producers are plant-like and have cell walls. Would a producer protist contain chlorophyll? Other protists are animal-like. In addition to being consumers, these protists are like animals because they show movement and don't have cell walls. **Diatoms** (DI uh tahmz) and protozoans (proht uh ZOH unz) are two types of protists that live in both fresh and salt water. Without diatoms and protozoans most of Earth's fish would die of starvation because diatoms and protozoans are the primary source of food for fish.

Fungus Kingdom. A **fungus** is a consumer with cell walls. A fungus may be one-celled or many-celled. Even though some fungi are many-celled, fungi are still considered simple organisms. Each cell in a fungus has a nucleus; some cells even have more than one. Since fungi (FUN ji) don't have chlorophyll, they can't make their own food. They must take in their food from their surroundings. Mushrooms, molds, mildews, and yeasts are types of fungi. Think of a place you have seen mold. Where was it getting its food?

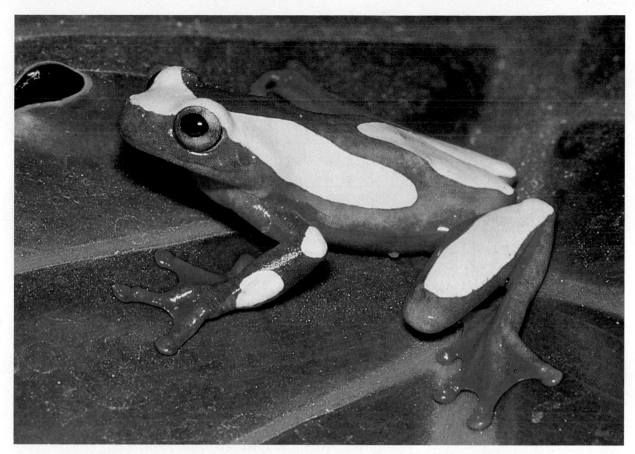

The rain forest has a blend of plant and animal life.

Plant Kingdom. Members of the plant kingdom are all around us. Because most of them contain chlorophyll, you know they are producers. Each plant cell has a nucleus and a cell wall. Plants are many-celled, complex organisms. Like the protists, the members of the plant kingdom are important as food to other organisms. Consumers need plants to survive. In fact, without plants and other consumers, there would be no consumers. What are some plants you eat?

Animal Kingdom. If it creeps, crawls, swims, flies, hops, or runs, it is probably a member of the animal kingdom. Animals are consumers; they can't make their own food. Animals, like plants, are many-celled, complex organisms. An animal cell has a nucleus and a nuclear membrane. But an animal cell doesn't have the rigid cell wall. You certainly know about many groups of animals, such as worms, insects, fish, birds, and mammals.

Name two ways in which plants and animals differ.

Table 1   Five-Kingdom Classification

	Simple Organisms			Complex Organisms	
	Monerans	Protists	Fungi	Plants	Animals
producers	some	some	no	most	no
consumers	some	some	yes	some	yes
one-celled	yes	yes	some	no	no
many-celled	no	no	most	yes	yes
nucleus	no	yes	yes	yes	yes
cell membrane	yes	yes	yes	yes	yes
cell wall present	most	some	yes	yes	no
cell organelles	no	yes	yes	yes	yes

Table 1 shows characteristics of organisms in the five kingdoms. Using the table, tell which kingdoms may be either one-celled or many-celled. Which kingdom does not have a nuclear membrane? Looking closely at each of the three general characteristics of organisms makes the first step in classifying organisms easier and faster. Which kingdoms are always consumers?

Lesson Summary

- Classification is the process of grouping organisms by similar characteristics.
- Moneran, protist, fungus, plant, and animal are the five kingdoms of organisms.

Lesson Review

1. What is classification?
2. Name the five kingdoms scientists use to classify organisms.
3. What three general characteristics do scientists look at to classify organisms into kingdoms?
4. What type of organism eats other organisms?
5. What type of organism contains chlorophyll?
★6. Would a very tiny animal, such as a flea, be a simple or complex organism? Explain your answer.

How can you use cells to classify organisms?

What you need

microscope
prepared slides A, B, C, D, E
reference books
pencil and paper

What to do

1. Focus the microscope on a cell on slide A. Compare the structures you see on the slide with the structures you see in picture A.
2. Draw one cell from slide A. Label the structures. Use reference books if needed.
3. Make a chart like the one shown to record the structures in each cell.

Observations of Cell Structures					
	A	B	C	D	E
nucleus					
cell membrane					
cell wall					
many-celled					

4. Repeat steps 1 and 2 using each pair of slides and pictures.
5. Identify the kingdom to which each cell belongs.

What did you learn?

1. Which cells did not have a nucleus?
2. Which cells have cell membranes? cell walls?

Using what you learned

1. Which cell was the simplest in structure? Why do you think so?
2. Which cells can make food? How do you know?

Scientific Naming

LESSON 3 GOALS
You will learn
● about a naming system used in classifying organisms.
● that each kind of organism has a scientific name.

Suppose as you're walking home on a crisp autumn day, you notice a tiny brown mouse in a nook on your front porch. It's so small that you suspect it may even be a baby mouse. It is half-hidden in some fallen oak leaves blown onto your porch. You move quietly toward the small mouse, so you can observe it. As you watch and listen you notice it's making noises you can barely hear. It reminds you of a pet hamster you once had. Yet there are some obvious differences between this small mouse and Mortimer, your pet hamster. As this wild mouse scurries away, you wonder what its name is. You learned in science class that all organisms are given a name—a scientific name. How do you find out more about this tiny brown mouse and its name?

There are some things you already know about the mouse that will help you learn its name. It obviously has many cells. You know it's a consumer because it feeds on other organisms. It's a member of the animal kingdom, but there are thousands of animals in this kingdom. How do you sort through all the animals in the kingdom to find out more about this one kind of mouse?

Scientists found that in studying so many organisms they needed to group organisms into smaller groups than kingdoms. Their classification system has a total of seven main groups. Why so many?

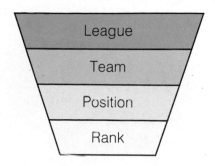

Your system for classifying your baseball cards would be organized in this way.

Let's think back to your baseball card sorting system. After you sorted your cards into National League and American League teams, would you want to sort them into smaller groups? How many smaller groups would you want to use in classifying the cards? You could sort the leagues into individual teams. Then you might want to sort players on each team into groups based on their playing positions— pitchers, infielders, or outfielders. You may even want to group your pitchers into starting pitchers or relief pitchers. In your classification you used four main groups—league, team, playing position, rank. Classifying your cards into these smaller groups will help you put them in order and make them easier to find. Using this system, you would have no trouble finding the card your friend Emilio wants—starting pitcher for the National League's 1989 New York Mets team, Dwight Gooden.

What is the plural of phylum? of genus?

The seven main groups in scientific classification help keep all Earth's organisms in order. Remember that the largest grouping of organisms is kingdom. Organisms in each kingdom are grouped into phyla. Each phylum is divided into classes, and each class is divided into orders. Organisms in each order are grouped into families. Families are divided into genuses. Each genus is divided into species. Because each species is a particular form of life, scientists won't divide a species into any more groups.

Organisms are classified in this system.

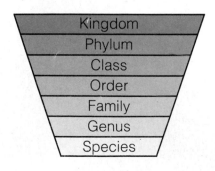

KINGDOM

Animalia – animals

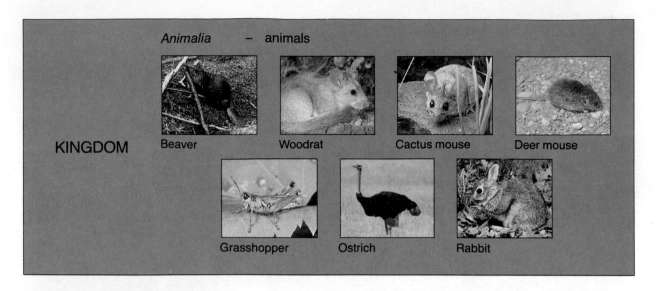

Beaver Woodrat Cactus mouse Deer mouse

Grasshopper Ostrich Rabbit

PHYLUM

Chordata – animals with backbones

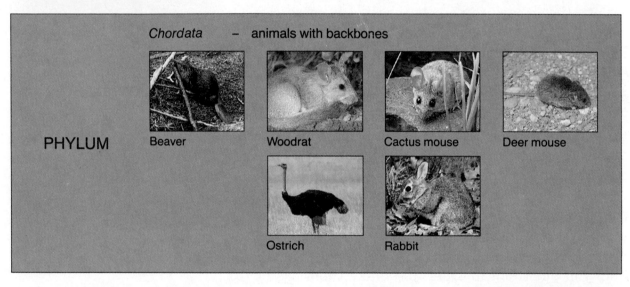

Beaver Woodrat Cactus mouse Deer mouse

Ostrich Rabbit

CLASS

Mammalia – animals that produce milk

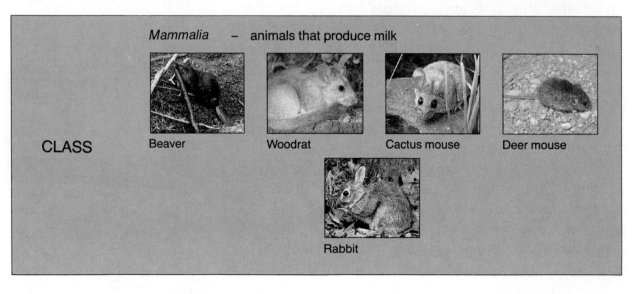

Beaver Woodrat Cactus mouse Deer mouse

Rabbit

Rodentia — animals that gnaw

Beaver   Woodrat   Cactus mouse   Deer mouse

ORDER

Cricetidae — small and medium-sized rodents

Woodrat   Cactus mouse   Deer mouse

FAMILY

Peromyscus — white-footed mice

Cactus mouse   Deer mouse

GENUS

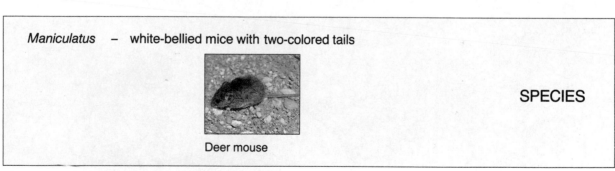

Maniculatus — white-bellied mice with two-colored tails

Deer mouse

SPECIES

Let's see what groups the brown mouse belongs to. Look at the chart on these two pages. It shows only a small sampling of the animals in each of the seven main groups in the classification system. The organisms at the top of the chart belong to the animal kingdom, along with the mouse. They all share very basic characteristics.

When the mouse is grouped into a phylum, one of its characteristics is looked at closely—in this case, whether it has a backbone or not. The organisms in the same phylum as the mouse all have backbones. They are in the phylum called *Chordata* (kor DAHD tuh). There are other phyla in the animal kingdom. Notice in the chart on page 306 that the grasshopper is not in the same phylum as the mouse. The grasshopper doesn't have a backbone.

Placing the mouse in the third grouping—a class—looks at yet another characteristic. The mouse is in the same class as other animals with backbones that produce milk—mammals. Notice in the chart that the ostrich isn't in the same class as the mouse. The ostrich is not a mammal.

Mammals can be grouped by looking at another characteristic. All mammals in the same order as the mouse gnaw their food. The mouse belongs to the order of gnawing mammals, *Rodentia* (roh DENCH uh). By looking at the pictures in the chart, you can tell that the animals in the same order have many more characteristics in common than the animals in the same class do. The primary characteristic that the animals in this class have in common is their gnawing.

What are the characteristics of animals in the order *Rodentia?*

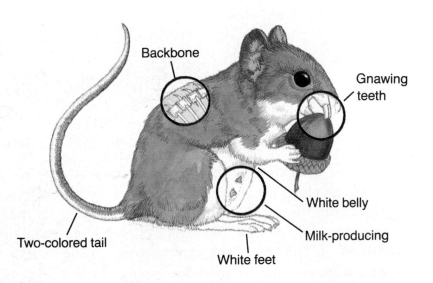

Backbone

Gnawing teeth

White belly

Two-colored tail

White feet

Milk-producing

Characteristics of a deer mouse

The next grouping of animals is the family. The mouse belongs to the *Cricetidae* (kruh SED uh dee) family. Animals in this group are small and medium-sized rodents. The next grouping places the mouse in the *Peromyscus* (per uh MISE kus) genus—white-footed mice. In this genus there are about 15 kinds of mouse. Each one is a different species of mouse. The mouse you found on your porch belongs to the *maniculatus* (muh nih kyew LAY tus) species, a kind of mouse with a white belly and a two-colored tail.

Scientists have given each particular organism a two-part name. This name is made up of its genus name and its species name. The mouse's scientific name is *Peromyscus maniculatus*. The name that people use in everyday speech for this kind of mouse is deer mouse. Deer mouse is the common name for your mouse. A scientist, however, would use the scientific name.

You notice that the genus comes first in the scientific name followed by the species. These names come from the Greek and Latin languages and are used by scientists all over the world. Can you tell why this system is helpful to all scientists?

Would You Believe?

It would take as many as 6,000 pages to print in an average-sized book all of the scientific names of known insects on Earth.

Buteo jamaicensis
Red-tailed hawk

Buteo brachyurus
Short-tailed hawk

Buteo lineatus
Red-shouldered hawk

The members of a particular species all have similar characteristics. But there may be variations in appearance within a species. You know that all dogs don't look alike. Some are large; some, small. There is a great variety of color in the coats of dogs. All deer mice look similar, but you probably couldn't find two that were exactly alike. Scientific naming is the way scientists point out the huge variety and uniqueness of all Earth's organisms.

Lesson Summary

- A classification system for organisms is used by people all over the world. The divisions in the system are kingdom, phylum, class, order, family, genus, and species.
- Each organism has a scientific name made up of its genus and species.

Lesson Review

1. Why do scientists need a naming system to classify organisms?
2. Name the divisions of the scientific classification system.
3. House cats belong to the order *Carnivora,* the family *Felidae,* the genus *Felis,* and the species *domesticus.* What is the scientific name for a house cat?
★4. Would a Siamese cat and a Persian cat have the same scientific name? Explain your answer.

Use Application Activity on pages 511, 512.

How are characteristics used in classification?

What you need

box of items
pencil and paper

What to do

1. Make a chart like the one shown.
2. Empty the contents of the box onto your desk.
3. Observe the objects. Pretend that they all belong to the same kingdom of objects. Think of at least one characteristic that they all have in common.
4. Give the kingdom a name based on the common characteristic. Write this name in your chart.
5. Divide the kingdom into 2 phyla based on differences among the objects. Name each phylum. Write the names in your chart.

6. Divide the objects in one phylum into 2 classes. Name each class. Write the names in your chart. List the objects in each class.
7. Repeat step 6 with the objects in your other phylum.

What did you learn?

1. What characteristics did you use to classify the objects into two phyla?
2. What characteristics did you use to classify the objects of the first phylum into two classes? the other phylum into two classes?

Using what you learned

1. At what level of classification did the objects included have the most characteristics in common?
2. At what level did the objects included have the fewest characteristics in common?

Classification of Objects				
Kingdom				
Phylum				
Class				

Viruses

LESSON 4 GOALS
You will learn
● that viruses are different from living things.
● how organisms produce antibodies that fight diseases caused by viruses.

Amy feels miserable. She has a headache, a stuffy nose, and a sore throat. In fact, she aches all over. She stayed home today because her mother says she has a virus. Shawn has a wart on his finger. He has been putting medicine on it, and it's beginning to go away. The wart was also caused by a virus. What are viruses, and how do they cause these changes in our bodies?

Scientists don't classify viruses as organisms because they don't have all the features of life. A **virus** has characteristics of both living and nonliving things. Viruses are made of some of the same substances found in living things. However, viruses are not made of cells. A virus can reproduce, but only if it's inside a living cell. A virus needs energy, which must be obtained from a cell. When a virus isn't inside a living cell, it can't carry on any life processes.

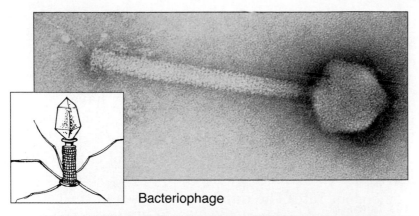

Bacteriophage

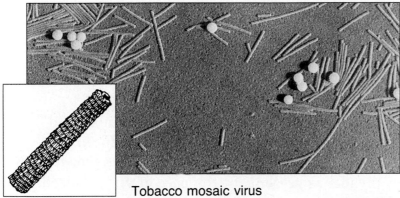

Tobacco mosaic virus

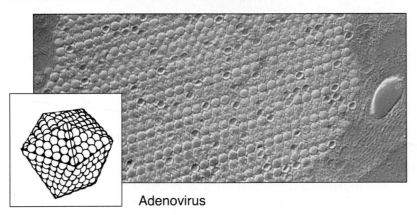

Adenovirus

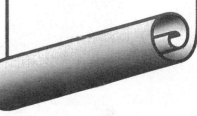
Viruses are extremely small. Scientists weren't able to see them until a powerful type of microscope called the electron microscope was invented. Remember that a moneran is the smallest living thing. Compare its size to that of a virus. Viruses have very odd shapes when compared with shapes of cells. They may be rod-shaped, round, or have many sides. Some viruses also have spikes or tails. Scientists identify viruses by these shapes and sizes.

313

How might viruses enter your body?

Now let's find out how a virus caused Amy to be sick. Perhaps she was standing near a friend who coughed or sneezed without covering her nose and mouth. Thousands of viruses from Amy's friend's body were thrown into the air. Amy may have breathed in some of the viruses or rubbed some into her eyes, mouth, or nose. Once inside her body, the viruses entered her cells and took control of the cells' activities. The viruses then began to reproduce at a tremendous rate. The number of viruses in the cell soon became so great the cell burst. The viruses were then free to enter other cells. Each cell entered by a virus was no longer able to carry out its function. These cells were finally destroyed. What can be done to stop all the cells in Amy's body from being destroyed by the virus?

When a virus enters the body of a human and most other animals, antibodies are produced. An **antibody** is a substance produced in the blood when an invader is present. In the case of virus-caused

ACTIVITY You Can...

Show How Viruses Are Spread

One way that viruses are spread is through air and water. Put a mirror near your mouth. Breathe through your mouth onto the mirror. Breathe through your nose onto the mirror. (This works best if the mirror is cool.) What do you see? Viruses are often present in this water vapor. Why do you think it's important to cover your mouth and nose when you cough or sneeze? Why do you think people may be advised to stay home when they have a cold or the flu?

314

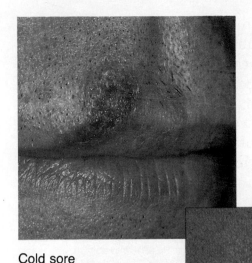

Cold sore

Chicken pox

diseases, the invader in the blood is a virus. Amy's body makes an antibody to fight the virus. As the antibodies destroy the viruses, Amy begins to feel better and eventually gets well. The antibodies produced by the cells in Amy's body stay in her blood even after she is no longer sick. They keep her from getting that particular virus again.

Perhaps you've been sick with chicken pox, a disease caused by a virus. When you got chicken pox, your body began making antibodies to destroy the viruses. As the viruses were destroyed by the antibodies, you began to get well. You will never get chicken pox again because you now have the antibodies for that disease in your blood.

Some of the same viruses that cause diseases in people make animals ill. For example, the virus that gives humans mumps makes cats, mice, and cows ill with leukemia.

People don't always have to have a disease for their bodies to create antibodies. Vaccines can be used to prevent diseases. Do you remember receiving a polio vaccine? A **vaccine** (vak SEEN) is a dead or weak virus used to help the body fight a certain disease. When a polio vaccine was put into your body, you didn't get polio. Your body made antibodies that destroyed the virus quickly. You now have polio antibodies in your blood and will never get polio.

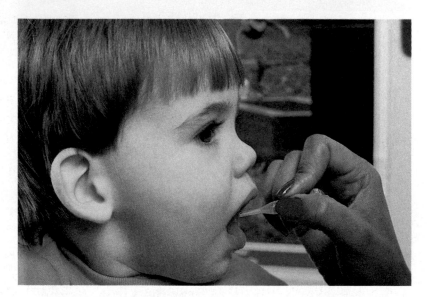

Lesson Summary

- Viruses have characteristics of both living and nonliving matter. They can't carry on life processes unless they are inside living cells.
- Some organisms produce antibodies that destroy the viruses that cause diseases.

Lesson Review

1. Why aren't viruses classified as organisms?
2. How do viruses compare in size to monerans?
3. How does a vaccine aid in keeping you healthy?
★4. Recall the example at the beginning of the lesson. How do you think the medicine works on the wart on Shawn's finger?

CHAPTER REVIEW
12

Summary

Lesson 1
- All organisms reproduce, grow, develop, use energy, need food, and are made of cells.
- The nucleus of a cell controls cell activities. A cell membrane holds the cell together and controls what passes into and out of it. A cell wall provides support for a plant cell.

Lesson 2
- Classification is the process of grouping organisms by similar characteristics.
- Moneran, protist, fungus, plant, and animal are the five kingdoms of organisms.

Lesson 3
- A classification system for organisms is used by people all over the world. The divisions in the system are kingdom, phylum, class, order, family, genus, and species.
- Each organism has a scientific name made up of its genus and species.

Lesson 4
- Viruses have characteristics of both living and nonliving matter. They can't carry on life processes unless they are inside living cells.
- Some organisms produce antibodies that destroy the viruses that cause disease.

Science Words

Fill in the blank with the correct word or words from the list.

organism
cell
nucleus
cell membrane
cell wall
producer
consumer
cyanobacteria

moneran
protist
fungus
virus
antibody
vaccine
diatoms

1. Anything that shows all the features of life is a(n) ____.
2. The basic unit of all living things is a(n) ____.
3. A one-celled organism with a nucleus is a(n) ____.
4. Dead or weak viruses that cause a certain disease are made into a(n) ____.

5. Matter that has characteristics of both living things and nonliving things is a(n) ____.
6. A stiff structure that provides protection and support for plant cells is the ____.
7. A consumer with cell walls and a nucleus is a(n) ____.

8. The flexible structure that holds the contents of a cell together is the ____.
9. A chemical produced in the blood when foreign matter is present is a(n) ____.
10. An organism that eats other organisms is a(n) ____.

Questions

Recalling Ideas

Correctly complete each of the following sentences.

1. All living things reproduce, grow, develop, use energy, are made of cells, and

   (a) make noise. (c) eat plants.
   (b) need food.   (d) make food.
2. The human body fights viral diseases by producing
   (a) monerans.
   (b) antiseptics.
   (c) vaccines.
   (d) antibodies.
3. Anything that shows all the features of life is a(n)
   (a) organism.
   (b) virus.
   (c) antibody.
   (d) animal.
4. A virus has the characteristics of
   (a) living matter.
   (b) nonliving matter.
   (c) both a and b.
   (d) an organism.
5. The last word in a scientific name is the
   (a) genus.   (c) species.
   (b) family.   (d) phylum.
6. Organisms that have cells that do not have a nucleus are
   (a) plants.   (c) fungi.
   (b) monerans.   (d) viruses.

318

7. The kingdom in which most of the organisms contain chlorophyll is
   (a) plant. (c) animal.
   (b) protist. (d) fungus.

Examining Ideas

Determine whether each of the following statements is true or false. Rewrite the false statements to make them correct.

1. Consumers use chlorophyll to capture the sun's energy and produce food.
2. One-celled organisms have nothing in common with many-celled organisms.
3. All living things can be grouped into five families.
4. Reproduction, growth, development, and energy use are all controlled by each cell's nucleus.
5. A structure that provides protection and support for a plant cell is a cell membrane.
6. Scientists classify organisms by grouping those that share places to live.
7. Vaccines cause the body to make antibodies that destroy viruses.
8. Animals use the sun's energy directly to make their own food.

Understanding Ideas

Answer the following questions using complete sentences.

1. Compare the organisms in the five kingdoms on the basis of cell structure and properties of the organisms.
2. Which have the most characteristics in common: animals in the same family or animals in the same class? Explain your answer.
3. Compare the characteristics of viruses with those of living things.
4. Explain why scientists use a classification system. What two important jobs are done by the modern classification system?
5. The scientific name for humans is *Homo sapiens,* therefore, you belong to the genus *Homo.* What species are you?

Thinking Critically

Think about what you have learned in this chapter. Answer the following questions using complete sentences.

1. Compare atoms and cells.
2. Defend the statement: All plants and animals get their energy from the sun.
3. Plants and animals are said to be the most complex organisms. Tell why you agree or disagree. Discuss cell structures and the six features of life in your statement.
4. You have just gotten the measles. Explain how your body is fighting this disease. How could this disease have been prevented?
5. How many species of organisms have the scientific name *Homo sapien?* Explain.

Simple Organisms

Do you have a pair of athletic shoes? Do you often wear the shoes without socks? What do you notice about the shoes after they have been worn over a long period of time?

Excessive sweat from your feet washes away the protective coating on the inside of the shoes, and bacteria begin to grow.

It's necessary to keep harmful bacteria under control. Some bacteria can cause illness and even death. Other bacteria are helpful and provide us with products such as cheese, yogurt, and penicillin.

ACTIVITY

Have You Ever...

Seen a Cell?

Use a flat-sided toothpick and scrape the inside of your cheek. Place the scrapings in a couple of drops of iodine solution on a slide. Examine the slide under a microscope. What do you see? Do you think that all cells in your body are the same?

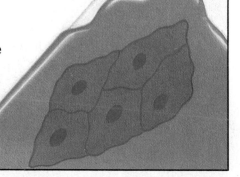

Monerans

Take a look at the clothes you are wearing. The next time you eat, look closely at your food. As you walk outside today, look carefully at soil and water. All of the things you see around you and on you have something in common. They are homes for simple organisms. These organisms live everywhere in your environment, and they play a very important part in your world.

Monerans are the simplest organisms and can't be seen by the naked eye. They're so very small that 300 of them could fit side by side across the period at the end of this sentence. They are one-celled organisms. They don't have a nucleus, but they do have nuclear material. They live on your body, in your body, in your clothes, in your food, and all around you. Most monerans are helpful. They may be a food source for other organisms, or they may help break down dead organisms. Some monerans cause disease.

All the things around you are homes for simple organisms.

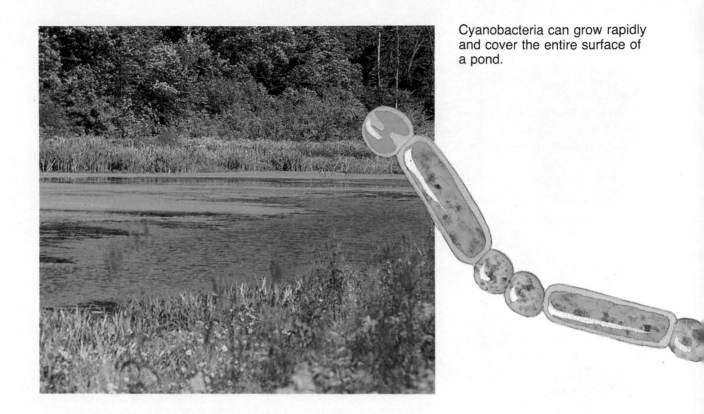

Cyanobacteria can grow rapidly and cover the entire surface of a pond.

Cyanobacteria

One kind of moneran is **cyanobacteria**. They live in water or other places where there is moisture. Cyanobacteria contain the green pigment chlorophyll. Chlorophyll allows the cyanobacteria to carry on photosynthesis, which is a process that allows them to produce their own food. These monerans serve as food for water animals. Because many of them are bluish green in color, they are often called blue-green bacteria. But not all cyanobacteria are blue-green. Others appear red, black, brown, or purple.

Have you ever seen a slimy green mass on the surface of a lake, pond, or swimming pool? This green mass may be made up of thousands of cyanobacteria. This growth may be a sign that the water is polluted. Many cyanobacteria produce a bad smell. The smell is a clue that the water isn't suitable for drinking or swimming. Cyanobacteria grow very well in many polluted lakes and ponds because they use the pollutants as food.

Where can cyanobacteria be found?

Bacteria

Another kind of moneran is **bacteria**. You may not have realized it, but you have probably eaten food that is produced with the help of bacteria. Have you eaten cheese or yogurt lately? Bacteria are very important in our environment. Some bacteria change the nitrogen in the air into a form that plants can use. Other bacteria break down dead organisms, which other living things can then use for food. They help produce not only cheese and yogurt but also butter, vinegar, and sauerkraut. Bacteria help in the processes used to make linen, rope, and leather.

Unlike cyanobacteria, which live mainly in moist places, bacteria can live in many different places. Some bacteria can live even where there is no oxygen or where temperatures are extremely hot or cold.

Some bacteria live inside the bodies of other organisms. They can be found in the digestive systems of some plant-eating animals, such as cows and goats. They help break down plant cell walls,

Would You Believe?

Some bacteria can live in water with temperatures close to 80°C and a pH of 2!

releasing the nutrients to the animals' systems. Did you know that you have bacteria that live in your intestines? In humans these bacteria make vitamins and produce materials that may kill harmful bacteria.

Many kinds of bacteria are harmful. For example, one type you may have heard of, *Salmonella* (sal muh NEL uh), is a cause of food poisoning. Harmful bacteria are often called "germs." Germs can cause illnesses such as ear infections and pneumonia (noo MOH nyuh).

Harmful bacteria spread among groups of people, causing diseases. A **communicable** (kuh MYEW nih kuh bul) **disease** is one that can be passed from one organism to another. Some diseases are spread by air when a person sneezes or coughs. Touching anything an infected person has touched can also spread the disease. Many diseases caused by bacteria are communicable. Have you ever had strep throat? It is a communicable disease that causes a sore throat and often a fever and a headache. Another communicable disease is tuberculosis, which results in a bad cough and breathing problems. Can you think of any other communicable diseases?

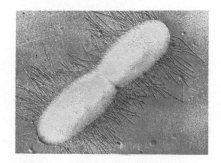

These bacteria live in human intestines and help with digestion.

What is a communicable disease?

Bacteria may spread among groups of people and cause diseases.

Controlling Growth of Bacteria

When you buy meat at a grocery store and you don't plan to cook it within a day or two, you should freeze it. Do you know why? Bacteria can cause food to spoil, and freezing the meat can help to prevent spoiling. The appearance and smell of food can sometimes help you to know if it is spoiled. Look at the picture of raw hamburger. Which package of hamburger would you choose to cook?

Although bacteria can grow in many places, each kind of bacteria has certain temperature and moisture levels and particular sources of food in which it grows best. Very high temperatures kill most bacteria. You may have seen someone put baby bottles or canning jars into boiling water. This is done to kill harmful bacteria. Another example of killing bacteria with high temperatures is when milk is pasteurized. **Pasteurization** (pas chuh ruh ZAY shun) is the process of heating and then quickly cooling milk to kill disease-causing bacteria. However, because the milk is not boiled, other bacteria do survive. That's why milk will eventually spoil, even if it's kept cold and sealed in a carton.

Why doesn't pasteurization kill all bacteria?

Another way of controlling the growth of bacteria is to lower the temperature of food. At five degrees Celsius or below, the growth of bacteria is slowed. Freezing will kill many bacteria, however, some are adapted to low temperatures. When you take food out of the freezer to thaw, the surviving bacteria will begin to grow.

Because bacteria need water to grow, removing moisture from food may slow their growth. For example, bacteria will not grow in dried fruit or dry cereals even if the lid is left off the container. The process of removing water from food is called **dehydration** (dee hi DRAY shun). Can you think of other foods that are often dehydrated in order to keep them from spoiling?

Another way to control bacteria is to use disinfectants. **Disinfectants,** such as rubbing alcohol and chlorine bleach, are chemicals that can kill bacteria. Many disinfectants are used in places such as hospitals and homes. Do you remember ever falling off your bike and cutting yourself? Someone probably used an antiseptic on your cut to kill the germs and to keep the cut from becoming infected. An **antiseptic** is a type of disinfectant used on living things to kill bacteria.

Why does dehydration slow bacterial growth?

Cyanobacteria and bacteria play an important role in your life and in the environment. One important part of knowing about monerans is knowing how they help us. Another part is knowing how to control their growth. Every day you use this knowledge to help prevent diseases and infections.

The small green cells are bacteria.

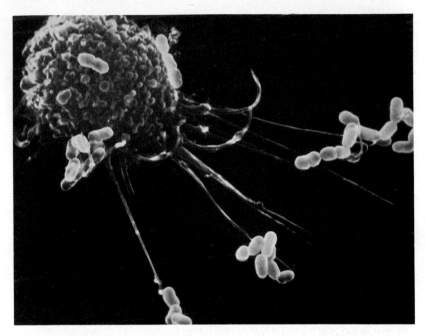

Lesson Summary

- Cyanobacteria are producers that live in water environments.
- Bacteria help produce food and other products. They can also cause disease.
- There are many ways of controlling the growth of bacteria.

Lesson Review

1. Why do cyanobacteria grow well in polluted lakes?
2. How do bacteria help people?
3. Why do communicable diseases spread so easily?
4. Why is it important for hospitals to use disinfectants to control the growth of bacteria?
★5. Explain why dehydration slows the growth of bacteria.

328

How can the growth of bacteria be controlled?

What you need

3 agar dishes with lids
masking tape
2 cotton swabs
tweezers or forceps
2 paper circles
antiseptic
hand lens

What to do

1. Label one agar dish A. Tape the dish shut.
2. Label another agar dish B and a third dish C.
3. Choose a place where you expect to find bacteria growing. Rub a swab across the surface several times. Lift the lid of dish B slightly. Rub the swab lightly over the entire agar surface in a zigzag pattern. Replace the lid. Tape the dish shut.
4. Soak a paper circle in antiseptic. Using tweezers, place the circle in the center of dish B. Lightly press it to the agar.
5. Choose a different source of bacteria. Repeat steps 3 and 4 with dish C.
6. Place all three dishes in a warm, dark place for five days.
7. After five days, use a hand lens to observe the dishes. **CAUTION:** *Do NOT open the dishes.*

What did you learn?

1. Describe the growth in each dish.
2. Which source supplied the most bacteria?
3. Which source of bacteria was most affected by the antiseptic?

Using what you learned

1. How can the growth of bacteria in your classroom be controlled?
2. How can the growth of bacteria on the body be controlled?

Protists

LESSON 2 GOALS
You will learn
● that various protists have different characteristics.
● how protozoans use certain structures to move.
● what part protists play in our environment.

Have you ever looked at a drop of lake water under a microscope? If you have, you probably saw many tiny organisms. Many of these organisms were protists, another kind of simple organism. Unlike the moneran, which you have already learned about, the protist is more complex. It has a nucleus, the control center for the cell's important activities. Protists can be plantlike or animal-like. Algae (AL jee) are examples of plantlike protists. Protozoans (proht uh ZOH unz) are examples of animal-like protists.

Algae

What are plantlike protists called?

Plantlike protists, also called **algae**, are producers and are important because they produce large amounts of oxygen for the air we breathe. Algae are also a source of food for most marine life. For example, the largest animal on Earth, the blue whale, has a diet that is made up only of algae.

Some algae are one-celled protists. Each has a nucleus, cell wall, and chlorophyll. Some algae live in fresh water, while others are adapted to ocean water. Algae are grouped by color, type of cell wall, and method of movement.

Some algae are one-celled protists that produce oxygen and food.

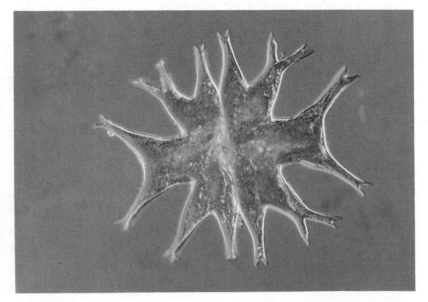

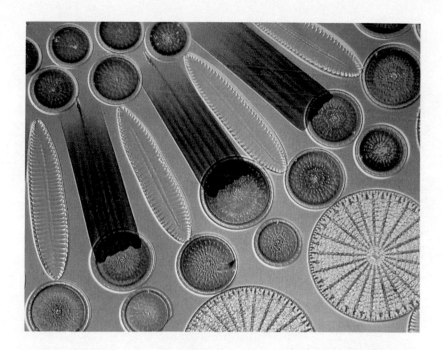

You may have cleaned out the kitchen sink or shined up your muddy bike using scouring powder. Did you know that your scouring powder was made from algae? Diatoms (DI uh tahmz) are algae found in fresh water and in the ocean. Diatoms are called "golden algae" because of the yellow pigment in the cells. They are covered with a fine shell. This shell has two parts. One part fits over the other part like a pillbox or a petri dish. Each shell has a very intricate design. When diatom cells die, their shells settle on the bottom of the ocean. These shell deposits are mined and are used to make products such as toothpaste, scouring powder, and cosmetics.

A type of algae that lives mostly in the ocean is a dinoflagellate (di noh FLAJ uh lut). A dinoflagellate has two flagella. **Flagella** (fluh JEL uh) are long, whiplike structures used for movement. The beating of these flagella cause the dinoflagellate to swim in a spinning motion. Some dinoflagellates have a red pigment that can give water a red color when there are a lot of them. A "red tide" is the rapid growth of dinoflagellates in the ocean. This growth can be harmful to ocean life. Poisons produced by a red tide can kill fish and other ocean animals.

SCIENCE AND . . .
Reading

If the prefix *mono-* means "1" and the prefix *di-* means "2," a diatom must have how many parts?
A. one
B. one and a half
C. two
D. two and a half

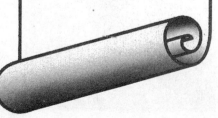

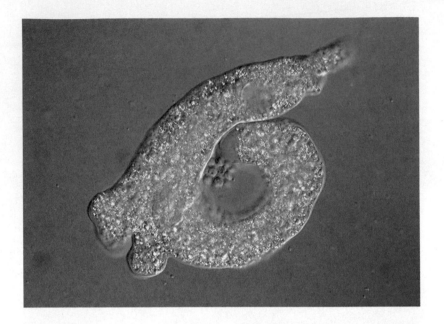

Pseudopodia make it possible for an amoeba to move and feed.

Protozoans

A **protozoan** is a one-celled, animal-like protist. Unlike algal protists, which produce their own food, protozoans are consumers. These protists live in water, soil, and on decaying matter. Some protozoans live as parasites within other organisms. Protozoans are grouped according to how they move.

One kind of protozoan moves by means of **pseudopodia** (sewd uh POHD ee uh). A pseudopodium is a fingerlike extension that lets the cell move and feed. An amoeba (uh MEE buh) belongs in this group.

A paramecium (per uh MEE see um) is one of a group of protozoans that move with their **cilia** (SIHL ee uh). Cilia are tiny hairlike structures that enable the paramecium to move and "sweep" food to its "mouth."

Other types of protozoans move by flagella, while still others don't move at all.

Just as there are helpful and harmful bacteria, there are helpful and harmful protozoans. Some protozoans live in the digestive systems of other living things, such as termites, to help them digest the food they eat. Others are a source of food for larger organisms. Skeletons of some protozoans form

What is a protozoan?

Cilia help the paramecium move and "sweep" food to its "mouth."

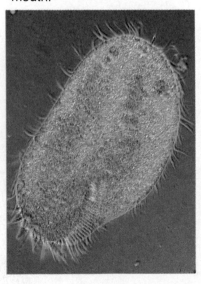

Skeletons of protozoans have formed much of the White Cliffs of Dover, England.

much of the limestone and chalk on Earth. The deposits are used to make cleaning products.

Although most of these simple organisms are so small they can be seen only with the aid of a microscope, they provide food and give us essential materials to make products that we use every day. Some protists, though, are harmful. For example, a protozoan in certain mosquitoes causes the disease called malaria.

Lesson Summary

- Protists can be plantlike—algae—or animal-like—protozoans.
- Protozoans are classified by how they move.
- Protists can be helpful or harmful in our environment.

Lesson Review

1. What is the main difference between algae and protozoans?
2. What are three ways that protozoans move?
3. Of what benefit are algae and protozoans?
★4. How are protists more complex organisms than monerans?

333

Fungi

LESSON 3 GOALS
You will learn
● about several kinds of fungi.
● how fungi help and hinder our environment.

Have you ever enjoyed a mushroom pizza? Do you like salad with Roquefort or blue cheese dressing? Do you get excited when you walk into a bakery and get a whiff of freshly baked bread? Or have you ever been aided in a quick recovery from an illness by penicillin? If you can answer yes to any of these questions, you know another kind of simple organism—fungi. Without fungi, none of these experiences would be possible.

Fungi, the plural word for fungus, are consumers that have no chlorophyll to enable them to photosynthesize. Fungi are classified in a separate kingdom from plants because they have no roots, they can't make their own food, and they aren't made up of tissues. Fungi live off living and once-living organisms. You may be familiar with different types of fungi such as molds, yeasts, and mushrooms. Fungi range in size from one-celled yeasts to large mushrooms.

Examples of fungi

ACTIVITY

You Can...

Find the Fungus "Amongus"

Look around the school grounds, a park, or a yard to find various kinds of fungi. Record where you find the fungi. Make drawings or take photographs of them. Obtain a field guide from the library to help you classify the fungi into groups. Observe the fungi again after one week. Record any changes you observe. What kinds of fungi did you find? Where does fungi seem to grow best? What caused any changes you observed? CAUTION: Never eat wild mushrooms or other wild fungi.

Like bacteria, fungi can be helpful or harmful organisms. Some fungi help clean up the environment by breaking down dead plant and animal matter. Fungi are also helpful in the food industry. Certain types of mushrooms are used as food for people. Mold is vital to the aging process of some cheeses to give them flavor. And another kind of fungus, yeast, is a key ingredient used to make bread.

If you become ill, fungi may help to make you healthy again. Some molds, such as *Penicillium,* are used to make particular kinds of medicine to kill bacteria that cause infection. What common medicine is made from Penicillium?

Fungi can also cause problems for people and the environment. If you have ever suffered from the itching and pain of athlete's foot or ringworm, you know the harm that fungi can do to human skin.

The mold *Penicillium* is a fungus used to make medicine.

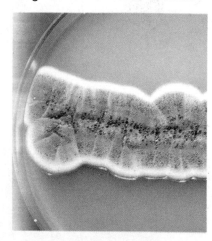

Many people with allergies are particularly sensitive to molds and yeasts. Certain fungi that live on crops, trees, plants, and animals cause destruction and even death.

Many foods can be affected by fungi. Fruit that is stored in a humid place is often spoiled by fungi. And have you ever been all set to make a sandwich for lunch only to find mold on the bread?

Lesson Summary

- Molds, yeasts, and mushrooms are kinds of fungi.
- Fungi help clean up the environment and help make food and medicine. Many plants and animals get diseases caused by fungi.

Lesson Review

1. Give an example of how each type of fungus is used in the food industry.
2. What is a common medicine that is made from fungi?
3. Name two conditions that humans suffer from because of fungi.
★ 4. Explain how some kinds of fungi serve as natural "recyclers."

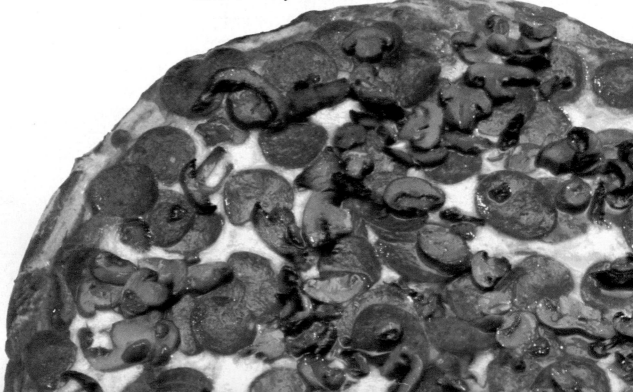

What are the growth needs of fungi?

ACTIVITY

What you need

4 plastic cups
masking tape
1 slice fresh bread
moldy bread
4 cotton swabs
4 squares of
   plastic wrap

4 rubber bands
dropper
distilled water
hand lens
pencil and
   paper

What to do

1. Label the cups A, B, C, and D.
2. Divide the fresh bread into four pieces. Put one piece in each cup.
3. Lightly brush a swab over the surface of the molded bread. Lightly rub this swab across the bread in cup A.
4. Repeat step 3 for cups B, C, and D. Use a new swab each time.
5. Use the dropper. Wet the bread in cups B and D with distilled water.
6. Cover each cup with plastic wrap. Secure it with a rubber band.
7. Place cups A and B in a brightly lit place. Place cups C and D in a dark closet.
8. Observe the bread each day for five days without removing the plastic wrap. Record your observations.

What did you learn?

1. In which cup did you observe the most mold growth?
2. What are the best growing conditions for mold?

Using what you learned

1. How should bread be stored to prevent the growth of mold?
2. What other variables might affect the growth of mold?

I WANT TO KNOW ABOUT...

"Flashlight" Fish

Do you know that some bacteria live deep beneath the ocean? They provide food and light for some of nature's most unusual creatures. Scientists have observed huge tubeworms up to 3.5 meters long living near volcanic vents in the ocean floor.

These tubeworms have a special relationship with bacteria. The bacteria live within the cells of the tubeworms. The bacteria get nutrients from the chemicals produced during underwater volcanic eruptions. These chemicals are the "food" that the tubeworms need to grow.

Bacteria can also be found in patches on the bodies of some fish. The bacteria obtain food from the water. As the bacteria break down their food, they begin to glow due to chemical reactions that take place. The glowing patches on the skin of the fish act like headlights, lighting the area around the fish. This glow allows the fish to locate food and attract others of their kind.

Predators may be attracted to brightly lighted fish. To escape predators, some fish can cut off the flow of blood to the bacteria. Without blood, it's impossible for the chemical reactions that produce the glow to occur. In other fish a flap of skin covers the bacteria until the danger has passed.

As deep sea exploration continues, scientists hope to find more animals that have developed ways of using bacteria for food or light.

Science and Technology

Summary

Lesson 1
- Cyanobacteria are producers that live in water environments.
- Bacteria help produce food and other products. They can also cause disease.
- There are many ways of controlling the growth of bacteria.

Lesson 2
- Protists can be plantlike—algae— or animal-like—protozoans.

- Protozoans are classified according to how they move.
- Protists can be helpful or harmful in our environment.

Lesson 3
- Molds, yeasts, and mushrooms are kinds of fungi.
- Fungi help clean up the environment and help make food and medicine. Many plants and animals get diseases caused by fungi.

Science Words

Fill in the blank with the correct word or words from the list.

monerans	fungi	antiseptic	communicable
bacteria	pasteurization	flagella	disease
algae	dehydration	pseudopodia	cyanobacteria
protozoan	disinfectant	cilia	

1. A chemical that kills many simple organisms is a(n) ____.
2. The process of heating and quickly cooling milk to kill disease-causing bacteria is ____.
3. The removal of water from a material is ____.
4. Fingerlike extensions of a cell that are used by an amoeba for movement and feeding are ____.

5. The long whiplike structures used by protozoans for movement are ____.
6. A disinfectant that is used on living things is a(n) ____.
7. A disease that can be passed from one organism to another is a(n) ____.
8. Small hairlike structures used by a paramecium for movement and feeding are ____.

Questions

Recalling Ideas

Correctly complete each of the following sentences.

1. Simple organisms provide food sources, make food, recycle matter, and
   (a) have special organs.
   (b) can cause disease.
   (c) do not reproduce.
   (d) all live in water.
2. Cyanobacteria are monerans that contain
   (a) a nucleus.
   (b) a flagellum.
   (c) chlorophyll.
   (d) pseudopodia.
3. Two methods used to control the growth of bacteria are dehydration and
   (a) reproduction.
   (b) pasteurization.
   (c) fertilization.
   (d) respiration.
4. Two types of algal protists are diatoms and
   (a) dinoflagellates.
   (b) amoebas.
   (c) fungi.
   (d) bacteria.
5. There are many kinds of fungi, such as mushrooms, mold, mildew, and
   (a) cyanobacteria.
   (b) amoebas.
   (c) protozoans.
   (d) yeast.
6. Some medicines are made from a genus of fungus called
   (a) *Escherichia.* (c) *Viola.*
   (b) *Penicillium.* (d) *Quercus.*
7. Because they contain chlorophyll, cyanobacteria are considered
   (a) parasites. (c) consumers.
   (b) edible. (d) producers.
8. The structures that a paramecium uses to move are
   (a) cilia. (c) flagella.
   (b) feet. (d) pseudopodia.
9. Mushrooms are
   (a) monerans. (c) flagellates.
   (b) fungi. (d) germs.
10. Algae are
    (a) protozoans. (c) monerans.
    (b) molds. (d) protists.

Examining Ideas

Determine whether each of the following statements is true or false. Rewrite the false statements to make them correct.

1. All cyanobacteria are harmful.
2. One-celled, animal-like protists are dinoflagellates.
3. Fungi are important because they produce large amounts of the oxygen that we breathe.
4. Bacteria can live only where there are mild temperatures and plenty of water.
5. Scarlet fever is caused by a fungus.
6. A red tide made up of dinoflagellates can be harmful.

7. Athlete's foot and ringworm are caused by fungi.
8. Masses of cyanobacteria in a pond or lake may be a sign that the water is polluted.
9. All protozoans are producers.
10. Bacteria in the digestive system of an animal will cause it to get sick.
11. Fungi are important producers because they have no chlorophyll.
12. Monerans have no nuclear material.

Understanding Ideas

Answer the following questions using complete sentences.

1. Identify two monerans and tell why each is important to the environment.
2. Identify one use of algal protists.
3. Compare and contrast algal protists and protozoans.
4. Describe the structures used for movement in algal protists and protozoans.
5. Explain several ways in which fungi are helpful and harmful to humans.
6. Distinguish between a disinfectant and an antiseptic.
7. Compare how algae and paramecia get their food.

Thinking Critically

Think about what you have learned in this chapter. Answer the following questions using complete sentences.

1. Why should foods made with meat, mayonnaise, eggs, or milk be kept in a cooler at a picnic?
2. Suppose a scientist has developed a product that will kill all fungi. The scientist is excited because food will be prevented from spoiling, and certain diseases will be eliminated. Do you share this scientist's excitement? Explain why or why not.
3. When milk is pasteurized, it is heated and then cooled quickly several times. Why do you think it is important to cool the milk quickly?

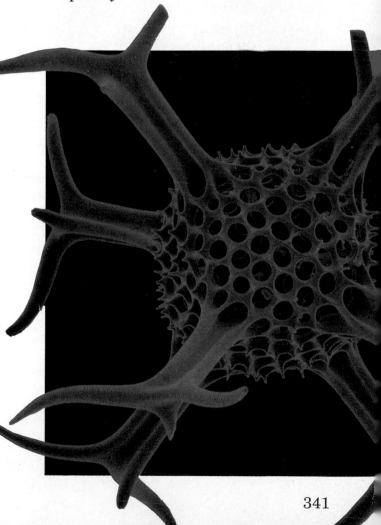

Growth and Reproduction

You probably eat a number of delicious foods for breakfast. Do you ever have eggs? An egg, if fertilized, will develop into an embryo. Although the embryo develops in the egg outside the mother, it needs nutrition, protection, and time to grow, just as a human embryo does.

The chicken, like most animals, is the product of the union of two parents. Some simple organisms can reproduce by a single parent.

Have You Ever...

Examined an Egg?

Gently crack open an egg. Place the contents in a dish. What does the yolk look like? Observe the shell. Break off a piece and pull inward to see the inner and outer shell membrane. Look for the chalazas, the small ropelike structures that anchor the yolk. Find the germ spot, an area lighter in color about the size of a pinhead on the upper surface. What do you think an embryo feeds upon while it is in the egg?

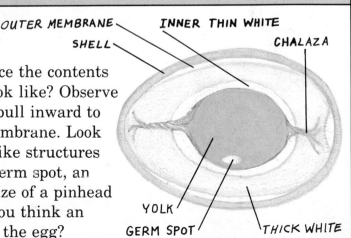

OUTER MEMBRANE

INNER THIN WHITE

SHELL

CHALAZA

YOLK

GERM SPOT

THICK WHITE

Cells and Organisms

LESSON 1 GOALS
You will learn
- the parts of a cell.
- how organisms grow.
- the stages of mitosis.

If someone asked you what a rose and a frog had in common, what would you say? Your first response might be "nothing." After all, they don't look or sound alike. A rose doesn't make any noise you can hear, while a frog can be quite vocal, given the right conditions. Roses and frogs don't smell the same either. Roses smell sweet, and frogs—well, frogs don't. As for taste, even though neither one is a popular menu item, you know they don't taste the same. A rose and a frog are different in many ways. However, that's not all there is to it. A frog and a rose are alike in an important way. They are both organisms. In other words they are both complete living things.

There are thousands of different kinds of organisms. Roses, frogs, mushrooms, amoebas, and bacteria are organisms. Each belongs to a different kingdom, but all organisms have a similar basic structure. And that brings us to another similarity between a frog and a rose. Like all organisms, both are composed of cells. An organism may be just a single cell such as an amoeba, a group of similar cells such as a mushroom, or a complex system of different kinds of cells such as a rose or a frog.

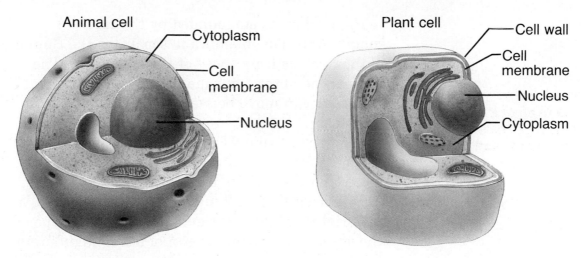

Animal cell

Cytoplasm

Cell membrane

Nucleus

Plant cell

Cell wall

Cell membrane

Nucleus

Cytoplasm

Plant and animal cells are similar, but they do have some differences.

Groups of similar cells make up the tissues of complex organisms. The muscles and skin of a frog or any other animal are made up of tissues. Organs are composed of different tissues. The heart and brain of a frog or any other animal are organs. The leaf of a rose or any other plant is also an organ made up of several different tissues. And the tissues of a leaf are made up of groups of certain types of cells. Each cell, tissue, or organ helps the organism survive.

Parts of a Cell

Every organism begins life as a single cell. An amoeba is a one-celled organism throughout its life — time. Complex many-celled organisms such as frogs, humans, or roses also begin life as one cell. All the complex tissues and organs of plants and animals develop from one cell.

All cells—both plant and animal—have similar parts. Look at the animal cell in the picture on this page. Like most cells, it has a dense, rounded nucleus. The jellylike liquid part of the cell that is outside the nucleus is called **cytoplasm** (SITE uh plaz um). You will recall that the entire cell is surrounded by a covering called the cell membrane. This membrane holds the parts of the cell together and regulates the movement of materials into and out of the cell.

The nucleus is surrounded by the **nuclear membrane**. This membrane separates the contents of the nucleus from those of the cytoplasm. The nuclear membrane has many tiny pores, so some materials can move between the nucleus and the cytoplasm.

The nucleus controls the activities of the cell by sending out chemical messages to the cytoplasm, where those activities mainly occur. Also, the nucleus contains **chromatin** (KROH muh tun), a material that controls the appearance and type of the organism. The chromatin of a frog is different from that of a rose or a mushroom. Each type of organism has its own type of chromatin within the nucleus. When a cell begins to divide, the chromatin becomes visible as fine threads called **chromosomes** (KROH muh sohmz).

Every body cell of an organism has the same number of chromosomes. Each chromosome has a partner, and together they form a pair. The chromosome partners in each pair are similar but

In what part of the cell is chromatin located?

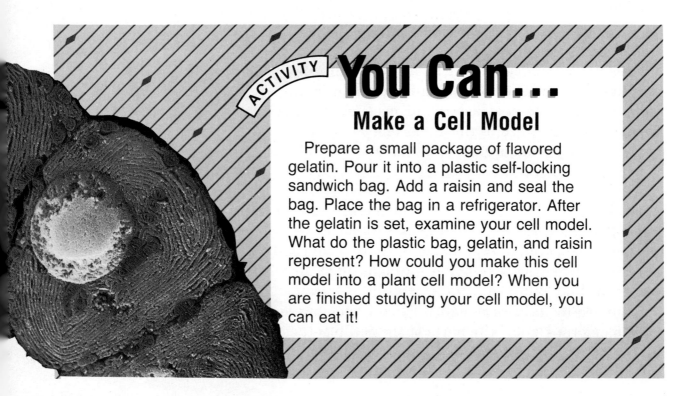

ACTIVITY

You Can...

Make a Cell Model

Prepare a small package of flavored gelatin. Pour it into a plastic self-locking sandwich bag. Add a raisin and seal the bag. Place the bag in a refrigerator. After the gelatin is set, examine your cell model. What do the plastic bag, gelatin, and raisin represent? How could you make this cell model into a plant cell model? When you are finished studying your cell model, you can eat it!

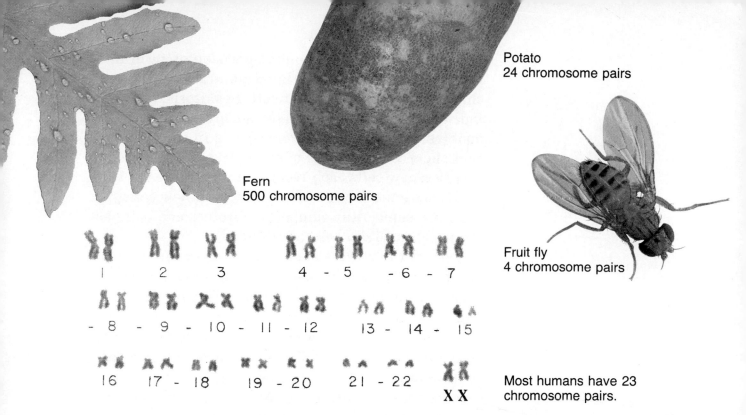

Potato
24 chromosome pairs

Fern
500 chromosome pairs

Fruit fly
4 chromosome pairs

Most humans have 23
chromosome pairs.

not identical. The number of chromosome pairs in different species of plants and animals varies widely. For example, there are 4 chromosome pairs in a fruit fly, 500 pairs in one species of fern, 24 pairs in a potato, and 23 pairs in humans. Look at the pairs of human chromosomes in the picture on this page. It shows that you have 46 individual chromosomes grouped into 23 pairs. There's something else you need to know about those individual chromosomes. Each one is able to make a copy of itself by splitting down its length.

Cell Division

You know that kittens grow up to be cats and oak trees grow from acorns. But why does that happen and how? The cells in the kitten's body divide to form new cells. As the number of cells in its body increases, it grows. The acorn grows into a tree in the same way. In fact, all many-celled organisms grow by cell division. When a cell divides, the chromosomes and the cytoplasm in the cell also divide.

347

Mitosis (mi TOH sus) is the division of a cell into two new cells, each with the same number of chromosomes as the parent cell. In mitosis, each individual chromosome makes a copy of itself. This doubles the number of chromosomes in the cell so that there are two pairs of each kind of chromosome. The two new cells each receive one pair of each kind of chromosome. The result is that both new cells have the same total number of chromosome pairs as the parent cell did before it divided.

Look at the process of mitosis in the picture on this page. To make it easy to follow, only three unpaired chromosomes are shown. The dividing cell passes through four stages of mitosis.

Stage 1. Each chromosome makes a copy of itself. On each chromosome there is a structure called the centromere. Each doubled chromosome is held together at the centromere. At the end of this stage, the nuclear membrane disappears.

Stage 2. The doubled chromosomes move to the center of the cell.

Stage 3. The centromeres split in half and each half moves to an opposite end of the cell.

Stage 4. The cytoplasm between the two sets of chromosomes becomes pinched apart. New cell membranes form between the two new cells. The cell

Mitosis has four stages.

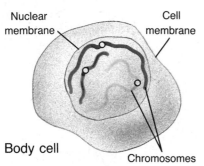

Nuclear membrane

Cell membrane

Body cell

Chromosomes

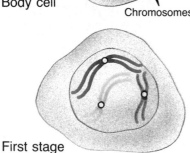

First stage

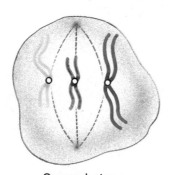

Second stage

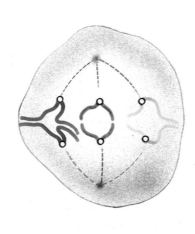

Third stage

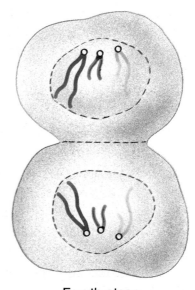

Fourth stage

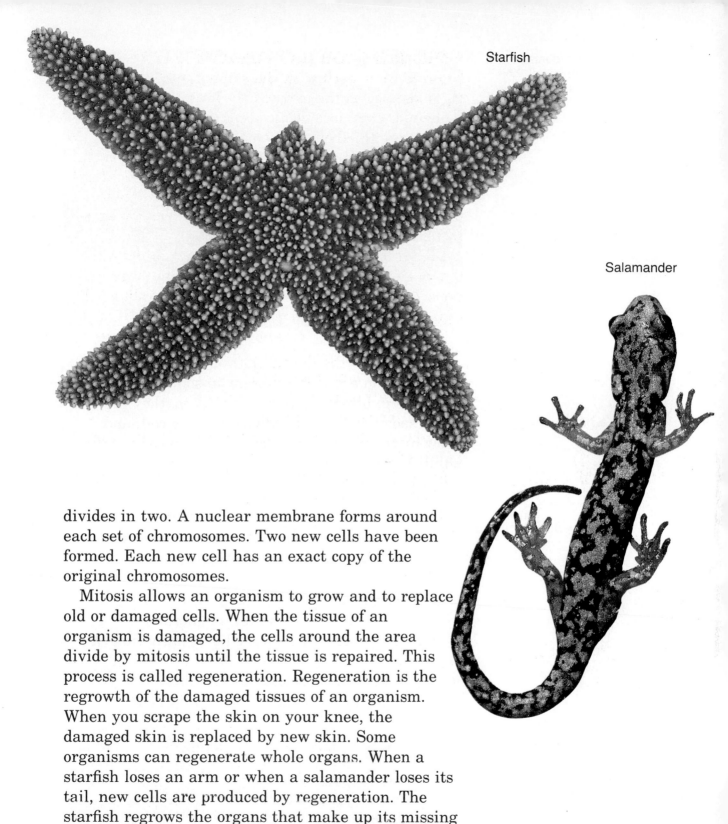

Starfish

Salamander

divides in two. A nuclear membrane forms around each set of chromosomes. Two new cells have been formed. Each new cell has an exact copy of the original chromosomes.

Mitosis allows an organism to grow and to replace old or damaged cells. When the tissue of an organism is damaged, the cells around the area divide by mitosis until the tissue is repaired. This process is called regeneration. Regeneration is the regrowth of the damaged tissues of an organism. When you scrape the skin on your knee, the damaged skin is replaced by new skin. Some organisms can regenerate whole organs. When a starfish loses an arm or when a salamander loses its tail, new cells are produced by regeneration. The starfish regrows the organs that make up its missing arm, and the salamander regrows its missing tail. Whole organs of plants such as roots and stems can also be regenerated.

Chickens, like all organisms, begin life as a single cell. This chicken egg is a single cell.

How are all organisms alike?

Even though the organisms you've learned about in this lesson are very different in some ways, they are alike in others. Like all organisms, they are composed of cells, begin life as a single cell, and grow by the process of mitosis. Thinking about these similarities will help you remember what you have learned in this lesson.

Lesson Summary

- Most cells are composed of a nucleus and cytoplasm. The nucleus and cytoplasm are separated by the nuclear membrane. The entire cell is surrounded by the cell membrane.
- Organisms grow by a method of cell division called mitosis.
- In mitosis, the chromosomes are copied and divided equally between the two new cells.

Lesson Review

1. What is chromatin?
2. How many pairs of chromosomes are in each human cell?
3. How many stages are there in mitosis?
★4. Does regeneration take place in humans? How do you know?

How do cells divide?

What you need

50-cm string   scissors
construction paper   tape
5-cm blue yarn (4)
5-cm yellow yarn (4)

What to do

1. Make a string circle on the paper. Place two blue yarns and two yellow yarns inside the circle.
2. Place two more blue yarns and two more yellow yarns in the circle. Tape two blue yarns together at their center points. Tape the other two blue yarns together at their center points. Also tape the centers of the yellow yarns.
3. Remove the string circle from the paper. Place the pairs of blue and yellow yarns in the center of the paper so the tapes form a line.
4. Cut each tape lengthwise to separate the yarn pairs. Move one pair of blue and one pair of yellow yarn pieces to opposite ends of the paper.
5. Cut the string in half. Use each half to make a circle on the paper around each set of four yarns.
6. Cut the paper in half between the two string circles.

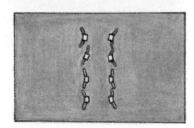

What did you learn?

1. What cell parts did the paper, string, yarns, and tape represent?

2. How do steps 1 and 6 in your model compare?

Using what you learned

1. Use your model to explain how cells divide.
2. Explain how organisms grow.

Reproduction

LESSON 2 GOALS
You will learn
● what reproduction means.
● methods of reproduction by one parent.
● the process of reproduction by two parents.

In the first lesson in this chapter, you learned how and why kittens grow up to be cats. In this lesson you'll learn how cats produce kittens. You'll also learn why they produce only kittens and not puppies, bunnies, or any other type of organism. Cats, like all organisms, begin life as one cell. This one cell can only be formed from other mature organisms.

Reproduction is the process of organisms producing new organisms of their own kind. This process of reproduction allows the characteristics of an organism to be passed on from parent to offspring. Reproduction may require one parent or two parents.

Organisms reproduce only their own species.

352

Reproduction by One Parent

Most one-celled organisms reproduce by splitting in half. **Fission** is the equal splitting by mitosis of a one-celled organism into two new one-celled organisms. Each cell grows and eventually reproduces again. Reproduction of organisms such as an amoeba or paramecium occurs by this simple method of mitosis. Reproduction by one parent is also common in bacteria and some algae. The offspring are exact copies of the parent.

How does an organism produced by fission resemble its parent?

Fission in bacteria

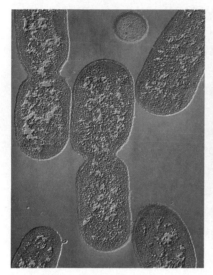
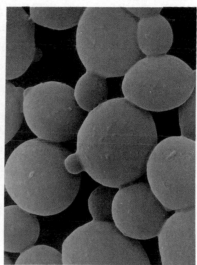

Budding in yeast

Another form of reproduction by one parent is budding. **Budding** is the production of offspring by outgrowths of the parent. Yeasts are one-celled organisms that reproduce in this way. A small budlike growth appears on the surface of a yeast cell. It grows and then pulls away to live as a separate organism. Budding also occurs in animals such as sea anemones. The buds appear on the animal's body wall, develop into young sea anemones, and eventually fall off. As in fission, offspring produced by budding are identical to the parent.

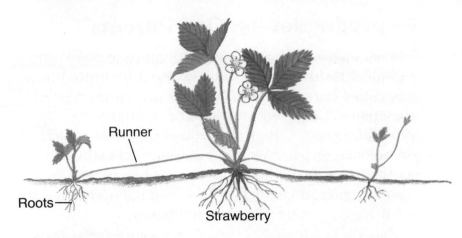

Runner

Roots

Strawberry

In plants, reproduction by one parent is common. New plants can develop from small pieces of a single plant. **Vegetative reproduction** is the formation of new plants from a body part of a single parent plant. These plants are exact copies of the parent plant. There are many kinds of vegetative reproduction. For example, look at the picture of strawberry plants on this page. These plants reproduce by means of runners. These runners are long, thin stems that grow from the main stem of the plant. At the end of the runner, a new plant grows. The new plant takes root in the soil, and eventually the runner connecting the new plant and the parent plant rots away. Runners are only one of many kinds of vegetative reproduction.

ACTIVITY

You Can...

Grow a New Plant

Divide a garlic bulb into cloves. Plant three cloves about 5 cm deep in a large pot of soil. Keep the soil moist but not wet. Wait two weeks. See what happens. Do garlic plants require one or two parents to reproduce?

Reproduction by Two Parents

Most species of plants, animals, and fungi reproduce by two parents. The offspring of this kind of reproduction are not exact copies of either parent. They have some characteristics of both parents. You will recall that all organisms develop from one cell. In organisms with two parents, this first cell is formed by combining one cell from each parent. These cells from the parents are formed by a kind of cell division called meiosis (mi OH sus).

Meiosis is the process of cell division that results in sex cells, which have half the number of chromosomes as the original cells. You have learned that body cells contain pairs of chromosomes. Now you will learn that each of those pairs is made up of one chromosome from each parent. Both chromosomes in a pair control the same characteristics. For example, one pair of a cat's chromosomes controls the color of its eyes.

What type of cell results from meiosis?

Chromosomes determine characteristics such as eye color.

In meiosis there are two cell divisions, not one as in mitosis. The first division is called meiosis I, and the second division is called meiosis II. The pictures here describe meiosis I and meiosis II.

Meiosis I

In meiosis I, the chromosome number is halved. There are four stages.

Stage 1. Pairs of similar chromosomes come together.

Stage 2. Each chromosome of each pair doubles by making a copy of itself. Each doubled chromosome is held together by the centromere. The pairs of chromosomes are not joined together, but are positioned side-by-side.

Stage 3. The pairs of doubled chromosomes move to the center of the cell.

Stage 4. The pairs of doubled chromosomes move apart so that half the chromosomes are present in each half of the cell. The cytoplasm between the two groups of chromosomes is pinched apart, and a new membrane forms between the two new cells. There are now two separate cells. This is the end of meiosis I.

First Division

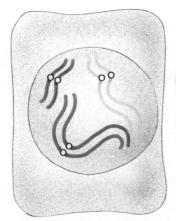

First stage

Second stage

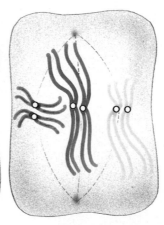

Third stage

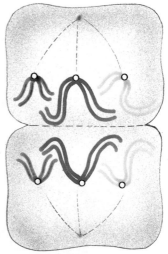

Fourth stage

356

Meiosis II

Meiosis II immediately follows meiosis I. In meiosis II, each of the two cells divides again. There are three stages, and they are similar to those in mitosis.

Stage 1. The centromeres of the doubled chromosomes line up.

Stage 2. Each pair splits, and the halves move toward opposite ends of the cell.

Stage 3. The cytoplasm between the two sets of chromosomes is pinched apart, and cell membranes form between the two cells. Four cells are produced at this stage.

Notice that each of the four cells has one half the original chromosome number. That means that each cell has only one chromosome of each kind, rather than two. In the males of a species, cells formed by meiosis are called **sperm** cells. In the females of a species, cells formed by meiosis are called **egg** cells. Remember, cells produced by meiosis contain half the chromosomes of cells produced by mitosis. In other words, sperm cells and egg cells contain one half the chromosomes of the parent cells.

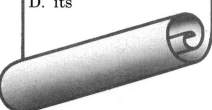
Second Division

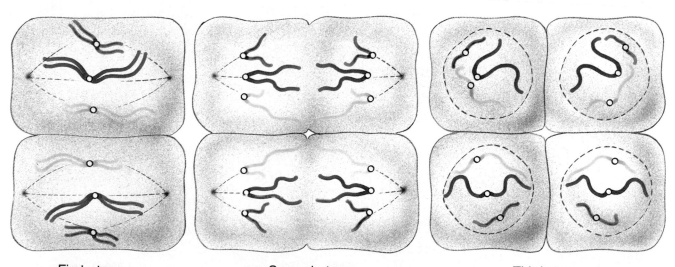

First stage   Second stage   Third stage

Sperm fertilizing an egg

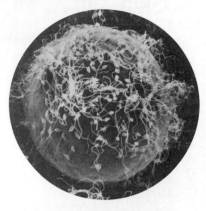

Zygote developing into an embryo

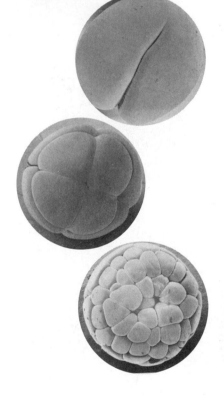

Most animals and some plants produce sperm cells in males and egg cells in females. Some species, such as earthworms and many plants, produce both sperm and egg cells in the same individual. In reproduction, one egg cell unites with one sperm cell, bringing the pairs of chromosomes back together. **Fertilization** is the uniting of an egg cell with a sperm cell to form a new cell. A **zygote** (ZI goht) is the cell formed from this fertilization. A new organism grows from the zygote.

The characteristics of both parents are mixed in the offspring. This causes the offspring to be different from each other and from their parents. That's why, for example, a kitten's fur may be a different color from the parents' fur. But the parents and offspring will be the same in one very important way—they will be the same species. If the parents are cats, the offspring will be kittens, not puppies or any other animal. The process of meiosis ensures that the offspring receive the same number of chromosome pairs as their parents.

In the early stages of growth, an organism is called an **embryo**. A mass of cells develops from the zygote as it divides by mitosis. Look at the series of pictures on this page. Observe the early divisions of the embryo. The mass of cells eventually develops into tissues and organs.

Many embryos are protected by a shell.

Mammals provide more parental care than most reptiles.

Developing embryos are usually protected in some way. The embryo may be protected by a layer of jelly, such as in fish or frogs. The fertilized eggs are laid in water to protect them from drying out. In reptiles and birds, the embryos are protected by a shell. The shell protects the embryo from drying out on land. In most mammals, embryos are protected by the body of the female parent.

The number of offspring and the amount of parental care for the young varies a great deal among animals. Fish and amphibians produce many more eggs than reptiles, birds, or mammals, and they generally provide very little care for the young. Mammals produce fewer offspring than reptiles and birds, but they provide more parental care for their young than other animals. This extra parental care increases the chances that the young will survive. As young animals grow, they learn to take care of themselves.

Plants also vary in how many offspring are produced and how well they are protected. Seed-bearing plants develop a thickened layer of cells called a seed coat around the embryo. Many seed plants produce a very large number of seeds. This increases the chances of reproduction. An oak tree may produce hundreds of acorns but only a few will survive to grow into adult trees. Many drop onto unsuitable soil, while others are eaten by animals. Plants with a large number of seeds have a better chance of reproducing than do those with few seeds.

Would You Believe?

A queen bee can lay as many as 3,000 eggs in one day.

What two processes are involved in reproduction by two parents?

In this lesson, you have learned many new terms and processes. But they can all be organized and understood as part of three general statements. First, all organisms begin life as a single cell. Second, organisms that are produced by one parent grow and reproduce by mitosis. Third, organisms produced by two parents grow by the process of mitosis and reproduce by the process of meiosis.

Lesson Summary

- Organisms reproduce organisms of their own kind.
- Fission, budding, and vegetative reproduction are methods of reproduction by one parent.
- Meiosis, fertilization of an egg cell by a sperm cell, and the growth of the zygote into the embryo are all parts of the process of reproduction by two parents.

Lesson Review

1. How do sea anemones and yeast reproduce by one parent?
2. What is a runner?
★3. In the picture below, how are the developing embryos protected? Why is it important that reptiles lay many eggs?

How do plants reproduce from one parent?

What you need

sweet potato
large glass jar
4 toothpicks
plant cutting
small glass jar
water
pencil and paper

What to do

1. Place a sweet potato in a large jar of water so that at least half of the potato is underwater. If needed, use toothpicks to hold the potato.
2. Keep the jar and potato in a dark place for a few days. After some roots have formed, place the jar in a warm, well-lit area.
3. Place the plant stem cutting in a small jar of water. Put the jar in a warm, well-lit area.
4. Observe the sweet potato and plant cutting several times a week for three weeks. Add water to the sweet potato when needed. Replace the water around the plant cutting every other day.
5. Record your observations each week.

What did you learn?

1. What changes did you observe in the sweet potato and plant cutting?

2. What was the new growth in the sweet potato?
3. What was the new growth in the plant cutting?

Using what you learned

1. If you planted the sweet potato and plant cutting in soil, what do you think would happen?
2. How many parent potato plants are needed to reproduce? What is the name for this type of reproduction?

361

I WANT TO KNOW ABOUT...

Summarizing Paragraphs

To summarize a paragraph, you need to determine its main idea. This idea may be stated in one or more sentences and may be located anywhere within the paragraph. The rest of the paragraph is made up of details that tell more about the main idea. When summarizing, select one or more details that provide an example of the main idea.

Read the following paragraph. The main idea is underlined.

Most one-celled organisms reproduce by splitting in half. **Fission** is the equal splitting by mitosis of a one-celled organism into two new one-celled organisms. Each cell grows and eventually reproduces

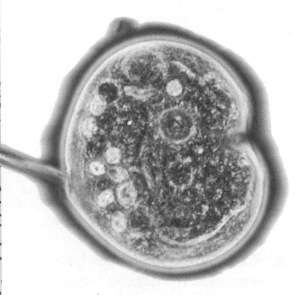

again. Reproduction of organisms such as an amoeba or paramecium occurs by this simple method of mitosis. Reproduction by one parent is also common in bacteria and some algae. The offspring are exact copies of the parent.

Now here's a summary of the paragraph that you just read.

Fission is the equal splitting by mitosis of a one-celled organism into two new one-celled organisms. Organisms such as an amoeba or paramecium as well as bacteria and some algae reproduce in this way.

Notice that the boldfaced term is part of the summary. Boldfaced terms should always be included in a summary. Sometimes they are part of the main idea, and sometimes they provide an important detail. Notice also that sometimes you have to combine information from two or more sentences for your summary. As much as possible, keep your summary simple and in your own words.

Now, you try it. Write a one- or two-sentence summary of paragraph 2 on page 353.

Language Arts

Summary

Lesson 1
- Most cells are composed of a nucleus and cytoplasm. The nucleus and cytoplasm are separated by the nuclear membrane. The entire cell is surrounded by the cell membrane.
- Organisms grow by a method of cell division called mitosis.
- In mitosis, the chromosomes are copied and divided equally between the two new cells.

Lesson 2
- Organisms reproduce organisms of their own kind.
- Fission, budding, and vegetative reproduction are methods of reproduction by one parent.
- Meiosis, fertilization of an egg cell by a sperm cell, and growth of the zygote into the embryo are all parts of the process of reproduction by two parents.

Science Words

Fill in the blank with the correct word or words from the list.

cytoplasm
nuclear
  membrane
chromatin
chromosome
mitosis
reproduction
fission
budding

vegetative
  reproduction
meiosis
sperm
egg
fertilization
zygote
embryo

1. The material that controls the kind and appearance of an organism is ____.

2. The production of a new organism from an outgrowth of the parent is known as ____.

3. The part of the cell outside the nucleus is ____.

4. In the male of the species, meiosis produces ____.

5. The cell that results when an egg and sperm unite is a(n) ____.

6. The formation of new plants from a body part of a single parent plant is ____.

7. The contents of the nucleus are separated from the cytoplasm by the ____.

8. A thread of chromatin that carries all the information about an organism is a(n) ____.
9. A cell divides into two cells, each having the same number of chromosomes as the parent cell, in the process of ____.
10. A many-celled organism in the early stages of development is a(n) ____.

Questions

Recalling Ideas
Correctly complete each of the following sentences.

1. The number of pairs of chromosomes that human body cells have is
   (a) 150.   (c) 23.
   (b) 46.   (d) 4.
2. Some organisms can repair damaged tissues or regrow body parts by
   (a) meiosis.
   (b) budding.
   (c) fission.
   (d) regeneration.
3. The control center for the cell is the
   (a) nucleus.   (c) centromere.
   (b) chromatin.   (d) cytoplasm.
4. The process of combining an egg cell with a sperm cell is
   (a) meiosis.
   (b) mitosis.
   (c) fertilization.
   (d) fission.
5. A potato reproduces by
   (a) fission.
   (b) budding.
   (c) vegetative reproduction.
   (d) bulbs.

6. Of the following, the living thing that is able to reproduce by one parent is
   (a) humans.   (c) cows.
   (b) giraffes.   (d) yeasts.
7. The part of a cell that is NOT part of the nucleus is
   (a) the cytoplasm.
   (b) the chromosome.
   (c) meiosis.
   (d) chromatin.
8. All of the following terms are involved in two-parent reproduction EXCEPT
   (a) meiosis.   (c) mitosis.
   (b) fertilization. (d) zygote.

Examining Ideas
Determine whether each of the following statements is true or false. Rewrite the false statements to make them correct.

1. Every organism begins with a single cell.
2. Fission and budding are both forms of reproduction by one parent.
3. Cytoplasm is the fluid part of the cell.

4. In meiosis, the cells produced have half the number of chromosomes as the cell that divided.
5. Many-celled organisms grow by mitosis.
6. Damaged tissues can be replaced by budding.
7. Groups of similar cells make up the organs of complex organisms.
8. Most of the activities of the cell take place in the nucleus.
9. Every body cell of an organism has the same number of chromosomes.
10. Meiosis results in two new cells that are identical to the parent.
11. An embryo develops from a zygote by meiosis.
12. Human egg and sperm cells each contain 23 pairs of chromosomes.

Understanding Ideas
Answer the following questions using complete sentences.
1. What is fertilization, and why is meiosis important in this process?
2. Briefly describe the process of meiosis.
3. How is the amount of protection an embryo has related to the number of embryos an organism produces?

Thinking Critically
Think about what you have learned in this chapter. Answer the following questions using complete sentences.
1. How are mitosis and meiosis alike? How are they different?
2. Why is it important that mammals provide more parental care for their young than do reptiles?
3. Explain why reproduction is important to the survival of the species.
4. Hypothesize why reproduction in which the offspring can get traits from two parents might be an advantage for the survival of the species.

Inheriting Traits

Can you roll your tongue? Some people can, but others can't, no matter how hard they try. Tongue-rolling is an inherited trait.

In your own family, you may have noticed that although no two members are identical, there are strong resemblances between family members. Do people who meet you for the first time tell you that you look like your mom? Or do they tell you that you look like your dad? Do you see any resemblance? Freckles, blue eyes, and curly hair are all examples of inherited traits controlled by your genes. For each trait, you receive two genes, one from each parent. Some genes, like the ones for freckles, are dominant. Other genes, such as the ones for blue eyes, are recessive.

ACTIVITY

Have You Ever...

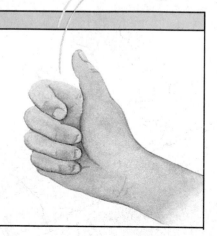

Wondered About Inherited Traits?

Flip a coin in the air. Does it land heads up or tails up? What are the chances of heads? What are the chances of tails? Repeat the activity ten times. Record your results. As a class, collect and compare the data. For the total number of coin flips, how many times did heads come up?

Heredity

LESSON 1 GOALS
You will learn
• that offspring inherit traits from their parents.
• that traits are controlled by genes.
• that genes may be dominant, recessive, or expressed equally.

When you were younger, you may have read stories about animals that had babies different from themselves. It was fun to think of an elephant hatching from a bird egg, or a swan hatching from a duck egg. But you knew these stories were fantasies. Organisms reproduce only their own kind and the offspring have characteristics like those of their parents.

If you look closely at a population of organisms, you will, however, notice individual traits. For instance, look at the population of students in your classroom. Unless there are identical twins in your class, no two students will look exactly alike. Every student has inherited different traits from his or her parents.

Remember that in reproduction, the traits an organism inherits are controlled by the chromosomes in the cell. Half of the chromosomes come from one parent and half come from the other parent. One child may inherit red hair, freckles, and a broad nose from his or her parents. A child of different parents may inherit black hair, dark skin, and a narrow nose. **Heredity** is the passing of traits from parents to offspring.

Traits are passed from parents to children.

Two dogs of the same breed produce puppies that are like the parents. This German shepherd was bred with another German shepherd. Their puppies have inherited the traits common to German shepherds. The puppies will grow up to be German shepherd dogs. What would you predict the puppies would be like if a German shepherd bred with a small white poodle? Would the puppies still be called dogs? The puppies would inherit some traits of German shepherds and some traits of poodles. Though the puppies might not look much like either of the parents, they would still have all the traits that make them dogs.

Inheriting Traits

Recall the puppies that were the offspring of two German shepherd dogs. Each puppy received half its chromosomes from the father's sperm cell and half from the mother's egg cell during fertilization. Since the parent dogs had chromosomes for similar traits, the puppies looked like the parents. If a small white poodle were the father and a German shepherd were the mother, the chromosomes the puppies received from each parent would be for different traits. Thus, some puppies could be large with curly white hair, while others could be small yet look like German shepherds. The combination of traits could create a large variety of possibilities.

From where did the puppies receive their chromosomes?

Genes determine the colors of fish.

How many genes control a particular trait?

The part of the chromosome that controls traits in an organism is a **gene.** One chromosome with its gene comes from the father. The other chromosome with its gene comes from the mother. Some traits are controlled by one pair of genes, but most traits are controlled by two or more pairs of genes. Fur color in dogs, height in humans, and leaf shape in many plants are all examples of traits controlled by more than one pair of genes.

For many years people did not understand how traits were passed from parents to offspring. The study of genes, or genetics, is a fairly new science. It began in a small Austrian school in the 1800s.

Expressing Traits

Gregor Johann Mendel was an Austrian monk who studied and taught science and math in a technical school. He had grown up on a farm with an orchard, and he had always liked working with plants. Mendel was interested in heredity. He wanted to discover how parent organisms passed traits to their offspring so he decided to do an experiment with garden pea plants.

Mendel had noticed that some pea plants were tall and some were short. None were ever of medium height. Mendel mated tall plants with other tall plants by collecting pollen from the flower of one tall plant then brushing it on the flower of another tall plant. When the pollinated flower formed a pea pod, he saved the seeds and planted them in his garden the next year. All the seeds produced tall plants. He tried this experiment for many years, always having the same result. Mendel's experiment proved that the tall plants could produce only tall plants. Mendel did the same experiment with short pea plants. When he mated short plants with short plants, the seeds they produced always grew into short plants.

What do you think happened when Mendel mated tall plants with short plants? The seeds from this cross produced all tall plants! What happened to the trait for shortness? It seemed to have disappeared. Mendel said the trait for tallness was stronger. He called it the **dominant** (DAHM uh nunt) **trait.** Dominant traits are controlled by genes on the chromosomes called **dominant genes.**

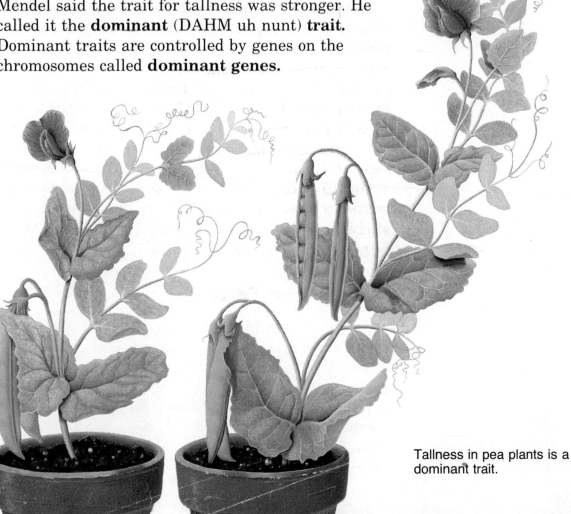

Tallness in pea plants is a dominant trait.

The genes present in chromosomes determine the fur color of Bengal tigers.

The shortness trait was hidden by the dominant tallness trait. Mendel called shortness in pea plants a **recessive trait**. Recessive traits are controlled by genes on the chromosomes called **recessive genes.** The seeds produced when the tall and short plants were mated had both the dominant and recessive genes. The plants that grew from these seeds were tall. The recessive gene for shortness was "hidden" by the dominant gene for tallness.

Remember that when Mendel crossed short pea plants with other short pea plants, their seeds produced short plants. That's because a recessive trait is seen only when both genes on a pair of chromosomes are recessive.

Let's look at another example of recessive genes being passed by parents to offspring. This white Bengal tiger is a rare animal. You know that most tigers are orange. The genes for fur color in Bengal tigers occur on a pair of chromosomes. Normally, one gene for orange fur comes from the chromosome of the mother, and one gene for orange fur comes from the father. As a result most tiger offspring have orange fur. If a tiger cub inherits a dominant gene for orange fur from one parent and a recessive gene for white fur from the other parent, it also would have orange fur. How, then, did this tiger come to have white fur? Both its mother and father carried a recessive gene for white fur. The cub inherited a pair of recessive genes, giving it white fur.

White fur in Bengal tigers is a recessive trait.

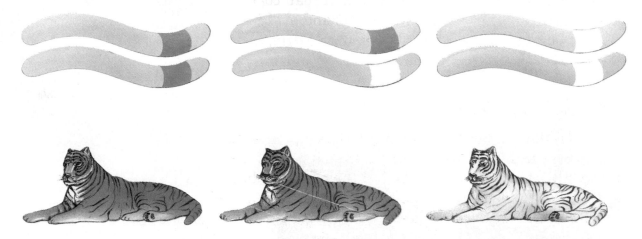

372

Roan cow

Some genes are neither dominant nor recessive. In cows with red or white coats, there are no dominant genes for coat color. What happens when a bull with a red coat breeds with a cow with a white coat? The calf that is produced has a coat with both red and white hairs. The hairs are intermingled, giving the coat a light red appearance. This mixed coloring is called roan. When there are no dominant genes for coat color, the genes are expressed together. A cow with a red coat has inherited only genes for a red coat. A cow with a white coat has inherited only genes for a white coat. But a cow with a roan coat has inherited genes for both a red coat and a white coat. If roan cattle breed with other roan cattle, a calf may be red, white, or roan.

Why are some cows roan?

Predicting Traits

Mendel did another experiment with pea plants. In this experiment he crossed violet-flowered pea plants with white-flowered pea plants. All the offspring had violet flowers. In this case the violet color was dominant and the white was recessive.

ACTIVITY

You Can...

Study Genetics With Peanuts

Get a bag of unshelled peanuts. Sort the peanuts according to how many seeds they have inside. Keep track of how many peanuts have one seed, two seeds, and so on. What is the most common number of seeds? What does this tell you about the inheritance of the number of seeds in peanuts?

Symbols are used to represent the genes found in chromosomes.

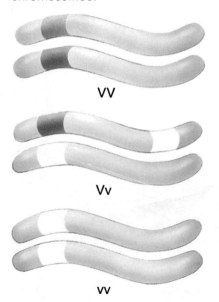

VV

Vv

vv

Remember that genes come in pairs because they are part of the chromosomes an organism inherits from its parents. You can use symbols to show how a pair of genes is inherited. First, mark both genes for a particular trait with the same letter. When a gene is dominant, use a capital letter. When a gene is recessive, use a lowercase letter. Let's use the pea flowers as an example. In the violet-colored plants, both genes are for the dominant violet color. You can write the symbol of these two dominant genes as *VV*. Now write *vv* for the symbol for the recessive genes for a white color. The gene pair for a cross between the two plants can be written as *Vv* because it has one gene for violet and one gene for white.

You can write the letter symbols on a diagram to help you predict what offspring will be like. The diagram is called a **Punnett square**. It was invented by Reginald C. Punnett, an English geneticist. This Punnett square shows the offspring of a cross between a violet-flowered pea plant and a white-flowered pea plant. The genes of the parents are shown outside the square. The violet-flowered parent is shown by two capital letters, *VV*. The white-flowered parent is shown by the lowercase *vv*.

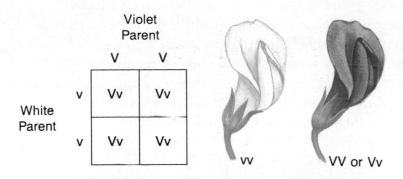

Violet
Parent

V   V

White
Parent

	V	V
v	Vv	Vv
v	Vv	Vv

vv   VV or Vv

The four boxes within the square show every possible combination of gene pairs that an offspring could inherit. Notice that all the offspring will have one dominant gene and one recessive gene for flower color. What color will the offspring be? Remember, a dominant gene hides a recessive gene. So the offspring will be violet. From a Punnett square such as this, you can predict the chances of offspring having a particular trait.

Let's do another example with a Punnett square. A dominant trait that some people have is free earlobes. The recessive trait is attached earlobes. Suppose both parents have one gene for free earlobes and one gene for attached earlobes. *L* is the dominant gene, *l* is the recessive gene. Using the Punnett square, predict the chances of an offspring having free earlobes and the chances of an offspring having attached earlobes.

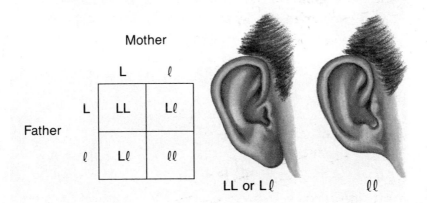

Mother

L l

	L	l
L	LL	Ll
l	Ll	$l l$

Father

LL or Ll $l l$

An offspring could receive a
dominant or a recessive trait.

SCIENCE AND . . .
Math

Suppose one parent of a child has only dominant genes for black hair. The other parent has only recessive genes for red hair. What are the chances that the child will have red hair?
A. one chance in four
B. four chances in four
C. no chance

Do you see that only one of the boxes has a recessive gene pair (*ll*)? A child that receives this pair will have attached earlobes. You can see that a child has a one in four chance of receiving two recessive genes from the parents. Thus, the chance of a child inheriting free earlobes is three times better than for inheriting attached earlobes.

Lesson Summary

- Offspring inherit traits from parents.
- Genes control traits inherited by offspring.
- If there is no dominant gene, traits are expressed equally.

Lesson Review

1. What is heredity?
2. Why is the white Bengal tiger rare?
3. Why is a roan calf produced when a red cow breeds with a white bull?
★4. Make a prediction using these facts and a Punnett square. Brown eyes are dominant. Blue eyes are recessive. Both parents have one dominant gene and one recessive gene for eye color. What are the chances that the offspring will have brown eyes? blue eyes?

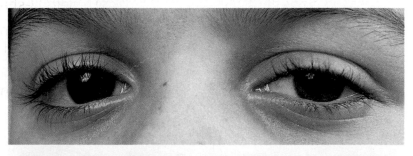

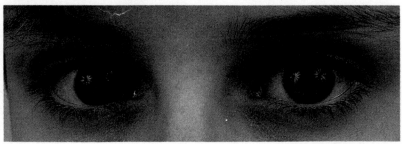

How common are dominant and recessive traits?

What you need

mirror
pencil and paper

What to do

1. Look at the traits in the table.
2. Observe and record the number of people in your class who show the dominant or recessive traits listed.
3. Use a mirror to look at yourself. Include your own traits in your observations.

Comparing Traits	
Dominant Trait	**Recessive Trait**
Dimples	No dimples
Free earlobes	Attached earlobes
Can roll tongue into U-shape	Cannot roll tongue into U-shape
Hair on middle section of finger	No hair on middle section of finger
Space between front teeth	No space between front teeth
Non-red hair	Red hair

What did you learn?

1. Which dominant traits are common in your class? which recessive traits?
2. Are dominant or recessive traits more common?

Using what you learned

1. Why do you think some dominant traits are not common?
2. If two parents have red hair, predict the hair color of all their offspring. Explain your answer.

Genetics in Populations

LESSON 2 GOALS
You will learn
- about gene mutations.
- how species evolve by natural selection.

Luis bought a cactus plant for his room. It was round with little golden hooks all over it. He thought it looked quite nice on his windowsill when the sun shone on the golden hooks. Every day he carefully watered it and watched to see if it had grown. It didn't seem to be getting any larger, and then one day he thought it appeared to be getting smaller! Perhaps it needed more water. The next day Luis was surprised to see the cactus had collapsed. It looked like an old wet bag covered with yellow hooks. Luis was sure his cactus was dead, but he didn't know why. Do you?

Organisms survive because they are adapted to their environments. Luis' cactus was adapted to live in the dry, hot conditions of the desert. But Luis changed the environment of the cactus. The cactus wasn't adapted to the new habitat and so it didn't survive.

This cactus needs to have the same environment as the one it has adapted to.

Changes in habitats are common. For example, a winter can be exceptionally cold or a summer exceptionally hot. Many changes are caused by humans. Can you think of some? Humans dam rivers, which floods valleys, cut down trees in forests, and plow fields and plant crops. Humans also pollute the air and the waters. All these things change the environment. If species of organisms can't adapt to changes in the environment, what will happen to them?

Mutations can eventually result in different varieties of apples.

Mutations

Sometimes an apple grower will find one apple on a tree that's different from the other apples. The shape or color of the apple may be different from the rest of the apples. Most of the time, these changes go unnoticed if they don't harm the taste or usefulness of the apple. But some changes are valuable if they cause improvement over the original. The different apple may be used to create a new apple variety.

Some mutations, such as curled wings, may be a disadvantage to an organism.

Name two causes of gene mutations.

What caused the difference in the apple? There was a change in the genes of an apple flower. This change is called a **mutation** and can cause a new trait to appear. Mutations can be spontaneous or caused by poisons or radiation. Most mutations produce very small changes in an organism. The effect of these small mutations may not be seen for several generations.

An apple tree is a cultivated plant. Its needs for food, light, and water are usually carefully tended to. Even a tree with a weak trunk may be encouraged to survive if it produces good fruit. In the wild, however, the traits passed to an organism may mean the difference between life and death for an organism. The traits may make it possible for it to survive and reproduce or cause it to die without producing offspring.

Remember, changes in the environment don't cause mutations. Gene mutations exist in organisms before the environmental changes occur. These mutations cause certain traits to appear. If the traits are the ones needed in the environment, they help the organism survive.

Natural Selection

Let's use a clover plant as an example as we look at how traits affect the survival of an organism. The clover plant has genes that control the number of hairs on its stem. The number of hairs on a clover plant stem may not be of any benefit to it. Possibly the hairs may not cause it any harm either. Genes that control the flower color are more important to the clover plant. Some clover plants may have red flowers, others white. If bees are attracted to the color red more than the color white, the red flowers may be pollinated more often than the white. The red-flowered clover may produce more seeds and eventually crowd out the white-flowered clover plants. Even though all the white-flowered clover plants may disappear, the gene for white flowers will still be present in some of the plants with red flowers. From time to time, a white-flowered plant will appear when a cross of two red plants produces the recessive white-flowered trait.

Remember that plants are producers. They use chlorophyll to make their own food. Sometimes a gene mutation causes a corn plant to be produced that contains no chlorophyll. It sprouts from its seed and grows until it has used all the food stored in the seed. Without chlorophyll to make more food, the seedling dies.

Bees are attracted to brightly colored plants.

The seedling died because of natural selection. **Natural selection** is the process by which organisms less adapted to their environment tend to die, and better-adapted organisms tend to survive. The white-flowered clover plants died out because of the process of natural selection. If a gene mutation causes a change that is helpful to an organism, it will help the organism survive. The longer an organism survives, the better chance it has to reproduce and pass on its genes. If a gene mutation causes a change that is harmful to an organism, the organism may die without producing offspring. Therefore, its genes won't be passed on, and neither will the mutation that caused it to die.

Let's look at a population of organisms that were able to change as their environment changed. In rural areas of nineteenth century England, there were many spotted moths called peppered moths. Most of the peppered moths were light colored. However, there were a few dark-colored peppered moths too. The dark color was the result of a gene mutation.

Light-colored moths were hard to see when they rested on the light-colored tree bark. In the 1800s, many factories were built in the northern cities of England. The smokestacks of these factories filled the air with pollution, which caused the bark of the nearby trees to turn dark. The light-colored moths no longer resembled the tree bark. Now the dark-colored moths blended into the tree bark better than the light-colored moths. Birds that fed on the moths could see the light-colored ones better than

What caused the tree bark to darken?

Peppered moths on tree bark

382

You Can...

Show How Natural Selection Occurs

Get some green paper. It should be about 22 x 28 cm. Get some green thread and at least three other colors of thread. Cut five 2-cm pieces of each color of thread. Scatter all the pieces of thread on the paper. Using tweezers, see how many pieces of thread you can pick up and put in a cup in 10 seconds. How many pieces of thread did you pick up? What color did you pick up the most? the least? Which "thread animals" are most likely to be safe from "tweezer predators"? How have you demonstrated natural selection?

the dark-colored ones. More dark-colored moths than light-colored moths survived because they were not so easily found and eaten by the birds. It was these surviving, dark-colored moths that reproduced and passed on their genes. So the mutated gene that carried the trait of dark color was passed on. By the 1950s, the peppered moths in cities with factories were mostly dark colored. Then another change in the environment occurred. In the 1960s, pollution control laws were passed and the air became cleaner. The tree bark became lighter in color because there was less soot covering it. The dark-colored moths became easier for the birds to see. The few remaining light-colored moths were able to escape the birds more easily. The number of light-colored moths soon began to increase as they survived and reproduced.

Why did more dark moths survive?

These whooper swans have adapted to survive in the cold.

Define evolution.

The peppered moths are an example of a species that changed over time, or evolved. The **evolution** of the peppered moth from light to dark and back to light again occurred because of natural selection.

The history of life on Earth includes the extinction of many species. These species died out because they didn't have the adaptations necessary to survive in their changing environments. The life you see around you today is the result of individual organisms surviving and their populations changing over time. And these organisms are still evolving today as their environments continue to change.

Lesson Summary

- Gene mutations cause new traits to appear in organisms.
- Natural selection is a process by which a population of organisms evolves through time.

Lesson Review

1. Explain why dark-colored peppered moths are now rare in rural England.
★2. Suppose a gene mutation causes a squirrel living in an arctic region to be born with white fur. Explain how natural selection might lead to the evolution of a population of squirrels with white fur.

Use Application Activity on pages 513, 514.

What are the chances for tallness?

What you need

masking tape
2 coins
pencil and paper

What to do

Part A

1. Tallness is a dominant trait in pea plants. Let *T* represent tallness. Let *t* represent shortness.
2. Two plants that are *Tt* for the tallness trait are mated. Draw a Punnett square to show the possible gene pairs that may occur in the offspring.

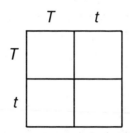

Part B

1. Put a piece of tape on each side of two coins. Let each coin represent one of the plants in Part A.
2. Mark a *T* on one side of each coin. Mark a *t* on the other side of each coin. The letters represent the genes of the plants.
3. Put one coin in each hand. Shake the coins loosely and drop them on a table.

4. Record both letters that are facing up on the coins. These two letters represent the genes of one offspring of the plants.
5. Repeat steps 3 and 4 nineteen more times.

What did you learn?

1. Look at your Punnett square. What is the chance that any one offspring will be tall?
2. How many of the offspring in Part B were tall?

Using what you learned

1. Are the 2 parent plants, *Tt*, tall or short? Explain.
2. If one parent had only dominant genes for tallness, *TT*, how many offspring would have been short?

Controlling Traits

LESSON 3 GOALS
You will learn
● why humans use selective breeding.
● that genes can be transferred between organisms.

Have you eaten sugar snap peas or one of the new super sweet corns? These new, delicious varieties of vegetables have been available for only a few years. They were produced by a process called selective breeding. In **selective breeding,** organisms with desirable traits are crossed with organisms with other desirable traits. The offspring produced have a combination of the desirable traits. Since people began to grow plants for food, over 11,000 years ago, they have selected plants with the most desirable traits. They saved the seeds from only the best fruits and vegetables to plant the following year. Plants were chosen for their resistance to disease, greater food production, and faster growth. Over thousands of years, this selection process has caused great changes in food plants.

Racehorses are selectively bred for speed.

Here's how a breeder uses selective breeding to produce an improved variety of an organism. The breeder starts with several parent organisms. The offspring of each parent organism are compared to the other offspring. Only the offspring with the most desirable traits are chosen to breed again. These offspring with desirable traits are crossed again. After several generations the desirable traits become more common. Eventually these traits will occur in almost all members of the breeder's population.

Using selective breeding, breeders have developed a type of wheat that can be grown in colder climates, cows that produce more milk, and horses that run faster. The outward appearance of dogs and cats has been changed through selective breeding.

Unlike natural selection, selective breeding does not necessarily make the organism better adapted to its natural environment. Some traits that are selected by people are often harmful to the plant or animal population. For example, selective breeding has helped produce seedless oranges. But how would seedless oranges reproduce in the wild? They couldn't. Seedless oranges can only be cultivated in orchards.

Name one way in which selective breeding and natural selection differ.

Seedless oranges

Another example is the hairless mouse. These mice were bred for laboratory research. Suppose several of these mice were accidentally released into the wild. Neither they nor their offspring could survive a cold winter outside the laboratory.

Transferring Genes

It took many years for breeders to develop the super sweet corn and the seedless orange. If a dog breeder wanted to develop a new coat color in poodles, it would take many generations to produce a pure strain with the new color. Until recently, it was not possible to select a desirable trait from one species and transfer it into another. Now, however, scientists can do this. How is this possible? Scientists move a single gene from an organism of one species to an organism of a different species. This process is often done in one-celled organisms such as bacteria and yeasts.

Insulin is a drug necessary to people with the disease diabetes. By transferring genes, scientists have been able to make large quantities of insulin. The gene that causes insulin to be produced in humans can be placed into bacteria. Since bacteria reproduce very quickly, they make large quantities of insulin in a short time period.

Transferring genes into bacteria has also been used to produce another drug—called interferon. Interferon is useful for treating viral diseases and cancer.

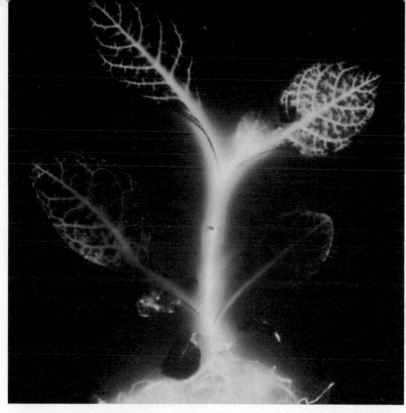

By transferring genes from a firefly to a tobacco plant, scientists have produced a tobacco plant that glows.

One type of gene transfer scientists are working on involves the bacteria in the roots of some plants such as peas and beans. These bacteria allow the roots to grow without nitrogen fertilizer. The bacteria take the nitrogen they use from the air. If corn and other plants can be developed with this ability, farmers will not need to use nitrogen fertilizers.

Lesson Summary

- Selective breeding has produced changes in traits of plants and animals that are useful to humans.
- Gene transfer results in organisms of one species having traits of organisms of another species.

Lesson Review

1. Explain how selective breeding might be used to produce racehorses.
2. How might selective breeding be harmful to organisms such as hairless mice?
★3. Does gene transfer make an organism better adapted to its environment? Explain.

I WANT TO KNOW ABOUT...

A Geneticist

Some people can't tell the difference between the colors red and green. You can imagine the problem this creates for them when looking at traffic lights. People who have this problem are color-blind.

Hanako Lam is a geneticist doing research on color-blindness. Hanako had already discovered the gene that makes color-vision molecules in the eyes of cows. How could she find the same gene in humans?

The molecule needed for seeing different colors resembles a spiral ladder. Hanako knew if the molecule was split at the "rungs" of the ladder, each strand would be able to combine with another strand. Using a new research method, she split a molecule obtained from a cow. Then she put a strand of a human molecule with it. The color-vision gene from the cow lined up with the genes from the human. Hanako was able to see where genes that produce color-vision molecules in humans are located.

Hanako's research will not eliminate color-blindness. Hanako wants to use her research technique to locate other genes that cause other inherited traits. The more scientists know about the work of each gene, the more they can detect harmful genes and correct the defects they cause.

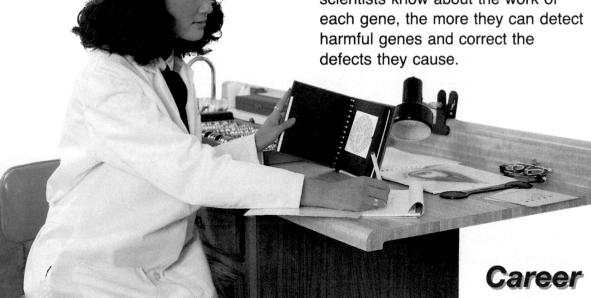

Career

390

Summary

Lesson 1
- Offspring inherit traits from parents.
- Genes control traits inherited by offspring.
- If there is no dominant gene, traits are expressed equally.

Lesson 2
- Gene mutations cause new traits to appear in organisms.

- Natural selection is a process by which a population of organisms evolve through time.

Lesson 3
- Selective breeding has produced changes in traits of plants and animals that are useful to humans.
- Gene transfer results in organisms of one species having traits of organisms of another species.

Science Words

Fill in the blank with the correct word or words from the list.

heredity	dominant
gene	trait
dominant genes	recessive
recessive genes	trait
mutation	Punnett
natural selection	square
evolution	
selective breeding	

1. The process by which organisms less adapted to their environment die and better adapted organisms survive is ____.
2. The passing of traits from parents to offspring is ____.
3. The crossing of organisms with desirable traits to produce offspring with a combination of these traits is called ____.
4. The part of a chromosome that controls the traits of an organism is a(n) ____.
5. Genes whose traits are always expressed are ____.
6. A change in genes that causes a new trait to appear is a(n) ____.
7. Genes that control hidden traits are ____.
8. The process by which a species slowly changes over time is ____.

Questions

Recalling Ideas

Correctly complete each of the following sentences.

1. A characteristic passed from parent to offspring is a
   (a) gene.　　　(c) zygote.
   (b) chromosome. (d) trait.

2. If the gene for white is dominant (W) and the gene for red is recessive (w), the offspring of a white flower (WW) and a red flower (ww) will be
   (a) all white.　　(c) all pink.
   (b) all red.　　　(d) red and white.

3. The portions of the chromosomes that control the traits of an organism are called
   (a) zygotes.　　(c) genes.
   (b) sperm.　　　(d) cells.

4. The crossing of organisms to produce certain desirable traits is
   (a) natural selection.
   (b) selective breeding.
   (c) mutation.
   (d) heredity.

5. A sudden change in a chromosome is known as
   (a) fertilization.
   (b) budding.
   (c) natural selection.
   (d) mutation.

6. Bacteria can be made to produce large quantities of the drug insulin by the process of
   (a) gene transference.
   (b) natural selection.

   (c) selective breeding.
   (d) fertilization.

Examining Ideas

Determine whether each of the following statements is true or false. Rewrite the false statements to make them correct.

1. The combination of a dominant gene and a recessive gene results in offspring that show both characteristics.

2. A Punnett square is used to predict the chance that an offspring will have a certain trait.

THE FAR SIDE　　　By GARY LARSON

© 1988 Universal Press Syndicate

When the monster came, Lola, like the peppered moth and the arctic hare, remained motionless and undetected. Harold, of course, was immediately devoured.

3. A pure gene is one whose trait is always expressed.

4. Natural selection is a change in genes that can cause a new trait to appear in a population.

5. Selective breeding makes an organism better adapted to its environment.

6. Changes in environment cause mutations.

7. Scientists can move a single gene from an organism of one species to an organism of a different species.

8. Natural selection ensures the passing on of traits that are most suited to a particular environment.

9. Evolution is the spontaneous change in a gene.

10. Gregor Mendel was an Austrian monk who developed a diagram to predict the traits of offspring.

11. Gene transfers must be made between organisms of the same species.

12. A trait caused by a mutation of a gene can be passed on to offspring.

Understanding Ideas

Answer the following questions using complete sentences.

1. When will the traits of recessive genes be expressed?

2. One parent has a pair of genes for long eyelashes; the other parent has a pair of genes for short eyelashes. An offspring has long eyelashes. Which gene is dominant?

3. In Mendel's experiments, could a short pea plant ever have a mixed gene pair? Explain your answer.

Thinking Critically

Think about what you have learned in this chapter. Answer the following questions using complete sentences.

1. Explain why it was important that Gregor Mendel use thousands and thousands of plants in his experiment.

2. A pure trait is one that results when genes in a pair are the same. A hybrid trait results when the gene pair is mixed. Suppose one parent has a hybrid trait (Tt), and the other parent has a pure trait (TT). What is the chance that the offspring will have the pure trait?

3. In a certain type of daisy, there is a gene for a red color (R) and a gene for white color (W). Neither gene is dominant, so if an offspring receives a mixed gene pair (RW), its color will be pink. Suppose two daisies have the genes RR and RW. Describe the appearance of each daisy. Then use a Punnett square to predict the appearance and gene makeup of the offspring of these two daisies.

Checking for Understanding

Write a short answer for each question or statement.

1. Name the five kingdoms and give one characteristic of each.
2. Classify each of the following organisms into the proper kingdom: spider, diatom, bacteria, mold, evergreen tree.
3. How is an algal protist different from a protozoan?
4. How are fungi helpful?
5. What characteristics do all living things have in common?
6. Why are viruses not classified as organisms?
7. How do scientists classify organisms?
8. Give several examples of communicable diseases.
9. Under what conditions can a virus reproduce?
10. Describe the major cell structures.
11. Explain the classification system used to name organisms.
12. What are some ways to control bacteria?
13. What are some examples of simple organisms?
14. What is the difference between a producer and a consumer?
15. Name some different ways organisms protect their embryos.
16. Where is chromatin found in a cell, and why is it important?
17. What is mitosis?
18. What is heredity?
19. How are traits passed from parents to offspring?
20. How does a recessive gene differ from a dominant gene?
21. How does natural selection differ from selective breeding?
22. What is a mutation?
23. How is fission related to regeneration?
24. If an organism has 500 pairs of chromosomes in each of its cells, how many chromosomes will be present in each new cell produced by meiosis?
25. What is the difference between a zygote and an embryo?

Recalling Activities

Write a short paragraph for each question or statement.

1. How can you use cells to classify organisms?
2. How are characteristics used in classification?
3. How can the growth of bacteria be controlled?
4. What are the growth needs of fungi?
5. How do cells divide?
6. How do plants reproduce from one parent?
7. How common are dominant and recessive traits?
8. What are the chances for tallness?

Project Ideas

1. What are warts? Find out about some of the causes and remedies for warts that have been suggested by folklore.
2. Make a collection of thirty to fifty different objects and discover how many ways you can group and name them.
3. Compare the rates of decay of different kinds of fruit such as dried, frozen, boiled, canned, fresh, and pickled. Hypothesize the factors that affect the different rates.
4. Find the smallest plant cutting that will regenerate a new plant.

Books to Read

Genetics: From Mendel to Gene Splicing by Caroline Arnold, Franklin Watts, Inc.: Danbury, CT, 1986.

Hidden Worlds: Pictures of the Invisible by Seymour Simon, Morrow, William, & Co., Inc.: New York, 1983.

The Story of Life on Earth by Michael Benton, Franklin Watts, Inc.: Danbury, CT, 1986.

Microbes and Bacteria by Francene Sabin, Troll Associates: Mahwah, NJ, 1985.

Human Body

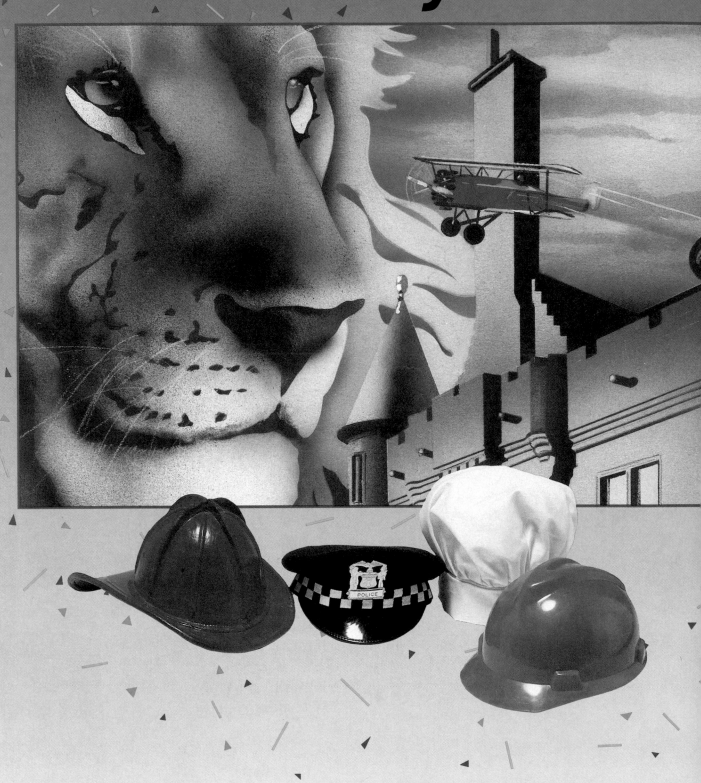

P eople always say to me
"What do you think you'd like to be
When you grow up?"
And I say "Why,
I think I'd like to be the sky
Or be a plane or train or mouse
Or maybe be a haunted house
Or something furry, rough and wild . . .
Or maybe I will stay a child."

"The Question"
Karla Kuskin

SCIENCE
In Your World

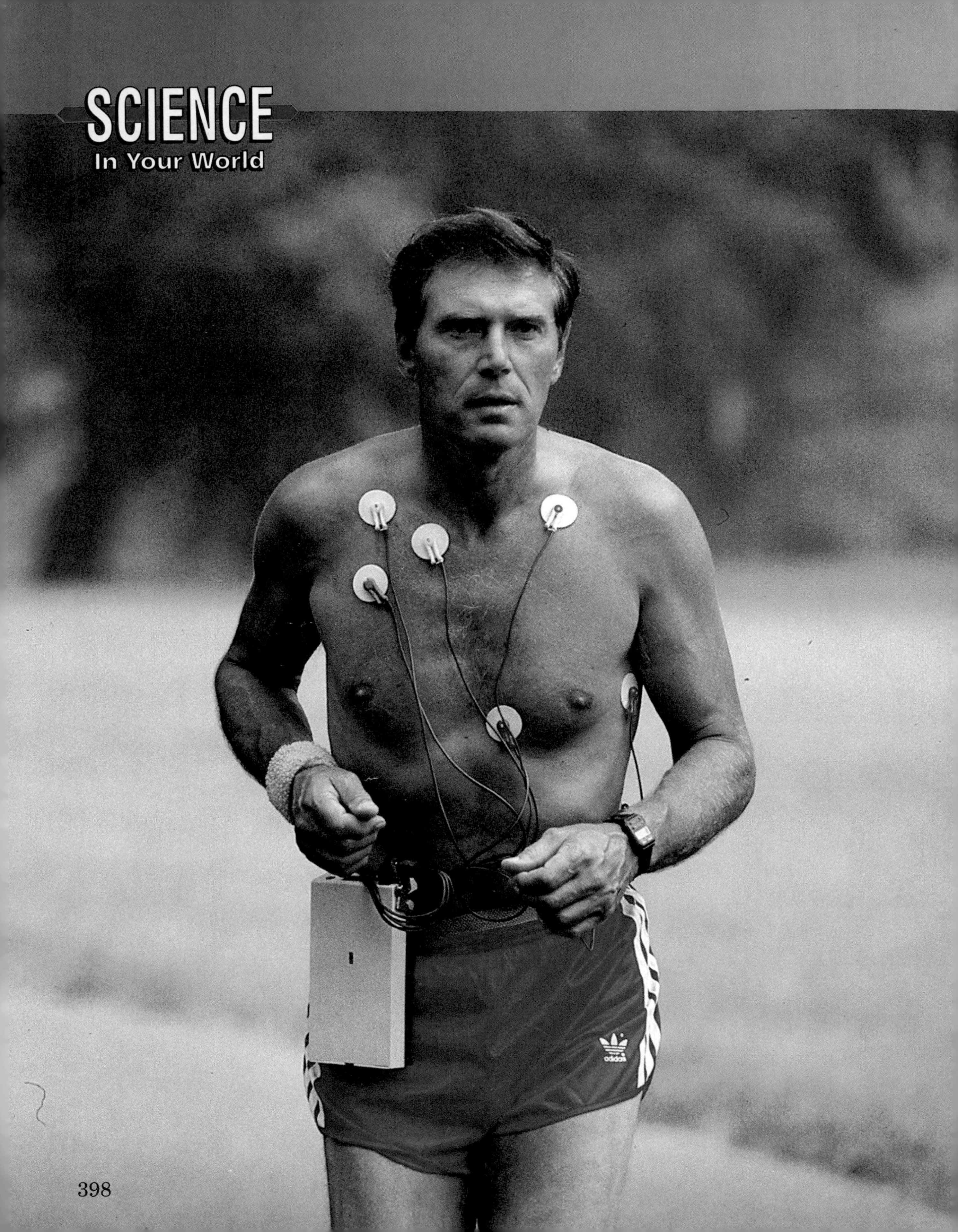

CHAPTER 16

Circulation and Respiration

Beating about 70 times a minute, your heart pumps blood to the brain, lungs, kidneys, and other vital parts of the body through the circulatory system. Arteries carry the oxygen-rich blood from your heart, and veins return the blood to your heart. As you increase your activity, your heart beats faster. The runner's heartbeat will increase as he runs and then return to normal when he stops running. The runner can check his heart monitor as he runs to determine his heart rate.

ACTIVITY

Have You Ever...

Measured Your Breathing Rate?

Place your hand on your chest and count for one minute the times your chest lifts as you inhale. Write down the number. Run in place for one minute. Check your breathing rate again. Write down the number. Take your breathing rate every two minutes. How much time passes before your breathing rate is the same as the initial count? How does exercise affect your breathing rate?

Circulation

Have you ever traveled on a bus or an airplane? People use such vehicles to travel or to send packages from one place to another. Buses and airplanes are part of what is known as a transport system. Can you think of other vehicles that belong to transport systems?

Communities have different transport systems to help move people and things from one place to another. A subway in a large city is another example of a transport system.

There are also transport systems in your body. The **circulatory system** is one of these. It's called a transport system because its job is to carry food and oxygen to your body cells. These substances are necessary to each cell's growth and repair. While cells grow and repair, wastes are produced. These wastes must be removed. Your circulatory system transports these wastes from your cells to organs that release the wastes from your body.

Transport systems remove waste materials.

Your body is made up of over 70 trillion cells. These cells are the basic building blocks of organisms. As a complex organism, you show all the features of life. You grow, develop, use energy, and need food. The trillions of cells that help you do these things are grouped into tissues, organs, and systems.

Muscles and blood are examples of tissues. They work together to form organs such as the brain, stomach, and lungs. When groups of organs work together, they form systems such as the circulatory system.

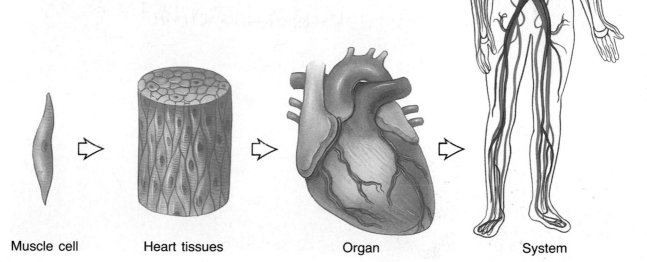

Muscle cell   Heart tissues   Organ   System

The Circulatory System

The circulatory system has three parts. First, there's the heart. Your heart is an organ made of muscle and nerve tissue. Your heart pumps blood, the second part of your circulatory system. And finally, there are the blood vessels. These vessels are tubes that transport the blood that your heart pumps.

A human heart beats more than 100,000 times a day at an average of 60 to 80 times a minute. The heart rate varies depending upon the individual and what he or she is doing. Your heart beats faster when you're exercising than when you're inactive. A heart beat is a result of your heart muscle contracting. If you make a fist of your hand and squeeze gently in and out, it is similar to what happens to the heart as it contracts and relaxes. With each contraction, your heart pumps blood through your blood vessels to body cells. Blood then flows back to your heart in other vessels. Your blood is constantly flowing through your blood vessels.

What determines your heart rate?

Your heart rate is determined by your age and your level of activity.

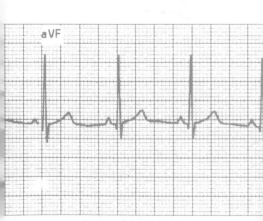

Your heart beats faster when you are exercising.

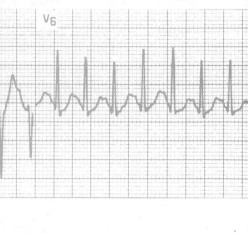

ACTIVITY

You Can...

Check Your Pulse

Place the tips of two fingers on the side of your neck. Feel for your pulse. Count the number of beats you feel in 10 seconds. Multiply the number of beats by 6 to figure your pulse for one minute. Record this number. Take your pulse in this same way two more times. Find the average of these three numbers. Use this number as your normal pulse. How could you find your exercise pulse? How would it compare with your normal pulse?

The Heart

Your heart is about the size of your fist and is located near the center of your chest behind your breastbone. The drawing shows the inside of a heart with its four chambers—two upper and two lower. The upper chambers are called the left **atrium** (AY tree um) and right atrium. The two lower chambers are called the left and right **ventricles** (VEN trih kulz). Find them in the drawing below.

As blood circulates, blood from your body cells returns to the right atrium. The atrium contracts and forces blood into the right ventricle. When blood enters the right ventricle, it also contracts and pumps blood to the lungs to pick up oxygen and release carbon dioxide. Blood rich in oxygen flows back to the heart and enters the left atrium. The atrium contracts and forces blood into the left ventricle. Blood is then pumped from the left ventricle through a network of blood vessels to all parts of your body.

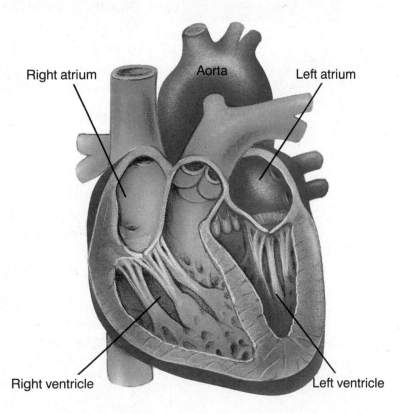

Right atrium
Aorta
Left atrium
Right ventricle
Left ventricle

The heart has four chambers.

Blood Vessels

Your body has three kinds of blood vessels—
arteries, veins, and capillaries.

Arteries are vessels that transport blood away
from your heart to all the parts of your body. They
are shown in red in the diagram below. The largest
artery is the aorta (ay ORT uh). It leads out of the
left ventricle and allows blood to flow into smaller
arteries throughout your body. As these arteries
become smaller, they branch into microscopic blood
vessels called **capillaries.**

If you could stretch out all your capillaries and
place them end to end, they would stretch 80,000
kilometers! Capillaries are in every tissue of your
body and are only one cell thick. Materials pass
through capillary walls into and out of body cells.
Food and oxygen pass from capillaries into body
cells, as waste materials, such as carbon dioxide,
pass out of body cells and into capillaries.

Capillaries connect arteries with veins, which are
colored blue in the diagram below. **Veins** carry blood
from body cells back to the heart. Valves in veins
prevent blood from flowing back and keep blood
flowing toward the heart.

Define arteries and veins.

What vessels connect the
arteries and veins?

The transfer of materials
between blood and body cells
takes place in the capillaries.

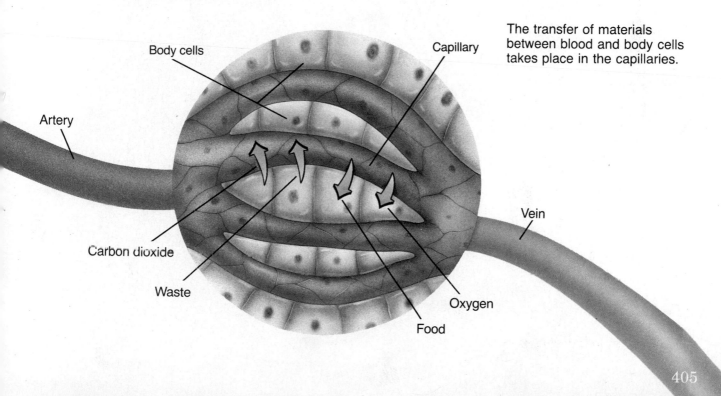

Body cells

Capillary

Artery

Carbon dioxide

Waste

Oxygen

Food

Vein

405

CIRCULATORY SYSTEM

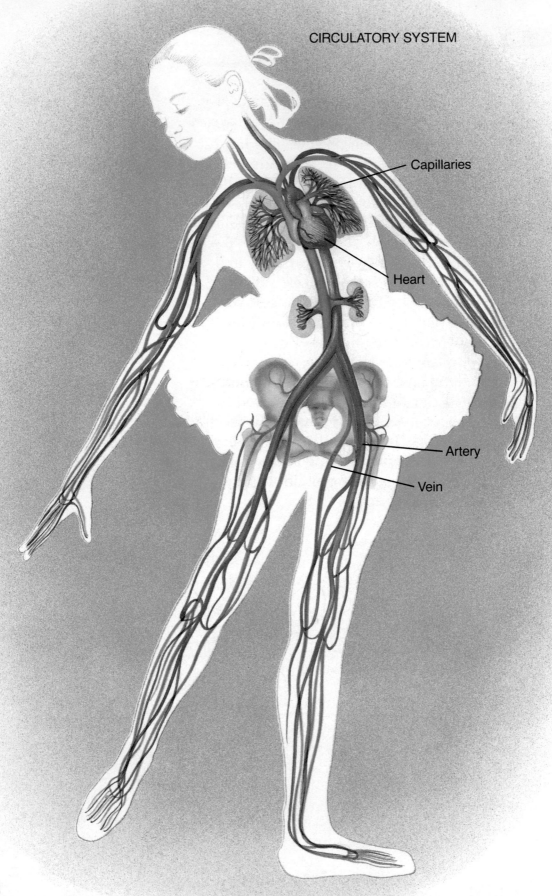

Capillaries

Heart

Artery

Vein

Blood

Blood is a mixture—it's composed of solid cells and a liquid. The liquid part is made mostly of water and is called **plasma.** Food and other materials are transported to your cells in the plasma, while wastes like carbon dioxide are removed.

The solid cells in your blood are all microscopic. There are red cells, white cells, and platelets. **Red cells** contain a chemical that combines with oxygen as the blood flows through lung tissue. As blood circulates through your body, it gives off oxygen and picks up the waste carbon dioxide.

White cells destroy germs and other foreign matter that enter your body. You might have seen white cells in the form of pus around a sore or a splinter that entered your skin tissue.

When you last cut yourself, did you notice that your blood quickly stopped flowing? It did so because a blood clot formed. But what caused the blood to clot? A blood clot forms because of small cells in the plasma called **platelets.** In the clotting process, platelets collect around injured tissue and produce chemicals that form a threadlike protein. It's this protein that forms a blood clot.

Would You Believe?

A drop of blood can completely circulate through your body in one minute.

Red blood cells in blood vessel

White blood cells

What is the function of the circulatory system?

As you can see, the circulatory system brings necessary materials to all of your body cells, as well as removing the "garbage" they produce. This transportation process is going on whether you're sleeping cozily in your bed, walking down the school hallway, or marching in the band. Your circulatory system is constantly at work.

Lesson Summary

- The circulatory system transports food and oxygen to each cell of your body. It removes wastes from each cell of your body.
- The heart, blood, and blood vessels make up the circulatory system.

Lesson Review

1. What are the functions of the circulatory system?
2. Name the three main parts of the circulatory system.
3. Trace the flow of blood from the right atrium to the left ventricle of the heart.
★4. Why does a scab form when you get cut? Why is it important?

What causes blood to circulate?

What you need

meat baster
thin rubber tubing
glass of water
empty water glass
pencil and paper

What to do

1. Attach one end of the rubber tubing to the baster. Put the other end into a glass of water.
2. Squeeze the bulb of the baster to suck up water.
3. Lift up the rubber tubing and put the other end into an empty glass.
4. Use the fingers of one hand to hold the tube in the glass. Lightly squeeze the rubber tubing.
5. Give a strong squeeze to the bulb of the baster.
6. Repeat steps 2 to 5 several times. Observe and feel the flow of water.

What did you learn?

1. What happened when the bulb of the baster was squeezed?
2. Where could you feel a pulse in this system?

Using what you learned

1. What part of the baster and rubber tubing system is like the left ventricle of the heart? the aorta? an artery? the blood?
2. What else would you need to make a complete model of the circulatory system?

Respiration

LESSON 2 GOALS
You will learn
● about the functions of the respiratory system.
● about the parts of the respiratory system.

The sixth graders at Clark Middle School were having a Career Fair. Guests were invited to come and talk about the ways they earned a living. Louisa invited her uncle to talk about his work as a marine biologist. Since he does some of his work underwater, he brought slides and examples of his diving equipment. During his talk he explained that divers wear air tanks so they can breathe and remain underwater for long periods of time.

After Louisa's uncle left, the class began its science lesson about the importance of oxygen to the body. The class read about people who had gone without food or sleep for periods of time. However, they learned that these people couldn't go without breathing for any length of time because their body cells constantly need oxygen. This was the reason Louisa's uncle used air tanks to breathe when he went underwater. The air in the tanks provided the necessary oxygen.

Louisa's teacher asked the class if they knew how oxygen is transported to body cells. Do you know? If you remember from the previous lesson that oxygen is transported to your body cells by red blood cells as your blood flows through your body, then you are correct. The question you and Louisa's class now have to answer is: How does the oxygen reach your blood? Let's read to find out.

For oxygen to reach your blood, another transport system of the body is involved—the **respiratory system.** This system transports gases into and out of your body. During the process of **respiration,** there is an exchange of gases.

What is the function of the respiratory system?

Glassblowers know how to control their inhaling and exhaling to do their job.

Oxygen in the air enters your body when you inhale, and carbon dioxide exits when you exhale. This process of inhaling and exhaling is called breathing. Place your hands on your rib cage, and take a deep breath, then exhale. What do you observe? As you inhale, your chest area expands. As you exhale, your chest area gets smaller.

The muscle helping you breathe is your diaphragm (DI uh fram). As you can see in the drawing below, the **diaphragm** is a muscle that separates your chest area from the lower part of your body. When you inhale, your diaphragm contracts and other muscles pull your ribs apart so that air can move into your lungs. When you exhale, your diaphragm relaxes and your ribs move together, forcing gases out of your lungs.

The respiratory system, like the circulatory system, is made up of several parts. Each has its own function.

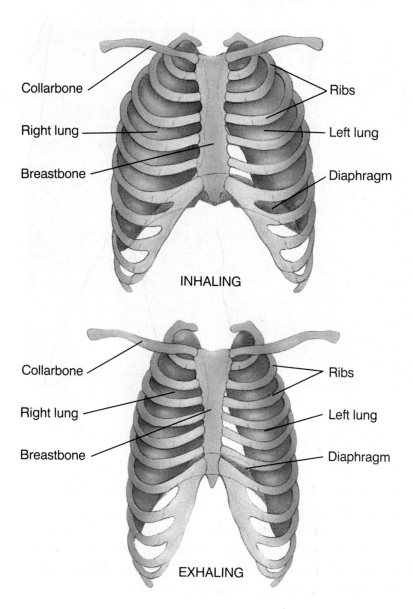

Collarbone

Right lung

Breastbone

Ribs

Left lung

Diaphragm

INHALING

Collarbone

Right lung

Breastbone

Ribs

Left lung

Diaphragm

EXHALING

Rib muscles work together with your diaphragm, causing air to enter and leave your lungs.

The Respiratory System

The air you breathe enters your body through your nose or mouth. From there it enters your nasal passages, where it's warmed and moistened. The nasal passages are lined with mucus (MYEW kus) and hairlike structures called cilia. **Mucus** is a moist, sticky fluid in the lining of your nasal passages. Mucus and cilia act as filters—they trap dust and other particles in the air you inhale. When dust and other particles accumulate in your nasal passages, you sneeze. Sneezing loosens and expels the trapped particles.

Like the filter worn in the picture, cilia in your nasal passages filter out particles in the air you breathe.

Look at the drawing on page 414. You can see that inhaled air passes into a stiff tube called the **trachea** (TRAY kee uh). Air passes from the trachea to the lungs. Mucus and cilia are also present in the trachea and trap small particles so they don't get into your lungs. If you are in a very dusty room, you may find yourself coughing. This happens because dust has become lodged in your trachea, where the mucus and cilia have trapped it.

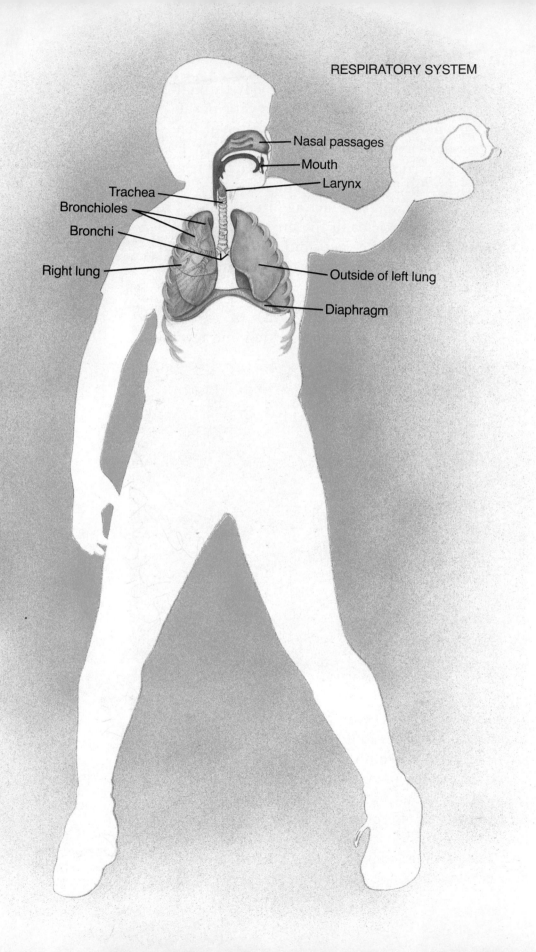

RESPIRATORY SYSTEM

Nasal passages

Mouth

Larynx

Trachea

Bronchioles

Bronchi

Right lung

Outside of left lung

Diaphragm

Look again at the drawing, and locate the **larynx** (LER ingks). As you can see, your larynx is at the upper end of your trachea. Your larynx contains your vocal chords. When air passes over your vocal chords, it causes them to vibrate and make sounds.

Define larynx.

Have you ever sung in a chorus or music class? Perhaps you had trouble singing some of the high notes. What did the music teacher tell you to do? Did he or she tell you to take a deep breath? If so, it was because the more air you inhale, the greater the vibrations when you exhale. These vibrations cause the vocal chords to make more sound. Listen carefully to your favorite singer. Trained singers not only take music lessons but also are trained to breathe properly in order to sing high and low notes.

Singers inhale and exhale more air so they can create a wider range of sounds.

415

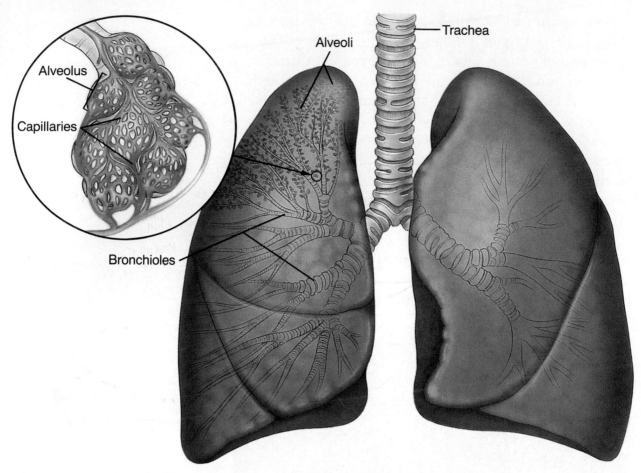

Alveolus

Capillaries

Bronchioles

Alveoli

Trachea

Oxygen and carbon dioxide are exchanged between air and blood in the alveoli.

If you trace the trachea in the drawing on page 414 with your finger, you will see that it branches into two tubes called **bronchi** (BRAHN ki). These bronchi are short tubes that carry air into your right and left lungs. Inside the lungs, the tubes branch many times, forming **bronchioles** (BRAHNG kee ohlz). The bronchioles lead into tiny air sacs called **alveoli** (al VEE uh li), shown in the drawing above. There are about 300 million alveoli in your lungs. If these air sacs were opened up and spread out, they would cover an area about the size of an average classroom floor. It is here, in each tiny alveolus, that gases are exchanged. Oxygen moves from the alveoli into the capillaries that surround each of these tiny air sacs, and carbon dioxide moves from the capillaries into the alveoli. In the drawing, blood vessels colored red indicate oxygen-rich blood. Blood vessels colored blue show blood rich in carbon dioxide.

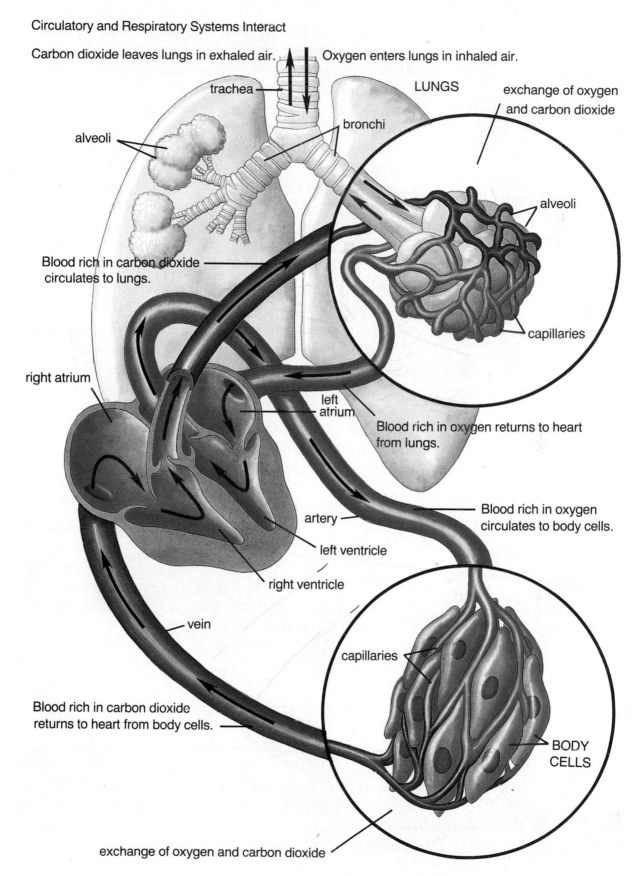

Circulatory and Respiratory Systems Interact

Carbon dioxide leaves lungs in exhaled air.

Oxygen enters lungs in inhaled air.

trachea

bronchi

LUNGS

exchange of oxygen and carbon dioxide

alveoli

alveoli

capillaries

Blood rich in carbon dioxide circulates to lungs.

right atrium

left atrium

Blood rich in oxygen returns to heart from lungs.

artery

Blood rich in oxygen circulates to body cells.

left ventricle

right ventricle

vein

capillaries

BODY CELLS

Blood rich in carbon dioxide returns to heart from body cells.

exchange of oxygen and carbon dioxide

Do you understand now why the circulatory and respiratory systems are called transport systems? Each system transports materials your body needs and each system also transports waste materials produced by your body cells. To help you understand how these two systems work together, look at the diagram on page 417. Follow the pathway of air into and out of the lungs and the pathway of blood as it circulates from the heart to the lungs and back to the heart. Then follow the pathway of blood as it circulates from the heart to body cells and back to the heart.

Why is it important to protect your respiratory system?

Like all the systems in your body, the respiratory system is essential to your life and can't always be repaired if it's damaged. It's also important to the quality of the life you lead, and the things you are able to do. People who suffer from lung problems such as emphysema do so because alveoli are clogged. Even though their blood circulates, the air can't get into the clogged alveoli. This causes shortness of breath. Many people with emphysema have difficulty doing such everyday activities as walking up the stairs.

Testing can help diagnose respiratory problems.

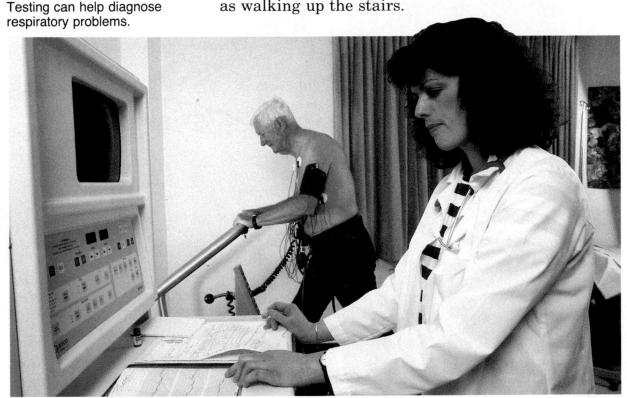

A scientist looks for asbestos in insulation. Asbestos was removed from many schools after it was linked to lung cancer.

Your respiratory system can be damaged if you're not careful. For example, people who choose to smoke risk developing lung cancer and other respiratory problems. In Chapter 18, you will be reading about other ways of keeping your body healthy.

Lesson Summary

- The respiratory system is a transport system. It transports gases into and out of your body. During the process of respiration, there is an exchange of gases.
- The respiratory system includes the nose, larynx, trachea, bronchi, bronchioles, and alveoli.

Lesson Review

1. Explain why living organisms need oxygen.
2. What happens to your diaphragm when you inhale? when you exhale?
3. What do mucus and cilia do in the respiratory system?
★4. Most men have longer and thicker vocal chords than women. How does this explain the differences between men's and women's voices?

What do we exhale?

What you need

safety goggles
graduated cylinder
limewater
2 test tubes
test tube rack
drinking straw
mirror
pencil and paper

What to do

1. Put on safety goggles. Pour 6 mL of limewater from the graduated cylinder into each of 2 test tubes in the test tube rack. Label one test tube C for control.
2. Place a drinking straw in the other test tube. Blow your breath out *gently* through the straw several times. A steady stream of air should bubble through the limewater. Continue this process for five minutes.
3. Observe any change in the limewater.
4. Take a deep breath through your nose. Blow your breath out onto a mirror that is held close to your mouth.
5. Observe what happens to the mirror. Rub your finger across the spot that has formed on the mirror. Observe your finger.

What did you learn?

1. What changes in the limewater did you observe after you exhaled into it?
2. Why did you need a control test tube?
3. Describe what you saw on the mirror.

Using what you learned

1. What do you exhale that could have caused the change in the limewater?
2. What evidence shows that we exhale water vapor?

Summary

Lesson 1
- The circulatory system transports food and oxygen to each cell of the body. It removes wastes from each cell of the body.
- The heart, blood, and blood vessels make up the circulatory system.

Lesson 2
- The respiratory system is a transport system. It transports gases into and out of your body. During the process of respiration, there is an exchange of gases.
- The respiratory system includes the nose, larynx, trachea, bronchi, bronchioles, and alveoli.

Science Words

Fill in the blank with the correct word or words from the list.

circulatory system

arteries	atrium
capillaries	ventricles
veins	trachea
plasma	larynx
red cells	bronchi
white cells	bronchioles
platelets	alveoli

respiratory system
respiration
diaphragm
mucus

1. The system that transports materials in the blood to and from the cells of the body is the ____.

2. A moist, sticky substance that lines the nose is ____.
3. Small blood vessels that connect arteries and veins are ____.
4. Blood vessels that carry blood to the heart are ____.
5. Blood vessels that carry blood away from the heart are ____.
6. The muscle that separates the chest area from the lower part of the body is the ____.
7. The exchange of gases is part of the process of ____.
8. Cells in the plasma that cause blood clots to form are ____.
9. Cells that destroy foreign matter in the blood are ____.
10. ____ is the liquid part of blood.

Questions

Recalling Ideas

Correctly complete each of the following sentences.

1. An example of tissue is
   (a) the heart.   (c) the lungs.
   (b) the blood.   (d) the brain.

2. The structures for air exchange in the lungs are
   (a) alveoli.   (c) veins.
   (b) nephrons.   (d) cilia.

3. Oxygen is added to the blood and carbon dioxide is released in the
   (a) lungs.   (c) liver.
   (b) heart.   (d) brain.

4. Each upper chamber of your heart is called
   (a) an aorta.   (c) a ventricle.
   (b) an artery.   (d) an atrium.

5. A muscle that helps control breathing is the
   (a) alveolus.   (c) diaphragm.
   (b) trachea.   (d) bronchioles.

6. All of the following structures are part of the respiratory system EXCEPT
   (a) lungs.   (c) alveoli.
   (b) bronchi.   (d) ventricles.

7. Air passes from the nose to the lungs through the
   (a) trachea.   (c) larynx.
   (b) aorta.   (d) bronchi.

8. When your ribs move up and out, you are
   (a) exhaling.   (c) transpiring.
   (b) inhaling.   (d) respiring.

9. Your vocal chords are contained in your
   (a) trachea.   (c) diaphragm.
   (b) larynx.   (d) bronchi.

10. The trachea branches into two tubes called the
    (a) bronchioles.   (c) alveoli.
    (b) bronchi.   (d) capillaries.

Examining Ideas

Determine whether each of the following statements is true or false. Rewrite the false statements to make them correct.

1. Your circulatory system transports food, water, and carbon dioxide to each cell of your body.

2. Veins transport blood from the heart to the lungs and all other parts of the body.

3. The largest artery in your body is the aorta.

4. Materials pass between your body cells and your blood mainly through the walls of arteries.

5. Your diaphragm relaxes as you inhale and contracts as you exhale.

6. Mucus and cilia lining the trachea trap small particles and move them away from the lungs.

7. Oxygen and carbon dioxide are exchanged between the capillaries and the alveoli of the lungs.

8. The branching tubes that carry air to the alveoli are the bronchi.
9. Platelets destroy foreign matter that enters your body.
10. Atria connect arteries and veins.
11. Valves in veins keep blood flowing away from the heart.
12. The right and left atria contract to pump blood away from the heart to the lungs and other parts of the body.
13. Groups of organs working together form systems.
14. All humans have the same heart rate.
15. The four parts of the circulatory system are the heart, the blood, the blood vessels, and the lungs.
16. Both the circulatory system and the respiratory system are transport systems.

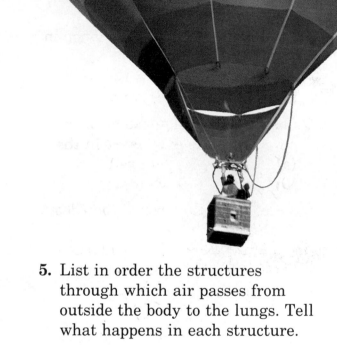

Understanding Ideas

Answer the following questions using complete sentences.

1. How do the circulatory system and the respiratory system work together?
2. What happens to inhaled air before it reaches the lungs?
3. What is the order in which blood flows through the chambers of the heart when it returns to the heart from the body?
4. Describe the parts of the circulatory system and explain the function of each. Explain the function of the circulatory system.

5. List in order the structures through which air passes from outside the body to the lungs. Tell what happens in each structure.

Thinking Critically

Think about what you have learned in this chapter. Answer the following questions using complete sentences.

1. How is the circulatory system like a transport system in a large city?
2. Smoking destroys the cilia in the nasal passages. Explain how you think this would affect the quality of the air that reaches the lungs of someone who smokes.
3. Trace the path of waste carbon dioxide from a cell in your leg until it leaves your body.

Digestion and Excretion

How many plastic containers do you have in your school and home? To mold each container, small granules of raw plastic are taken into the plastic factory, changed into a liquid, mixed with chemicals, and then poured into a mold.

Your body has a similar factory, called the digestive system, that takes in food. You use your teeth to grind the food. Then enzymes throughout the system change starches to sugar and digest protein and fat so they can provide nourishment for your body.

ACTIVITY

Have You Ever...

Wondered About Digestion?

Fill two baby-food jars with water. Drop a whole sugar cube in one jar and a crushed cube in the other jar. Put the lid on each jar and shake. How long does it take for the sugar to dissolve? Now think about the process of chewing and swallowing food. What effect do you think saliva has on food? Do you think digestion speeds up if food is chewed into small pieces before being swallowed?

Digestion

LESSON 1 GOALS
You will learn
● about enzymes and how they aid digestion.
● about the parts of the digestive system.
● how food is digested and passed into the blood.

What's your favorite food? Perhaps it's pizza. Do you know why you eat pizza, or for that matter any other kind of food? You eat because you, like all organisms, need energy. Every cell in your body is constantly using energy. You get the energy your cells need from the food you eat.

Let's find out how one bite of pizza helps supply the energy your cells need. You know that a cell can't use pizza straight from the delivery box. Your body needs to change it into a usable form. When you take a bite of pizza, it begins a long journey through a continuous tube of organs in your digestive system. Your digestive system includes all the parts of your body that break down food. Besides the organs that form the tube, there are other organs in the digestive system that produce chemicals called enzymes. **Enzymes** are substances that speed up a chemical reaction in your body and help break down the food you eat. With the help of enzymes, your body can digest most foods in a few

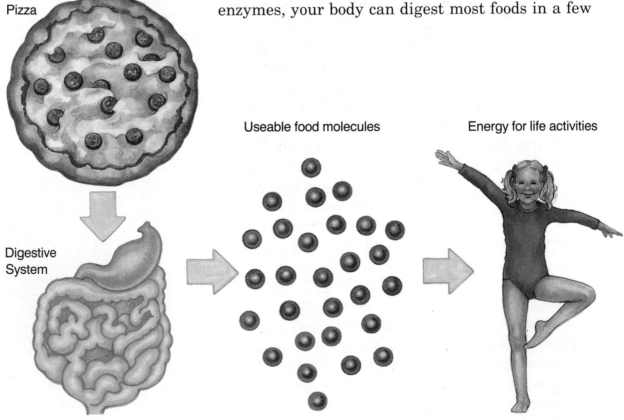

Pizza

Digestive System

Useable food molecules

Energy for life activities

hours. Through the process of digestion, your body changes food to molecules that your cells can use for all of life's activities. Within your cells, these molecules combine with oxygen to release energy.

As you chew your food, it is physically broken down into smaller and smaller pieces and mixed by the action of your teeth and tongue with the liquid in your mouth called **saliva** (suh LI vuh). Saliva is produced in glands that surround your mouth. From these glands, saliva flows into your mouth through tubes called ducts. Saliva begins to chemically break down the food in your mouth. It also helps moisten the food, making it easier to swallow. After being thoroughly chewed and moistened, the pizza is ready to leave your mouth, and you swallow.

Place your fingers under your chin and swallow. Can you feel the downward movement of the muscles? As you swallow, these muscles push the food into your esophagus (ih SAHF uh gus), another organ that is part of the digestive tube. Your **esophagus** is a muscular tube that connects your mouth with your stomach.

What is digestion?

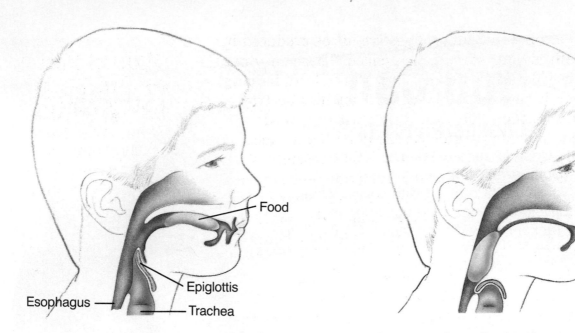

As you study the drawing that shows the esophagus and trachea, notice how close together they are. Find the **epiglottis** (ep uh GLAHT us). This is a flap of tissue that covers your trachea when you swallow food. When your epiglottis is closed, it prevents food from going into your trachea and causing you to choke. Have you ever had someone tell you a funny joke when you were swallowing food? When you suddenly laughed, your epiglottis opened to allow air to be pulled into your lungs. If a crumb of food slipped past your epiglottis, you felt as if you were choking.

After safely passing the epiglottis, the food continues to move toward your stomach. You can't control the muscles in your esophagus. The muscles contract and relax, always moving the food downward. If any food remains stuck in your esophagus after the first wave of muscle contractions, a second wave will carry it on down to your stomach.

Do you know where your stomach is? Your stomach tells you its location every time you're hungry. Your **stomach** is a small, saclike organ at the end of the esophagus that holds and digests food. The muscles of your stomach contract and relax, causing a churning action that breaks the food you have eaten into even smaller particles. At the same

What's the function of the epiglottis?

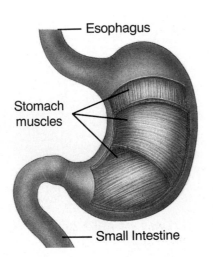

time, enzymes and other digestive juices produced in the walls of your stomach are added. These enzymes and other digestive juices mix with the food, helping to break it down into molecules. They also destroy bacteria that entered your mouth with the food.

About four hours after you swallowed your food, it is ready to leave your stomach. It now resembles a soupy mixture. Muscular movement of your stomach pushes the mixture to the next organ in your digestive tube, your small intestine. Why do you think you often feel hungry about four hours after your last meal?

Food enters your **small intestine** through a narrow opening at the lower end of your stomach. The opening is controlled by a group of muscles that allows food to flow into your small intestine in small spurts. Most of the chemical processes of digestion take place in your small intestine. In spite of the fact that it is called *small* intestine, it's really quite long—about seven meters. How can your body hold an organ that's seven meters long? Your small intestine fits inside your abdomen because it's arranged in many coils. You can see in the drawing on page 431 how it fits in a very small space.

It's in your small intestine that the food is finally changed into a molecular form that can be used by your body cells. The walls of your small intestine produce more enzymes. Other organs in your body also produce enzymes and digestive juices and flow them to your small intestine to aid digestion.

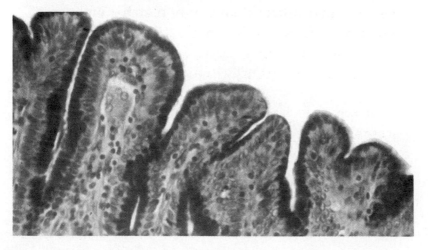

Cutaway view of a small intestine

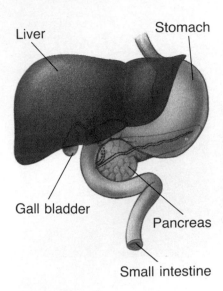

Liver

Stomach

Gall bladder

Pancreas

Small intestine

Ducts lead from the gall bladder and pancreas into the small intestine.

How does the liver aid in digestion?

One organ that is very important to digestion is your **liver**. The digestive fluid it makes is called bile. Bile is a yellowish green fluid made in the liver and stored in the gall bladder. It travels through ducts to the small intestine. Some foods you eat, such as peanut butter, bacon, and margarine, contain fats. Bile breaks fats into small droplets. These droplets are easier for the enzymes to break down into molecules. Find the liver and gall bladder in the drawing of the digestive system on page 431.

Your **pancreas** is another organ that sends enzymes and digestive juices to the small intestine. Find the pancreas in the drawing. It lies close to the stomach. A duct carries the enzymes and digestive juices from the pancreas to the duct that brings bile from the gall bladder. The juices move together to the small intestine.

The food is now in a molecular form that can be used by your cells. But how do the food molecules move from the digestive system to the cells where they are used? Most food molecules enter the blood from your small intestine. A few substances enter from your stomach. Inside the walls of your stomach and small intestine are many capillaries. Food molecules pass from the digestive system into your blood by **diffusion** (dihf YEW zhun). In diffusion molecules move from where they are present in large amounts to where they are present in small amounts. Since there are many food molecules in your stomach and small intestine, they diffuse into the capillaries, which have only a small amount of food molecules.

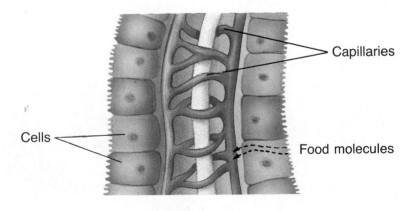

Capillaries

Cells

Food molecules

Food molecules pass through the walls of the small intestine into the bloodstream.

DIGESTIVE SYSTEM

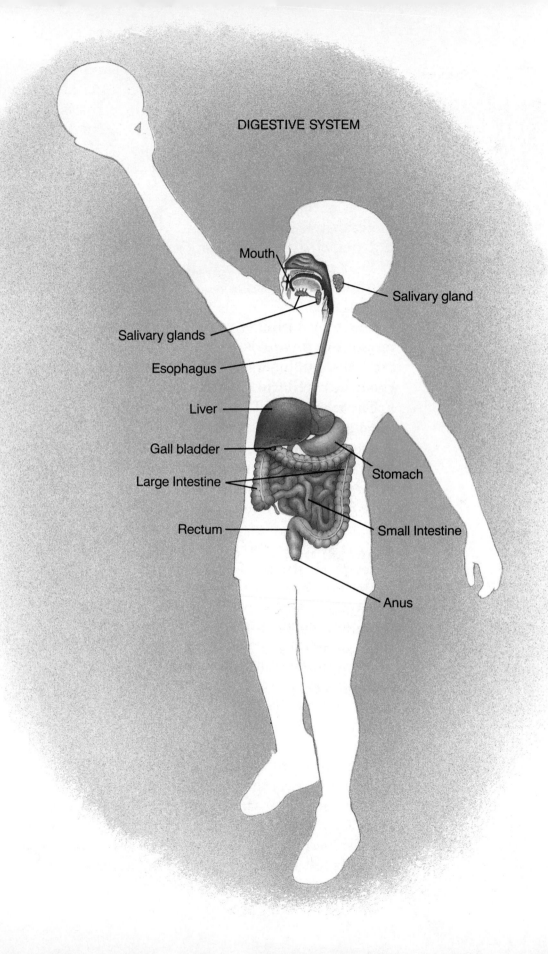

Mouth

Salivary gland

Salivary glands

Esophagus

Liver

Gall bladder

Large Intestine

Rectum

Stomach

Small Intestine

Anus

431

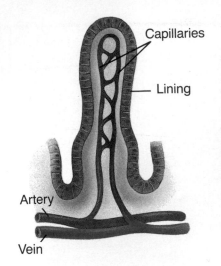

Capillaries

Lining

Artery

Vein

The inner lining of your small intestine has millions of tiny folds called **villi** (VIHL i). The villi are like tiny fingers. Inside the villi are capillaries. Find the capillaries in the drawing of the villus. Food molecules diffuse through the villi walls into the capillaries and are circulated by your blood to all your body cells. The photo above shows a magnified view of the inside of the small intestine. The millions of tiny villi give the intestine wall a velvet appearance.

Food That's Not Digested

Your body doesn't digest some of the food you eat. Undigested food moves into your **large intestine** from your small intestine. Another name for the large intestine is colon. This is the last organ in the digestive tube that food will pass through before leaving your body. The large intestine, which is about two meters long, forms a loop and partly covers the small intestine. Find the large intestine in the drawing on page 431.

Your large intestine doesn't contain villi. Its smooth walls contain many blood vessels that absorb most of the water that remains in the undigested food. By the time food gets to your large intestine, the usable nutrients have diffused into your blood. What is left is waste material, or materials that are difficult or impossible to digest.

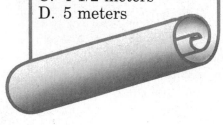

SCIENCE AND . . .
Math

If a small intestine is 6 3/4 meters long, how much longer is it than a large intestine that is 2 1/4 meters long?
A. 3 1/2 meters
B. 4 meters
C. 4 1/2 meters
D. 5 meters

Bacteria that live in your large intestine work further on undigested food. Your body benefits from the presence of the bacteria, since they produce vitamin K and some B vitamins your body needs.

The foods that aren't easily digested, called high-fiber foods, are a very important part of your diet. High-fiber foods help keep the muscles of your digestive tube healthy. Some examples of high-fiber foods are popcorn, broccoli, and whole-grain bread. Study the photo below of high-fiber foods to discover more healthful foods you can add to your diet.

Solid wastes that remain in your large intestine move into your rectum for storage until they leave your body in a bowel movement. The **rectum** is a very muscular part of the digestive tube. It enables the waste material to be pushed from the body through the anus (AY nus). Usually it takes about 20 hours for food to move through your entire digestive system, but this time varies from person to person.

Name two ways you benefit from bacteria in your intestines.

Why are high-fiber foods important?

High-fiber foods

433

Table 1   Organs of Your Digestive System

Digestive Organ	How Organ Processes Food
Mouth	Chews, grinds, moistens with saliva
Esophagus	Moves food to stomach
Stomach	Churns, adds enzymes and digestive juices, digests some food, moves food to the small intestine
Small Intestine	Adds enzymes, digests food, diffuses food to blood through villi, moves undigested food to large intestine
Large intestine	Bacteria breaks down food wastes here, makes vitamin K and some B vitamins, removes most of remaining water, eliminates wastes

Use the table above to review the organs of your digestive system and answer these questions. In which organ do almost all the food molecules diffuse into the blood? Which organ adds saliva to the food? Which organ moves the food into the stomach? Now close your book, and have a classmate use the table to ask you some more questions.

Lesson Summary

- Enzymes are substances that speed up chemical reactions such as the process of digestion.
- The mouth, esophagus, stomach, small intestine, and large intestine, along with the liver, gall bladder, and pancreas, form the digestive system of your body.
- The digestive system breaks down food into molecules so it can be used by your body cells.

Lesson Review

1. In what parts of the digestive system are enzymes made?
2. What happens to food in the small intestine?
★3. Why are villi so important to your body?

Use Application Activity on pages 515, 516.

How does diffusion take place?

What you need

2 paper cups
starch solution
water
safety goggles
apron
iodine solution in dropper bottle
dialysis tubing, 2 15-cm lengths
2 marbles
2 small wide-mouth jars
2 pencils
string
paper towels
pencil and paper

What to do

1. Tie the bottom of each length of tubing shut. Put a marble in each. Fill the tubing half full of water. Tie the top of each length tightly shut. Then tie one length of tubing to each pencil.
2. Place the pencils on the jars. The tubing should hang down freely.
3. Fill one jar almost to the top with starch solution. Fill the other jar with water.
4. Let the jars stand overnight. Remove the tubing from the jars. Dry off the outside of each.
5. Pour some of the water from one length into a cup.
6. Put on safety goggles and an apron. Put 3 drops of iodine solution in the cup. **CAUTION:** *Do not touch the*

iodine solution. Iodine turns blue when starch is present. Record what you observe.
7. Repeat step 6 with the other bag.

What did you learn?

1. How did the bags compare when you removed them from the jars?
2. What did you observe when you put iodine solution in the cups?

Using what you learned

1. What process did you observe? Explain.
2. What happens to starch in your body?

435

Excretion

LESSON 2 GOALS
You will learn
● what excretion is.
● about organs needed for excretion.
● about structures of the urinary system.

Have you ever prepared a meal from scratch or helped someone else do it? Let's imagine a menu of chicken, potatoes, applesauce, and green beans. First, you might put the chicken in an oven to bake. You might peel the potatoes and apples before cooking them. Then, you might remove the stems and tips from the green beans. What happens to the peelings and stems you removed from your food before cooking or the chicken bones that were left after you ate? These are all waste materials that you probably just throw away.

Just as you removed some wastes from the food as you prepared your meal, your body must remove the wastes that build up within its cells. As your body cells use food molecules and oxygen, wastes build up. If these wastes aren't removed, your health will be affected. Your body removes these wastes in a process called excretion.

You know that solid wastes from digestion leave your body through your anus. You also know that cells produce carbon dioxide. Your body must also get rid of extra water and salts. Did you ever think of your skin as an organ for waste removal?

436

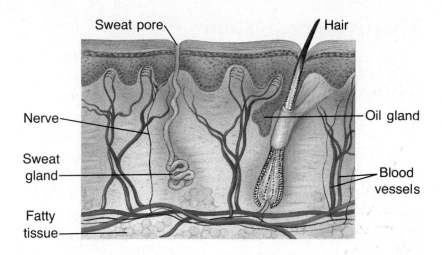

Sweat pore — Hair

Nerve —

Oil gland

Sweat gland —

Blood vessels

Fatty tissue —

The Skin

Perhaps you haven't even thought of your skin as an organ. It doesn't seem very much like your heart or stomach. But your skin is the largest organ in your body. Besides covering and protecting your body, your skin is also an organ of excretion.

What does your skin excrete? Study the cut-away view of a section of skin. Find a sweat gland. You've noticed sweat on your skin many times on hot days or after you've been playing hard. Sweat glands in your skin secrete a mixture of water and salts and move this liquid through ducts to pores on the surface of your skin. The liquid that your sweat glands excrete is called sweat or perspiration. As air passes over your skin, the sweat evaporates. The evaporation cools your skin. On a hot day or during vigorous exercise, the constant dampening of your skin by sweat helps keep your body temperature normal.

Sweat contains salts and urea (yoo REE uh) that your body must get rid of. **Urea** is a waste product that contains nitrogen produced by your cells. If you've ever tasted sweat, you know it tastes salty. The salts and urea collect on your skin until they are washed away. You can help keep your skin healthy by regularly washing away these wastes with soap and water. How do you think clean skin would help your body with excretion?

How does sweat help keep you cool?

Would You Believe?

Perspiration and urine are odorless; the bad smell results from bacteria that invade the wastes as they leave the body.

The Urinary System

Not all your body's liquid waste is removed by your skin. Most of it is removed by your **urinary** (YOOR uh ner ee) **system.** Your urinary system is made up of your kidneys, ureters (YOOR ut urz), bladder, and urethra (yoo REE thruh). Let's look at each of these organs and see how they aid your body in waste removal.

Find the position of your kidneys in the drawing of the urinary system on page 440. Place your hands on your back just above your waist. Your hands are now covering your **kidneys.** Each of these bean-shaped organs is about the size of a man's fist. An artery brings a constant flow of blood containing waste materials to each of your kidneys. As blood circulates through your kidneys, waste materials are filtered out, and the cleansed blood is sent through veins back into your circulatory system.

As your kidneys collect wastes, they produce urine. **Urine** is about 95 percent water in which urea, salts, and some other wastes are dissolved. Your kidneys filter all the blood in your body more than 50 times each day. In spite of all this filtering, only about 1.5 liters of urine are produced in 24 hours.

KIDNEY

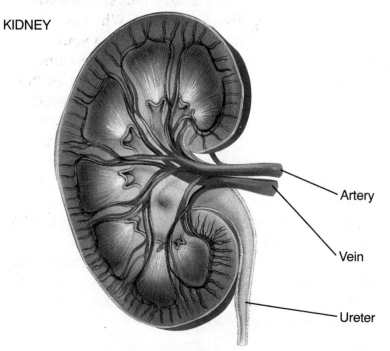

Artery

Vein

Ureter

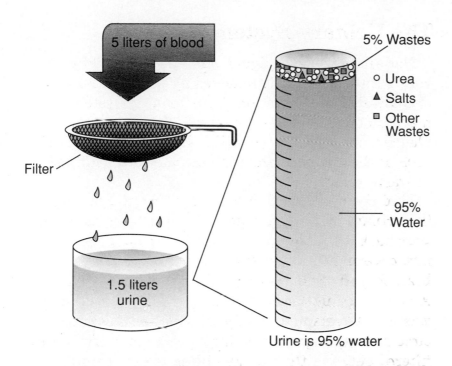

5 liters of blood

Filter

1.5 liters urine

5% Wastes

○ Urea
▲ Salts
□ Other Wastes

95% Water

Urine is 95% water

Your kidneys don't store urine. Urine is constantly leaving your kidneys through tubes called **ureters.** Ureters collect the urine, and then the smooth muscles in the walls of the ureters move it along by wavelike contractions to your bladder. The **bladder** is an organ that collects and temporarily stores urine. Find the bladder in the drawing on page 440. Notice its pouchlike shape. Your bladder is elastic, and it stretches as it fills with urine. When it becomes full, your nerves send a signal to your brain. Your brain then tells you it's time to empty your bladder. A strong ring of muscles encircles the lower end of the bladder, keeping it tightly closed. You learned to control these muscles when you were very young. When you allow them to relax, urine flows out of your body through a tube called the **urethra.** The process of emptying your bladder is called urination.

You can help keep your urinary system healthy by replacing the water lost through urination. Drink plenty of water and fruit juices. Remember that your health is affected if waste materials are not removed from your body. It's important to keep your urinary system functioning properly.

How can you help keep your urinary system healthy?

EXCRETORY SYSTEM

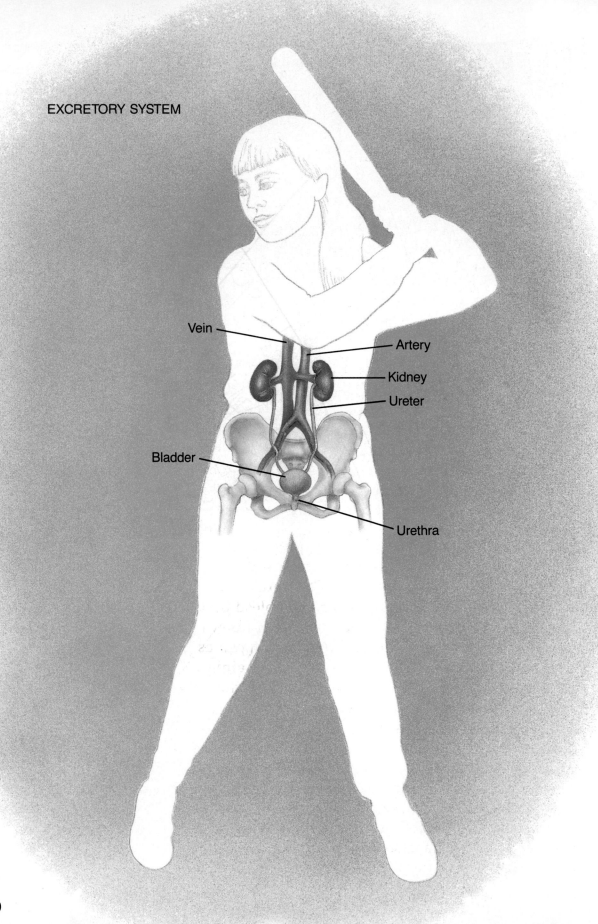

Vein

Artery

Kidney

Ureter

Bladder

Urethra

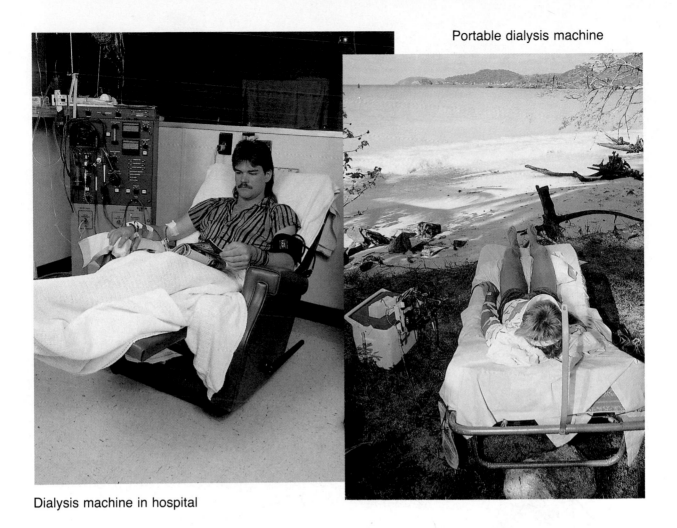

Portable dialysis machine

Dialysis machine in hospital

You know that your kidneys are extremely important in keeping you healthy. They are constantly filtering the wastes from your blood that could poison your cells. But sometimes one kidney may no longer be able to work. This may happen as the result of an accident or illness. If the remaining kidney is still healthy, it may enlarge and do the work of both. But if both kidneys fail to work properly, a person may be placed on a dialysis machine. This machine filters a person's blood as the kidneys normally would. First, a tube is connected to one of the person's arteries. As the person's heart pumps, blood flows into the machine, and the wastes are removed. Then, another tube carries the blood back into one of the person's veins. Dialysis is usually done two or three times a week.

What is a dialysis machine?

441

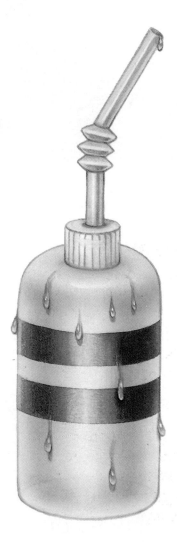

Your body needs to get rid of wastes through the process of excretion. Review how wastes are excreted from your body by studying these four steps.

Step 1. The wastes are removed from your cells.

Step 2. Your blood transports the wastes to your organs of excretion.

Step 3. Wastes move from your blood into your organs of excretion for removal.

Step 4. Wastes leave your body.

Washing your skin regularly with soap and water and drinking plenty of liquids are good ways to help your body stay healthy.

Lesson Summary

- Excretion is the process in which wastes are removed from the body.
- The organs of excretion include the lungs, the large intestine, the skin, and the kidneys.
- The structures of the urinary system are the kidneys, the ureters, the bladder, and the urethra.

Lesson Review

1. List the excretory organs that remove each of these wastes from the blood: water, salts, urea.
2. What happens if one of a person's kidneys fails?
★3. Hogs have no sweat glands. Explain why a hog would like to wallow in mud on a hot day.

How do kidneys work?

What you need

filter paper
funnel
jar
artificial blood sample
water
pencil and paper

What to do

1. Fold the filter paper in half. Then fold it again, almost in half. Refer to the diagram below.
2. Open the folded filter paper to form a cone. Now place the cone in the funnel. Moisten the top of the filter paper so it will stick to the inside of the funnel.
3. Place the funnel in a jar.
4. Slowly pour a sample of artificial blood into the funnel lined with filter paper. Be careful not to get any of the sample above the top of the filter paper. Record your observations.

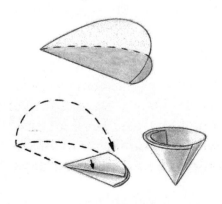

What did you learn?

1. What changes did you observe in the artificial blood when it passed through the filter paper?
2. What substance does the material that was filtered out of the artificial blood represent?

Using what you learned

1. How would the substance that the material in the funnel represents be removed from the body?
2. How does this activity represent the action of kidneys?

I WANT TO KNOW ABOUT...

Kidney Transplants

More than 80,000 people in the United States suffer from some kind of continual kidney failure. If kidneys fail, waste materials build up in the blood. If the increased amounts of water, urea, and salt are not removed, they will become poisonous to the body. Often, it's necessary to have a kidney transplant.

A kidney transplant means placing a healthy donor's kidney into a patient who has suffered kidney failure. Some people carry an organ donor card that allows a doctor to remove the kidneys from their body if they should die. Sometimes a close relative will donate a kidney. The patient's body then is less likely to reject the kidney. The donor survives using the remaining kidney. After the transplant, both the donor and patient usually continue to live healthy, active lives.

Sometimes kidney rejection becomes a problem. Our bodies react to germs and other foreign tissue by attacking them. This helps us fight off disease. However, the transplant patient's body will also try to fight the new kidney. Scientists are now developing drugs to keep the patient's body from rejecting the new kidney.

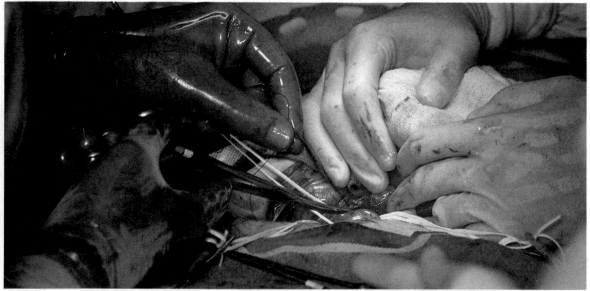

Science and Technology

Summary

Lesson 1
- Enzymes are substances that speed up chemical reactions such as the process of digestion.
- The mouth, esophagus, stomach, small intestine, and large intestine, along with the liver, gall bladder and pancreas, form the digestive system of your body.
- The digestive system breaks down food into molecules so it can be used by your body cells.

Lesson 2
- Excretion is the process in which wastes are removed from the body.
- The organs of excretion include the lungs, the large intestine, the skin, and the kidneys.
- The structures of the urinary system are the kidneys, the ureters, the bladder, and the urethra.

Science Words

Fill in the blank with the correct word or words from the list.

bladder	esophagus	pancreas	stomach	urethra
diffusion	kidneys	rectum	urinary system	urine
enzymes	large intestine	saliva	urea	villi
epiglottis	liver	small intestine	ureters	

1. The group of organs that remove liquid wastes from the body make up the ____.

2. The movement of molecules from where they are present in large amounts to where they are present in small amounts is ____.

3. The tube through which urine leaves your body is the ____.

4. The tube that connects your mouth with your stomach is the ____.

5. Substances that speed up a chemical reaction are ____.

6. The pair of bean-shaped organs in your back that filter wastes from your blood are ____.

7. A small saclike organ that holds and digests food is the ____.

8. A liquid made up mostly of water containing urea, some salts, and other wastes is ____.

9. The tubes that carry urine from a kidney to the bladder are the ____.

10. A cell waste product that contains nitrogen is ____.

Questions

Recalling Ideas

Correctly complete each of the following sentences.

1. Food is changed to forms your cells can use by the
   (a) circulatory system.
   (b) digestive system.
   (c) large intestine.
   (d) capillaries.

2. Food moves from your mouth to your stomach through your
   (a) epiglottis. (c) esophagus.
   (b) ureter. (d) aorta.

3. All of the following are body waste products EXCEPT
   (a) enzymes. (c) urea.
   (b) water. (d) carbon dioxide.

4. The movement of molecules from where they are present in large amounts to where they are in smaller amounts is called
   (a) circulation. (c) excretion.
   (b) diffusion. (d) digestion.

5. All of the following organs are involved in the excretion of body wastes EXCEPT the
   (a) kidneys. (c) lungs.
   (b) stomach. (d) skin.

6. Digested food diffuses into the blood from the
   (a) small intestine. (c) stomach.
   (b) large intestine. (d) bladder.

7. All of the following are parts of the digestive system EXCEPT the
   (a) tongue. (c) villa.
   (b) skin. (d) pancreas.

8. Bile is a digestive juice that is produced by the
   (a) stomach.
   (b) kidneys.
   (c) liver.
   (d) bladder.

9. Water is absorbed in the
   (a) small intestine.
   (b) large intestine.
   (c) esophagus.
   (d) gall bladder.

Examining Ideas

Determine whether each of the following statements is true or false. Rewrite the false statements to make them correct.

1. The large intestine is a narrow, tubelike organ about 7 meters long.

2. The process of digestion is completed in the large intestine.

3. The kidneys act as storage containers for urine.

4. Saliva is an enzyme produced by glands in the mouth.
5. Solid wastes from digestion leave the body through the ureters.
6. Urine is produced in the bladder.
7. The skin is an organ of excretion.
8. Urea is a chemical that speeds up digestion.
9. The liver and pancreas secrete digestive juices into the stomach.
10. Digested food is absorbed from the small intestine into the cells.
11. The urethra carries urine from the kidneys to the bladder.

Understanding Ideas

Answer the following questions using complete sentences.

1. How does your skin excrete body wastes?
2. What happens to the water in food while food is in the large intestine?
3. What are the functions of the stomach?

4. Describe how the body gets rid of
   (a) solid wastes.
   (b) liquid wastes.
5. List the organs of the excretory system and give one function of each.
6. Define and describe the function of enzymes. Give two examples of digestive enzymes and tell where they are produced and how they aid digestion.
7. Explain the difference between urea and urine.
8. Why should you chew your food thoroughly before swallowing it?

Thinking Critically

Think about what you have learned in this chapter. Answer the following questions using complete sentences.

1. Explain how the food digested in the small intestine gets to the cells of the body.
2. It is claimed that a person could live without a stomach but not without a small intestine. Explain why this might be true.
3. Swimmers used to be told not to go into the water for one hour after eating to allow their food to digest. Explain why this advice doesn't make much sense and is no longer recommended.
4. Why does food need to be digested? How is food changed by digestion?
5. Explain why skin is classified as an organ of the excretory system.

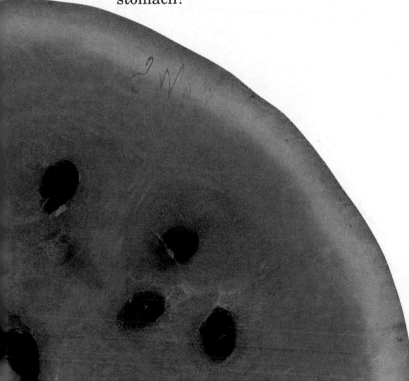

CHAPTER 18

Caring For Your Body

A balance beam used in gymnastics is not a very wide surface on which to jump, leap, or turn. Performing feats such as these requires the desire to succeed, long hours of practice, and a thorough understanding of the hows and whys of each movement.

Caring for your body's systems requires an understanding of how they work and what is needed to keep them working properly. A balanced diet, proper rest, and exercise will help your body to grow strong and healthy.

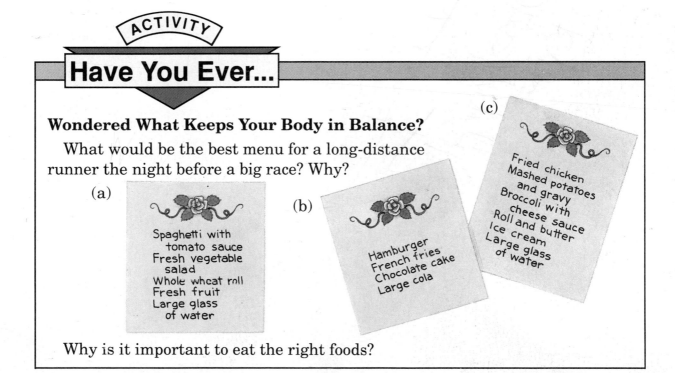

Healthful Eating

LESSON 1 GOALS
You will learn
● why having a balanced diet is important for your health.
● the definition of a balanced diet.
● the food groups that provide a balanced diet.

What's your favorite food? Is it considered healthful for your body? If it is, you're lucky. Sometimes our favorite foods aren't particularly nutritious. That's why it's important to eat a variety of foods. The more variety you have in your diet, the more likely you are to eat the kinds of foods you need for a strong mind and body. A healthy diet is a key to physical fitness.

Imagine sitting in the lunchroom with several of your friends. Jason is eating potato chips and drinking a soft drink. Sara brought a peanut butter and jelly sandwich, an apple, and some milk. Mitch is trying to lose weight, so he is skipping lunch altogether. Tina is eating yogurt and drinking milk. She is planning to buy an ice cream bar for dessert. What would you say to each of these friends if you wanted to help them eat a more healthful lunch? This lesson will help you answer this question and develop healthful eating habits.

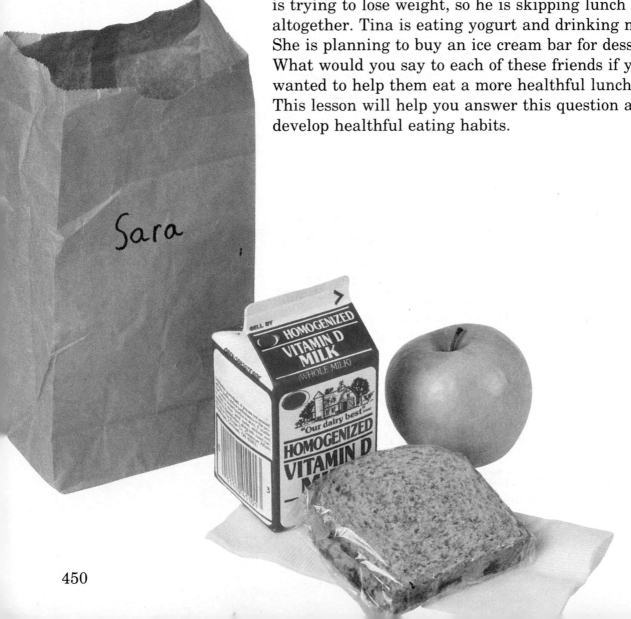

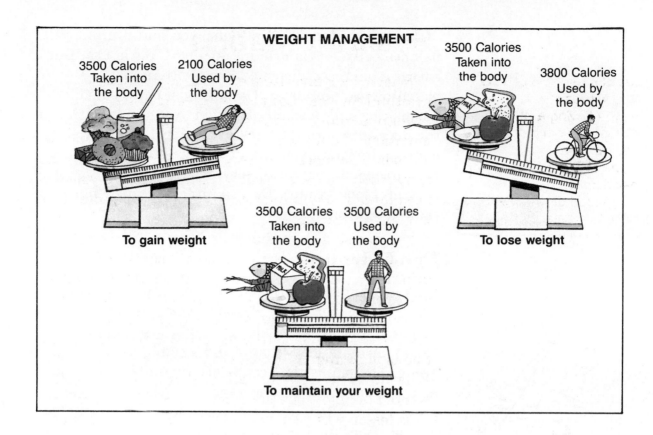

WEIGHT MANAGEMENT

3500 Calories Taken into the body

2100 Calories Used by the body

To gain weight

3500 Calories Taken into the body

3800 Calories Used by the body

To lose weight

3500 Calories Taken into the body

3500 Calories Used by the body

To maintain your weight

A Balanced Diet

The foods you eat are sources of energy for your cells. They're used to build and maintain all your body systems. Your body size, your age, your sex, and the activities you do each day determine the amount of energy you actually need. Energy in foods is measured in units called Calories. A good diet provides you with the number of Calories you need for good health. If you don't get enough Calories, you won't grow as you should. If you take in too many Calories, you may gain too much weight.

Define Calorie.

The intake and use of Calories work like a scale. If you want to gain weight, you must take in more Calories than your body uses. If you want to lose weight, you must take in fewer Calories than your body uses. To maintain your body weight, you need to take in the same number of Calories as your body uses.

Eating a **balanced diet** helps you maintain a balance between Calorie intake and Calorie use. But eating a balanced diet means more than just watching the number of Calories you eat. It also means choosing foods that provide your body with the nutrients you need to stay healthy. A balanced diet results when your daily diet contains the recommended number of servings from four healthful food groups. Do you already know what these food groups are?

Food Groups

What are two things to consider when planning your diet?

As you know, Calories aren't the only important thing to consider when planning your diet. A balanced diet also includes the right types of foods from four main food groups and a combination group. The main food groups are the milk group, the meat group, the fruit and vegetable group, and the grain group. Pizza and casserole dishes are examples of foods from the combination group. This group contains foods from two or more of the other four groups. To be sure that your body gets the nutrients

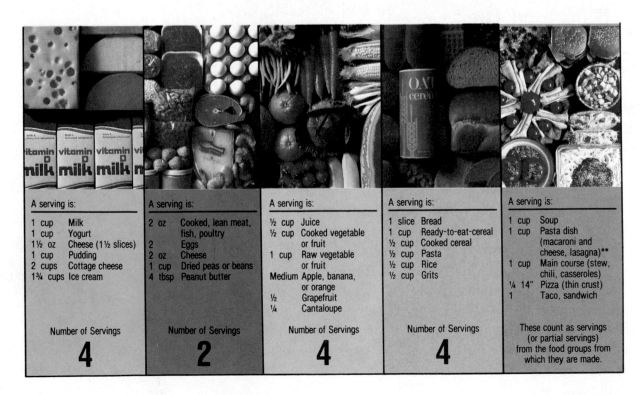

A serving is:

1 cup	Milk
1 cup	Yogurt
1½ oz	Cheese (1½ slices)
1 cup	Pudding
2 cups	Cottage cheese
1¾ cups	Ice cream

Number of Servings
4

A serving is:

2 oz	Cooked, lean meat, fish, poultry
2	Eggs
2 oz	Cheese
1 cup	Dried peas or beans
4 tbsp	Peanut butter

Number of Servings
2

A serving is:

½ cup	Juice
½ cup	Cooked vegetable or fruit
1 cup	Raw vegetable or fruit
Medium	Apple, banana, or orange
½	Grapefruit
¼	Cantaloupe

Number of Servings
4

A serving is:

1 slice	Bread
1 cup	Ready-to-eat-cereal
½ cup	Cooked cereal
½ cup	Pasta
½ cup	Rice
½ cup	Grits

Number of Servings
4

A serving is:

1 cup	Soup
1 cup	Pasta dish (macaroni and cheese, lasagna)**
1 cup	Main course (stew, chili, casseroles)
¼ 14"	Pizza (thin crust)
1	Taco, sandwich

These count as servings (or partial servings) from the food groups from which they are made.

it needs, you should eat four servings from the milk group, two servings from the meat group, four servings from the fruit and vegetable group, and four servings from the grain group.

The next time you go to a restaurant, choose kinds of foods that will make you healthy.

Why is it important to eat a balanced diet with foods from all the food groups? Foods from each of the food groups provide your body with certain kinds of nutrients. For example, the fruit and vegetable group provides many vitamins, and the milk group provides calcium and protein. If you don't eat foods from each group, your body will not be getting some of the nutrients it needs to stay healthy. Without calcium and protein, you won't have strong bones. Without the vitamins that the fruit and vegetable group provides, you would have little resistance to infections and you might find that cuts and other wounds don't heal easily.

You may be wondering what groups foods such as candy, potato chips, and soft drinks belong to. These foods belong to the "others" group. Foods in this group are generally high in Calories and low in nutritional value. They add few of the nutrients you need to stay healthy to your diet. Because they are often high in Calories, they may "fill you up" and make you less likely to eat foods from the four main food groups.

Would You Believe?

Americans' favorite vegetable is the potato.

453

INGREDIENTS: rolled oats, sugar, natural flavors, salt, calcium carbonate, guar gum, iron, vitamin A, and B vitamins.

NUTRITION PER SERVING
Serving Size: 43 grams
Servings per box: 10

Calories	140
Protein	4 g
Carbohydrate	30 g
Fat	2 g
Cholesterol	0 mg
Sodium	370 mg

PERCENTAGE OF RECOMMENDED DAILY ALLOWANCES

Protein	6
Vitamin A	25
Vitamin C	0
Niacin	15
Calcium	15
Iron	25
Vitamin B_6	20

Flavored cereal

INGREDIENTS: rolled oats, salt, calcium carbonate, guar gum, caramel flavor, iron, vitamin A, and B vitamins.

NUTRITION PER SERVING:
Serving Size: 43 grams
Servings per box: 10

Calories	120
Protein	6 g
Carbohydrate	27 g
Fat	2 g
Cholesterol	0 mg
Sodium	400 mg

PERCENTAGE OF RECOMMENDED DAILY ALLOWANCES

Protein	8
Vitamin A	35
Vitamin C	0
Niacin	20
Calcium	20
Iron	65
Vitamin B_6	30

Plain cereal

Have you ever had trouble concentrating on a difficult job? Has your skin been dry or your hair dull and brittle? Or have you had days when you felt quite nervous? All of these things could be caused by not eating a proper, balanced diet. Providing your body with all the nutrients it needs by eating a balanced diet can help you feel better every day.

But how do you determine the nutritional value of foods you like to eat? Labels on food packages give nutrition information that can help you plan a healthful diet. Look closely at the labels on the two cereal boxes above. They are from two varieties of the same brand of breakfast cereal. Find out the cereals' ingredients. They are listed in order, according to their weight. What is the main ingredient in both cereals? What ingredient comes next in the plain variety? in the flavored variety? How many grams make up a single serving? Which variety—plain or flavored—has fewer Calories in one serving? Which variety would you choose if you wanted to reduce your sugar intake? Which variety would give you more iron per serving?

All of the reasons for eating a balanced diet encourage you to make wise choices about the foods you buy. Advertisements for snacks—a snack bar, for example—want to convince you that if you eat the snacks, you will build muscle or increase your energy. But remember that an advertisement is designed to convince you to buy a product. Before you buy a snack, read the label. Find out about the ingredients, Calories, and vitamins. After reading a label, you can decide if the food is a nutritious one.

As you have learned in this lesson, eating a balanced diet is an important habit to develop. It will help you stay healthy and feel better every day. Think again about Jason, Mitch, and Tina from the beginning of this lesson. Are they providing their bodies with the nutrients they need to stay healthy and feel good? What can you do to develop the habit of eating a healthy, balanced diet?

Lesson Summary

- A balanced diet is important for maintaining a healthy body.
- A balanced diet includes the recommended number of servings from the main food groups.

Lesson Review

1. Name the basic food groups. State how many daily servings you should have from each group.
2. If you were going to pack a healthy lunch, what might you pack?
★3. Plan a day's menu, making sure you have the recommended number of servings from each food group.

The label on this snack bar says it will build your body. Read the ingredients. What do you think?

INGREDIENTS: Milk chocolate (sugar, milk, cocoa butter, chocolate, vanilla), granola (almonds, rolled oats, crisp rice, honey, coconut), corn syrup, sugar, butter, partially hydrogenated coconut and palm oil, cocoa, semi-sweet chocolate, peanuts, flour, salt.

Exercise

LESSON 2 GOALS
You will learn
● that exercise is needed for muscle strength, endurance, and flexibility.
● that exercise, sleep, and rest are important in maintaining a healthy body.

Have you ever gone swimming in the ocean or hiked in the mountains? Do you ever take walks with a friend or your family? Have you ever played tag or touch football on a cool autumn evening? What do all these activities have in common? For one thing, they're fun to do. It's enjoyable to be with friends and family, to play games, and to explore nature. What you may not think about is that all these activities are good for you because they are forms of exercise. And exercise, along with a balanced diet, is another key to physical fitness.

Exercise and Your Muscles

Exercise strengthens your muscles, and muscle strength helps you do activities such as running, jumping, skating, or swimming. Your muscles will become weak if you don't exercise them. When your muscles are strong, you can more easily lift, push, pull, jump, and bend. Strong muscles enable you to do activities without tiring easily. Muscle strength allows you to perform better in sports and helps you feel better. You are also more likely to have good posture when your muscles are strong. In general, exercise will help you look and feel better.

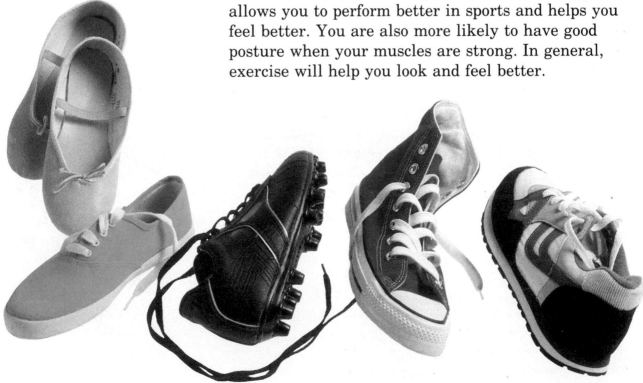

Stretching before exercising protects your muscles.

You can do different exercises to help different parts of your body. You may do many of these exercises just for the fun of it! Some exercises involve tightening muscles without moving your body. Simply tightening muscles—for example, lying on your back and tightening your stomach muscles—will strengthen them. Other types of exercises involve tightening muscles while moving your body. Familiar activities such as swimming, walking, running, and biking strengthen your muscles and help them move more easily. These kinds of exercises are particularly good for your heart. Using weight machines like the ones found in health clubs and gyms is another way to strengthen muscles.

No matter how you exercise, it's important to warm up by doing simple muscle stretches before you begin. By slowly and gently stretching and warming up before any vigorous exercise, you help protect your muscles from overstretching and help prevent muscle injuries during exercise.

Why is stretching necessary?

SCIENCE AND . . .
Writing

What error, if any, is in the underlined section? Gradually running longer distances helps you to gain <u>endurance. Muscles become more flexible.</u>
A. Spelling
B. Capitalization
C. Punctuation
D. No mistake

Endurance and Flexibility

When scientists talk about healthy muscles, they use not only the word "strength" but also "endurance" and "flexibility." If you were going to run a long-distance race, you would start practicing for it by first running short distances. Later, you would increase your time and distance. By doing this, you would build up muscle endurance. **Endurance** is the ability to continue using muscle strength. When you have muscle endurance, you can exercise for long periods of time without becoming tired.

Do you play volleyball or tennis? Or perhaps you practice gymnastics. These activities, along with most other sports, require flexibility. Muscle **flexibility** allows you to move your body easily into different positions. The more active you are, the more flexible you are. The more flexible you are, the less likely you are to injure yourself during physical activities.

Exercise, Rest, and Your Body Systems

Besides helping your muscles, exercise helps your body systems function as they should. As a result, more energy is used and your body stores less fat. Exercise also helps balance your Caloric intake. Remember that exercise strengthens your muscles. As you have learned, your heart is made of muscle tissue. Like your other muscles, your heart will be strengthened by regular exercise. A strong heart pumps more blood through your body with each beat, and it beats fewer times per minute. Other parts of your circulatory system are also improved through regular exercise.

How does exercise affect your overall heart rate?

Do you remember how you felt at the end of a day of playing outside? You've probably noticed that you often sleep better after a day in which you exercise a lot. Exercise helps your body relax and enables you to sleep well.

Why is sleep necessary?

Rest and sleep help your body to continue to grow and also help build you up again after each day's activities. During sleep, your muscles relax and your body systems slow down. A chemical that aids in tissue repair is released into your bloodstream as you sleep. All these things are important in keeping your body healthy.

Lesson Summary

- Exercise is needed to gain muscle strength, endurance, and flexibility.
- Many different types of exercises help you gain healthy muscles.
- Healthy body systems require exercise and enough rest and sleep.

Lesson Review

1. How can muscle strength be increased?
2. How do endurance and flexibility differ?
3. Why is it important to have enough sleep and rest?
4. What kinds of exercises can you do to help improve your flexibility?
★5. Explain how jumping rope might benefit your circulatory system.

What happens when muscles are overworked?

What you need

book
clock with second hand
pencil and paper

What to do

1. Hold your arm down at your side. Feel your biceps muscle with your other hand. Record whether it feels hard or soft.
2. Bend your elbow so that your forearm is straight out in front of your body. The palm of your hand should be facing up. Record how your biceps muscle feels.
3. Pick up a book and balance it on your open palm. Hold it there for 10 seconds. Record how your biceps feels now.
4. Put down the book and rest your arm for one minute.
5. Balance the book on the open palm of the same hand for 20 seconds. Rest for 5 seconds. Balance the book for 20 more seconds.
6. Repeat step 5 several times, until your arm is too tired to hold the book.

What did you learn?

1. How did your biceps muscle feel when your arm was down at your side?
2. How did it feel when you first held the book?

3. How many times could you hold the book, rest, and hold the book before your arm was too tired?

Using what you learned

1. What could you do so that you could hold the book longer? hold a heavier book?
2. How would you expect your results to change if you tried to hold a heavier book? if you "warmed up" your muscles before holding the book?

461

Prescription and Over-the-Counter Drugs

LESSON 3 GOALS
You will learn
● why medicines are drugs and how they affect your body.
● the difference between prescription and over-the-counter drugs.
● the importance of using medicines properly.

Mr. Diaz picked up his son Tomas from school after the school nurse had called to say he was ill. Tomas had a fever, a headache, and a sore throat. Mr. Diaz had already made a doctor's appointment for his son, and soon Tomas found himself in the doctor's office telling Dr. Garcia about his symptoms. After examining Tomas, she wrote out some prescriptions for medicine. On the way home, Mr. Diaz had the prescriptions filled at the drugstore.

When they arrived home, Mr. Diaz read the medicine labels carefully before giving Tomas any medication. He reminded Tomas that it is very important to follow the instructions on the labels. Mr. Diaz also told Tomas's sister not to bother the medicine. He said the medicine bottles had Tomas's name on them, which meant they were for Tomas only.

By carefully following Dr. Garcia's directions and taking his medicine correctly, Tomas began to feel better soon.

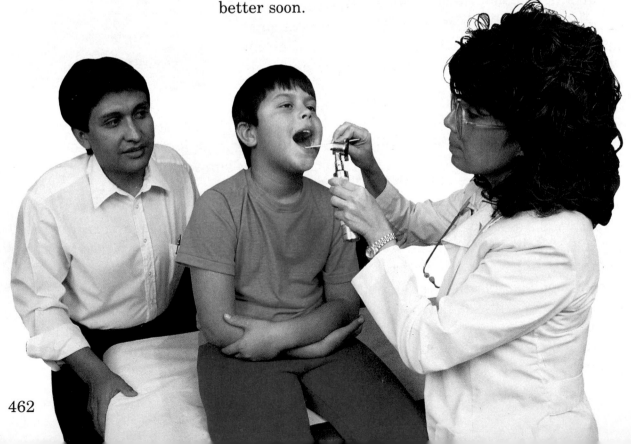

462

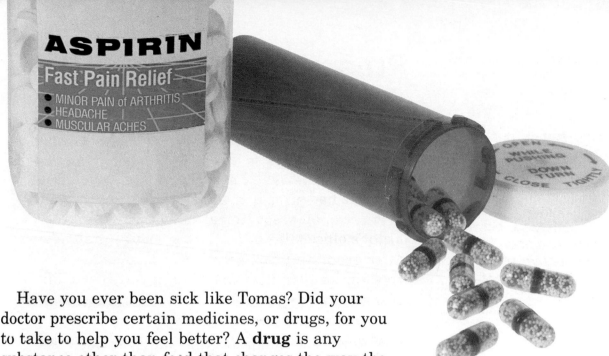

Have you ever been sick like Tomas? Did your doctor prescribe certain medicines, or drugs, for you to take to help you feel better? A **drug** is any substance other than food that changes the way the body works. **Medicines** are legal drugs used to cure, treat, or prevent illnesses. There are two types of medicines. One type is a prescription drug. The other type is an over-the-counter drug. Medicines such as the ones Dr. Garcia ordered are **prescription drugs.** Aspirin and cough syrup are examples of drugs sold in stores as **over-the-counter drugs.**

Both prescription drugs and over-the-counter drugs should be taken only with your parents' or guardian's permission. Both types come in containers with labels that must be read carefully. The directions on medicine labels must be followed exactly since taking too much or not enough medicine can be harmful.

On most labels, warnings and side effects are listed. A **side effect** is an unwanted change in the body that occurs after using a medicine. Many over-the-counter drugs can cause you to feel sleepy. This is a side effect and would usually be listed on the label. Understanding the side effects of drugs is important. For example, if a person didn't know that taking a particular drug causes sleepiness, it could be dangerous if that person attempted to ride a bike, drive a car, or use power tools. And both prescription drugs and over-the-counter drugs can be dangerous if more than one drug is used at the same time.

Define over-the-counter drugs.

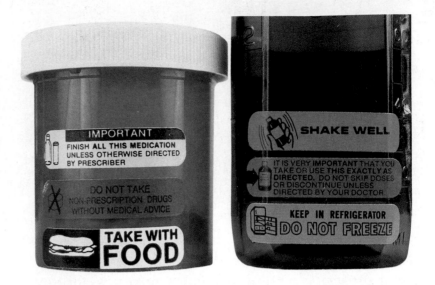

Medicines can improve the quality of our lives. Many of us have realized the benefits of prescription drugs or over-the-counter drugs. It's important to remember that these medicines should be taken only as directed by a doctor or with your parents' or guardian's permission. We must always be careful to read and follow all instructions precisely, just like Mr. Diaz and Tomas.

Lesson Summary

- Medicines are legal drugs used to cure, treat, or prevent illnesses.
- Prescription drugs must be ordered by a doctor, but over-the-counter drugs can be purchased without a doctor's order.
- It's important to carefully follow label directions on prescription and over-the-counter drugs.

Lesson Review

1. Why are medicines considered drugs?
2. Give some reasons why it's necessary to carefully read medicine labels.
3. What are some examples of side effects from medicines?
★4. What types of information would you find on a medicine label?

What drugs are found in over-the-counter medicines?

What you need

empty cartons and bottles of over-the-counter medicines
index cards
pencil and paper

What to do

1. Study the label of each empty medicine carton or bottle. Record the name of each medicine on an index card.
2. Record the purpose of the medicine and its main ingredient.
3. Record any warnings about possible side effects.
4. Sort the cards into groups based on the general purposes of the medicines.

purpose. What side effect(s) do you find listed on more than one card in the group?

What did you learn?

1. How many general purposes of medicine did you record?
2. Was there any one ingredient listed in every medicine for the same purpose? Circle the ingredient on each card in that group.
3. Look at one set of cards of medicines used for the same

Using what you learned

1. Why do medicine labels have information about dosages?
2. For whom are the directions on a medicine label intended?
3. Why should you never take a medicine without an adult's help?

465

Effects of Drugs

LESSON 4 GOALS
You will learn
● how drugs can have harmful effects on your body.
● about caffeine, alcohol, nicotine, marijuana, and cocaine and their effects.

Scene 1:
Maria's mother asked her to buy some soft drinks at the store. She reminded Maria to make sure everything she bought was labeled "caffeine-free" because the family was trying to cut down on their caffeine intake. Do you know why?

Scene 2:
Alec and Joey, two sixth-graders, sat on Joey's porch one hot summer day. Joey offered Alec something to drink. Joey said he thought that some fruit juice would be good, but Alec said he had something else in mind. Alec wanted a cold beer. Joey told Alec that he wouldn't give him any even if there was some in his house. Then they argued about whether or not beer was good for you. What do you think?

Scene 3:
Robert hadn't been to the dentist for a few years. He had been having problems with his teeth, so he finally decided to make an appointment. When the

dentist examined Robert's teeth, she looked concerned. She told Robert that he had some loose teeth that would have to come out. Robert was shocked and asked the dentist what caused this. The dentist asked Robert how long he had been chewing tobacco. Robert admitted that he had been chewing tobacco for ten years. The dentist said that there were white spots on his gums as a result of the tobacco juice, and she was going to have to test Robert's gum tissue to find out if he had cancer.

What are two possible effects of chewing tobacco?

Scene 4:

One day Tina met her six-year-old sister Teri running from the park after school. Teri was out of breath and told Tina that they needed to get out of the park quickly. Tina asked her sister what was wrong. Teri explained that some older kids were trying to sell marijuana and other drugs to the younger kids. Tina put her arm around her sister and told her that they would go home and talk to their mom and dad about it.

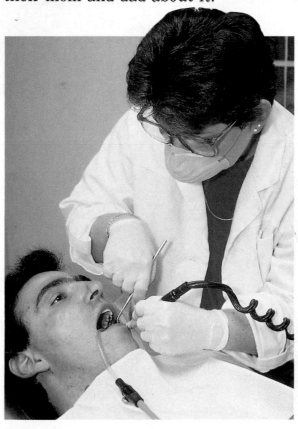

Situations like these may or may not happen to you or people you know. Yet, they do happen every day in large cities and in small towns. It's important to know how to deal with these kinds of situations and to make good decisions about what you should do. In this lesson you'll learn how drug use can be harmful to you.

Caffeine

Maria's family is decreasing caffeine intake. Her family is doing this because **caffeine** is a stimulant. A **stimulant** is a drug that speeds up the nervous system. The heart rate increases and blood pressure is affected. Caffeine helps people stay awake. This is the reason some people like drinking caffeine drinks.

You Can...

Take a Caffeine Survey

Read the labels of foods you have at home. Make a list of all the foods you find that contain caffeine. Ask people how they feel when they eat these foods. Read books to learn about caffeine. What foods contain caffeine? Why do foods contain caffeine? How does caffeine affect people? How could a person be getting too much caffeine without knowing it? Why do you think people eat foods that contain caffeine?

Caffeine is a drug found in some medicines and also in chocolate, coffee, tea, and many soft drinks. Caffeine use has side effects that may be harmful to some people. One side effect is that it's addictive, or habit-forming. The body grows to depend on the way caffeine affects it. Maybe you know people who always need "their cup of coffee" first thing in the morning. Their bodies have become dependent on the way caffeine affects them. Caffeine-free products are available to help a person reduce caffeine intake.

What does "addictive" mean?

Alcohol

People mistakenly think that alcohol isn't a drug or that it won't harm them. However, alcohol is a drug, and it can affect a person's health. A person can become dependent on alcohol.

Alcohol may be one of the most abused drugs in our country today. Alcohol is illegal for those under twenty-one. It is against the law in every state for someone your age to drink alcohol.

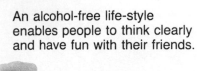

An alcohol-free life-style enables people to think clearly and have fun with their friends.

Alcohol is a depressant drug found in beer, wine, whiskey, and some other kinds of beverages. It's called a **depressant** because it slows down the brain and other parts of the nervous system. It can also harm the liver and other body organs. When a person drinks beer, for example, the alcohol in the beer enters the stomach the same way food does. About 20 percent of the alcohol is absorbed into the bloodstream through the walls of the stomach. The rest is absorbed through the walls of the small intestine. When alcohol in the bloodstream reaches the brain, the senses of sight, taste, touch, smell, and hearing are dulled.

Senses help keep a person safe. If they are dulled, accidents are more likely to happen. Studies show that over 50 percent of all fatal accidents and more than 70 percent of all drownings involve people who have been drinking alcohol. Now go back to Scene 2 at the beginning of the lesson. What do you think Alec and Joey should drink?

Nicotine

Another common drug is nicotine (NIHK uh teen). **Nicotine** is a colorless, odorless drug in tobacco products. Nicotine is a stimulant that's addictive. It enters the body when smoke from a burning cigarette is inhaled or tobacco is chewed. Nicotine affects the heart and causes it to work harder to supply body cells with oxygen. When a cigarette is smoked, a smoker's heart rate actually increases by as many as twenty beats per minute.

Some people, like Robert in Scene 3, think they are safe from the dangers of nicotine because they use smokeless tobacco. Smokeless tobacco comes in two forms—chewing tobacco and snuff. Both forms have the same harmful ingredients as the tobacco in cigarettes. The use of smokeless tobacco also increases the risk of cancer of the mouth. This was the reason Robert's dentist was going to test him for cancer.

Another substance associated with cigarette smoke is tar. Tar causes harmful changes in a person's body. **Tar** is a sticky substance that lines the lungs of a smoker. Tar irritates and clogs the lungs and increases the risk of lung problems, including cancer.

The next time you see a pack of cigarettes, read the warning label. Pay attention to that warning and remember the dangerous effects of nicotine and tar.

How does nicotine affect the heart?

Cigarettes

Warning: The Surgeon General Has Determined That Cigarette Smoking Is Dangerous to Your Health.

Marijuana

Marijuana (mer uh WAHN uh) is an illegal drug made from the crushed leaves, flowers, seeds, and stems of the hemp plant. People who use marijuana usually smoke the dried leaves and flowering tops of the plant. Marijuana is not only illegal but also dangerous. It contains hundreds of harmful ingredients. One of the most harmful is THC, which causes many of the effects of marijuana.

The short-term effects of using marijuana can include memory loss and slowed reaction time. Because marijuana enters the bloodstream and goes directly to the brain to be stored, it interferes with the ability to concentrate. It acts both as a stimulant and as a depressant. As a stimulant, marijuana makes the heart beat faster. As a depressant, it lowers the body temperature and slows down a person's ability to react. The simple act of crossing the street or riding a bicycle can become dangerous. Studying, recalling facts, and making decisions become difficult after smoking marijuana.

Marijuana

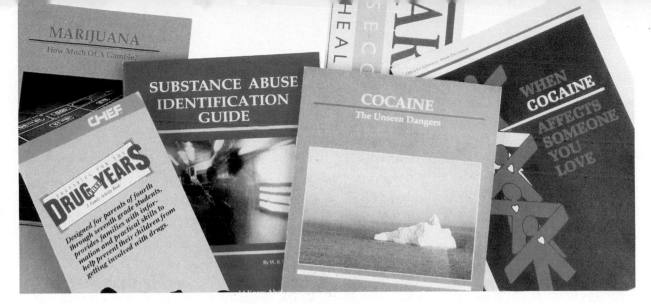

You can find information about drugs from many sources.

Scientists have shown that marijuana smoke contains more harmful products than cigarette smoke. Because the smoke is inhaled deeply and held in the lungs for a long time, lung tissue can be destroyed.

In Scene 4, Teri is only six years old. Think of the dangers to her if the older kids persuaded her to try marijuana. Besides the short-term effects, the long-term effects are also serious. Marijuana seems to weaken the body's ability to fight germs. Marijuana smokers seem to get sick more easily than people who do not smoke this drug. The constant inhaling of smoke also increases the risk of developing respiratory infections and lung cancer. These are risks both Tina and Teri plan to avoid. They are risks everyone should avoid.

Cocaine

Cocaine is an illegal and dangerous drug that acts as a stimulant. It's obtained from the leaves of coca shrubs and enters the body when it is sniffed or snorted through the nose. Cocaine powder can also be treated and changed to a form that can be smoked. It's a dangerous drug because it stimulates the nervous system to dangerous levels, causing increased heart rate and blood pressure. A person can die by using cocaine just one time.

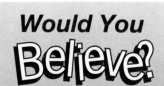

Would You Believe?

Prior to our knowledge of their dangers, marijuana and cocaine could be legally bought from any druggist in the United States.

What are some effects of cocaine use?

Anyone who survives the first use of this drug can quickly become addicted to it. People who continue to use this drug face respiratory tract infections, heart attacks, seizures, and strokes. Cocaine users who try to break their addiction face months of painful recovery.

Think again about the definition of the word *drug:* any substance other than food that changes the way the body works. All of the drugs discussed in this lesson can do harm and even cause death. When a drug is illegal, such as marijuana and cocaine, it's against the law to make, sell, grow, or possess the drug. Laws against illegal drugs exist to protect you from harming yourself and others. Penalties for breaking these laws can be very severe. It's important that you know about the harmful effects of drugs—illegal and legal. This knowledge, along with what you've learned from previous lessons about maintaining a balanced diet and getting plenty of exercise, will allow you to make intelligent and informed decisions to help you be the best person you can be.

Just like Alec and Joey, you and your friends can make healthful decisions.

474

A drug-free life-style helps you achieve your goals.

Lesson Summary

- Caffeine and nicotine are addictive stimulants found in some drinks and in tobacco products.
- Alcohol is a depressant found in beer, wine, whiskey, and other beverages. It can be addictive and can cause harm to the brain, liver, and other body organs.
- Marijuana and cocaine are illegal, addictive drugs. They increase heart rate, impair muscle coordination, impair thinking, and cause memory loss. Cocaine can cause death.

Lesson Review

1. How do nicotine and caffeine affect the body?
2. What are some products that contain caffeine?
3. What would you say to a smokeless-tobacco user to convince him or her that using tobacco is dangerous?
★4. Recall Joey in Scene 2. What would you do if you were Joey and facing the same situation?

I WANT TO KNOW ABOUT...

A Pharmacist

Suzette Smith is a pharmacist at a large city hospital. Working in a hospital pharmacy is much different from working in a pharmacy in a drug store. In a drug store, a pharmacist works directly with each patient, following the doctor's orders and making sure that the patient understands the instructions for taking a drug. As a hospital pharmacist, Ms. Smith works only with the hospital staff. She reads and interprets physicians' orders for medicines. Using these orders, she prepares drugs by following specific rules. She then sends the medicines to the correct floor or area of the hospital for use by patients.

In order to become a pharmacist, Ms. Smith had to go to college for five years. During her first two years, she took courses in chemistry, economics, accounting, life science, math, and physics. These courses were required before she could apply to pharmacy school. After being accepted to pharmacy school, Ms. Smith spent three years taking pharmacy courses. After graduation, she took a test given by the Board of Pharmacy in her state. When she passed the test, she was licensed to work as a pharmacist.

Career

476

Summary

Lesson 1
- A balanced diet is important for maintaining a healthy body.
- A balanced diet includes the recommended number of servings from the main food groups.

Lesson 2
- Exercise is needed to gain muscle strength, endurance, and flexibility.
- Many different types of exercises help you gain healthy muscles.
- Healthy body systems require exercise and enough rest and sleep.

Lesson 3
- Medicines are legal drugs used to cure, treat, or prevent illnesses.
- Prescription drugs must be ordered by a doctor, but over-the-counter drugs can be purchased without a doctor's order.

- It's important to carefully follow label directions on prescription and over-the-counter drugs.

Lesson 4
- Caffeine and nicotine are stimulants that can be found in some drinks and in tobacco products. These drugs can be addictive.
- Alcohol is a depressant found in beer, wine, whiskey, and other beverages. It can be addictive and can cause harm to the brain, liver, and other body organs.
- Marijuana and cocaine are two kinds of illegal, addictive drugs. They can produce harmful effects such as increased heart rate, impaired muscle coordination, impaired thinking, and memory loss. Cocaine can cause death.

Science Words

Fill in the blank with the correct word or words from the list.

endurance	over-the-counter
flexibility	drugs
drugs	side effect
medicines	caffeine
prescription drugs	stimulant
balanced diet	

alcohol	tar
depressant	marijuana
nicotine	cocaine

1. ____ are not considered food, but they cause changes in the body.
2. ____ is an illegal drug made from the hemp plant.

3. If the ____ of your muscles is good, you are less likely to be injured during physical activity.
4. An unwanted change that occurs in the body after taking a medicine is a(n) ____.
5. Aspirin and cough syrup are examples of ____.
6. Any substance that slows down the brain and other parts of the nervous system is called a(n) ____.

7. ____ is a sticky substance in tobacco smoke that irritates and clogs the lungs and increases the risk of cancer.
8. A drug that speeds up the nervous system is a(n) ____.
9. An addictive stimulant found in many soft drinks is ____.
10. ____ are any legal drugs used to treat or prevent illnesses.

Questions

Recalling Ideas
Correctly complete each of the following sentences.

1. All of the following are major food groups EXCEPT the
   (a) fiber group.
   (b) milk and meat groups.
   (c) grain group.
   (d) fruit and vegetable group.
2. An example of an over-the-counter drug is
   (a) marijuana. (c) aspirin.
   (b) cocaine. (d) heroin.
3. Cigarette smoking is addictive because tobacco contains the drug
   (a) alcohol. (c) nicotine.
   (b) caffeine. (d) tar.
4. All of the following drugs are addictive EXCEPT
   (a) aspirin. (c) nicotine.
   (b) alcohol. (d) a and c.
5. Alcohol is all of the following EXCEPT
   (a) a stimulant.
   (b) absorbed in the stomach.
   (c) addictive.
   (d) a depressant.
6. Regular exercise is necessary to develop muscle
   (a) strength. (c) endurance.
   (b) flexibility. (d) all of the above.
7. Not eating a balanced diet can affect your
   (a) skin. (c) nerves.
   (b) thinking. (d) all of the above.

Examining Ideas
Determine whether each of the following statements is true or false. Rewrite the false statements to make them correct.

1. If you take in too many Calories, you may gain weight. If you take in too few, you won't grow as you should.
2. Everyone whose age, sex, and body type are the same as yours

478

probably requires the same number of Calories as you do.

3. Potato chips are an example from the fruit and vegetable group.

4. Skipping a meal is a good way to cut down on the number of Calories you eat.

5. Eating a balanced diet will ensure that you are physically fit.

6. In order to lose weight, you must use more energy than is provided by the food you eat.

7. Marijuana is made from the leaves of the coca plant.

8. An unwanted change that occurs in the body after using a medicine is called an overdose.

9. Two portions of food supplying the same number of Calories have the same nutritional value.

Understanding Ideas
Answer the following questions using complete sentences.

1. Identify the four main food groups and give three examples from each.

2. Explain why exercise and the proper amount of sleep are just as important to good health as a balanced diet.

3. Explain the difference between prescription drugs and over-the-counter drugs.

4. Make a chart showing the commonly abused drugs, where they come from, and how they affect the body.

5. Explain the difference between drugs and medicine.

Thinking Critically
Think about what you have learned in this chapter. Answer the following questions using complete sentences.

1. Explain what people must do to use medicine safely.

2. Suppose you have a friend who wants to gain weight so he can play football. What would you suggest that he do? What would you tell him NOT to do?

3. Explain how to determine the nutritional value of an item you purchase at the grocery store.

Checking for Understanding

Write a short answer for each question or statement.

1. Five body systems are described in this unit: circulatory, digestive, respiratory, excretory, and urinary. Match the structures or descriptions below to the appropriate system.

   (a) produces bile
   (b) exchanges oxygen and carbon dioxide in the lungs
   (c) the heart, the blood, and the blood vessels
   (d) produces enzymes that aid in food breakdown
   (e) the esophagus, small intestine, and pancreas
   (f) alveoli, bronchi, and trachea
   (g) the kidneys, bladder, ureters, and urethra
   (h) changes food into a form the body can use
   (i) skin and lungs
   (j) the aorta, capillaries, atria, and ventricles
   (k) the diaphragm
   (l) forms urea

2. List the main food groups and give three examples from each.
3. What happens to digested nutrients in the small intestine?
4. What is a balanced diet?
5. How is food energy measured?
6. Why are exercise and the proper amount of sleep important for good health?
7. Beginning at the mouth, trace food through the structures of the digestive system.
8. How can drugs be harmful to the body?
9. Why is it better to breathe through your nose than through your mouth?
10. Name the main parts of the blood and tell what each one's job is.
11. Distinguish between stimulant drugs and depressant drugs and give two examples of each type.
12. Which body systems are most affected by smoking tobacco? Describe the effects.
13. Why is it hazardous for nonsmokers to be in the same room with smokers?
14. Why would it be dangerous for a person to drive a car after drinking alcohol?

Recalling Activities

Write a short paragraph for each question or statement.

1. What causes blood to circulate?
2. What do we exhale?
3. How does diffusion take place?
4. How do kidneys work?
5. What happens when muscles are overworked?
6. What drugs are found in over-the-counter medicines?

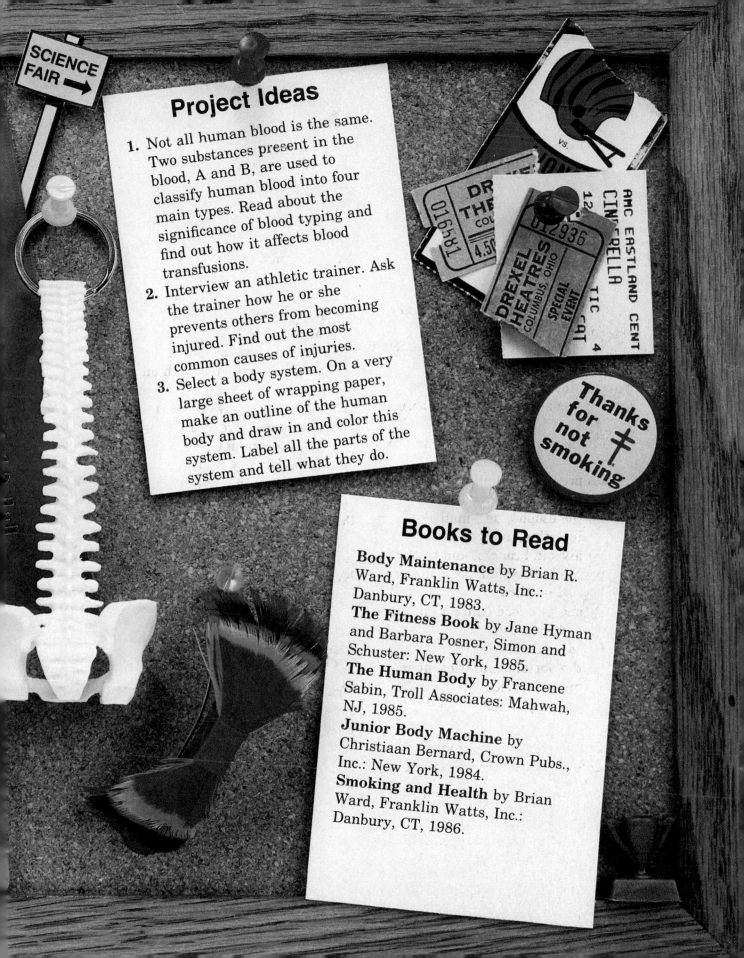

Project Ideas

1. Not all human blood is the same. Two substances present in the blood, A and B, are used to classify human blood into four main types. Read about the significance of blood typing and find out how it affects blood transfusions.

2. Interview an athletic trainer. Ask the trainer how he or she prevents others from becoming injured. Find out the most common causes of injuries.

3. Select a body system. On a very large sheet of wrapping paper, make an outline of the human body and draw in and color this system. Label all the parts of the system and tell what they do.

Books to Read

Body Maintenance by Brian R. Ward, Franklin Watts, Inc.: Danbury, CT, 1983.

The Fitness Book by Jane Hyman and Barbara Posner, Simon and Schuster: New York, 1985.

The Human Body by Francene Sabin, Troll Associates: Mahwah, NJ, 1985.

Junior Body Machine by Christiaan Bernard, Crown Pubs., Inc.: New York, 1984.

Smoking and Health by Brian Ward, Franklin Watts, Inc.: Danbury, CT, 1986.

SCIENCE FAIR ➡

Thanks for not smoking

Activities

Application Activities

Process & Problem Solving Activities

Some people think that they can learn about science by memorizing a lot of scientific facts. A real understanding of science also involves using many kinds of skills to do science activities. As you learn these skills, you begin to have a better understanding of why and how something happens, and you can use them to solve problems.

These activities were written to help you practice science skills. They were also written so you can use your imagination. Let's begin the journey to better understanding.

TABLE OF CONTENTS

PROCESS SKILL MODELS

Predicting	485	Controlling Variables	491
Interpreting Data	487	Hypothesizing	493
Defining Operationally	489	Experimenting	495

PROBLEM SOLVING ACTIVITIES

The Sink/Float Dilemma	497	Water Watch	507
Cat Burglar	499	Living or Nonliving?	509
The Great Egg Drop	501	Animal Scramble	511
To Take or Not To Take?	503	The Genie Game	513
Don't Refuse Refuse	505	Digestive Detective	515

Predicting

Definition   Predicting is proposing possible outcomes of an event or experiment. Predictions are based on earlier observations and inferences.

Example   Kim did an experiment to find out what happens to air when it is heated. She found that air rises as it becomes warmer. After thinking about her results, Kim predicted that the air temperature of a room would be higher at the ceiling than at the floor.

She decided to test her prediction. To do this, Kim taped a thermometer to the end of a stick and raised it to the ceiling of her living room. She kept an identical thermometer close to the floor. After 5 minutes she recorded the temperatures. She did this in two other rooms and recorded her results in the table below.

*R*oom Temperature

	Living Room	Dining Room	Bedroom
Ceiling	22°C	23°C	23°C
Floor	20°C	20°C	21°C

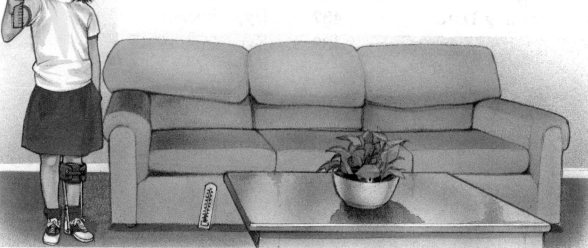

Practice

1. What was Kim's prediction? Was it correct?
2. What observations or inferences led Kim to make her prediction?
3. When you have your body temperature checked, it normally is 37°C. Predict the temperature a thermometer will show after you breathe on it for five seconds. Record your prediction.
4. Obtain a sterile thermometer and test your prediction. Place the thermometer bulb near your mouth. Breathe in and out slowly, directing your breath toward the bulb. Record your results.
5. How close was your prediction to your results? Based on what observation or inference did you make your prediction?
6. Predict the temperature of the thermometer after you hold the bulb between your thumb and forefinger. Record your prediction.
   Try it for five seconds. CAUTION: Be careful not to break the thermometer. How close was your prediction?

Interpreting Data

 Definition   Interpreting data is explaining the meaning of information that has been collected.

 **Example**   Mr. Bush's students were learning how to determine the humidity in the air. First, they found the temperature of the air using a dry-bulb thermometer. The temperature measured 25°C. Next, they found the temperature using a wet-bulb thermometer. It measured 18°C. The difference between the two readings is 7°C.

In order to determine the humidity, they had to interpret the data they collected and the data in the table on the next page. The dry-bulb thermometer reading (left-hand column) was 25°C. The difference between the wet- and dry-bulb readings (top row) was 7°C. Reading across and down, they found the humidity to be 50 percent.

Humidity Table

Example

Dry-Bulb Thermometer Readings (°C)	Difference Between Wet- and Dry-Bulb Thermometer Readings (°C)									
	1	2	3	4	5	6	7	8	9	10
	%	%	%	%	%	%	%	%	%	%
10	88	77	66	55	44	34	24	15	6	
11	89	78	67	56	46	36	27	18	9	
12	89	78	68	58	48	39	29	21	12	
13	89	79	69	59	50	41	32	23	15	7
14	90	79	70	60	51	42	34	26	18	10
15	90	80	71	61	53	44	36	27	20	13
16	90	81	71	63	54	46	38	30	23	15
17	90	81	72	64	55	47	40	32	25	18
18	91	82	73	65	57	49	41	34	27	20
19	91	82	74	65	58	50	43	36	29	22
20	91	83	74	66	59	51	44	37	31	24
21	91	83	75	67	60	53	46	39	32	26
22	92	83	76	68	61	54	47	40	34	28
23	92	84	76	69	62	55	48	42	36	30
24	92	84	77	69	62	56	49	43	37	31
25	92	84	77	70	63	57	50	44	39	33
26	92	85	78	71	64	58	51	46	40	34
27	92	85	78	71	65	58	52	47	41	36
28	93	85	78	72	65	59	53	48	42	37
29	93	86	79	72	66	60	54	49	43	38
30	93	86	79	73	67	61	55	50	44	39

Example ▶

Practice

1. Suppose the dry-bulb reading is 27°C and the wet-bulb reading is 24°C. Find the humidity. Explain how you got your answer.

2. Look at the dry-bulb thermometer readings in the table. What interpretation can you make about the humidity data as you read from the top of any one of the % columns to the bottom?

3. Compare the percentages as you move from left to right on the table. How do you interpret this data?

Defining Operationally

Definition   Defining operationally is forming a definition that is based on what you do or what you observe. An operational definition tells how something acts, not what it is.

Example   Sue dropped a sugar cube in a glass of water and stirred the water. She noticed that the sugar cube lost its shape and seemed to disappear. When Sue tasted different parts of the water, she found each part to be sweet. Sue concluded that the sugar dissolved and spread evenly throughout the water. Therefore, Sue defined dissolving as "spreading evenly throughout water." She decided to test other materials according to her operational definition. She made a table displaying her results.

Dissolving

Substance	Spread Evenly Throughout Water
iron filings	no
boullion cube	yes
food coloring	yes
pebbles	no

Practice

1. What is Sue's operational definition of dissolving?
2. What is the basis of Sue's operational definition?
3. Give an operational definition for the following:
   a. flying
   b. swimming
   c. burning
4. Obtain an ice cube, a square of butter, a piece of wax, and a block of metal. Using these materials, give an operational definition of melting.

Controlling Variables

 **Definition**   Controlling variables is making sure that everything in an experiment stays the same except for one factor.

 **Example**   Theresa and Ken were arguing about which paper would be best for making "long distance" paper airplanes. They decided to conduct a test to find out. They made three planes out of different kinds of paper. One was made of thin paper, one was made of medium paper, and one of heavy paper. All the pieces of paper were the same size. The folding pattern was also the same. They launched each plane from the same place and with the same amount of force. The plane made of the medium paper flew the longest distance.

 **Practice**   **1.** Which of the factors, or variables, did Theresa and Ken keep the same in their test?
2. Which variable did they change?
     Follow the directions on the next page for making a helicopter. Then make the table shown below. Drop your helicopter from the following heights and record the time it takes to hit the floor.

*H*elicopter Flights

Height	Time
1.0 meters	
1.5 meters	
2.0 meters	

491

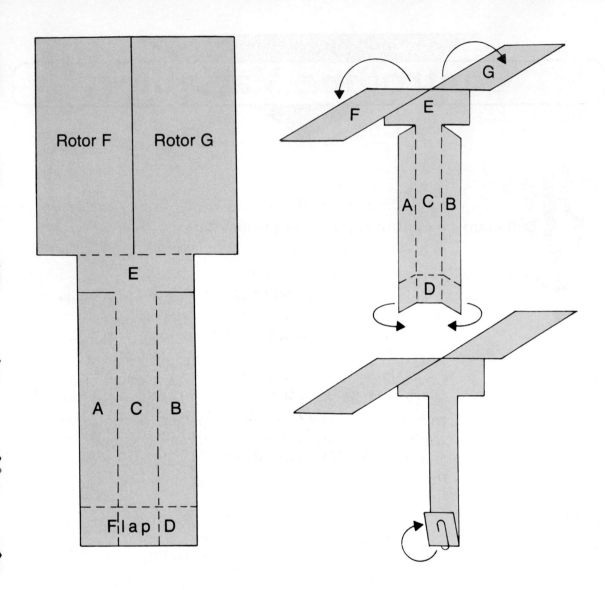

Construct a paper helicopter by following the directions shown here. Cut on all the solid lines. Fold along the dotted lines as follows: part A on C, part B on C, flap D upward, rotor F toward you, and rotor G away. Add a paper clip to flap D.

3. Which variables did you keep the same?
4. Which variable did you change?
5. Which variable might you change to make your helicopter fall faster? Try it.

Hypothesizing

Definition   Hypothesizing is making an educated guess about how or why something happens. A hypothesis can be tested to see if it is supported or not supported.

Example   Joe noticed that when it was raining his bicycle didn't stop as fast as it did when it was dry. He hypothesized that water reduced the effectiveness of the brakes.

Joe designed an experiment to test his hypothesis. He turned his bike upside down. He cranked the pedal by hand for one full turn. Then he applied the brakes and used a stopwatch to time how long it took for the wheel to stop turning. Next, he poured water on the wheel and repeated the test. He did this for three trials and recorded the results in the table on the next page.

493

Brake Effectiveness

Trials	Stopping Time (Dry)	Stopping Time (Wet)
1	2.0 seconds	3.9 seconds
2	2.3 seconds	3.5 seconds
3	2.5 seconds	3.7 seconds

Practice

1. What was Joe's hypothesis?
2. Was his hypothesis supported by his experiment? Why or why not?
3. Suppose you had a tank of pet goldfish that looked sick. State two or three hypotheses that might explain why they looked that way.
4. Explain how you might test each of your hypotheses.

Experimenting

 **Definition**   Experimenting is testing hypotheses or predictions. In an experiment, all variables must be kept the same except one.

 **Example**   Marco always gets his clothes dirty when he works on his bike. Plus, he can never seem to get rid of the grease stains. He saw an advertisement for a new laundry soap developed especially to remove grease. Marco thought that if this were true, the new soap would get his clothes cleaner than would his regular soap.

Marco tried an experiment. He put the same amount of grease on two identical rags. First, he washed one rag with his regular soap. Then, in the same washer, he washed the other rag with the new soap. The amount and temperature of the water and the time were kept the same for each washing. Sure enough, his clothes were cleaner with the new soap!

Practice   1. Make a copy of Table 1 shown below. Identify the different parts of Marco's experiment.

Table 1

Marco's Soap Experiment	
Hypothesis	
Variable that was changed	
Variables that were kept the same	
Results and conclusions	

2. Design and carry out an experiment to test one of the hypotheses listed below. Or, develop your own hypothesis and experiment about something you wish to test. Then make and complete Table 2 as shown.

Hypothesis A	Hypothesis B
dishwashing liquid A makes more bubbles than liquid B	glue X holds wood together better than does glue Y

Table 2

My Experiment	
Hypothesis	
Variable that was changed	
Variables that were kept the same	
Results and conclusions	

The Sink/Float Dilemma

Use after page 25.

Background   You may not realize it, but science plays a part in your life each day. In fact, people often use science to help solve everyday problems. Engineers are people who use science to solve problems on the job. It is the job of some engineers to design and build products for people to use. In doing so, they need to know many things about the properties of matter.

Problem   Imagine that you are a design engineer. You work for a company that makes underwater diving equipment. Your job is to design something with the following requirements.

1. When placed in water, it sinks immediately.
2. It remains completely underwater for 30 seconds.
3. After 30 seconds, all or part of the device returns to the surface and floats!
4. After the device is placed in the water, you may not touch it or add anything to the water.

Materials   aquarium or other large tank of water • various household junk • white glue • vinegar • cork • balloon • washers • baking soda

Solution   The list of materials contains items that can be used to build at least two devices that meet the requirements. However, they are not listed in any particular order. You must first figure out a design, or designs, based on the "clues" given in the materials list. Then build and test your device! Lastly, describe and draw your device by making and completing the table below.

Sink/**F**LOAT **D**EVICE

Materials Used
How It Works
Design

Cat Burglar

Use after page 84.

Background   Many buildings have a burglar alarm. If an intruder enters the building, the alarm sounds. Some burglar alarms are designed so that a nearby police station is automatically alerted when the alarm sounds.

Problem   You keep some of your favorite objects in a box in your room. Unfortunately, your cat likes these objects too! You want to know when your cat is on the prowl. So, you decide to rig your box with a burglar alarm.

Materials   1.5-V dry cells (2) • insulated bell wire • bell or buzzer • box such as a shoe box or cigar box • wire strippers • materials of your choice

Solution   Your burglar alarm must involve an electric circuit. Design it so that

1. when your box is opened by an intruder, the bell or buzzer is sounded.
2. when the box is opened by you, the alarm is not sounded.

Draw the plans for your burglar alarm. List the materials used and explain how the alarm works. Describe your alarm by making and completing a form like the one shown below.

Burglar Alarm

Design	
Materials Used	
How it Works	

The Great Egg Drop

Use after page 225.

 Background Travel in space is very different from travel on Earth. Because of this, space vehicles have many unusual design requirements. Designers and engineers are continually faced with challenging problems. These include developing strong but lightweight metals, efficient fuels, and equipment and supplies that can operate in a weightless environment.

 **Problem** You are a NASA design engineer. Your assignment is to design a module that will land astronauts safely on the moon. You realize that the moon does not have an atmosphere. So, wings or parachutes will not help. Your budget is very limited. You must use common objects to build your prototype, or model. These are the rules and regulations.

1. You will use a raw egg to represent an astronaut.
2. The landing module must be dropped from a height of three meters without the egg being broken.
3. If your module can be dropped successfully from more than three meters, you will be eligible for the Top Designer Award.

Materials  6 raw eggs • materials of your choice to build your landing module

Solution Draw the plans for your module. Make a table like the one shown below to record the results of your test landings. If your design does not work, change it and try again. Good luck!

*E*gg-*Drop Module Trials*

Trial	Height	Design Changes	Results
1	3 m		
2			
3			
4			

To Take or Not To Take?

Use after page 226.

Background   The moon has properties very different from Earth. There are no weather conditions on the moon because it has no water or atmosphere. The absence of air also means that there is no sound. People must communicate by means of radio signals. Due to its small mass, its gravitational force is much less than that of Earth. The moon has a rugged surface. It has mountains, craters, valleys, and plateaus.

Problem   You are a member of a crew exploring the unlighted side of the moon. Your spaceship develops mechanical problems and you are forced to land. Your base is 150 km away on the lighted side of the moon. It can be reached only by walking.

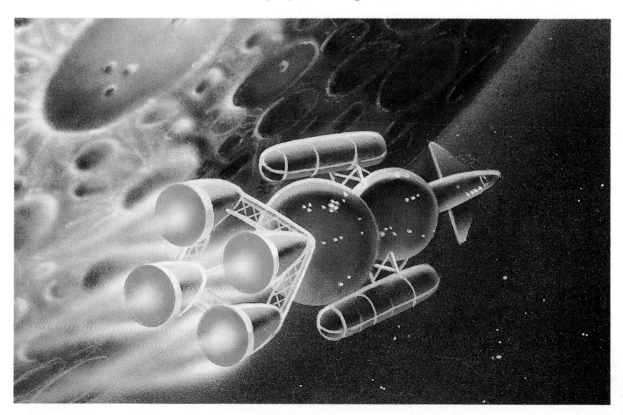

Your ship contains the 15 items listed below. However, only five of these items can be taken on the trip back to the base.

- pack of matches
- food concentrate
- 15 m of nylon rope
- silk parachute
- portable stove
- two pistols
- case of dehydrated milk
- two tanks of oxygen
- map of moon's stars
- life raft
- magnetic compass
- 24 L of water
- first-aid kit
- solar-powered FM receiver-transmitter
- signal flares

Materials   none

Solution 1. First, each member of your group (crew) must rank the items in order of importance. The item you feel would be most important should be marked 1 and the least important 15. Reasons for choices must be given. This is to be done individually without consulting anyone.

2. You and your crew must now decide as a group which five items you will take. In order to make this decision, your group must reach agreement about the ranking of all 15 items. Each group member must be given opportunities to express ideas and question those of others. Do not reach agreement by voting, but rather by discussion.

Don't Refuse Refuse

Use after page 252.

Background   Many waste items are reused by means of recycling. Paper and aluminum cans are two such items. In order to be recycled, a waste material usually must be processed in some way. For example, aluminum must be melted and then reshaped into new products. Used paper must be chemically treated and then pressed into new paper. Wastes that cannot be recycled must be hauled away and dumped someplace, such as in a landfill. All of this requires the use of energy and other resources.

Problem   Because of the increased costs of recycling and collecting refuse, your town has announced a large increase in taxes. To avoid this increase, your friends and neighbors have started a campaign to cut down on the amount of refuse that needs to be collected. For the campaign to be successful, people must find uses for many of the things they now throw away. Your problem is to help them find uses for items that commonly make up refuse.

Materials

refuse such as used film cans, perforated strips of computer paper, foam packing pellets, gum wrappers
- materials of your choice

Solution

You must think of and demonstrate a use for at least five items that are usually thrown away. One rule is that the items cannot be reused for their original purpose. For example, a gum wrapper cannot be used to wrap gum again. Another rule is that dangerous items, such as glass, and possible health hazards, such as food items, are excluded from this activity. Make a table like the one shown below. Write down the items you have chosen. Describe how each item can be reused.

*R*eusable Refuse

Refuse Item	Reuse
computer paper strips	
gum wrappers	
foam pellets	
film cans	

Water Watch

Use after page 272.

Background   There has been a drought in your area lately. No rain has fallen in a long time, and the lakes and reservoirs are drying up. A new industry has moved into town. Many people are moving into your area. The growing population requires more and more water. A serious water shortage is on the horizon.

Problem   There are two parts to this problem. The first is to determine approximately how much water is used each day at school by students and teachers. You may ignore water used in the school kitchen. You may also ignore any water used to water the school grounds.

   The second part of this problem is to devise a plan to conserve water. You must estimate how much water your plan would save each day.

Materials materials of your choice

Solution
1. Make a list of ways students and teachers use water each day.
2. Devise a plan for finding out how much water is used for each of these purposes.
3. Make a table like the one shown below. Record your data. Also list your plans to conserve water and the amount you estimate can be saved. Don't forget to total each column.

*W*ater Watch

Use of Water	Amount Used	Conservation	Amount Saved

Living or Nonliving?

Use after page 295.

Background   People consider Earth to be a unique place because it has living things. Living things, as we know them, have certain features that distinguish them from nonliving things. Living things are made up of cells. They have the ability to reproduce, grow, and develop. Living things require food as a source of energy. Energy is used to maintain all of these life processes. The search for life on other planets usually focuses on these same kinds of features.

Problem   You are a visitor from another planet. Your mission is to gather evidence of living things on Earth. Your spaceship has landed in a field with a sign that says, "Sam Brown's Alfalfa Farm." You suspect that this strange thing called alfalfa is a life form. However, you cannot take any living things back to your planet. Your instructions:

1. Find something that you think is a living thing.
2. Prove that it has at least four of the six features of living things listed in the Background.
3. Display your proof, or evidence, to your classmates.

Materials   4–5 alfalfa seeds • 4–5 alfalfa sprouts • other materials of your choice

Solution   1. Make a table like the one shown below. Plan and carry out a series of tests or experiments to prove that alfalfa shows at least four of the six features listed in your table. Describe your tests and record your results.
2. Display your evidence to your classmates, and give a brief explanation of your results.

*F*eatures of Living Things

Feature	Test	Result
1. Growth		
2. Reproduction		
3. Development		
4. Food		
5. Energy		
6. Cells		

Animal Scramble

Use after page 310.

Background   A classification system can be an important tool in studying living things. The same general classification system is used by all scientists. This system places living things into groups based on different characteristics. Each group has a name. The table below shows the groups and group names for three different animals.

Problem   You are a scientist studying animal classification. A package arrives with information from a fellow scientist. You need this information for a speech about animals. When you open the package, a disorganized pile of index cards falls onto the floor. Each card contains a group name and characteristic used to classify one of the animals. You must organize the cards—your speech is in an hour!

Materials   16 index cards

Solution   Copy each card shown on the next page onto an index card. Use the clues on the cards to classify them into three groups. Then make the table shown below and fill in the correct card numbers.

*A*nimal Scramble

Group-Name	Group-Name	Group-Name
KINGDOM-Animal PHYLUM-Chordata CLASS-Mammalia ORDER-Carnivora FAMILY-Felidae GENUS-*Felis* SPECIES-*domestica*	KINGDOM-Animal PHYLUM-Chordata CLASS-Mammalia ORDER-Ungulata FAMILY-Equidae GENUS-*Equus* SPECIES-*caballus*	KINGDOM-Animal PHYLUM-Chordata CLASS-Mammalia ORDER-Carnivora FAMILY-Canidae GENUS-*Canis* SPECIES-*latrans*
Animal A	Animal B	Animal C
card numbers:	card numbers:	card numbers:

Card 1 ORDER: Animal lives on all continents. They are flesh eaters or predatory animals, but some eat plant materials.	**Card 9** ORDER: Animal has a single toe on each foot.
Card 2 GENUS: It usually weighs between 14 and 23 kg.	**Card 10** GENUS: It has five toes and shearing teeth to facilitate the cutting of flesh.
Card 3 SPECIES: Animal has eyes that are shaped like a vertical slit.	**Card 11** SPECIES: It looks like a rather large, grayish collie dog or a pale yellowish small German shepherd dog with a drooping tail.
Card 4 FAMILY: Animal typically feeds on small mammals and birds.	**Card 12** GENUS: Its weight ranges between 136 and 1182 kg.
Card 5 GENUS: Equine is a word relating to or resembling this animal.	**Card 13** SPECIES: Animal has long legs and averages 1.8 m in height.
Card 6 ORDER: Since the pelts of many are valuable furs, this group is called the principal fur bearers.	**Card 14** SPECIES: Its entire body is covered with hair, or fur.
Card 7 FAMILY: It has feline, or catlike qualities.	**Card 15** SPECIES: This is a group of domesticated animals; that is, tame and living close to people.
Card 8 SPECIES: This animal is also known as a brush wolf, American jackal, and little wolf.	**Card 16** SPECIES: Its color varies from bay or brown, black, chestnut, gray to white.

The Genie Game

Use after page 384.

 Background   There is a genie in your neighborhood. But the genie will only appear if its hereditary traits are revealed.

 Problem   Your group will be given a Genie Sheet that lists eight heredity traits of your genie. The problem is to collect four pairs of trait cards that will produce four of these traits.

 Materials   16 blank index cards ● red and blue pencils

 Solution
1. Copy each card shown on the next page onto separate index cards to make a deck of trait cards. Each trait will have two kinds of cards: dominant (D) and recessive (R).
2. Work in groups of four. Two of your group members will shade their cards red. These cards will represent genes from the genie's mother. The other two will use blue to represent genes from the genie's father. Make a deck of 64 cards.
3. Shuffle the deck and deal ten cards to each player. Turn up the top card of the deck.
4. Play moves clockwise. The player to the left of the dealer can either pick up that card or draw from the deck. You must discard a card at the end of your turn.
5. Each player tries to match four red cards with four blue cards having the same trait. The object is to collect four pairs of cards that will produce four of the eight traits listed.
6. When you have collected the necessary cards in your hand, lay them down and announce "genie appear." If you have matched them correctly, you win this hand.

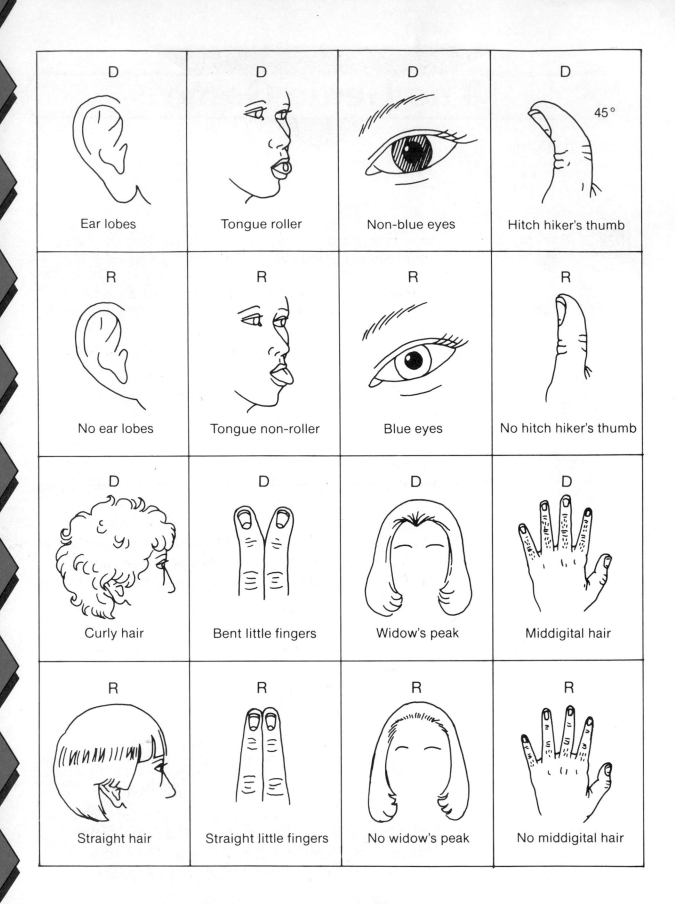

D	D	D	D
Ear lobes	Tongue roller	Non-blue eyes	Hitch hiker's thumb 45°

R	R	R	R
No ear lobes	Tongue non-roller	Blue eyes	No hitch hiker's thumb

D	D	D	D
Curly hair	Bent little fingers	Widow's peak	Middigital hair

R	R	R	R
Straight hair	Straight little fingers	No widow's peak	No middigital hair

Digestive Detective

Use after page 434.

 Background   Humans, like other animals, cannot make their own food as plants do. Food must be taken into the body from the outside. Food is broken down and then absorbed by the body cells through a process known as digestion. Part of the digestive system is the food canal. It is made up of the mouth, esophagus, stomach, small intestine, and large intestine. These organs work together to help change food to a liquid that can be used by the cells of the body.

 **Problem**   You are a doctor in charge of a hospital emergency room. An ambulance has just arrived with a sixth-grade student who attends a nearby school. The student complains that she has severe pains in the stomach area. She tells you she was on a class picnic and became ill. After X rays are taken of the student, you must compare and interpret them so that you can diagnose the problem.

 Materials   tracing paper ● pencil

 Solution   1. Examine each of the X rays shown on the next page.
2. Carefully trace the parts of the digestive system—in their correct positions—on your sheet of tracing paper. Draw any sections that overlap as a dotted line. Then label each part of the digestive system.
3. Examine the complete X ray. Locate the source of your patient's pain. Then write your diagnosis.

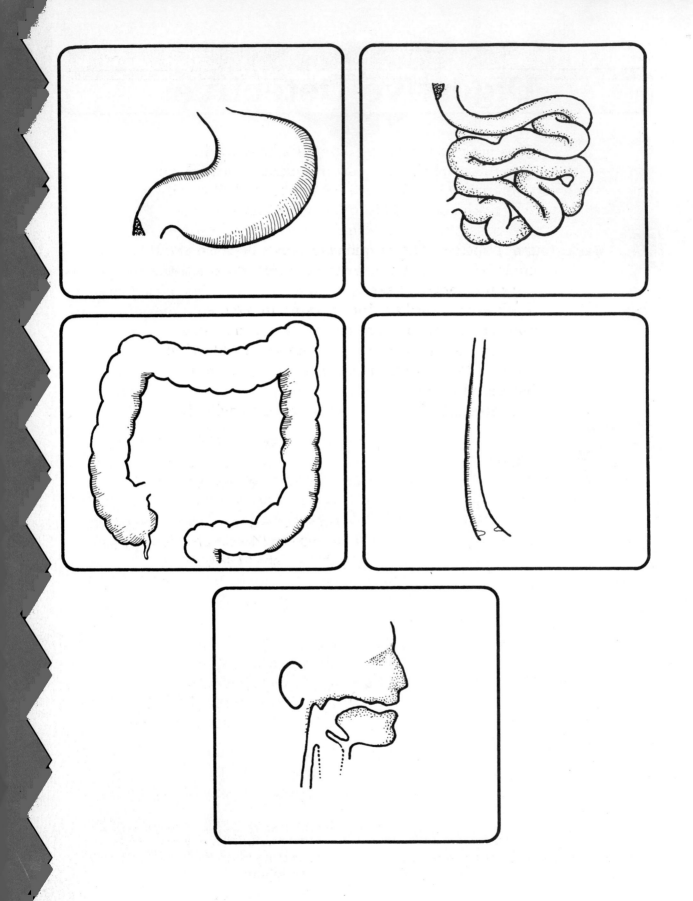

516

Glossary

This book has words you may not have read before. Many of these words are science words. Some science words may be hard for you to read. You will find the science words in **bold print.** These words may appear two ways. The first way shows how the word is spelled. The second way shows how the word sounds. The list below shows the sounds each letter or group of letters makes.

Look at the word **antibody** (ANT ih bahd ee). The second spelling shows the letters "ee." Find these letters in the list. The "ee" has the sound of "ea" in the word "leaf." Anytime you see "ee," you know what sound to say.

The capitalized syllable is the accented syllable.

a . . . back (BAK)
er . . . care, fair (KER, FER)
ay . . . day (DAY)
ah . . . father (FAHTH ur)
ar . . . car (KAR)
ow . . . flower, loud (FLOW ur, LOWD)
e . . . less (LES)
ee . . . leaf (LEEF)
ih . . . trip (TRIHP)
i (*or* i + *consonant* + e) . . . idea, life (i DEE uh, LIFE)
oh . . . go (GOH)
aw . . . soft (SAWFT)
or . . . orbit (OR but)
oy . . . coin (KOYN)

oo . . . foot (FOOT)
yoo . . . pure (PYOOR)
ew . . . food (FEWD)
yew . . . few (FYEW)
uh (*or* u + *consonant*) . . . comma, mother (KAHM uh, MUTH ur)
sh . . . shelf (SHELF)
ch . . . nature (NAY chur)
g . . . gift (GIHFT)
j . . . gem, edge (JEM, EJ)
ing . . . sing (SING)
zh . . . vision (VIHZH un)
k . . . cake (KAYK)
s . . . seed, cent (SEED, SENT)
z . . . zone, raise (ZOHN, RAYZ)

A

acceleration (ihk sel uh RAY shun): any change in speed or direction of an object

acid rain: rain with a low pH caused by the combination of sulfur and nitrogen oxides with water in the atmosphere

acids: substances that form hydrogen ions as they dissolve in water

action-reaction forces: two forces that have equal strength but opposite directions

alcohol (AL kuh hawl): a drug that slows down the way the body works

algae (AL jee): plantlike protists that produce large amounts of oxygen

alveoli (al VEE uh li): tiny air sacs in the lungs

antibody (ANT ih bahd ee): a chemical produced in the blood when foreign matter is present

antiseptic (ant uh SEP tihk): a disinfectant used on living things

arteries (ART uh reez): blood vessels that carry blood away from the heart

artificial satellites: objects placed in Earth's orbit by people

astronomers (uh STRAHN uh murz): scientists who study the stars, planets, and other objects in space

atoms (AT umz): the tiny particles that make up all matter

atrium (AY tree um): one of the two upper chambers of the heart

average speed: distance traveled divided by time

B

bacteria: monerans that live in a wide range of habitats

balanced diet: a diet that provides the body with the nutrients needed for good health

base: a substance that forms hydroxide ions as it dissolves in water

battery: an object that produces an electric current as a result of a chemical reaction

big bang theory: a model stating that all matter in the universe was together in one place about 20 billion years ago and then exploded, scattering pieces of matter everywhere in a constantly expanding pattern

biocontrols: organisms that prevent other organisms from harming crops

biodegradable (bi oh dih GRAYD uh bul) **waste:** waste that can be broken down into harmless compounds by organisms

black dwarf: a star that has lost all its energy and no longer gives off heat or light

black hole: a collapsed neutron star with gravity so great that light cannot escape

bladder: a saclike organ that stores urine for a few hours

bronchi (BRAHN ki): two short tubes that carry air from the trachea to the lungs

bronchioles (BRAHNG kee ohlz): tiny branching tubes in the lungs

budding: the reproduction of a new organism from an outgrowth of the parent

C

caffeine (ka FEEN): a drug that speeds up the nervous system

capillaries (KAP uh ler eez): small blood vessels that connect arteries and veins

cells: the basic units of life

cell membrane: a flexible structure that encloses a cell and holds the contents of the cell together

cell wall: a stiff structure that provides protection and support for most plant cells

chemical family: elements that have a similar arrangement of electrons in their atoms; a column of the periodic table

chemical properties: properties that relate to the way a substance changes to a new substance

chemical reaction: the process by which a chemical change occurs

chlorine: a chemical added to water supplies to kill bacteria

chromatin (KROH muh tun): material in a cell that controls the appearance and type of an organism

chromosomes (KROH muh sohmz): threads of chromatin that carry all the information about an organism

cilia (SIHL ee uh): tiny hairlike structures that enable movement

circuit (SUR kut) **breaker:** an automatic safety switch that breaks an electric circuit when wires are carrying too much current

circulatory (SUR kyuh luh tor ee) **system:** a system that transports materials in the blood to and from the cells of the body

Clean Water Act: a United States law that fights water pollution

clear cutting: the removal of all trees from an area of forest

cocaine (koh KAYN): an illegal drug made from coca leaves that causes an increase in blood pressure and heart rate

communicable (kuh MYEW nih kuh bul) **disease:** a disease that can be passed from one organism to another

compost (KAHM pohst): a mixture of decaying organic matter that can be used as a natural fertilizer

compound: a substance formed from the chemical combination of two or more atoms

conclusion (kun KLEW zhun): an answer to a problem or question

conductors (kun DUK turz): materials through which electrons flow easily

constellation (kahn stuh LAY shun): a star group with a recognized pattern or arrangement

consumer (kun SEW mur): an organism that eats other organisms

contour planting: planting crops in rows that follow the shape of the land

controlled burning: a forest management method used to control certain insects and diseases and to clear the forest floor of dry materials

cover crop: a fast-growing plant with many shallow roots that help keep topsoil from becoming dry and being eroded

crest: the high point of a wave

crop rotation (roh TAY shun): a method of replacing soil nutrients by planting one crop one year and a different crop the next year in the same soil

current electricity: the flow of electrons through a material

cyanobacteria (si uh noh bak TIHR ee uh): monerans that contain chlorophyll; also known as blue-green bacteria

cytoplasm (SITE uh plaz um): the part of a cell outside the nucleus

D

data (DAYT uh): recorded observations

dehydration (dee hi DRAY shun): the removal of water from a material

density (DEN sut ee): the amount of mass that a material has for its volume

depressant (dih PRES unt): a drug that slows down the brain and other parts of the nervous system

diaphragm (DI uh fram): a sheet of muscle between the chest and the lower part of the body that aids in breathing

diatoms (DI uh tahmz): plantlike protists that are a primary source of food for fish

diffusion (dihf YEW zhun): the movement of molecules from where they are present in large amounts to where they are present in small amounts

disinfectants (dihs ihn FEK tunts): chemicals that kill many simple organisms

dominant (DAHM uh nunt) **genes:** genes whose traits are always expressed

dominant (DAHM uh nunt) **trait:** a trait that hides another trait

drug: a chemical that can cause a change in the body

E

efficiency (ih FIHSH un see): a measurement of the work put into a machine compared with the amount of work done by the machine

effort force: the force applied to a lever to overcome resistance

egg: a cell produced by meiosis in female organisms

electric circuit: a continuous path over which electrons move

electric force: the force created by an electric charge

electric motors: machines that make use of several electromagnets to do work

electromagnet: a machine that produces a magnetic field as a result of a current passing through an iron core wrapped with a coiled wire

electromagnetic (ih lek troh mag NET ihk) **spectrum:** an arrangement of electromagnetic waves according to their wavelengths

electromagnetic waves: waves that do not have to travel through matter in order to transfer energy

electrons (ih LEK trahnz): particles with a negative electric charge that move around the nucleus of an atom

elements: substances that are made of just one kind of atom

embryo (EM bree oh): an organism in the early stages of growth

endurance (ihn DOOR uns): the ability to continue using muscle strength without becoming tired

enzymes (EN zimez): molecules that speed up a chemical reaction in an organism

epiglottis (ep uh GLAHT us): a flap of tissue that covers the trachea during swallowing

erosion: the wearing away of land

esophagus (ih SAHF uh gus): a tube that connects the mouth with the stomach

evolution (ev uh LEW shun): the changing of a population of organisms through time; species of organisms adapt to their changing environment and, therefore, evolve

experiment (ihk SPER uh munt): a test that is done to solve a problem or answer a question

F

fertilization (furt uh luh ZAY shun): the uniting of an egg with a sperm to form one cell

fertilizers (FURT uh li zurz): natural or synthetic materials added to the soil to replace nutrients

first law of motion: a law that states that objects at rest stay at rest and objects in motion stay in motion unless acted on by a force

fission (FIHSH un): the equal splitting by mitosis of a one-celled organism into two new one-celled organisms

flagella (fluh JEL uh): long whiplike structures used for movement

flexibility (flek suh BIHL ut ee): the ability to move the body easily into different positions

fluorine: a chemical added to water supplies to help prevent tooth decay

force of gravity: the pulling force of every object on every other object

forces: pushes or pulls that bodies exert on one another

formula (FOR myuh luh): a group of symbols used to show the elements in a compound

frequency: the number of waves that pass a point in a given period of time

friction (FRIHK shun): a force that slows down and stops moving objects

fulcrum (FUL krum): the point at which a lever rocks back and forth

fungi (FUN ji): plural of *fungus*

fungus (FUNG gus): a consumer with a cell wall

fuse: a safety device with a metal strip that can break an electric circuit when too much current flows through it

G

galaxy (GAL uk see): a large group of stars, gas, and dust

gamma (GAM uh) **rays:** waves with the shortest wavelength in the electromagnetic spectrum; released in nuclear reactions

gene (JEEN): a part of a chromosome that controls a trait of an organism

generators: machines that produce electric current by rotating coils of wire through a magnetic field

greenhouse effect: the warming of the atmosphere due to heat trapped by carbon dioxide and other gases

groundwater: underground water supply

H

hazardous (HAZ urd us) **waste:** refuse that is poisonous or radioactive; toxic waste

herbicides (UR buh sidez): substances used by farmers to kill weeds

heredity (huh RED ut ee): the passing of traits from parents to offspring

humus (HYEW mus): the dark organic material in soil

hydrocarbon (hi druh KAR bun): an organic compound that contains only carbon and hydrogen

hypothesis (hi PAHTH uh sus): an idea that has not been proved and can be tested in an experiment

I

inclined plane: a simple machine made up of a slanted surface

indicator (IHN duh kayt ur): a compound that changes color when added to acids and bases

infrared (ihn fruh RED) **wave:** an electromagnetic wave with a wavelength slightly shorter than that of microwaves; used in heat lamps and in detecting certain tumors and heat loss from buildings

inorganic (ihn or GAN ihk) **compounds:** all compounds made from any elements, except those carbon compounds classified as organic

insulators (IHN suh layt urz): materials through which electrons do not flow easily

ionic compounds: compounds formed when charged atoms combine

ions (I ahnz): atoms that have gained or lost an electron

J

joule (JEWL): another name for *newton-meter*

K

kidneys (KIHD neez): two bean-shaped organs that filter waste from the blood

kilowatt-hour: the energy produced by 1,000 watts of power in one hour

L

large intestine: the large tube below the small intestine where water from undigested food is absorbed

larynx (LER ingks): the organ at the upper end of the trachea that contains the vocal cords

laser (LAY zur): a device that produces an intense light beam of one wavelength that travels in only one direction

law of conservation (kahn sur VAY shun) **of mass:** a law that states that mass is neither created nor destroyed in a chemical reaction

lever: a simple machine made up of a bar that turns around a fixed point

light: the portion of the electromagnetic spectrum that is visible to humans

light-year: the distance light travels in one year, or 9.5 trillion kilometers

liver: the digestive organ that produces bile

Local Group: a cluster of galaxies of which the Milky Way Galaxy is a member

M

marijuana (mer uh WAHN uh): an illegal drug made from hemp that causes an increase in blood pressure and heart rate

mass: the amount of matter that is in an object

mechanical (mih KAN ih kul) **advantage:** the amount that a machine can increase a force

mechanical wave: a wave that transfers energy as it travels through matter

medicines: legal drugs used to treat, cure, or prevent illness

meiosis (mi OH sus): the process of cell division that results in cells with half the number of chromosomes of the parent cells

metals: shiny elements that are good conductors and can be bent or hammered

microwaves: radio waves with a wavelengths between one millimeter and 30 centimeters; useful in heating food, communication, and radar

Milky Way Galaxy: a spiral galaxy to which our sun and the planets belong

mitosis (mi TOH sus): the division of a cell into two new cells, each with the same number of chromosomes as the parent cell

mixture: a combination of substances that forms without a chemical reaction

molecule (MAHL ih kyewl): a particle formed when two or more atoms combine by sharing electrons

moneran (muh NIHR un): a one-celled organism with no nucleus

motion: the changing of position

mucus (MYEW kus): a moist, sticky fluid that is found, for example, in the nasal cavity

mutation (myew TAY shun): a change in genes that can cause a new trait to appear

N

natural resource: a material from Earth's atmosphere or crust that is useful to people

natural selection: the process by which organisms less adapted to their environment tend to die and better-adapted organisms tend to survive

nebulas (NEB yuh luz): large clouds of dust and gas in space

neutral (NEW trul): having a pH of 7; neither acid nor basic

neutrons (NEW trahnz): particles in the nucleus of an atom that have no electric charge

neutron star: a very small dense star formed from particles left over from a supernova

newton: a unit for measuring weight

newton-meter: the metric unit for work; also known as a joule

nicotine (NIHK uh teen): a drug found in tobacco products that speeds up the nervous system

nonmetals: dull, brittle elements that are poor conductors

nuclear (NEW klee ur) **membrane:** a cell structure that separates the contents of the nucleus from that of the cytoplasm

nucleus (NEW klee us): the core of an atom; the control center of a cell

O

optical (AHP tih kul) **telescope:** a tube with magnifying lenses or mirrors that collect, transmit, and focus light

organic (or GAN ihk) **compounds:** compounds that contain carbon

organisms (OR guh nihz umz): things that have all the features of life

over-the-counter drugs: drugs that can be bought without a doctor's prescription

oxide (AHK side): a compound of oxygen and one other element

P

pancreas (PANG kree us): the digestive organ that produces enzymes and dumps them into the small intestine

parallel circuit (PER uh lel ● SUR kut): an electric circuit in which the current can flow through more than one pathway

parent material: rocks from which soil is formed

particulates (par TIHK yuh luts): solid particles, such as those found in smoke from factory smokestacks; such particles are pollutants

pasteurization (pas chuh ruh ZAY shun): the process of heating and quickly cooling milk to kill disease-causing bacteria

periodic (pihr ee AHD ihk) **table:** a chart used by scientists to classify elements

pesticides (PES tuh sidez): chemicals used to kill organisms that harm crops

pH scale: a scale used to indicate the strength of acids and bases

physical change: a change in the size, shape, or state of matter that does not cause a new substance to be formed

physical properties: properties that can be observed without referring to another substance

plasma (PLAZ muh): the liquid part of blood

platelets (PLAYT luts): small cells in plasma that cause blood clots to form

Polaris (puh LER us): the North Star

position: the place or location where a person or object is

power: the rate at which a device uses energy

prescription drugs: drugs prepared after they are ordered by a doctor

pressure: a measure of the amount of force applied to a given area

prism: an object that bends light and separates it into colors

producer (pruh DEW sur): an organism that makes its own food

protist (PROHT ust): a one-celled organism with a nucleus

protons (PROH tahnz): particles in the nucleus of an atom that have a positive electric charge

protozoan (proht uh ZOH un): one of several kinds of one-celled animal-like protists that are grouped by how they move

pseudopodia (sewd uh POHD ee uh): fingerlike extensions of a cell that enable movement and feeding

pulley: a simple machine made up of a wheel with a grooved rim in which a rope runs

pulsar: a spinning neutron star that gives off radio waves

pulsating (PUL sayt ing) **theory:** a model stating that the universe will expand and shrink, over and over

Punnett square: a chart used to predict the outcomes of a genetic cross

R

radar: a device in which radio signals sent out from a transmitter bounce off objects and are received by an antenna; used to locate objects

radio telescope: an antenna used to collect radio waves from space

radio waves: waves that have the longest wavelengths in the electromagnetic spectrum

recessive (rih SES ihv) **genes:** genes that control hidden traits

recessive trait: a trait hidden by a dominant trait

rectum: the muscular part of the large intestine that pushes undigested food from the body

recycling: reusing items or resources

red cells: cells in plasma that transport oxygen to the body cells and carbon dioxide away from the body cells

red giants: very large expanding stars that glow red

reproduction (ree pruh DUK shun): the process by which organisms produce new organisms of their own kind

reservoir (REZ urv wor): a large artificial or natural lake used to collect and store water

resistance (rih ZIHS tuns) **arm:** the end of the lever where the resistance force rests

resistance force: the force exerted by the object that a lever moves

respiration (res puh RAY shun): a process that combines oxygen with food molecules in a chemical change that releases energy

respiratory (RES pruh tor ee) **system:** the system of tissues and organs that brings oxygen into the body and removes waste materials such as carbon dioxide

S

saliva: liquid in the mouth that begins the chemical digestion of food

salt: a compound formed when an acid and a base combine

sanitary (SAN uh ter ee) **landfill:** a waste disposal site where trash is placed in a hole and covered with soil

satellite (SAT uh lite): an object that orbits or revolves around a larger object

saturated solution (SACH uh rayt ud ● suh LEW shun): a solution in which no more of a substance can be dissolved at a given temperature

screw: a simple machine made up of an inclined plane wrapped in a spiral around a cylinder

scrubber: a device in a smokestack or chimney that uses water to remove particulates and some polluting gases

second law of motion: a law that states that an object's acceleration depends on the mass of the object and the size and direction of the force acting on it

selective breeding: the crossing of organisms with desirable traits to produce offspring with a combination of these desirable traits

selective cutting: a method of removing only mature trees from a forest so that small trees can continue to grow

series circuit (SUR kut): an electric circuit in which the electric current flows through only one pathway

sewage: liquid and solid wastes carried in sewers and drains

shelter belt: a row of trees or shrubs planted to prevent wind from blowing soil away

side effect: a change in the body other than the change desired when using a drug

small intestine: the digestive tube below the stomach in which most chemical digestion takes place

soil: a mixture of weathered rocks and organic matter in which plants grow

solution (suh LEW shun): a mixture in which a substance is spread evenly throughout another substance

space probe: a spacecraft sent beyond Earth to gather information about space objects

space shuttle: a system composed of a giant fuel tank, two large rockets, and an orbiter that can glide and land like a plane; the orbiter can be launched and returned to Earth many times

space station: a spacecraft used for living and working in space

sperm: a cell produced by meiosis in male organisms

static electricity: the positive or negative electric charges on objects

stimulant (STIHM yuh lunt): a drug that speeds up the nervous system

stomach: a small saclike organ that holds and digests food

strip cropping: the planting of several rows of a cover plant between rows of a main crop

subsoil: the second layer of soil; contains clay

substance: pure matter that is always the same in composition

supernova (sew pur NOH vuh): a very large exploding star

suspension (suh SPEN chun): a mixture in which the substances are not dissolved

T

tar: a substance associated with cigarette smoke that causes harmful changes in the body

thermal pollution: the dumping of hot water into a body of cooler water

third law of motion: a law that states that for every action force there is an equal and opposite reaction force

topsoil: the top layer of soil; contains organic matter

trachea (TRAY kee uh): a stiff tube through which air passes to and from the lungs

trash-burning power plants: facilities at which trash and coal are mixed and burned, producing energy that is used to provide electricity

trough: the low point of a wave

U

ultraviolet (ul truh VI uh lut) **waves:** electromagnetic waves with a wavelength just shorter than that of visible light

universe (YEW nuh vurs): space and all matter and energy in it

urea (yoo REE uh): cell waste containing nitrogen

ureters (YOOR ut urz): tubes leading from the kidneys to the bladder through which urine passes

urethra (yoo REE thruh): a duct through which urine leaves the body

urinary (YOOR uh ner ee) **system:** a group of organs that remove liquid wastes from the body

urine (YOOR un): a liquid produced by the kidneys and made up of water, urea, salts, and other wastes

V

vaccine (vak SEEN): a dead or weakened virus that is used to help the body produce antibodies to fight a certain disease

vegetative (VEJ uh tayt ihv) **reproduction:** the formation of new plants from a body part of a single parent plant

veins (VAYNZ): blood vessels that carry blood to the heart

velocity (vuh LAHS ut ee): the speed and direction of a moving object; an object's velocity changes as its speed or direction changes

ventricles (VEN trih kulz): the two lower chambers of the heart

villi (VIHL i): tiny folds in the small intestine where food molecules pass into the blood

virus (VI rus): a particle that has characteristics of both living and nonliving matter

volume (VAHL yum): the amount of space that matter occupies

W

watt: a unit used to measure power

wavelength: the distance from one wave trough to the next wave trough

wedge: a simple machine composed of one or two inclined planes

weight: the measure of the force of gravity acting on an object

weightlessness: the absence of feeling the pull of gravity; the condition of objects that are falling freely in space

wheel and axle: a simple machine composed of a large wheel (wheel) and a small wheel (axle) that turn together

white cells: cells in plasma that destroy foreign matter in the blood

white dwarfs: very old shrinking stars that glow white

work: the result of a force moving an object through a distance; work equals force times the distance an object moves

X

X rays: electromagnetic waves having a wavelength just shorter than that of an ultraviolet wave and able to penetrate many solid materials

Z

zygote (ZI goht): a cell that results from the combination of one egg with one sperm cell

A

Acceleration, 141, 144–145; *act.,* 145

Acid rain, 275–276, 282

Acids, 64–70; *act.,* 57; indicators, 66, 69–70; *act.,* 66, 69

Action-reaction forces, 142–143

Air, conservation, 278–280; pollution, 274–278, 280–281; *act.,* 281

Alcohol, 469–470, 475

Algae, 330–331, 333, 353, 362; *illus.,* 330; diatoms, 300, 331; *illus.,* 331

Alveoli, 416, 419; *illus.,* 416–417

Animal kingdom, 298, 301–302

Antibodies, 314–316

Antiseptic, 327

Arteries, 399, 405; *illus.,* 405–406

Artificial satellites, 214–215, 218

Astronomers, 178–180

Atoms, 32–35, 41–46; structure of, 33–35; *act.,* 35; *illus.,* 34

Atrium, 404; *illus.,* 404

Average speed, 126–129; *act.,* 129

B

Bacteria, 299, 321, 324–329, 335, 338, 353, 362; *illus.,* 325, 328; controlling growth of, 326–329; *act.,* 329

Bases, 64–70; indicators, 66, 69–70; *act.,* 66, 69

Batteries, 81–85

Big bang theory, 196–197

Biocontrols, 270

Biodegradable wastes, 250; *act.,* 253

Biologists, 282

Black dwarfs, 184; *illus.,* 185

Black holes, 187–189; *illus.,* 187–188

Bladder, 439, 442; *illus.,* 440

Blood, 399, 407–408, 438, 442; *illus.,* 407; vessels, 402, 405

Bronchi, 416, 419; *illus.,* 414, 417

Bronchioles, 416, 419; *illus.,* 414, 416

Budding, 353, 360; *illus.,* 353

C

Caffeine, 466, 468–469, 475; *act.,* 469

Capillaries, 405; *illus.,* 405–406

Cause and effect relationships, 254

Cell; 293–295, 314–316, 344–351; chromatin, 346; cytoplasm, 345–346, 348, 350, 356–357; division of, 347–351, 353, 355–358; *act.,* 351; *illus.,* 348, 356–357; egg, 357–358, 360; membrane, 294–295, 345, 348; nuclear membrane, 346, 348–350; nucleus, 294–295, 299–302, 322, 330, 345–346; parts of, 345–347, 350; *act.,* 346; *illus.,* 345; red, 407, 411; *illus.,* 407; sperm, 357–358, 360; structure of, 294–295; *act.,* 303; *illus.,* 294–295; wall, 294–295, 301–302; white, 407; *illus.,* 407; zygote, 358, 360; *illus.,* 358

Changes, physical, 25

Chemical families, 37, 40; *table,* 38–39

Chemical properties, 21–22, 25

Chemical reactions, 22–23, 25, 81; *illus.,* 22; conservation of mass, 23, 25; *illus.,* 23

Chlorine, 266, 268

Chromatin, 346

Chromosomes, 346–350, 355–358, 368–372; *illus.,* 347

Cilia, 332; *illus.,* 332

Circuit breakers, 88–89

Circuits, 82–89, *act.,* 85, 499–500; *illus.,* 82–84; parallel, 83–85; series, 83–85

Circulatory system, 399–409; *act.,* 403; *illus.,* 406, 407

Classifications, 291, 296–311; *act.,* 291, 303, 311, 511–512; *illus.,* 305–307; *table,* 302

Clean Water Act, 270

Clear cutting, 244

Cocaine, 473–475

Communicable diseases, 315, 325

Composts, 252

Compounds, 42–47, 57, 69; acids, 64–70; bases, 64–70; classifying, 58–62; formation of, *act.,* 47; formulas for, 45–46, 59; hydrocarbons, 60; inorganic, 61–62; *illus.,* 61; ionic, 44–46; *illus.,* 44; molecular, 42–43, 46; *illus.,* 42;

organic, 59–60, 62; *illus.*, 60; oxides, 61–62; *act.*, 63; salts, 67–68

Conclusions, 9–11

Conductors, 80, 82

Conservation, of clean air, 278–280; of clean water, 266–272; *act.*, 507–508; of forests, 244–247; *illus.*, 245; of mass, 23, 25; *illus.*, 23; of soil, 238–243; *illus.*, 239–240

Constellations, 204–209, *act.*, 206; *illus.*, 204–205, 207–208

Consumers, 299–302, 304

Context clues, 41

Contour planting, 240; *illus.*, 240

Controlled burning, 246

Cover crops, 239

Crests, 104; *illus.*, 104

Crop rotations, 241

Current electricity, 80–95; in circuits, 82–85; *act.*, 85, 499–500; *table*, 84; *illus.*, 82–84; in your home, 86–94; measuring, 92–94; *table*, 93; in motors, 91; *act.*, 95; *illus.*, 91

Cyanobacteria, 299, 323, 328; *illus.*, 323

Cytoplasm, 345–346, 348, 350, 356–357

D

Data, 9; *act.*, 487–488

Definitions, *act.*, 489–490

Dehydration, 327

Density, 15–16, 18–19; *act.*, 19; *illus.*, 16

Depressants, 470, 472, 475

Diaphragm, 412; *illus.*, 412, 414

Diatoms, 300, 331; *illus.*, 331

Diet, balanced, 451–455

Diffusion, 430; *act.*, 435

Digestive system, 425–435; *act.*, 425, 427, 435, 515–516; *illus.*, 431; *table*, 434

Diseases, communicable, 315, 325

Disinfectants, 327

Dominant genes, 371–375

Dominant traits, 371; *act.*, 377

Drugs, 462–475; effects of, 466–475; over-the-counter, 463–465; *act.*, 465; prescription, 462–464

E

Efficiency, 158–159

Effort forces, 161–162

Egg cells, 357–358, 360

Electric circuits, 82–89; *act.*, 85, 499–500; *illus.*, 82–84; parallel, 83–85; series, 83–85

Electric current, measuring, 92–94; *table*, 93

Electric forces, 132

Electricity, 75–96; current, 80–95; *act.*, 85, 499–500; *illus.*, 82–84; *table*, 84; electric forces, 132; in your home, 86–94; measuring, 92–94; *table*, 93; and motors, 90–91; *act.*, 95; *illus.*, 91; in pacemakers, 96; static, 75–80; *act.*, 75, 77; *illus.*, 76–79

Electric forces, 132

Electric motors, 90–91, *act.*, 95; *illus.*, 91

Electromagnetic spectrum, 104–106, 108, 113; *illus.*, 104–105

Electromagnetic waves, 102–115; *illus.*, 104–105,

Electromagnets, 90; *illus.*, 90

Electrons, 33–35 76–78, 80–82; *act.*, 35

Elements, 31–40; *table*, 33; classifying, 36–40; *table*, 38–39;

Embryos, 358–360; *illus.*, 358

Endurance, 458, 460

Energy, 426–427, 451; transfer of, 102–106

Enzymes, 426, 429–430, 434

Epiglottis, 428, 434; *illus.*, 428

Erosion, 233, 238–241, 243–244; *act.*, 233, 243

Esophagus, 427–428, 434; *illus.*, 428, 431

Evolution, 384

Excretion, 436–443; skin, 437–438; *illus.*, 437; urinary system, 438–443; *act.*, 443; *illus.*, 440

Exercise, 456–461; *act.*, 461; and body systems, 459–460; and endurance, 458, 460; experts, 168; and flexibility, 458, 460; and muscles, 456–460; and rest, 459–460

Experiments, 9–10; *act.*, 495–496

F

Fertilization, 358, 360; *illus.*, 358

Fertilizers, 242, 270

First law of motion, 140, 144

Fission, 353, 360, 362; *illus.*, 353

Flagella, 331–332

"Flashlight" fish, 338

Flexibility, 458, 460

Fluorine, 267

Food, 449–453; *act.*, 449; groups, 452–453

Forces, 130–145; action–reaction, 142–143; *act.,* 143; *illus.,* 142–143; effort, 161–162; electric, 132, friction, 132–134, 158–159; *act.,* 159; gravity, 17–18, 130–131, 187–188; and pressure, 135–137; magnetic, 131; resistance, 161–162; and work, 152–157, 160–165; *act.,* 167

Forests, conserving, 244–247; managing, 245–247; national, 246–247

Formulas, 45–46, 59

Frequency, 104–108, 110, 112

Friction, 132–134, 158–159; *act.,* 159

Fulcrums, 161–162, 166

Fungus kingdom, 298, 300, 302, 335–337; *act.,* 335, 337

Fuse, 88–94

G

Galaxies, 179, 190–193, 195, 196–198; *act.,* 198 *illus.,* 190–193

Gamma rays, 115

Generators, 81

Genes, 370–376; dominant, 371–375; and mutations, 379–380, 384; recessive, 372–376; transferring, 388–389

Geneticists, 390

Genetics, 367–390; *act.,* 367, 374, 377, 385, 513–514; in populations, 378–384

Gravity, 17–18, 130–131, 187–188

Greenhouse effect, 277; *illus.,* 277

Groundwater, 260–262, 265

H

Hazardous wastes, 249

Healthful eating, 450–455

Heart, 399, 402–404, 408; *illus.,* 404

Herbicides, 264

Heredity, 367–390; *act.,* 367, 374, 377, 385, 513–514

Humus, 237

Hydrocarbons, 60; *illus.,* 60

Hypothesis, 9–10; *act.,* 493–494

I

Inclined planes, 160, 163–164, 166

Indicators, 66, 69–70; *act.,* 66, 69

Infrared waves, 112, 115, 277; *illus.,* 112

Inorganic compounds, 61–62; *illus.,* 61

Insulators, 80

Ionic compounds, 44–46; *illus.,* 44

Ions, 44–46, 64–65, 68

J

Joules, 153–154

K

Kidneys 438–444; *act.,* 443; *illus.,* 438, 440; transplants, 444

Kilowatt-hours, 92–94

Kingdoms, 297–307; *table,* 302; animal, 298, 301–302; fungus, 298, 300, 302, 335–337; moneran, 299–300, 302, 313, 322–330; plant, 298, 301–302; protist, 330–333

L

Large intestine, 432–434

Larynx, 415, 419; *illus.,* 414

Lasers, 116–117

Law of conservation of mass, 23, 25; *illus.,* 23

Laws of motion, 138–145; *act.,* 143, 145

Levers, 160–162, 166; *act.,* 167; *illus.,* 160–162, 166

Life, classification of, 296–310; *act.,* 303; features of, 292–295; *act.,* 509–510; reproduction of, 343, 352–362; *act.,* 343, 354, 361; scientific names for, 304–310; *act.,* 311; simple organisms, 321–338; *act.,* 321, 329, 335, 337

Light, 104, 113–114; *act.,* 114, 118; lasers, 116–117

Lightsailing, 226

Light-years, 180

Liver, 430, 434; *illus.,* 430–431

Local Group, 192–193

M

Machines, 151, 156–168; *act.,* 151; advantages of, 156–159; efficiency of, 158–159; simple, 160–167; *act.,* 167; *illus.,* 160–166

Magnetic forces, 131

Marijuana, 467, 472–473, 475

Mass, 15–18; conservation of, 23, 25

Matter, measuring, 12–19; properties of, 20–26; *act.,* 26; states of, 20, 24

Measurements, 12–19; density, 15–16; *act.,* 19; electric current, 92–94; mass, 15–18; volume, 13–16, 18; weight, 17–18; work, 153–155; *act.,* 155

Mechanical advantage, 156–157, 159

Mechanical waves, 102–103, 106; *illus.,* 102–103

Medicines, 463–465; *act.,* 465

Meiosis, 355–357, 360; *illus.,* 356–357

Metals, 37, 40–41

Microwaves, 105, 110–111

Milky Way Galaxy, 179, 190–193; *illus.,* 192

Mitosis, 348–351, 353, 358, 362; *act.,* 351; *illus.,* 348

Mixtures, 48–52; solutions, 49, 51; separating, 50–52, *act.,* 52; suspensions, 50–51

Molecular compounds, 42–43, 46

Molecules, 42–44; *illus.,* 42

Moneran kingdom, 298–300, 302, 313, 322–330; bacteria, 299, 321, 324–329, 335, 338, 353, 362; *act.,* 329; *illus.,* 325, 328; cyanobacteria, 299, 323, 328; *illus.,* 323

Motion, 123–129; first law of, 140, 144; Newton's laws of, 138–145; research, 146; second law of, 141, 144–145; *act.,* 145; third law of, 142–143; *act.,* 143

Motors, 90–91; *act.,* 95; *illus.,* 91

Mucus, 413

Muscles, 456–461; *act.,* 461; and endurance, 458; and flexibility, 458; and rest, 459–460

Mutations, 379–380, 384

N

National forests, 246–247

Natural resources, 234; air, 274–281; forests, 244–247; soil, 233–243; water, 259–273

Natural selection, 381–384; *act.,* 383

Nebulas, 183–185; *illus.,* 183, 185

Neutral substances, 67

Neutrons, 33, 35, 187

Neutron stars, 187, 189; *illus.,* 187

Newtons, 17–18

Newton's laws of motion, 138–145; *act.,* 143, 145

Nicotine, 471, 475

Nonmetals, 40

Nuclear membrane, 346, 348–350

Nucleus, of atoms, 33–34; of cells, 294–295, 299–302, 322, 330, 345–346

O

Observations, 7–11; *act.,* 7

Optical telescopes, 210–213; *illus.,* 210–211

Organic compounds, 59–60, 62; *illus.,* 60; hydrocarbons, 60

Organisms, 292–311; cells and, 344–351; *act.,* 346, 351; *illus.,* 345; features of, 292–295; *act.,* 509–510; grouping, 296–310; *act.,* 303; growth of, 347, 358–359; *act.,* 329, 335, 337; and heredity, 367–390; *act.,* 367, 377, 383, 385; and reproduction, 343, 352–362; *act.,* 343, 354, 361; scientific naming of, 304; simple, 321–338; *act.,* 321

Organs, 401

Over-the-counter drugs, 463–465; *act.,* 465

Oxides, 61–62; *act.,* 63; *table,* 62

P

Pacemakers, 96, 226

Pancreas, 430, 434; *illus.,* 430

Parallel circuits, 83–85; *illus.,* 83–84

Parent material, 236–237, 242; *illus.,* 236

Particulates, 275, 279

Pasteurization, 326

Periodic table, 36–42; *table,* 38–39

Pesticides, 264, 270

pH scale, 67, 70; *illus.,* 67

Physical changes, 25

Physical properties, 24–25; *act.,* 497–498

Physical therapists, 476

Plant kingdom, 298, 301–302

Plasma, 407

Platelets, 407

Polaris, 205; *illus.,* 205

Pollution, air, 274–281; *act.,* 281; *illus.,* 274–276; thermal, 263, 265, 270; water, 260–265, 276; *act.,* 259, 262, 270; *illus.,* 262–265

Position, 124–126

Power, 92; from trash, 250

Predictions, *act.,* 485–486

Prescription drugs, 462–464

Pressure, 135–137; *illus.,* 135–137

Prisms, 113, 194; *illus.,* 113

Probes, 216–218; *act.,* 219

Producers, 299–302

Protist kingdom, 298, 300–302, 330–333; algae, 330–331, 333, 353, 362; *illus.,* 330–331; protozoans, 300, 332–333; *illus.,* 300, 332–333

Protons, 33–35, 77

Protozoans, 300, 332–333; *illus.,* 300, 332–333

Pseudopodia, 332; *illus.,* 332

Pulleys, 160, 165–166; *illus.,* 165

Pulsars, 187, 212

Pulsating theory, 197

Pulse, *act.,* 403

Punnett squares, 374–375; *illus.,* 375

R

Radar, 105, 110–111

Radio telescopes, 212–213; *illus.,* 212–213

Radio waves, 105, 108–112, 187, 212–213; microwaves, 105, 110–111

Rays, gamma, 115; X, 104, 115

Recessive genes, 372–376

Recessive traits, 372; *act.,* 377

Rectum, 433

Recycling, 251–252; *act.,* 251, 505–506

Red cells, 407, 411; *illus.,* 407

Red giants, 184–189; *illus.,* 185, 187

Refuse, disposing of, 248–253

Reproduction, 343, 352–362; *act.,* 343; by one parent, 353–354, 360–362; *illus.,* 353; *act.,* 354, 361; by two parents, 355–360; *illus.,* 356–357. See also Budding; Fission; Meiosis; Mitosis; Vegetative reproduction

Reservoirs, 266

Resistance arm, 161

Resistance forces, 161–162

Respiration, 410–420

Respiratory system, 410–420; *act.,* 399, 420; *illus.,* 414, 416–417

S

Saliva, 427

Salts, 67–68

Sanitary landfills, 248–249; *illus.,* 249

Satellites, 214–218; *act.,* 203; artificial, 214–215, 218

Saturated solutions, 49

Scientific methods, 6–11; *act.,* 485–496; *illus.,* 8–9

Scientific naming, 304–311; *illus.,* 306–307

Screws, 160, 163–164, 166

Scrubbers, 279

Second law of motion, 141, 144–145; *act.,* 145

Selective breeding, 386–389

Selective cutting, 245

Series circuits, 83–85; *illus.,* 83–84

Sewage, 263–265, 267–269, 272

Shelter belts, 240

Shuttles, 223–224; *illus.,* 223

Side effects, 463

Simple machines, 160–167

Skin, 436–438; *illus.,* 437

Small intestines, 429–432, 434; *illus.,* 429, 431

Soil, 233–243; conserving, 238–243; *act.,* 233, 243; profile, 236–237, 242; *illus.,* 236; scientists, 70

Solutions, 49, 51; saturated, 49

Space, 177–231; constellations, 204–209; *act.,* 206; *illus.,* 204–205, 207–208; expanding universe, 194–197; *act.,* 198; galaxies, 179, 190–193, 196–198; *act.,* 198; *illus.,* 190–193; lightsailing in, 228; location in, *act.,* 181; people in, 220–227; *act.,* 227, 501–504; probes, 216–218; *act.,* 219; satellites, 214–218; *act.,* 203; shuttles, 223–224; *illus.,* 223; stars, 177–197, 204–209; *act.,* 177, 189; *illus.,* 182–188; stations, 223–224, 226–227; technology, 225–226; telescopes, 203, 210–213; *illus.,* 210–213; vastness of, 178–181; *illus.,* 179

Speed, average, 126–129; *act.,* 123, 129

Spectrum, electromagnetic, 104–106, 108, 113; *illus.,* 104–105; of stars, 194–195; *illus.,* 195

Sperm cells, 357–358, 360

Stars, 177–197, 204–209; black dwarfs, 184; *illus.,* 185; constellations, 204–209; *act.,* 206; *illus.,* 204–205, 207–208; kinds of, 184–189; *act.,* 177, 189; *illus.,* 182, 185, 187; life cycles of 183–185; *illus.,* 185; neutron, 187, 189; Polaris, 205; red giants, 184–189; white dwarfs, 184–185, 189

Static electricity, 75–80; *act.,* 75, 77; *illus.,* 76–79

Stimulants, 468, 471–473, 475

531

Stomach, 428–429, 434; *illus.*, 428, 430–431

Strip cropping, 239; *illus.*, 239

Subsoil, 236–237, 242; *illus.*, 236

Substances, 21–25; *table*, 21; chemical properties of, 21–22, 25; *act.*, 26; chemical reactions of, 22–23, 25; composition of , 32–35; physical properties of, 24–25; *act.*, 497–498

Summarizing paragraphs, 362

Supernovas, 186–189; *illus.*, 186–187

Suspensions, 50–51; *illus.*, 50

Systems, 400–401; *illus.*, 401; circulatory, 399–409; *act.*, 403, 409; *illus.*, 406, 417; digestive, 425–435; *act.*, 425, 427, 435, 515–516; *illus.*, 431; respiratory, 399, 410–420; *act.*, 399, 420; *illus.*, 414, 416–417; urinary, 438–443; *act.*, 443; *illus.*, 440

T

Tar, 471

Telescopes, 203, 210–213; optical, 210–213; *illus.*, 210–211; radio, 212–213; *illus.*, 212–213

Thermal pollution, 263, 265, 270

Third law of motion, 142–143; *act.*, 143; *illus.*, 142–143

Topsoil, 236–240, 242; *illus.*, 236

Trachea, 413, 419, 428; *illus.*, 414, 416–417

Traits, controlling, 386–389; dominant, 371, 377; expressing, 370–373; inheriting, 369–370; predicting, 373–376; *act.*, 385; recessive, 372, 377

Trash, 248–253; power from, 250; recycling, 251–252; *act.*, 251, 505–506; types of, 249–250; *act.*, 253

Trash-burning power plants, 250

Trough, 104, 106; *illus.*, 104

U

Ultraviolet waves, 104, 114–115

Universe, 179–180; movement in, 194–195; *act.*, 198; origin of, 196–197

Urea, 437–439, 444

Ureters, 439, 442; *illus.*, 438, 440

Urethra, 439, 442; *illus.*, 440

Urinary system, 438–443; *act.*, 443; *illus.*, 440

Urine, 438–439; *illus.*, 439

V

Vaccines, 316

Variables, controlling, 491–492; *act.*, 491–492

Vegetative reproduction, 354, 360–361; *act.*, 354, 361

Veins, 399, 405; *illus.*, 405–406

Velocity, 127–128

Ventricles, 404; *illus.*, 404

Villi, 432, 434; *illus.*, 432

Viruses, 312–316; *act.*, 314; *table*, 315; *illus.*, 313

Volume, 13–16, 18

W

Wastes, 248–253; biodegradable, 250, 253; *act.*, 253; hazardous, 249; power from, 250; recycling, 251–252; *act.*, 251, 505–506

Water, 259–273; *illus.*, 260–261; conservation, 266–272; *act.*, 273, 507–508; pollution, 260–265, 276; *act.*, 259, 262, 270; *illus.*, 262–265

Watts, 92–93

Wavelengths, 104–108, 111–117; *illus.*, 104

Waves, 101–118; electromagnetic, 102–115; *illus.*, 104–105; higher frequency, 112–115; infrared, 112, 115, 277; light, 104, 113–114; mechanical, 102–103, 106; *illus.*, 102–103; properties of, 104–105, 107; *act.*, 107; *illus.*, 104; radio, 105, 108–112, 187, 212–213; *act.*, 101; ultraviolet, 104, 114–115

Wedges, 160, 163–164, 166

Weight, 17–18

Weightlessness, 222

Wheel and axles, 160, 164–166

White cells, 407; *illus.*, 407

White dwarfs, 184–185, 189; *illus.*, 185

Work, 152–156; *act.*, 155

X

X rays, 104, 115

Z

Zygote, 358, 360; *illus.*, 358

Photo Credits

Kerins; **220, 221,** NASA; **222,** Johnson Space Center; **224,** NASA; **225,** Kenji Kerins; **227,** Studiohio; **228, 231,** NASA; **232,** Bob Daemmrich; **233,** Diane Graham-Henry and Kathleen Culbert-Aguilar; **237,** Lefener/Grushow from Grant Heilman; **238,** D.P. Burnside/Photo Researchers; **239,** (l) Larry Lefever from Grant Heilman, (r) Grant Heilman Photography; **240,** David R. Frazier; **242,** Kenji Kerins; **244,** (l) Kenji Kerins, (r) Grant Heilman Photography; **246,** Gilbert Grant/Photo Researchers; **247,** Nathan Bilow/Stock Imagery; **248,** Kenji Kerins; **250,** courtesy of Signal Environmental Systems, Inc.; **252,** Kenji Kerins; **254,** Larry Hamill; **256,** Shannon Moore; **258,** James Blank/Stock Boston; **262,** (t) Tim Courlas, (b) Kenji Kerins; **263,** Grant Heilman Photography; **264,** Tom Myers; **265,** Alan Pitcairn from Grant Heilman; **266,** Grant Heilman Photography; **267,** (l) courtesy City of San Diego Dept. of Water Utilities, (r) Hal Harrison from Grant Heilman; **268–269,** Kenji Kerins; **269,** (l) Kenji Kerins, (r) Dennis MacDonald/Photri; **270,** (t) General Biological Inc., (c) James Westwater, (b) Grant Heilman Photography; **271,** (l) Alan Pitcairn from Grant Heilman, (r) Frank S. Balthis; **272,** Bob Daemmrich; **273,** Kenji Kerins; **274,** C.D. Miller; **275,** John Verde/Photo Researchers; **276,** (tl) Doug Martin, (tr) G. Zimbel/Monkmeyer Press, (b) Herman Kokojan/Black Star; **277,** Steve Lissau; **278,** Michael Bush/Stock Imagery; **279,** Lawrence Migdale; **280,** George Anderson; **282,** Ted Rice; **284,** Bob Daemmrich; **286–287,** Aaron Haupt/Merrill photo; **288,** Dean Christake/FPG; **290,** Bob Daemmrich; **291,** Animals Animals/Robert Pearcy; **293,** Maslowski Photo; **294,** Dr. Jeremy Burgess/Science Photo Library; **295,** Dwight R. Kuhn; **296,** Kenji Kerins; **297,** (l to r, t to b) Stephen J. Krasemann/DRK Photo, Carolina Biological Supply, Aaron Haupt/Merrill photo, Roger K. Burnard, Thomas Russell, Thomas Russell, Dr. G. Murti/Science Photo Library/Photo Researchers; **298,** John Colwell from Grant Heilman; **299,** Roger K. Burnard; **300,** (t) Eric Grave/Photo Researchers, (b) Larry Cameron/Photo Researchers; **301,** David M. Dennis; **305,** Studiohio; **306, 307,** (beaver) Stanley Schoenberger from Grant Heilman, (woodrat) Phil A. Dotson/Photo Researchers, (cactus mouse) William Weber, (deer mouse) Paul E. Taylor/Photo Researchers, (grasshopper) Alvin Staffan, (ostrich) Leonard Lee Rue III/Photo Researchers, (rabbit) Alvin Staffan; **309,** (l) Roger K. Burnard, (c) Anthony Mercieca/Photo Researchers, (r) Lynn M. Stone; **310,** William D. Popejoy; **311,** Brent Turner/BLT Productions; **312,** Studiohio; **313,** (t) B. Heggeler/Biozentrum/University of Basel/Science Photo Library/Photo Researchers, (c) Biology Media/Photo Researchers, (b) CNRI/Science Photo Library/Photo Researchers; **314,** Kenji Kerins; **315,** (l) Camera M.D. Studios, (r) CDC; **316,** Pictures Unlimited; **318,** Brian Parker/Tom Stack & Associates; **320,** Kenji Kerins; **322,** Lawrence Migdale; **323,** Roger K. Burnard; **324,** Shay/Gerard Photography; **325,** (t) CNRI/Science Photo Library/Photo Researchers, (b) Joseph DiChello; **326, 327,** Shay/Gerard Photography; **328,** Lennart Nilsson © Boehringer Ingelheim Ltd. Gmb H./"The Body Victorious", Delacorte Press, Dell Publishing Company, NY; **329,** Shay/Gerard Photography; **330,** Alex Rakosy/Black Star; **331,** (t) Biophoto Associates/Science Source/Photo Researchers, (b) Manfred P. Kage/Peter Arnold, Inc.; **332,** M. Abbey/Photo Researchers; **333,** (l) Photri, (r) Eric Grave/Photo Researchers; **334,** (tl) William D. Popejoy, (cl) Lynn M. Stone, (bl) Rich Brommer, (tr) David M. Dennis, (br) Stephen J. Krasemann/DRK Photo; **335,** William Ferguson; **336,** Elaine Shay; **338,** Fred McConnaughey/Photo Researchers; **341,** Manfred P. Kage/Peter Arnold, Inc.; **342,** Stephen Frisch/Stock Boston; **343,** Andy Sacks/TSW-CLICK/Chicago; **344,** (l) Stock Imagery, (r) Images Colour Library/Stock Imagery; **346,** Lennart Nilsson "The Incredible Machine," National Geographic Society; **347,** (tl) Chris Rogers/Stock Imagery, (tc) Cliff Beaver, (tr) Runk/Scheonberger from Grant Heilman, (b) Russell Lappa; **349,** (l) Runk/Schoenberger from Grant Heilman, (r) Rich Brommer; **350,** Kenji Kerins **353,** Science Photo Library/Photo Researchers; **354, 355,** Kenji Kerins **358,** (tl) Dr. Mia Tegner, Scripps Institute of Oceanography, (br) Animals Animals/Zig Lesczynski, (others) "SEM In Biology", R.G. Kessel & C.Y. Shih © Kessel/Shih 1976; **359,** Bob Daemmrich; **362,** Walker England/Photo Researchers; **366,** Kenji Kerins; **367,** Norman Mosallem/The Stock Shop; **368,** (l) Aaron Haupt/Merrill photo, (r) Studiohio; **369,** (l) Walter Chandoha, (r) Studiohio; **370,** William Curtsinger/Photo Researchers; **372,** Gary Randall/Tom Stack & Associates; **373,** D.K. Langford; **376,** Ted Rice; **377,** Studiohio; **378,** (l) Studiohio, (r) Lynn M. Stone; **379,** Studiohio; **381,** William J. Weber; **382,** Animals Animals/Breck P. Kent; **383,** Daniel A. Erickson; **384,** Teiji Saga—PPS/Photo Researchers; **386,** Daniel A. Erickson; **387,** Brent Jones; **388,** (l) Daniel A. Erickson, (r) NIH/Science Source/Photo Researchers; **389,** Keith Wood, courtesy of University of California at San Diego; **390,** Cobalt Productions; **394–395,** Aaron Haupt/Merrill photo; **396,** Diane Graham-Henry and Kathleen Culbert-Aguilar; **398,** Robert Rathe/Stock Boston; **399,** Patrick Watson/Medichrome; **400,** (l) Steve Lissau, (r) Cobalt Productions; **401,** Makr Burnett/Merril photo; **402,** Aaron Haupt/Merrill photo; **403,** (t) Pictures Unlimited, (b) Studiohio; **407,** (l) Lennart Nilsson, (r) Secchi-Lecaque/Roussel-UCLAF/CNRI/Science Photo Library/Photo Researchers; **408,** James Westwater; **409,** Studiohio; **410,** Steve Small/Stock Imagery; **411,** Cobalt Productions; **413,** Lawrence Migdale; **415,** Paul Shambroom/Photo Researchers; **418,** Larry Mulvehill/Photo Researchers; **419,** James Holmes/Thomson Laboratories/Science Photo Library/Photo Researchers; **423,** Dwaine Patton/Stock Imagery; **424,** Kenji Kerins; **425,** Diane Graham-Henry and Kathleen Culbert-Aguilar; **427,** Studiohio; **429,** Photri; **432,** John Hansen, Ohio State University; **433,** file photo; **435,** Studiohio; **436,** Shay/Gerard Photography; **441,** (t) Dan McCoy/Rainbow, (b) SIU/Photo Researchers; **442,** Studiohio; **444,** Hank Morgan/Photo Researchers; 446–447, Elaine Shay; **448,** Diane Johnson/TSW–CLICK/Chicago; **449,** Gabe Palmer/The Stock Market; **450,** Studiohio; **452,** Nat'l. Dairy Council; **453,** (l) Mary Lou Uttermohlen, (r) Studiohio; **456,** Studiohio; **457,** Daniel A. Erickson; **458,** David Brownell; **459,** Mark Kozlowski; **460,** Hank Morgan/Rainbow; **461,** Studiohio; **462,** Bob Daemmrich; **463,** Studiohio; **464,** Aaron Haupt/Merrill photo; **465,** Studiohio; **466,** (l) Kenji Kerins, (r) H.M. DeCruyenaere; **467,** (l) Robert Brenner, (r) Ted Rice; **468, 469,** Studiohio; **470,** (l) Studiohio, (r) Tim Courlas; **471,** Larry Hamill; **472,** (l) Bill Bachman/Photo Researchers, (r) David M. Dennis; **473,** Studiohio; **474,** H.M. DeCruyenaere; **475,** David Madison/DUOMO; **476,** Doug Martin; **479,** David Madison; **480–481,** Aaron Haupt/Merrill photo; **501,** NASA; **505,** Larry Hamill; **507,** Tom McHugh/Photo Researchers.